WISHBONE

WISHBONE
OKLAHOMA FOOTBALL, 1959–1985

WANN SMITH
FOREWORD BY JAY WILKINSON

UNIVERSITY OF OKLAHOMA PRESS : NORMAN

This book is published with the generous assistance of the Wallace C. Thompson Fund, University of Oklahoma.

Library of Congress Cataloging-in-Publication Data

Smith, Wann.
  Wishbone : Oklahoma football, 1959-1985 / Wann Smith ;
foreword by Jay Wilkinson.
     p. cm.
  Includes bibliographical references and index.
  ISBN 978-0-8061-4217-3 (hardcover : alk. paper) 1. Oklahoma Sooners
(Football team)—History. 2. University of Oklahoma—Football—
History. I. Title.
  GV958.U585S55 2011
  796.332'630976637—dc22

                    2011006028

The paper in this book meets the guidelines for permanence and durability of the Committee on Production Guidelines for Book Longevity of the Council on Library Resources, Inc. ∞

1 2 3 4 5 6 7 8 9 10

To Greta, Erin, and Madeline

Contents

List of Illustrations ix

Foreword, by Jay Wilkinson xi

Acknowledgments xiii

Introduction 3

1. The Recession Begins, September 1959–January 1960 9

2. Into the Chasm, September 1960–October 1961 25

3. Fighting Back, November 1961–January 1963 37

4. Bud's Last Hurrah, January 1963–January 1964 53

5. Gomer, January 1964–December 1965 63

6. Renaissance in Norman: Jim Mackenzie, December 1965–April 1967 79

7. Changing of the Guard: Chuck Fairbanks, May 1967–January 1968 97

8. Stability, Decline, and Crisis, February 1968–October 1970 105

9. The Magnificent 'Bone, October 1970 119

10. Ascent, October 1970–January 1972 127

11. Conference Champions! October 1972–January 1973 141

12. Switzer-Land, January 1973–December 1973 153

13. Playing in the Dark: Part One, January 1974–January 1975 171

14. Playing in the Dark: Part Two, January 1975–November 1975 183

15. Back to the Summit, November 1975–January 1976 195

16. Transition and Resurrection, January 1976–January 1979 205

17. Julius Caesar and the Sooner Empire, January 1979–January 1981 237

18. New Decade, New Formation, January 1981–January 1984 253

19. Back to the 'Bone and Back to the Top, January 1984–January 1986 277

Epilogue: A Tempest Past 295

Notes 301

Bibliography 319

Index 321

Illustrations

1. Bud Wilkinson   6
2. The 1961 offensive line fires off the mark   43
3. Jim Grisham and Bud Wilkinson   45
4. President Kennedy at the 1963 Orange Bowl   50
5. Ralph Neely and Gomer Jones   66
6. Sooners on White House tour, September 1964   68
7. Jack Ging   78
8. Jim Mackenzie and his staff, 1966   82
9. Jim Mackenzie   85
10. The unstoppable Owens   103
11. Split-t formation   120
12. Wishbone formation   121
13. Greg Pruitt in Cleveland Stadium, 2010   135
14. Dave Robertson drawing a crowd, 1972   143
15. Leon Crosswhite   149
16. Athletic Director Wade Walker   154
17. Barry Switzer, 1968   155
18. Tinker Owens punishing Texas, 1973   166
19. Rex Norris and the Selmon Brothers at the OU-Texas game, 1973   167
20. Elvis Peacock, 2010   173
21. Kenny King, 2010   208
22. Lott, King, and Ivory in action   211
23. Oklahoma offensive line on the eve of the Sooner-Buckeye showdown   221
24. "The Kick"   225
25. Thomas Lott, 2010   236
26. Bob Stoops in pursuit of Billy Sims   240
27. Spencer Tillman, 2010   270
28. Tillman at Iowa State   282
29. Barry Switzer at home, 2010   297

Foreword

JAY WILKINSON

The Wishbone offense changed the face of college football. The offensive scheme's high reward was not without risk, but at its most efficient it was virtually unstoppable for much of its two decades of popularity. Wann Smith's *Wishbone: Oklahoma Football, 1959–1985*, details the history of the Sooner program from the Bud Wilkinson years through the Barry Switzer era, including the adoption of the Wishbone offense and the remarkable success the program enjoyed as a result. It explains the success that Oklahoma achieved in the 70s and 80s, winning three national championships and dominating the Big Eight Conference during Switzer's sixteen-year tenure as head coach.

The book's many compelling stories and anecdotes illustrate what it was like to go through the recruiting process and the practice routines and to take the field as a Sooner. The names of the OU players and coaches involved are now legendary; the games—runaways and nail-biters alike—are historic; and many of the records, both team and individual, have yet to be broken.

Smith provides the reader firsthand behind-the-scenes descriptions of important historical football events such as University of Texas coach Darrell Royal's decision in 1970 to help the OU coaching staff learn the secrets of the Wishbone offense. At that time, the Sooners' fortunes were floundering, and the entire Oklahoma coaching staff was in jeopardy of being fired. The fact that Coach Royal was willing to pass along "trade secrets" demonstrates how the coaching profession in those days differed from the world of big business.

The book also examines how close Oklahoma's Wishbone came to be shelved before it became one of the most explosive and prolific attacks in college football history. It was only after the 1970 Sooners' season got off to yet another mediocre start that OU coaches, led by Barry Switzer, decided to adopt the new offense. Smith reveals how the Wishbone's eventual success was never a walk in the park and how there were significant growing pains involved. The book's commentary details how the Sooners' experiment with the Wishbone offense came within a cat's whisker of extinction.

Wishbone investigates the challenges faced by the Oklahoma football program not only in instituting the initial change in offensive philosophy, which required convincing players already on the roster to buy in to the scheme, but also in recruiting athletes with the specific skills and talents to master the Wishbone's many intricacies. Bud Wilkinson's smashing of racial barriers in the 1950s set the stage for the influx of blue-chip African American players during the years immediately preceding the adoption of the Wishbone and during its heyday, and Barry Switzer's well-documented ability to communicate and bond with these athletes played a pivotal role in the offensive formation's success.

While the Switzer era was important for Oklahomans, it was also an extraordinary period for football in general, and there is no other book that focuses on this era with such historical depth as does *Wishbone*. This is a story of determination, foresight, triumph, and more than a little serendipity, reported by a fine writer who captures the accomplishments, pitfalls, and personalities that contributed to one of football's, and all of sport's, best all-time records of achievement on the playing field.

Acknowledgments

Researching and writing a retrospective analysis of University of Oklahoma football extending over half a century could not have been successfully accomplished without the eager cooperation of those closest to the program. Very special thanks go out to Leon Cross, Johnny Tatum, and J. D. Roberts not only for their trust and patience but also for those lunches at O'Connell's. Also, my sincerest and fondest gratitude must be extended to Barry Switzer for the countless hours he spent patiently on the phone with me, the home visits, and that rare opportunity to help him chase his wandering German shepherd pup, Jazz, down the street. Appreciation also goes to Steve and Tinker Owens for making their time my time; to Eddie Crowder, whose help in the early stages of the project aided its development immeasurably; and to Eddie Hinton, Gene and Donna Hochevar, Merv Johnson, Jackie Lee and Apache Ging, Larry Lacewell, Thomas Lott, Kenny King, Derland Moore, Jay O'Neal, Tom Osborne, Homer Rice, Darrell and Edith Royal, Bobby Warmack, Joe Washington, Jay Wilkinson, and Uwe von Schamann for their time, patience, and friendship.

I would also like to acknowledge the contributions of Claude and Nancy Arnold, Emory Bellard, Dean Blevins, Bobby Boyd, George and Barbara Brewer, Jimmy Carpenter, Glen Condren, Jay Cronley, Leon and Trisha Crosswhite, Tony DiRienzo, Marcus Dupree, Jimbo Elrod, Rudy Feldman, Dan Gibbens, Archie Griffin, Jim and Mattie Grisham, Galen Hall, Jimmy Harris, Bob Harrison, Victor Hicks, Scotty Hill, Jamelle Holieway, Bobby Drake Keith, Rex Kern, Johnny Majors, Carl McAdams, Mike McClellan, Ken Mendenhall, Ralph Neely, Chuck Neinas, Rex and Melinda Norris, Elvis Peacock, Jerry Pettibone, Bobby Proctor, Greg Pruitt, Steve Rhodes, Jim Riley, Dave Robertson, J. D. Sandefer, Dewey Selmon, Ron Shotts, Billy Sims, Anthony Stafford, Keith and Sybil Stanberry, Jim Terry, Clendon Thomas, Helen Thomas, Jerry Thompson, Spencer Tillman, Mike Treps, Jerry Tubbs, Wade and Jean Walker, Joe Washington, John Sayle Watterson, J. C. Watts, and Steve Zabel, each of whom shared their experiences and their time.

Furthermore, I would like to extend my deepest appreciation to the Associate Director and Editor-in-Chief of the University of Oklahoma Press, Chuck Rankin, for his comments, guidance, and suggestions, and to my late editor, Kirk Bjornsgaard, who was taken from his friends, family, and colleagues far too early; his vision was instrumental in getting this project off the ground. Thanks go to Special Projects Editor Alice Stanton, Amy Hernandez in Marketing, Editorial Administrative Assistant Connie Arnold, Managing Editor Steven Baker, Staff Assistant Anna María Rodríguez, and Kelly Parker for working her copyediting magic. Their contributions simply cannot be overestimated. I am also grateful for the support of Joe Castiglione, Kenny Mossman, and the staff of the Sports Information Department at the University of Oklahoma in allowing me access to their football archives—the "Holy of Holies"—to facilitate my research.

I appreciate the support given me in the preparation of this manuscript by Sam Threadgill, whose help in its nascent stages was critical; my appreciation and regards also go out to Carl and Lorie Bailey, Rhonda Baldwin, Lee Bobbitt, Ken Champion, Kelly Eisenhart, Eric Schneider, William Roy Equels, Sr., Douglas M. Harper, Perry Lightfoot, Charlie Northcott, Laura Pritchett, Mary Pritchett, Mark Pugh, Mark and Deidre Ross, Mike Rusk, Liz Schneider, and W. E. and Betty Smith.

And above all, my gratitude goes to my children, Greta, Erin, and Madeline Smith, for allowing me to retreat to my office to work on this project these past three years, and to my wife, Iris, who displayed preternatural patience while reading the manuscript and offered invaluable and indispensable advice, which resulted in the finished product being a far better one than it otherwise might have been.

WISHBONE

Introduction

By the middle of 1945, the Second World War had ended. Germany, Italy, and their European Axis partners had been vanquished by early May, and Japan raised a tattered white flag in mid-August. And while the Allied Powers had won the war, by the end of the 1945 season, football fortunes at the University of Oklahoma had taken an ugly turn.

In December, the Oklahoma Sooners had just completed their fifty-first season of college football. Owen Field, once a venue to such notable coaches as Bennie Owen and Tom Stidham, sat quietly, as if pensive over the trials of recent seasons past. The echoes of historic successes had been suppressed, temporarily forgotten on the heels of the last game played weeks before: a 47–0 loss to in-state rival Oklahoma A&M. It was the Sooners' second consecutive defeat at the hands of the Aggies, a team to whom Oklahoma had not previously lost since 1933. And to compound the problem, the loss had topped off a disappointing 5–5–0 season.

Bennie Owen, the stadium's founder and namesake, had led the team for twenty-two years, from 1905 through 1926, and in that time Owen's Sooners stormed through four undefeated seasons while amassing a win/loss record of 122–54–16. Additionally, in 1906 Owen ensured his place among the pantheon of Sooner legends by being the first coach in the midlands to effectively incorporate the forward pass into his offense.[1]

From 1937 to 1940, Tom Stidham compiled an impressive 27–8–3 record while leading the Sooners to their first Big Six Conference title in 1938. Stidham's Sooners finished the season with their first national ranking, placing fourth in the fledgling Associated Press poll and fifth in the now-defunct Dickinson poll. Under Stidham, Oklahoma accepted its first bowl invitation and traveled to Miami, Florida, in late December to play General Robert Neyland's Tennessee Volunteers in the fifth Orange Bowl, a penalty-ridden game the Sooners would lose 17–0.

Despite the success he had achieved in Norman, Stidham departed in January 1941 to accept the head coaching position at Marquette University.[2]

Eleven days later, Dewey "Snorter" Luster, a Sooner alumnus who had captained the 1920 Oklahoma squad, was tapped to take over. His 1941 squad posted a promising 6–3–0 record, but its season ended on an inauspicious note with a 7–6 loss to Nebraska in Lincoln—a mere eight days prior to the Japanese attack on the American naval base at Pearl Harbor, Hawaii. Despite the fact that Luster's five-year sojourn on the Oklahoma sidelines produced an overall record of 27–18–3 including two more Big Six titles, his Sooners were never able to defeat Texas, and back-to-back losses to Oklahoma A&M in 1944 and 1945[3] created a situation unacceptable to Sooner fans and university administration alike.

In November 1945, Coach Luster, citing ill-health, turned in his resignation to university president George Lynn Cross.[4] As Oklahoma regent Lloyd Noble saw it, the head coaching vacancy afforded the university the opportunity to create a stronger foundation, a chance to reinvent its football program. Noble realized that with the war over there would be a massive influx of experienced, mature athletes returning from the military; he knew that the Sooners needed just the right man to lure the cream of that crop to Norman.

University of Oklahoma athletic director Lawrence E. "Jap" Haskell, who had been director of intercollegiate athletics at the Jacksonville Air Station, had met James M. Tatum years earlier when Tatum was hired as an assistant to Don Faurot, the head coach of the Jacksonville Naval Air Station team. Remembering Tatum to be a dynamic, driven coach, he invited him to Norman for an interview. Tatum requested and was granted permission to bring his colleague at Iowa Pre-Flight along for the process: Charles Burnham "Bud" Wilkinson.[5] During the course of the interview, the committee was so taken with young Wilkinson that when it finally offered Tatum the position, it was contingent upon Wilkinson accompanying him to Norman.

Bud Wilkinson had run the gamut of experiences in his first thirty years. While a senior at the University of Minnesota in 1936, he played on renowned head coach Bernie Bierman's Gopher team that won the very first Associated Press national championship. By the completion of his college career, Wilkinson had twice earned All-American status and had been awarded Minnesota's highest honor for combined scholarship and sports, the Big Ten Medal. In the summer following his graduation, Wilkinson also led the collegiate team to a

7–0 victory over the Green Bay Packers in the College All-Star Game.[6] After his graduation in the spring of 1937, Wilkinson spent the summer cruising across the Atlantic to Europe as the sports deck director on board a Holland America Line cruise ship. Upon his return, he moved to Syracuse, New York, where he received a master's degree in English and served as a part-time assistant coach under Ossie Solem. In the summer of 1938, he married Mary Shifflett in Grinnell, Iowa.

In the summer of 1941, Wilkinson returned to Minneapolis as an assistant under Bierman but joined the navy several months later after the United States entered the Second World War. In 1943, he was assigned to the Iowa Pre-Flight School, a preparatory program for aspiring naval pilots, where he became an assistant football coach under head coach Don Faurot. Faurot had developed a revolutionary offensive scheme that he had already employed at the University of Missouri: the Split-t formation.[7] Using the Split-t, Faurot's Tigers had gone from relative mediocrity to an 8–2–0 season and the seventh spot in the final ranking of the 1941 Associated Press poll. It was while at Iowa Pre-Flight that Wilkinson first encountered fellow assistant coach Jim Tatum.

In 1944, the Iowa Pre-Flight program was terminated and Bud Wilkinson was reassigned to the aircraft carrier USS *Enterprise*. While aboard, he served as flight deck officer and saw action in both the Iwo Jima and Okinawa campaigns.[8] After the war, Wilkinson moved his family back to Minneapolis, where he went into business with his father as a mortgage broker; but soon after returning home, his career was cut short by a telephone call from Tatum. Always the persuasive salesman, Tatum convinced Wilkinson to join him in Norman, Oklahoma, as his assistant coach in 1946. During Tatum's first and only season at the Sooner helm, he led the refurbished Crimson and Cream to an 8–3–0 record while finishing fourteenth in the final AP poll. At the end of the regular season, the Sooners were invited to attend their second bowl game, a January 1, 1947, Gator Bowl joust with North Carolina State in Jacksonville, Florida.

Three days prior to the bowl game, Oklahoma regent Lloyd Noble phoned university president George Cross to inform him of a rumor circulating that, despite his assurances to the contrary, Tatum was planning to jump ship to

Bud Wilkinson. Photo from *Look* magazine, courtesy Jay Wilkinson.

the University of Maryland along with his staff and a contingent of players. Cross immediately flew to Jacksonville to offer Wilkinson the position should Tatum choose to leave. A three-year contract was offered by Cross but was altered to four years because Wilkinson wanted a guarantee that he would be able to see at least one of his recruiting classes through to graduation. As a postscript, Wilkinson had confirmed that the rumor had been true; Tatum was headed to Maryland along with most of the coaching staff.[9] Jim Tatum continued to negotiate with both Maryland and the University of Oklahoma through the first few weeks of 1947, but when it became obvious that Oklahoma would not meet his demands, he tendered his resignation. On February 1, 1947, the university issued a press release stating that Tatum had resigned to accept the position of head coach at the University of Maryland. It was also announced that Bud Wilkinson would become the thirteenth head coach at the University of Oklahoma.

Over the next twelve seasons, Bud Wilkinson's Oklahoma teams scaled unprecedented heights in college football. With the help of players such as Darrell Royal, Myrle Greathouse, George Brewer, Tommy Gray, Leon Manley, Wade Walker, Charlie Surratt, the Burris brothers—Paul, Bob, Kurt, and Lynn—Merrill Green, Demosthenes Andrecopolous (Dee Andros), Jack Mitchell, Claude Arnold, Leon "Mule Train" Heath, Jim Owens, Tom Catlin, Jim Weatherall, Buddy Leake, Eddie Crowder, Buck McPhail, the O'Neal brothers—Pat, Jay, and Benton—Billy Vessels, J. D. Roberts, Jack Ging, Darlon "Doc" Hearon, Roger Nelson, Billy Pricer, Bill Krisher, Gene Dan Calame, Max Boydston, Jimmy Harris, Tommy McDonald, Clendon Thomas, Jerry Tubbs, Bo Bolinger, Wayne Greenlee, J. D. "Jakie" Sandefer, Ed "Beaky" Gray, Prentice Gautt, Bob "Hog" Harrison, and scores of others, Wilkinson's Sooners would:

- Win national championships in 1950, 1955, and 1956;

- Win twelve consecutive conference titles from 1947 through 1959 (under Wilkinson, Oklahoma did not lose a conference game until October 31, 1959);

- Win thirty-one consecutive games from October 2, 1948 through January 1, 1951; and

- Win forty-seven straight games from October 10, 1953 through November 16, 1957—an NCAA record that still stands in the twenty-first century.

For the first twelve years of Bud Wilkinson's regime, the University of Oklahoma's football team swept across the land like an angry wind, toppling other programs in its wake. From early 1953 through late 1957, the Sooner storm had encountered nothing that could withstand its force and fury. But by 1959, the lightning had passed, the thunder had subsided.

A new era was dawning on Sooner football.

1 The Recession Begins

SEPTEMBER 1959–JANUARY 1960

At the conclusion of the 1956 season, the University of Oklahoma was basking in the glow of its second consecutive national title. The football team had grown accustomed to the limelight, having won three NCAA championships over the past seven years. And while team honors abounded, there was no shortage of individual awards garnered. Clendon Thomas had won the national scoring title followed by Tommy McDonald, who had placed second. McDonald had also won the Maxwell Award, and he and Jerry Tubbs had placed third and fourth respectively in the Heisman balloting. Tubbs also won the Walter Camp Award as the nation's most outstanding college football player. Four Sooners were selected to All-American first teams: Jerry Tubbs, Tommy McDonald, Bill Krisher, and Ed "Beaky" Gray. Additionally, Jerry Tubbs was invited to participate in the annual East-West Shrine game. Playing alongside Jerry on the team was Paul Hornung, 1956 Heisman Trophy winner and quarterback of the Notre Dame team the Sooners had destroyed 40–0 in South Bend two months earlier.

After the first team meeting preceding the Shrine game, Hornung approached Tubbs and suggested that since Tubbs would be doing the deep snapping and Hornung the punting, perhaps they should go to the practice field for a few reps. As the two men walked onto the field, Tubbs asked in his slow, Texas drawl, "Paul, about how far do you stand back from the line of scrimmage when you're punting?"

"About fourteen or fifteen yards, I suppose," replied Hornung. Tubbs slowly shook his head as he continued walking and said, "Well, I don't know if I can get it back that far to you." To Hornung's surprise, Tubbs's first snap dropped two feet short. The second try, while picking up distance, still dropped just out of reach. Hornung retrieved the ball, tucked it beneath his arm, walked over to Tubbs, and asked, "Jerry, I'm a little confused. Weren't you the starting center on Bud Wilkinson's last two national championship teams?" Tubbs hesitated, looked Hornung in the eye, and replied, "Yeah, Paul, but we never had to punt."[1]

While Tubbs's remark was something of an exaggeration, it accurately illustrated both the ability and the attitude of those marvelous mid-fifties Sooner squads. From 1954 through 1956, Tubbs and his teammates had never tasted defeat; indeed, in the two years that Tubbs and his quarterback-partner Jimmy Harris had been battery mates, they had never mishandled a single snap. Following the 1956 season, Wilkinson's 1957 and 1958 teams appeared to have been cut from the same cloth. They would play twenty-two games, win two Orange Bowls, and lose only twice—once per season. The '57 team finished fourth in the final wire service polls, and the '58 team came in fifth.

In 1959, Oklahoma's economy was booming, the state ego had never been stronger, and the future appeared bright for Sooner football. Oklahoma was ranked second in the preseason Associated Press poll, and the national media was replete with praise fueling high hopes for what was expected to be another Sooner national title run. But Wilkinson had done his job too well. For the past six years, he had taken his teams to unprecedented heights, and the state of Oklahoma had gone along for the ride. As a result, no one was prepared for what was to occur at the decade's end; no one in the state could have anticipated that the Sooners were on the brink of the worst period since 1929–1933 when Oklahoma head coaches Adrian Lindsey and Lewie Hardage produced a combined record of 19–25–8. From September 25, 1959, through October 28, 1961, Bud Wilkinson's teams would lose games at an unheard-of pace as they tumbled to a 10–14–1 record. In 1959, Wilkinson's Sooners posted a 7–3–0 record, the worst since his first year as head coach. In 1960, the Sooners struggled through a 3–6–1 season, and in 1961 they lost their first five games. In order to reach any understanding of this complex problem, several possible causes must be examined.

Some have suggested that Wilkinson's involvement in the Coach of the Year Clinics may have provided a distraction detrimental to his responsibilities as head coach at the University of Oklahoma. By the mid-1950s, he had reached the zenith of national fame; from 1954 through 1956, Sooner football was an irresistible force that had encountered no immovable objects. During this time,

Wilkinson joined Michigan State head coach Duffy Daugherty in organizing and presenting the Coach of the Year Clinics. These clinics, held in January and February of each year—critical recruiting periods for any college coach—were conducted by Wilkinson, Daugherty, and the annual winner of the Coach of the Year award. Preparation and travel for these clinics required an inordinate amount of time, and since Daugherty and Wilkinson were doing the lion's share of the work, the demands on Wilkinson's time produced a significant distraction from his recruiting duties in Norman. Bud's son, Jay, commented on the clinics:

> They were annual weekend workshops for high school and college coaches and were held in three cities at once with the clinic staff rotating in and out of those three cities. These clinics involved a tremendous amount of travel and they were exhausting. Consequently, there were some occasions when potential recruits were on the Norman campus and Dad wouldn't be there. Boys who had come to meet him were often disappointed, and that undoubtedly hampered the recruiting effort. Some of the players felt that Dad's heart wasn't in recruiting to the degree it had been previously.[2]

The rigorous demands of administering these clinics were felt by other coaches as well. After winning his first Coach of the Year award at the University of Texas in 1961, Darrell Royal participated in the clinic and found it so demanding he swore he would never do it again.[3] And Wilkinson's business partner, Duffy Daugherty, who had led his Michigan State Spartans to top-ten finishes in the final Associated Press polls in 1955, 1956, and 1957, suffered a fate similar to that of Wilkinson and his Sooners; as Daugherty's involvement in the Coach of the Year Clinics increased, his MSU teams fell to 3–5–1 in 1958 and 5–4–0 in 1959.[4]

It has also been suggested that Wilkinson's appointment as director of President Kennedy's Council on Physical Fitness in March 1961 further impacted his schedule. Prior to accepting President Kennedy's offer, Wilkinson polled university president Cross and the board of regents and was given the green light.[5]

"Shortly after he was elected President, JFK appointed Bud director of the President's Council on Physical Fitness," recalls Sooner assistant coach Jay O'Neal. "Bud held the position from 1961 through 1963." O'Neal explains that when Wilkinson went to Washington to evaluate the program, he had found a Byzantine network of physical fitness programs funded through Washington, all widely dispersed under the control of different agencies. "Bud organized and put them all together, a feat which deeply impressed President Kennedy. He and Bud became quite close."[6]

Wilkinson's appointment was received with nearly unanimous national enthusiasm. White House reporter Helen Thomas was of the opinion that Wilkinson would set the tone and raise the national awareness in physical fitness; she believed that Bud fit the administration's formula for "viguh."[7] But the man on the street in Oklahoma who bled crimson and cream was not quite as enthusiastic about the appointment, fearing that a slipping football program, so long the major source of pride in the state, would require more of Bud's concentration, not less.

The ability of opposing defenses to diminish the effectiveness of Oklahoma's Split-t offense may also have played a salient role in the decline of Wilkinson's fortunes from 1959 through the first half of the 1961 season. Although the Sooners dominated college football in the 1950s using this offense, there had been other successful variations of it on the national scene that made their mark during that era. Bobby Dodd's Georgia Tech squads produced top-ten teams running the Belly-t; Army ran the Bear-t; and Texas, later under Darrell Royal, ran a modified version of the Wing-t. And, as is the norm in football, each of these variations resulted in defensive adjustments by opponents who, in many cases, adopted the very 5–4 defensive formation created by Bud Wilkinson and Gomer Jones—a defense that is still known today as the "Oklahoma defense." But, as TCU proved while taking the Sooners to the wire before succumbing 21–16 on September 25, 1954, when attempting to corral the Split-t offense, quality of personnel is at least as important, if not more so, than defensive formation.

"TCU had talented athletes that were disciplined and well coached," comments former Oklahoma Outland Trophy winner and coach John David "J. D." Roberts. "While defenses may have been catching up with the Split-t, their effectiveness against us was probably more attributable to their talent than to their set. And by 1959, teams were beginning to develop ways to defend the Split-t more effectively. Coach Wilkinson had wanted to develop some new wrinkles that we could run from our basic offense to keep defenses off guard."[8] Former Sooner championship quarterback Jimmy Harris also believes that teams were beginning to catch up with the Split-t. "Bud was already aware of it because he had us doing a few spreads, the swinging gate, and so on."[9] But although defenses and talent may have been gaining on Wilkinson during the latter stages of the 1950s, it is unlikely that Oklahoma's decline was precipitated by that factor. The Split-t had proven itself a resoundingly flexible mode of attack, having gone through a remarkable evolution in Norman. The formation had been predominantly a rushing offense while Jack Mitchell and Darrell Royal were under center; it had become an effective passing offense with Claude Arnold and Eddie Crowder; and by the mid-fifties, with Jimmy Harris and Jay O'Neal, it had morphed into a combination of both, with a large dollop of halfback pass tossed in.

Some have also proffered the theory that changes in coaching personnel in the latter part of the decade might have contributed to a dilution of strategic philosophy. During Wilkinson's first years at Oklahoma, his coaching staff was comprised of men who had cut their teeth in other regions, men who had brought a divergence of experience and opinion along with them to Norman. While OU assistant coaches Frank "Pop" Ivy, Bill Jennings, Frank Crider, and Dee Andros had each played for and graduated from the University of Oklahoma, Ray Nagel had coached at UCLA, Pete Elliott had quarterbacked the 1948 Michigan Wolverines to an undefeated national championship season, Dutch Fehring and Bill Canfield hailed from Purdue, John Shelly had coached under Red Blaik at Army, Ted Youngling had coached at Duke, Gomer Jones and George Lynn had played for Ohio State, and Wilkinson himself was a product of the University of Minnesota.

∵

Sooner running back Clendon Thomas suggests that the loss of long-established coaches in the second half of the decade may have had an effect on the team:

Pete Elliott left for Illinois, Sam Lyle went to the Edmonton Eskimos and Pop Ivy also went to Edmonton before going on to the Chicago Cardinals and then to the New York Giants. We lost a significant core group of coaches that had been so instrumental in keeping the team motivated. And later in the decade, Bud began to hire some of the players who had completed their eligibility and remained at the University to finish degrees. As a result, I think the staff may have become a bit insular. While they were fine coaches to a man, their experience was derived from playing on the collegiate level whereas had Coach Wilkinson brought in outsiders, he might also have imported some new ideas, which never hurts.[10]

Thomas's opinion is shared by Jimmy Harris. "Bud surrounded himself with a group of his ex-players, and I suppose that has its negatives along with its positives."[11] Harris's comments must be afforded an extra measure of credibility since he falls into the very category he calls into question, having been an undefeated Sooner quarterback from 1954 through 1956 and a member of Wilkinson's staff in 1959. However, J. D. Roberts disagrees with this theory. Roberts points out that during the 1950s, while there may indeed have been an influx of former Sooner players on the staff, there had also been a consistent contingent of coaches without Oklahoma roots on campus as well. Roberts suggests that if there had been a problem arising from a lack of new ideas on the staff that it was far more likely to have occurred in 1964–65 under head coach Gomer Jones.[12] During Jones's tenure, his coaching staff was composed almost exclusively of ex-OU players in Jay O'Neal, Carl Allison, Bob Cornell, Brewster Hobby, Dick Heatly, Joe Rector, and Jerry Thompson. However, to conclude that the 1964 and 1965 teams suffered under Gomer because of the homogeneous nature of the coaching staff would be highly questionable. While it is correct that Gomer's coaches were OU products, they were hardly just out of pads; Jerry Thompson had spent time coaching with Frank Kush at Arizona State, Joe Rector had coached at Texas Western, Brewster Hobby had taught high school ball in Oklahoma City, and Dick Heatly coached at Washington. Also, Bobby Drake Keith, who had coached for Bear Bryant at Alabama, joined

Wilkinson's staff in 1963 and remained with Jones through 1965.

From the renaissance of Oklahoma football in 1946 through the end of Bud Wilkinson's regime in 1963, the Sooners concentrated their recruiting efforts in Oklahoma and northern Texas. Could Wilkinson's failure to expand recruiting on a national scale have caught up with him and contributed to the slump? In the 1950s, it was extremely difficult to gather information about high school players outside the region, but on a few notable occasions Wilkinson did bring in players from parts of the country the Sooners normally did not prospect. Wade Walker from North Carolina (who joined Wilkinson and Tatum in 1946), Buddy Leake from Tennessee, and Tommy McDonald, Leon Cross, and Ralph Neely, all from New Mexico, were notable exceptions to Wilkinson's regional recruiting policy. But this failure to expand Oklahoma's recruiting efforts into other parts of the country certainly left the Sooners susceptible to periodic talent droughts. In the late 1950s and early 1960s, the pool of talent produced within Wilkinson's target regions dropped off, leaving the team with fewer quality athletes coming in to fuel the machine.

Former Sooner Charley Mayhue believed that the recruiting suffered somewhat due to Wilkinson's loss of enthusiasm, and former Sooner player, Oklahoma assistant coach, and University of Colorado head coach and athletic director Eddie Crowder expressed similar feelings. "We had been drawing our players from Oklahoma and northwest Texas, but this wasn't sufficient anymore," said Crowder. "So we started going outside. Also, the Texas schools began to recruit more intensely. I felt that after our 47-game winning streak ended, our entire staff underwent a decline in motivation. And I thought I could discern in Bud a waning of his usual coaching exuberance."[13] J. D. Roberts describes what he also observed to be a decline in Wilkinson's enthusiasm, "In my opinion, Coach Wilkinson didn't seem to have the same fire that he'd displayed earlier in the decade. It was difficult, at times, to get him to accompany us on recruiting trips; his time was so taxed by his other commitments."[14] After leaving Oklahoma, Wilkinson himself reflected on the subject: "It would have been different if I'd been a little more farsighted. At the time, I'd not realized that Oklahoma had earned enough publicity and enough accolades that we could recruit beyond our own geographic area. We felt our recruiting [area] was the state of Oklahoma and the Texas panhandle. [During that period] I didn't have the normal athletic talent graduate from high school in our region. Had I been more farsighted, we could have expanded the recruiting area quite a bit, but at that time, I didn't do it."[15]

In addition to the paucity of incoming fresh high school talent, attrition likely played a role in the Sooners' slump. In 1955, the program was placed on a two-year probation for lending an automobile to a player, paying medical expenses for a player's immediate family member, and providing players miscellaneous fringe benefits. However, as a result of what the NCAA considered "the excellent cooperation and assistance" extended to its investigating committee, the penalties were relatively light and resulted neither in bans on television appearances nor on participation in bowl games.[16]

Three years later, the Sooners found themselves embroiled in another controversy involving ex-Sooner coach Bill Jennings who was, at the time, the head coach at the University of Nebraska. In late April 1958, highly regarded Lexington tackle and Nebraska High School Player of the Year Monte Kiffin contacted Bud Wilkinson by letter expressing an interest in attending OU. When Jennings learned of Kiffin's interest in the Sooners, he dashed off a letter to Wilkinson threatening that, should Kiffin become a Sooner, he would reveal information to the NCAA that he claimed would compromise Oklahoma. Wilkinson immediately brought university president George Cross into the matter, and it was decided to reply to Jennings by informing him that if he indeed possessed such compromising information, he should present it to the NCAA immediately regardless of where Kiffin enrolled. Wilkinson sent copies of his reply to chancellor Clifford M. Hardin at the University of Nebraska and to Walter Byers at the NCAA. Byers became involved and questioned Dr. Cross about a fund handled by an Oklahoma accountant named Arthur L. Wood that was purportedly used for recruiting. When questioned, Wood openly admitted that he had been in charge of such a fund and that his connection at OU had been Jennings himself, who had been the Sooner assistant personally responsible for monitoring and directing Wood to disburse the monies from 1952 through 1954. Wood further claimed that the fund had been discontinued in 1954 when Jennings had resigned from OU to go into private business. When Byers learned of this development, he requested confidential access to the fund's records, but Wood declined, stating that as an accountant he could not legally, ethically, or professionally disclose the records of his clients. As a result, in January 1960, Oklahoma was placed on an indefinite NCAA probation, which prohibited both postseason games and television appearances. Stipulated within the probation was the provision that if and when Wood allowed access to his books, the probation would be lifted.[17] Wood finally relented the next season, and the probation ended.[18]

"Unquestionably, this second probationary period during a single decade was a major factor in what was to be a decline in the quality of OU football," opined Dr. Cross. "The recruitment of exceptional athletes became more difficult, and the morale of those already on the campus seemed to be affected."[19] In fact, the probation imposed on Oklahoma in 1960 would have a far greater effect on Gomer Jones's tenure as head coach four years later. But the loss of players does appear to have played a role with the remaining athletes, who failed to mature and contribute to the team in their last two seasons of eligibility. "We had some linemen we'd recruited that didn't come through for us in '59," recalls Roberts. "We fell off quite a bit at center, linebacker, and fullback."[20] Clendon Thomas also felt that the natural ebb and flow in the quality of recruiting classes played a role in the Sooners' decline. He explains:

Each year you have a group of high schoolers coming out and you make a list of kids who could potentially make strong contributions to your program. The quality of those kids, even though you might get the best of the best, is not always the same year after year. The quality comes and goes, and I think Coach Wilkinson suffered somewhat from this dynamic during that period. They might have recruited the twenty best players from our part of the country and yet in the end, they weren't Jerry Tubbs, and they weren't Jimmy Harris, and they weren't Tommy McDonald. I think that the talent pool fell off through some of those years.[21]

Bud Wilkinson's desire and drive in the years preceding the slump have also been called into question, but it is unlikely that Wilkinson suffered any lapse in motivation during the time the '56 and '57 classes were recruited; these incoming high school players were superb athletes lured by the successes of the past three seasons. If Bud Wilkinson did, in fact, experience diminished passion for recruiting and/or coaching, it likely would have occurred, as Eddie Crowder contended, after the November 1957 streak-ending loss to Notre Dame in Norman. If Wilkinson's enthusiasm dampened at that time, it would have put a damper on recruiting classes after 1957, and in all likelihood the effects would not have been evident until 1960 and 1961, precisely when his decline was in the deepest valley. And while Wilkinson's failure to extend the Sooners' recruiting efforts nationwide unquestionably caused problems for Oklahoma, this also did not begin to pose serious problems until the early sixties.

The probations of 1955 and 1960, despite President Cross's statement to the contrary, were unlikely to have created major problems for Oklahoma by themselves; the negatives coming to bear on recruiting by the probation of 1955 were more than compensated for by the lure of the back-to-back national titles the Sooners won in 1955 and 1956 combined with the continuing on-field success of the 1957 and 1958 squads. However, combined with the distractions Wilkinson was experiencing with his Coach of the Year Clinic responsibilities and, to a lesser degree, his participation in President Kennedy's Council on Physical Fitness after 1960, the impact of the probation of 1960 undoubtedly played a role in the decline of the early sixties.

That the Sooner coaching staff failed to keep pace with advancing defensive trends vis-à-vis the Split-t offense is unlikely to have played a pivotal role in Oklahoma's late-fifties ebb. As TCU demonstrated as early as 1954—and as J. D. Roberts explained—a defense's ability to stop the Split-t was far more dependent upon the personnel manning that defense than on the defensive scheme itself; the Horned Frogs had a viable and effective game plan designed to wreak havoc on the Split-t, but they were also blessed with gifted athletes. The problems encountered by Oklahoma from 1959 through 1961 had less to do with opponents' use of innovative defensive strategies than with an overall decline in available talent in Norman.

The tendency to focus blame on one specific cause responsible for the Sooners' slump must be considered short-sighted and myopic, much like the actions of the characters in the poem by John Godfrey Saxe, "The Blind Men and the Elephant." In the poem, six blind men from Indostan try to determine what an elephant looks like by grasping different parts of the animal. In an effort to describe the creature, the sixth blind man grasps its tail and concludes that the creature must be very much like a rope. To attribute the dip in fortunes of 1959–1961 to any one factor would be errant; the problem was created by a patchwork of concurrent negatives, the most significant of which seems to have been a decline in available talent during the down years of '59, '60, and '61—a decline caused by the attrition suffered by the 1956 and 1957 recruiting classes. For a variety of reasons, many players from these classes who were depended upon to play key roles failed to live up to expectations during their junior and senior seasons. According to former Sooner player John Tatum, the prospect of playing sophomores was anathema to Bud Wilkinson; Tatum recalls that "Bud was of the opinion that for every sophomore that started, he'd lose a game."[22]

∵

The mosaic of problems influencing the fate of Wilkinson's squad required a catalyst to set the wheels of decline into motion. That catalyst occurred on September 26, 1959, when Oklahoma traveled to Evanston, Illinois, to play the Northwestern Wildcats. Despite their fabled forty-seven-game winning streak of the mid-fifties and their impressive bowl victories over highly rated nonconference foes, the accusation had long been leveled at the Sooners that the caliber of Big Seven competition fell well below that of other conferences—primarily the Big Ten.[23] Speculation had been vociferous and loud that Oklahoma would have had trouble dominating Ohio State or Michigan as they had been doing the other six members of the Big Seven Conference. And the facts were difficult for Wilkinson to dismiss. From 1950 through 1958, five of the Big Seven Conference schools—Kansas, Kansas State, Missouri, Iowa State, and Nebraska—had posted only twelve winning seasons among them. Colorado, consistently the best team in the conference during that time besides Oklahoma, posted nine winning seasons. And in 1954 and 1955, the Sooners' two national title years, Colorado was the only other conference team to post winning records both seasons.

The Big Ten Conference, on the other hand, had long established itself as a bastion of college football power. Since Wilkinson had assumed command of the Sooners in 1947, the Big Ten had won four national titles—Michigan State in 1948 and 1952 and Ohio State in 1954 and 1957—while the Big Seven had taken home three—1950, 1955, and 1956, all by Oklahoma. In addition, during that twelve-year period, eight of the Big Ten teams had finished in the final top-ten of the wire service polls thirty times; in the Big Seven, no other team had placed in the final top ten except the Sooners. And entering the 1959 season, at least five Big Ten teams entertained realistic national aspirations—Wisconsin, Purdue, Iowa, Ohio State, and Northwestern.

The Sooners' first game of 1959 would provide an opportunity for second-ranked Oklahoma to silence those critics. Northwestern was coached by Ara Parseghian, who would later rise to prominence as the head coach at Notre Dame. In 1958, the stars had fallen into alignment for Parseghian as his Wildcats defeated Michigan for the first time since 1951 and Ohio State for the first time since 1948—the only game the Buckeyes would lose that season—while only narrowly losing to eventual Big Ten and Rose Bowl champion Iowa. And in 1959, Northwestern welcomed back twenty-nine of its best thirty-three players.

Still, in Oklahoma, confidence abounded. The Sooner nation had no reason to doubt that Wilkinson would lead his team on another furious run at the national title. University of Illinois and Chicago Bears star Red Grange, the "Galloping Ghost," wrote in *Sports Illustrated*, "Oklahoma has become synonymous with victory and the reasons are simple. Coach Bud Wilkinson is a football perfectionist who recruits only the best players and insists on speed in his line and backfield. If Oklahoma can get safely by Northwestern in its opening game, the Sooners should march through the Big Eight on their way to an unbeaten season."[24]

Three days prior to the Northwestern game, the Sooners departed from Oklahoma City en route to Evanston, Illinois. The flight was not a smooth one, and several members of the team struggled with airsickness. The Sooners checked into the Orrington Hotel in Evanston Wednesday evening and went through a light workout on Thursday morning before dressing for dinner and a show at the Chez Paree Supper Club. Founded in the 1930s, the Chez Paree was the hottest night spot in Chicago, hosting entertainers such as Dean Martin and Jerry Lewis, Liberace, Sophie Tucker, Jimmy Durante, Nat "King" Cole, and Mae West. Known for its celebrity, after Thursday, September 24, the Chez Paree would become somewhat notorious among college football fans for its role in the Oklahoma football team food poisoning incident.

As the Sooner football team filed into the nightclub, they were greeted by a blonde hostess and two older gentlemen. Brewster Hobby explained, "As we went in, these gentlemen introduced the woman to each of the players. She was very quick to ask 'What position do you play?' Of course, everyone was trying to be polite so we told her what position we played and what team we were on [e.g., first or second]. Then they began serving the fruit salad and instead of just going down the row like they normally do, *they served it sporadically through-out the area* (author's italics). Evidently, the drug was in those salads. They got twenty-two of the top thirty-three players."[25]

Starting quarterback Bob Boyd became ill almost immediately after taking his first bite. "I was one of the first guys to reach the bathroom," recalls Boyd. "And by the time I'd thrown up a couple of times the entire restroom was full of players."[26] Also poisoned at the Chez Paree that evening was assistant coach Jimmy Harris. "I had my stomach pumped that evening," he remembers. "By game time on Saturday two days later, I was sitting up in the booth with Eddie Crowder and I still felt horrible, unsteady. I told Bud before the game that I didn't think our guys could perform anywhere near full speed or strength because most of them were still very sick and dizzy."[27]

Harris could not have been more right. On unsteady legs, the Sooners took the field on a Saturday afternoon whose threatening, cloudy sky soon gave way to driving rain. Oklahoma won the toss, took the wind, and kicked off. The game was nationally televised by NBC with color provided by Lindsey Nelson and Red Grange, and, from the outset, it was obvious to the viewers that something was seriously wrong with Oklahoma.

"OU's trip to Northwestern was a debacle," comments O'Neal. "I watched the game on television and there was absolutely no question in my mind that whatever it was that those players had ingested was still affecting their balance, their equilibrium. Guys were doing crazy things on that field."[28] Oklahoma lost five of twelve fumbles that day in a shocking and unprecedented 45–13 loss.

The postgame investigation of the poisoning incident subsequently raised more questions than it resolved. After departing the Chez Paree, the affected members of the team traveled by taxi to the Louise A. Weiss Memorial Hospital, where seven of thirteen were admitted and nine had their stomachs immediately pumped. When OU team physician Dr. D. G. Willard arrived at the hospital, nurses in the emergency room informed him that the boys were ill from "food intoxication." He was also informed at that time that one of the players, quarterback Bob Page, had suffered circulatory collapse. The affected players' stomach washings, along with blood and urine specimens, were collected and saved by hospital staff.[29] "The substance that we'd been given in our food was apomorphine," says Bobby Boyd. "They tested us for it at the hospital and that's how I know."[30]

Dr. Willard was assured by representatives of the Chicago Board of Health (CBOH) that lab reports reflecting the results of the tests conducted on the samples would be mailed to the University of Oklahoma the following Monday. However, on Friday following the incident, the CBOH informed him that all specimens had come back showing no sign of any poisoning or any chemical intoxication. Additionally, Dr. Willard was told that samples of the food served to the team on Thursday evening had also been examined and had also returned negative.[31]

Next, according to Dr. Willard, the CBOH attempted to place the blame on the turkey sandwiches served the players at the Orrington Hotel during the lunch service on Thursday, but this was ruled out as a possibility because Jimmy Harris—who had been severely affected by food poisoning at the Chez Paree—had not eaten the turkey; Harris had eaten lunch with the coaching staff in a separate room. At that point, the CBOH decided to place the blame on the Braniff Airways flight Wednesday evening, but this possibility was also ruled out because three of the players who had become violently ill at the Chez Paree had been so airsick on the incoming flight that they had declined the airline's entrée.[32] Despite assurances from the CBOH that further extensive tests would be made followed by a thorough investigation, the matter was dropped when Dr. Willard was informed that the vials containing the evidence had mysteriously disappeared.[33]

In a letter to Dr. Willard from the chief of the Oklahoma State Department of Health, Dr. F. R. Hassler, it was indicated that the players' illness was the result of antimony poisoning.[34] Bud Wilkinson and Dr. Willard were convinced and later privately stated that they believed the poisoning incident was intentional and probably the result of Mafia intervention or influence.[35]

The significance of the 45–13 loss to the Wildcats must not be underestimated. While the Sooners emerged from the fiasco at Evanston relatively unscathed physically, the damage to their psyche was significant. Under Wilkinson, Oklahoma had never lost a game by such a decisive margin; indeed, since 1946, the Sooners had never lost a contest by more than a touchdown, and the average margin of defeat was a mere 4.7 points. Great football teams never allow opponents forty-five points, nor do good teams unless there are exceptional extenuating circumstances. Such circumstances occurred when the Sooners suffered food poisoning prior to the Northwestern game in September 1959. After being ranked number two in the AP poll prior to the contest, the Sooners dropped completely off the charts. In the wake of such a complete disaster, the team could not hope to maintain its trademark spirit of supreme confidence: the same spirit that had carried them through a decade of dominance. And with its confidence compromised, the team's swagger diminished.

Two weeks following the Northwestern game, Oklahoma lost for the second consecutive year to traditional rival Texas, and for the first time since 1953 the Sooners had started a season with a losing record. Bud Wilkinson's teams had never lost to a Big Seven opponent and were enjoying a run of seventy-two consecutive unbeaten conference games, but in mid-October 1959 the Sooners were a team in trouble. Therefore, when Missouri hosted Oklahoma on October 17, like a shark circling wounded prey, it detected blood. But, although second-year head coach Dan Devine's Tigers were in a position to take over the conference lead with a victory and despite the high hopes afoot in Columbia, Oklahoma once again prevailed, 23–0, and the Sooners' undefeated conference streak climbed to seventy-three.

The following week Oklahoma faced a another challenge to its conference hegemony when former Sooner quarterback "General" Jack Mitchell brought his Kansas Jayhawks to Norman. OU led 7–0 in the third period when Jayhawk quarterback Dave Harris took the ball sixty yards for the equalizing score. Certain that their streak had come to an end, the Sooners were spared when Harris's two-point conversion attempt failed as his pass, intended for KU's Jim Jarrett, struck an official in the back of the head, careened into the air, and was intercepted by Oklahoma's Bob Cornell.[36] Thus, an early incidence of "Sooner Magic" enabled Oklahoma to escape with a narrow 7–6 victory.

The conference unbeaten streak stood at seventy-four, but it was teetering on the edge of oblivion as the Sooners traveled to Lincoln on October 31, 1959. Lack of concentration leading to mental mistakes combined with a resolute and determined Nebraska team spelled disaster for Wilkinson and his Sooners as the Cornhuskers dealt Oklahoma its first conference defeat in thirteen years, 25–21. The Halloween Massacre in Lincoln signaled the end of Sooner dominance over their conference rivals, a dominance that had extended over 74 games and 296 quarters and a dominance that saw Oklahoma outscore all foes by a total of 2,690 points to 572. The loss in Lincoln added another nail to the coffin containing the myth of Sooner invincibility.

If, as Jay O'Neal maintains, the Northwestern game set the tempo for the remainder of the year,[37] then the 1959 season set the tempo for the next two years. Oklahoma dropped out of the top twenty after the upheaval in Lincoln but managed to climb back to the fifteenth spot in the AP poll by season's end. The Sooners would move through the last four games in 1959 without a hitch; Kansas State fell 36–0, Army surrendered 28–20, Iowa State dropped 35–12, and Oklahoma State succumbed 17–7. Oklahoma claimed its twelfth consecutive conference title, and by so doing, once again provided some measure of relief and confidence for the future.

But little did Wilkinson or the Sooner nation realize that Oklahoma football was on the precipice of the worst thirteen-month period in its history.

2 Into the Chasm

Although 1959 had been Bud Wilkinson's worst year since his first as head coach in 1947, hope still sprang eternal among the ranks of Sooner fans as the 1960 season approached. Both the summer college football preview issue of the *Saturday Evening Post* and *Street and Smith*'s college football annual touted Oklahoma as a title contender and ranked it sixth in the nation.

Over the summer, Sooner athletic advisor and wrestling coach Port Robertson served as coach of the United States Olympic freestyle wrestling team participating in the seventeenth Olympiad in Rome. Robertson's team earned three gold medals while defeating four world champions, three of them Russian.[1] In March, during the Big Eight Conference track meet in Kansas City, University of Oklahoma pole-vaulter J. D. Martin cleared a 15' 7" bar to set a new collegiate indoor record.[2] Suddenly, Wilkinson's Sooners found themselves in the unfamiliar position of trying to live up to the accomplishments of both Robertson's Olympic wrestlers and J. D. Martin's indoor pole-vaulting feats.

Attrition would play a critical role in the upcoming season for the Sooners as starting players Bob Boyd, Brewster Hobby, Prentice Gautt, Wahoo McDaniel, Gilmer Lewis, Jerry Thompson, Jim Davis, and Billy Jack Moore were all lost to graduation. Consequently, the 1960 Sooner team would be a predominantly young one as underclassmen occupied eighteen of the twenty-two positions. On the positive side, Leon Cross, a resilient player who had hung tough for three years without playing a down because of persistent injuries (the team had given Leon the nickname "The Old Rugged Cross"), was finally healthy and ready to play a starting role alongside Ronny Payne, Billy White, Jim Byerly, Karl Milstead, Jerry Tillery, and Tom Cox. Oklahoma's stable of running backs appeared to be a strong one with Mike McClellan at left halfback, Ronnie Hartline at fullback, and Don Dickey at right halfback.

Although the Sooner nation had high expectations for their team as the season approached, Wilkinson was unable to share their optimism. As early as late spring 1960, he knew that in addition to concerns with his squad's immaturity, he had another serious problem. Wilkinson had planned to start Bob Page at quarterback in 1960, but Page suffered a serious shoulder injury in spring practice that sidelined him for the coming season. So, in late May 1960, Wilkinson asked Abilene, Texas, running back Jimmy Carpenter if he would be willing to play under center. Carpenter had been no stranger to gridiron success himself; while Wilkinson and company had been busy racking up a collegiate record forty-seven-game winning streak from 1953 through 1957, Carpenter's high school football team had been mirroring that success 235 miles southwest of Norman. During the mid-fifties, the Abilene Eagles, with Jimmy Carpenter in the backfield, had won forty-nine straight games, setting a Texas high school record. After graduating in May 1957, Carpenter had cast his lot with the Sooners.

Historically, Wilkinson's quarterbacks had been special to him. Since coaches were not allowed to call plays from the sidelines, Bud considered his quarterbacks extensions of himself on the field and had spent an inordinate amount of professional and personal time with them going over game situations while grilling them on every conceivable combination of events to which they would need to react with split-second timing. Jack Mitchell, Darrell Royal, Claude Arnold, Eddie Crowder, Gene Dan Calame, Jay O'Neal, and Jimmy Harris had each been more than a player to Wilkinson; their relationships had been more like father-to-son than coach-to-player. Unfortunately, with existing rules preventing Carpenter from practicing over the summer, he would have only two weeks in September to prepare himself for the demands of the approaching season. To further complicate the situation, Carpenter still dealt with a hamstring tear he had suffered while playing baseball in the spring of 1959; the injury had required surgery and had kept him sidelined for the 1959 season, and as the 1960 season drew near, it still bothered him. "In late May of 1960, Bud asked me if I would be willing to play quarterback," recounts Carpenter. "I told him I'd never played the position before but I'd be happy to try even though my leg hadn't completely healed from the surgery. I had lost a step and still had a slight limp; I was a long way from 100 percent."[3]

The Sooners' first game would be a rematch against 1959's opening opponent, the Northwestern Wildcats. Oklahoma would be striving to prove that the previous season's blowout loss had been a fluke, and Northwestern was determined to prove that it had not.

Shortly after the game started, the Sooners tantalized the 61,500 partisans in the stadium by drawing first blood on a thirty-five-yard Karl Milstead field goal. But the enthusiasm would not last as Wildcat quarterback Dick Thornton blistered the home team for two passing touchdowns complemented by two field goals as Northwestern went home with a 19–3 victory.[4] Carpenter had played well at quarterback, but the young Sooners had been worn down by Northwestern. Coach Wilkinson stated after the game, "Northwestern has an excellent football team. However, the big disappointment was our lack of mental and physical toughness in the fourth quarter after playing quite well for forty-five minutes."[5]

The disappointment over the loss was palpable within the state of Oklahoma. National championship hopes, while not dead, had taken a serious hit. With one loss in hand and a team that was struggling for identity and confidence, Wilkinson was faced with the task of preparing his team for visiting Pittsburgh and its star tight end Mike Ditka. Ditka, a senior, led the team in receiving and was destined for enshrinement in both the College Football Hall of Fame and the NFL Hall of Fame. Pittsburgh had opened the season with a disappointing 8–7 loss to UCLA in Los Angeles followed by an equally demoralizing tie with Duffy Daugherty's Michigan State Spartans. So after beginning their season ranked seventh in the AP poll, the Panthers were a talented and frustrated 0–1–1 team exuding desperation from every pore.

Oklahoma took an early 7–0 lead on a thirty-yard pass from Jimmy Carpenter to Ronny Payne only to watch it vanish as the Panthers grabbed the momentum and the lead by scoring six-pointers in quarters two and three. However, when Pitt had the ball on the Sooner three-yard line late in the third period and failed to score, the momentum shifted. In the fourth quarter, Sooner end Phil Lohmann blocked a Panther punt, and the ball was recovered by Oklahoma's Marshall York at the Pitt twelve. Wilkinson, showing confidence in his alternate team, sent them in, and two plays later Don Dickey bulled in from the five-yard line for the score. The Sooners lined up for the point after kick, but instead of kicking, Bennett Watts took the snap, skirted right, and carried two Pittsburgh tacklers with him across the goal line. Oklahoma took the lead and the game, 15–14.[6] Ditka had been effectively corralled; the Sooner defense had limited him to two catches for twenty-three yards.

The victory infused the Sooners and their fans with a cautious sense of optimism; their young team had played well, and spirits were high in anticipation of their annual showdown with Texas in Dallas. The Longhorns, after dropping their season opener 14–13 to Nebraska in Austin, had posted back-to-back shutouts against Maryland (34–0) and Texas Tech (17–0). Texas coach Darrell Royal had won two straight from Bud Wilkinson and was determined to take the hat trick as well as the Hat Trophy back to Austin.

Texas posted a field goal and a touchdown in the first quarter and took a 10–0 lead to the halftime locker room. The Longhorns scored the only touchdown in the third quarter and returned an intercepted pass seventy-eight yards for a fourth-quarter tally in the 24–0 win.[7] Although the statistics indicated that the Sooners had been competitive, they were misleading; Oklahoma had only crossed midfield twice and did not mount a threat inside the Steer's red zone until the game was out of hand, and even that drive resulted in a Sooner fumble. Unlike Wilkinson, Royal had the benefit of depth; Texas played three different squads an almost equal amount of time during the game (the first team played for twenty minutes, the second team for twenty-one, and the third team for nineteen).[8]

The 1–2 Sooners then began preparation for their contest with Kansas. Coach Jack Mitchell's team had come within a hairbreadth of defeating Oklahoma in Norman the previous year and was an odds-on favorite to defeat the Sooners in 1960. Kansas entered the game ranked ninth in the nation with victories over TCU and Kansas State; its sole loss had come at the hands of the previous season's national champions, the Syracuse Orangemen.

The two teams fought to a 13–13 tie, as KU, with the ball at the Sooner two-yard line with thirty-four seconds remaining in the game, eschewed a shot at six points and elected instead to go for the game-winning field goal. The Jayhawk kicker's foot stubbed the turf before striking the ball, and the resulting kick fell well short of the crossbar. The Sooners had been forced to rely upon

Sooner Magic to get past Kansas for the second straight year. During any other season, Kansas would have considered a tie with Oklahoma a tremendous moral victory (when it became the first team to score on the national champion Sooners in 1956 in a 34–12 loss, the crowd in Lawrence stormed the field and tore down the goalposts), but times had changed. As the two squads left the field on October 15, 1960, Oklahoma had been relieved to have escaped a trap, and Jack Mitchell and his Jayhawks, having felt as though they had outplayed their southern opponents, were dejected.

By mid-October, Oklahoma's record stood at 1–2–1. Although the going had been rough thus far in 1960, salvation appeared to be at hand. The Sooners had avoided a loss in Lawrence, were looking ahead to their annual game with Kansas State—a game that was usually the equivalent to a free space on a bingo card—and would then proceed into the heart of their conference schedule. But as the Sooners prepared to ford the Big Eight Conference river—a runnel that had been exceedingly kind to them in seasons past—they were to find the waters in 1960 had become deeper, swifter, and more treacherous.

The Kansas State game played out as expected. Just the tonic for an ailing club, the Wildcats were held to sixty-nine yards of total offense and five first downs as the Sooners resembled one of Bud's showcase teams of old while amassing 450 yards of offense and 28 first downs. However, disturbing signs of disarray still loomed. Oklahoma had fumbled seven times (losing two), and while just punting twice on the afternoon, it had averaged only twenty-seven yards per kick. Showing remarkable prescience, Oklahoma guard Karl Milstead remarked in the postgame locker room, "Our first team can't play like we did today and expect to win next week against Colorado."[9] In the quiet of Bud's office after the game, it had been clear to him that the landslide victory was more the result of a poor Kansas State team's inability to compete than of the Sooners' skill.

The following week's trip to Boulder would set the tone for the remainder of the season. Colorado, as has been stated, was consistently the second-best team in the conference during the nineteen-fifties and was responsible for some of the closest games in which Oklahoma was involved during that time. Dallas "Dal" Ward, Colorado's exemplary coach, had resigned after the 1958 season to accept a faculty position, and his successor, Sonny Grandelius, had struggled. But in 1960, the Buffaloes appeared to have awakened. After dropping its season opener to Baylor in Waco, Colorado had won four consecutive games against Kansas State, Arizona, Iowa State, and Nebraska.

The Sooners played the Buffs on a day when the weather offered a hodge-podge of options ranging from rain to sunshine to snow. Early in the game, the Buffs mounted a sixty-one-yard drive for the game's only points in their 7–0 victory. Oklahoma crossed midfield only three times while being held to seven first downs and 193 total yards. The loss came one year to the day after Oklahoma's first conference loss under Wilkinson to Nebraska in 1959. Also, it was Oklahoma's first conference shutout since 1942 when Dewey Luster's team lost to Kansas 7–0. The loss elevated Colorado into a tie for first place in the conference with Missouri and eliminated Oklahoma from Big Eight title contention. Bud Wilkinson was guaranteed his worst season in Norman.

Oklahoma had survived many tense games in Boulder before, so the loss in the Rockies, especially in a season when the Sooners entered the game 2–2–1, was not particularly shocking. Yet even though OU now stood at a disappointing 2–3–1, no one—even Wilkinson himself—expected the ensuing meltdown. The following three weekends saw Oklahoma suffer an unprecedented free fall through the conference with losses to Iowa State, Missouri, and Nebraska. Only the November 26 victory over Oklahoma State—a sort of "welcome to the conference party" for the recently inducted Cowboys—helped to assuage the pain of the season just completed.

Leon Cross believes that the absence of on-field leadership hurt the Sooners in 1960: "It [the leadership] simply wasn't there in 1960. Everybody was worried about 'me' and not the team. Bud was very frustrated with that squad. On one occasion he called us all a bunch of quitters, just trying to motivate us. But we didn't have the talent that year. We had people who didn't make their grades and an unusual number of injuries. I think sometimes you go through these cycles. We won for so long and then we found ourselves with some people who really didn't seem to want to pay the price."[10]

Once again, attrition reared its ugly head. "In 1960, we had lost some players for a variety of reasons," remembers Jimmy Carpenter. "The vast majority of the guys in my freshman class were no longer on the team, for one reason or another."[11] Sooner center John Tatum comments on how the attrition affected the team psychologically:

> The 1957 recruiting class was a great one but almost all of them either got hurt or, for one reason or another, quit, making 1960 absolutely the worst senior class that Coach Wilkinson ever had during his time at OU. We were young, inexperienced, and struggling to adapt to major college football that season. What got us down was, here we were at the University of Oklahoma playing for arguably the greatest coach in major college football, and all of a sudden we're losing games and more of them that he'd ever lost before. I think a lot of us felt like we were letting down the tradition. I was a sophomore that year and most of the guys who should have been seniors were no longer there. It created a genuine leadership problem; and a couple of the seniors still on the team had serious attitudes—they were the kind of guys who could hand someone a thousand dollars and still piss 'em off. If you look at the freshman class of '59, at the end of their three years of eligibility in 1962, there were only eight of us that were three-year lettermen, and *that was unheard of at OU.* Wayne Lee, Paul Lea, Melvin Sandersfeld, Gary Wylie, Dewayne Cook, John Porterfield, Monte Deere all started in '60 as sophomores; which also explains why our '62 team was so much better.[12]

"There were only three games we should have actually lost in 1960," says Leon Cross, "Northwestern, Texas, and Missouri. The Iowa State game was unquestionably the low point of the year for us. But still, we never gave up, never quit during that season."[13]

∵

The football teams of the Big Eight Conference entered 1961 with more collective national notice than they had received in decades. The "six dwarfs" of the Big Seven Conference had existed from 1948 through 1958 under Oklahoma hegemony, so as the Sooners' star began to descend, the fortunes of Missouri, Kansas, and Nebraska started to ascend. Even though Missouri had gone undefeated in 1960, Kansas was the only conference team to make an appearance in the 1961 preseason AP poll; the Jayhawks had earned their number eight spot largely on the strength of their triple-option quarterback, John Hadl. A star high school recruit from Lawrence, Kansas, Hadl had considered taking his talents to Norman in 1958 after bonding with Sooner players in an off-season Fellowship of Christian Athletes meeting.[14] But in the end, Hadl knew he was destined to be scoring his collegiate touchdowns in the Sunflower State.

Losing Hadl in 1958 had been half of a one-two punch that continued to affect the Sooners at quarterback in years to come. When Bud's son, Jay Wilkinson, graduated from Norman High School in May of 1960, he had been one of the most highly sought prep school boys in America. He had earned honors as the Oklahoma co–All State Player of the Year while playing quarterback in the Split-t at Norman High School. Also, Jay had been named a first-team All-American his senior season, was Boomer Conference Player of the Year in both his junior and senior years, and had been voted the most outstanding player in the 1959 Oklahoma All-State game. Jay had also played on Oklahoma's 1960 Oil Bowl team, defeating the Texas All-Stars 14–13—only the second time Oklahoma had won the game since 1945. So it was perfectly understandable that Sooner fans everywhere expected to see Jay Wilkinson don the crimson and cream.

But, as dearly as the people of Oklahoma wanted Jay to enroll at OU and as desperately as the team needed a blue-chip quarterback, Bud Wilkinson had other plans for his sons. He had always insisted that Jay and his brother Pat matriculate outside the state of Oklahoma. And while Jay was deciding where to attend college, the need for talent—specifically at quarterback—at the University of Oklahoma, had reached critical mass.

"It had always been dad's wish that Pat and I would go away to college," recalls Jay. "Dad was an icon in the state of Oklahoma and he realized that had I decided to stay in Norman, the expectations on me would have been staggering."[15] So Jay Wilkinson departed for Duke and his brother Pat to Stanford.

As the Sooners began preseason practice in 1961, they once again faced a shortage of talent. Halfback Don Dickey suffered a knee injury early in practice and was lost for the season; Bill Meacham, also a halfback, quit the team because of a recurring knee injury; center Jim Byerly had left school; and three heralded newcomers were declared academically ineligible on the eve of the new season. Unable to settle on a single quarterback, Wilkinson decided to rotate three into the slot: Bill Van Burkleo, Bob Page, and Monte Deere. On the plus side of the ledger, Tom Cox, Leon Cross, Wayne Lee, Billy White, and Ronny Payne all returned. Jay O'Neal joined Wilkinson's staff in December 1960 when Bob Blaik, son of Army coaching legend Earl "Red" Blaik, departed to go into the oil business with his brother in Oklahoma City. As spring practice began in 1961, O'Neal and his fellow coaches found themselves faced with not only evaluating and training the available talent but also assuaging wounded egos and self-confidence resulting from the past two seasons.

"When we arrived as players in the mid-fifties," recounts O'Neal, "winning was just a given at the University of Oklahoma. It was accepted by everyone on the team that we would win. However, when the players came in after the '59, '60, and '61 seasons, I think that expectation became weakened, diluted. There existed a seed of doubt, perhaps a suspicion that maybe they *wouldn't* suc-ceed."[16] Indeed, the players on campus for spring practice in 1961 were coming off of a year unprecedented at the University of Oklahoma; the 3–6–1 record been a personal low for Wilkinson, and the Sooners had not lost that many games since their war-depleted team in 1931 posted a 4–7–1 mark. Adding insult to injury, the coaching staff was experiencing not-so-friendly fire from the state media, and Wilkinson was being openly criticized for the first time since the season opening loss to Santa Clara in 1948. O'Neal discusses the situation going into the 1961 season:

> Spring practice gave us an opportunity to rebuild the team's psyche. We had to get people into the right positions to enable them to achieve their full potential. And after everyone and everything had been evaluated in the spring, we made the appropriate adjustments in the fall. In 1961 we were handicapped by today's standards; we didn't have players on campus during the summer then like we do now. Players didn't arrive until early September because we couldn't start practicing until two weeks before our first game and in '61 we opened on Sept 30, against Notre Dame in South Bend.[17]

The Fighting Irish had been the bane of Bud Wilkinson's existence. The two teams met for the first time in 1952 in a game broadcast on NBC—the first nationally broadcast college football game in the history of the sport. Although the Irish won the game in a 27–21 thriller, Billy Vessels blistered the Irish defense for 195 yards rushing—a performance that has been acknowledged to have played a key role in Vessel's becoming Oklahoma's first Heisman Trophy winner. The next season, the Irish traveled to Norman for Oklahoma's season opener. Notre Dame was ranked number one in the nation, and Oklahoma was ranked sixth in spite of having suffered heavy losses to graduation. Again, Notre Dame overcame the Sooners, 28–21, in a classic back-and-forth match. The 1953 loss to the Irish would be the last time Oklahoma would lose a game until November 16, 1957, when their fabled forty-seven-game winning streak came crashing down on a blustery fall afternoon as the heavily favored Sooners lost a 7–0 game to their nemesis from South Bend, the University of Notre Dame.

Due to errors resulting from Sooner inexperience, the 1961 Oklahoma–Notre Dame game bore little resemblance to past games between the two teams. The Irish and the Sooners traded punches, leading to an early 6–6 tie, but later, as the Sooners were moving in for the go-ahead score, an errant pitchout gave Notre Dame the ball inside their own five-yard line. Assistant coaches Jay O'Neal and Rudy Feldman were scouting Texas that weekend and were watching the Sooners play the Irish from their hotel room. "Rudy was a fiery, emotional coach," says O'Neal. "His nickname was 'The German.' When he saw our team fumble that ball while trying to score the touchdown, he blew up and threw his glass of water at the television set!"[18] In the 19–6 loss, Oklahoma's starting squad had played 80 percent of the game and had fought the Irish to a virtual standoff; the Sooner alternates, however, had played a mere 20 percent of the time while allowing 160 net yards, an average of 14.5 yards per play. "With a defensive yield like that," said Wilkinson, "it is almost impossible to win."[19]

It had also been impossible to win the next weekend when Iowa State came to town bringing its 2–0 record. Oklahoma would achieve what Wilkinson would refer to as "the low-water mark" of his career in Norman as it allowed ISU to take a 21–0 lead in the first quarter. In that quarter alone, Oklahoma would lose five of six fumbles and toss an interception.[20] Although the Sooners regained their poise and outscored the Cyclones 15–0 during the remainder of the game, they still suffered their second defeat of the season, 21–15. Losses to Texas, Kansas, and Colorado followed in rapid and painful succession as Oklahoma limped to its worst five-game start in the history of the program.

When the Sooners walked off of Owen Field on October 28, 1961, their record stood at 0–5; even worse, over the past twelve months—since October 29, 1960—Oklahoma's record had been 1–9. The Sooners had bottomed out; they could not go any lower. They would not go any lower.

Bud would not allow it.

3 Fighting Back

On October 1, 1932, the New York Yankees were playing the Chicago Cubs at Wrigley Field in game three of the World Series. The game was tied at four runs each in the fifth inning as George Herman "Babe" Ruth approached the batter's box. As he walked to home plate, he was mercilessly harangued by Chicago players from the Cubs' dugout. Cubs' pitcher Charlie Root's first pitch to the Babe just nipped the outside corner of the plate for strike one. Ruth casually looked toward the Cubs' dugout and raised his right hand, extending his index finger. Root's next two pitches were balls. His fourth pitch was another strike. The Babe then looked at the Cubs' dugout and held up two fingers. At this point, Ruth then tapped the dirt from his cleats, narrowed his eyes, looked again to the Cubs' dugout, and then pointed to the center field bleachers. Root's next pitch was a curveball, high and inside, which the Babe blasted over 440 feet past the flagpole in center field, precisely where he had pointed.

Ruth's heroic histrionics have long been the subject of debate over whether his gesture was designed to indicate the destination of his home run. Whatever the truth might have been in game three of the 1932 World Series, Bud Wilkinson's declaration on his television show twenty-nine years later, on October 29, 1961, could not be misinterpreted. After discussing the previous day's loss to Colorado with host Howard Newman, Wilkinson turned his attention to the five remaining games on the schedule. The elephant in the studio loomed large; both Newman and Wilkinson realized that the 0–5 Sooners faced an equally daunting second half of the schedule with games against defending Big Eight champion Missouri in Columbia, Army in Yankee Stadium, and Nebraska in Lincoln. Additionally, two games that usually amounted to little more than scrimmages, with Kansas State and Oklahoma State, posed serious concerns as well.

As Wilkinson's show unfolded, he shocked Newman and the viewing audience by declaring that his Sooners would win their five remaining games. "When Bud made the televised comment that we'd win the rest of our games in

1961, I'm not sure how many of his coaches believed it," comments Jay O'Neal. "The next morning at the coaches meeting we were sort of shaking our heads and laughing about it when someone asked 'What the heck was he thinking?'"[1] As shocking as Wilkinson's proclamation had been, he knew exactly what he was doing. The scores of the first five losses told a story of a team that could easily have been 4–1 rather than 0–5; Bud knew that if the mental errors his team had been making could be eliminated, they would win. "Coach Wilkinson was always upbeat, never down," continues O'Neal. "He knew that if we eliminated the errors we would win games. And that's what he told the team. It gave the players a terrific burst of confidence."[2]

Wilkinson's televised endorsement of his players' capabilities in the midst of a winless season served another important purpose; he was openly expressing confidence in his team and, by making the pronouncement on television, had put his own reputation on the line as a gesture of that confidence. It was a tactic that would be successfully employed later by first-year coaches Barry Switzer in 1973 and Bob Stoops in 1999. Switzer used the draconian probation assessed against the departed Chuck Fairbanks's Sooners after the 1972 season as motivation to propel his first team to a 10–0–1 record and a Big Eight title in 1973, and when Bob Stoops was introduced to the media as Oklahoma's twenty-first head coach in 1999, he openly eschewed the philosophy of "rebuilding," stating instead that his team's goal was to win immediately. Stoops and Switzer each knew that by expressing confidence in their players, they would be imbuing them with a self-confidence of their own.

"Hearing Bud declare that we were going to win the rest of our games after that fifth straight loss was really important to us," says Mike McClellan. "I think mentally, we were simply all tired of getting beaten. After that Colorado loss we had some young guys that finally came around and began to play sound football."[3]

Game six in the 1961 season saw the Sooners travel to Manhattan, Kansas, to play the Kansas State Wildcats. True to form, after beginning the season with victories over Indiana and Air Force, the wheels had fallen off of the Kansas State jalopy as it dropped its next four games before hosting Oklahoma. At halftime, the Sooners held a tenuous 10–0 lead that would shrink to 10–6 late in the second half. However, Mike McClellan's eighty-two-yard fourth-quarter touchdown run sealed the deal, and Wilkinson clinched his first victory since the 1960 Oklahoma State game, forty-nine weeks earlier. Wilkinson's bold televised declaration was beginning to assume an air of cautious prescience.

The next team in Oklahoma's path was Missouri. The Tigers had finished the previous season undefeated, ranked fourth in the country, and had won the Big Eight Conference. Dan Devine's Tigers entered the November 11, 1961, game with the Sooners in Columbia ranked tenth in the country; they had allowed an average of only five points per game to their first seven opponents and had posted three shutouts—one against the previous season's national champions, the Minnesota Golden Gophers. The Tigers had not lost a game in Columbia in over two years; coincidentally, the last time they had lost on their home field was on October 17, 1959, when they had been embarrassed by Oklahoma 23–0.

Wilkinson had not been pleased with practice the week preceding the Missouri game. "After Wednesday evenings after practice," reflects O'Neal, "Bud would usually say 'the hay's in the barn,' and he would have the coaches over to his house for a drink. We would also review anything that needed reviewing and if Volney Meece, John Cronley, and other media people he trusted were in town, he would invite them over, too."[4] But on the Thursday prior to the Missouri game, the hay was evidently not yet in Wilkinson's barn. John Tatum recalls what occurred:

The week of the Missouri game, the practices were just a comedy of errors for the alternate starting unit. It was so bad that on Thursday, Coach Wilkinson stopped practice and demoted our alternate starting unit to last team, and we had about fourteen different teams. Then he dismissed the rest of the squad and kept the alternates out late to work with the last unit. He'd *never* done this before. So after we'd gone through practice with the last team again, he called us together and told us how disappointed he was in us because we were making so many mistakes, and he was right. There were fumbles, guys jumping offsides, center snaps on the wrong snap count, receivers dropping passes, backs hitting the wrong holes . . . you name it. He even said that if there was any way that he could have left us behind for the trip to Columbia, he would have. When we met the bus to take us to Max Westheimer Field for the flight to Columbia the next day, Gomer wouldn't let our unit board the starters' bus. He stopped me as I was starting to board the bus and said, "Johnny, Coach Wilkinson wants you on that other bus . . . he doesn't want you around the starting team." So we got on the other bus and when we got to the airport, we had to fly on the second airplane. In Columbia, he had us staying in a different wing of the hotel and we weren't even allowed to eat with the starters. He totally segregated us because we'd been screwing up so badly.[5]

The heavily favored Tigers won the coin toss and elected to receive the ball. As Wilkinson and the Sooner nation had feared, Missouri moved the ball in workmanlike fashion downfield, four-to-five yards at a clip, until a forty-eight-yard pass completion set them up at the Sooner two-yard line with a first and goal. At this point, Wilkinson called a time-out and gathered the team around him on the sideline. Tatum continues, "Bud called the alternates over and he told us in no uncertain terms that it was *our* fault that Missouri was moving the ball on the other team because of our poor practicing habits the prior week. Then he told us that we had to get out on the field and that if Missouri was going to score, they could score on *us*. When we went into the game, I swear, the Green Bay Packers couldn't have scored on us. We held them on downs and took over."[6]

"Dad told me later," says Jay Wilkinson, "that Missouri had had four cracks at our goal line on that first series. He said that they attacked inside twice and outside twice, and he told me that his coaches had guessed correctly on all four defensive calls."[7] Jimmy Carpenter also reflects on the pivotal game:

We stopped them three or four times right at the goal line during that game. Dennis Ward and those guys made some great plays. On our touchdown, we were on their fifteen-yard line when Bob Page called an option play to the right and pitched it out to me. Just as I caught the ball, I got drilled right in the center of my chest by a Missouri lineman and as

I was going down, out of the corner of my eye, I noticed my roommate, Mike McClellan, skirting the right side, so I flipped out to him and he scored. We called him "Iron Hands," but he had no trouble handling that pitchout. After the season ended, I played in a few All-Star games with some of those Missouri players and they were still chapped about that loss. They had been highly rated nationally at the time . . . at least they were until they played us.[8]

With less than two minutes to play in the game, the Sooners, leading by only seven points, faced a fourth-down punting situation from their own twenty-eight-yard line. Wilkinson had instructed his team well on dealing with just such a scenario, and center Johnny Tatum followed those instructions to perfection; he did not snap the ball. Instead, Tatum took a series of delay-of-game penalties in order to run out the clock (unlike today's rules, in 1961 the clock was restarted after a delay-of-game penalty). When the clock finally expired, Oklahoma had pulled off an unlikely 7–0 road victory over a powerful Missouri team. Dan Devine, furious because of the way Wilkinson had managed the clock in the game's waning seconds, stormed off the field; during the off-season, he became instrumental in getting the delay-of-game timing rule changed.

The 1961 victory over Missouri was a watershed event for the Oklahoma Sooners. Although the team stood at 2–5 for the season, the Sooners' confidence in themselves and in one another had been revalidated. Beating Missouri on the road represented a psychological and emotional turning point for Wilkinson and his Sooners. With three games remaining on their schedule, they began to prepare with a purpose; once again, the Sooners started *expecting* to win. Jerry Pettibone, future Oklahoma assistant coach and world-class recruiter, was a senior on the 1961 squad. He comments, "The team never got down through that entire period although we were frustrated because we knew we weren't playing up to potential. The coaching staff never got down on us or lost faith in us as players."[9]

Oklahoma's next game would be played the weekend prior to Thanksgiving. The venue was Yankee Stadium, located in the northernmost of the five New York

City boroughs. The Sooners would be facing the United States Military Academy. Finding themselves underdogs to the 6–2 Cadets, the Crimson and Cream reverted to a play they had used with deadly effectiveness in the last decade: the no-huddle, "go-go" offense.

"Bud had noticed that Army had a habit of emerging from their defensive huddle somewhat slowly, so we decided to run a quick snap play on them," recalls Carpenter. "On our first counter play, I gained about ten yards, then Page called the same play again and we picked up a couple more." On the next play, while Army was still trying to break their defensive huddle and get into position, Carpenter took the snap directly from center and, before the Cadets were set, pitched it out to McClellan who ran straight ahead for seventy-nine yards and a touchdown. "Army adjusted pretty darned quick after that play, but we still won the game, 14–8."[10]

Win number three in Wilkinson's unlikely prophecy had come to pass, and the Sooners began preparation for their Turkey Day showdown with the Cornhuskers in Lincoln. After winning twelve games against Nebraska in his first twelve seasons as head coach, Bud Wilkinson found himself mired in a two-game losing streak to his former assistant coach and not-so-friendly adversary Bill Jennings. Jennings, in year five of a five-year contract, had yet to produce a winning season and knew that to have any chance at being retained in Lincoln, beating the Sooners was a must.

By halftime it appeared that Nebraska had nothing to fear. On the strength of touchdowns in the first two quarters, the Huskers led Oklahoma 14–0. To make matters worse, only two teams had scored more than fourteen points on Nebraska's defense all season long. In the locker room, Wilkinson vented his frustration in uncharacteristic fashion. Tatum recalls Wilkinson's halftime tirade:

Coach Wilkinson was livid. It was the only time in my five years at OU that I ever heard him single out guys by name and criticize them. He was upset not only because of the way we were playing but because of who was beating us. He said, "You guys are an embarrassment to the tradition of Oklahoma football. I wish I could watch the rest of this game from the press box so I couldn't be seen associating with this team." After the referee came in for the five-minute warning, Ronny Payne stood up and said, "Okay guys, let's go out and kick their asses!" Coach Wilkinson turned and said, "Ronny, sit down. That's the problem with this team. You guys are all talk and no do." Then he turned to Gomer and said, "Gome, give me a two or three minute head start and then you bring these guys out; I don't want to be seen with them."[11]

The 1961 offensive line fires off the mark. *Left to right:* Dale Perini, Leon Cross, Karl Milstead, John Tatum, Claude Hamon (obscured by Tatum), Billy White, Ronny Payne. Courtesy John Tatum.

Wilkinson's fury was contagious. Oklahoma took the second-half kickoff and, in only three plays, scored its first touchdown of the day on a thirty-yard pass from Bob Page to Ronny Payne. Later in the same period, a nineteen-yard punt return by Monte Deere set the Sooners up for their second score, a nine-yard scamper by Jimmy Carpenter. The game remained tied until, early in the fourth quarter, Nebraska's league-leading punter, Dennis Claridge, boomed a towering kick over Oklahoma's punt coverage team that rolled dead at the Sooner two-yard line. Oklahoma then began the game-winning drive—a marathon push toward Nebraska's goal line that burned over twelve precious minutes off the game clock. When Jimmy Carpenter finally covered the last few yards for the touchdown, there was scarcely enough time for the deflated Huskers to stage a comeback. Oklahoma had prevailed 21–14.

"We went out in the second half and scored three times to win the game," smiles Tatum. "In the dressing room afterwards, Coach Wilkinson told us, 'you guys have got more heart and courage than any team I've ever been associated with.'"[12]

Only one final game stood between Wilkinson and the fulfillment of his October 29 prophecy. From a historical perspective, playing Oklahoma State in Norman was generally not a source of great concern; however, the Sooners had not won a home game all year, and the pressure was on.

After a respectable struggle, Oklahoma State finally relented to Oklahoma, 21–13. With their fifth victory in a row, the Sooners had turned a 0–5 disaster into an unlikely 5–5 salvation and found themselves voted the Comeback Team of 1961 by the Associated Press. Wilkinson's bold October gambit had paid off for Oklahoma. No major college football coach had ever gone from 0–5 to 5–5 in the same season. His feat of turning the Sooners around in 1961 against daunting odds had been nothing short of pure coaching alchemy. Darrell Royal said of Wilkinson's 1961 accomplishment, "I believe that was probably the best coaching job Bud Wilkinson has ever done in Norman."[13]

⁙

While the hopes of the Sooner nation were bolstered during the winter of 1962 by their team's resurgence, Bud Wilkinson was pondering his future. He had confided in university president George Cross that his interest and enthusiasm for coaching was waning, and further compounding his dilemma was an interest in politics he had developed while serving as the director of the President's Council on Youth Fitness and through his close association and friendship with President Kennedy. However, his brief sojourn in Washington had left him ambivalent about a role in politics; he was both fascinated by the opportunities presented by government service and repulsed by its petty intrigues.[14]

In 1962, Wilkinson was enthusiastic about the incoming group of sophomores ready to step into the fray. Headlining the group of second-year players were Ralph Neely, Eddie McQuarters, Jim Grisham, Norman Smith, Butch Metcalf, Glen Condren, Ron Fletcher, Lance Rentzel, Newt Burton, Charley Mayhue, and

Jim Grisham and Bud Wilkinson. Courtesy Jim and Mattie Grisham.

Rick McCurdy. This group of comparative youngsters would bolster and support the returning contingent of upperclassmen including Leon Cross, Wayne Lee, Johnny Tatum, Paul Lea, Virgil Boll, Monte Deere, James Parker, Jimmy Payne, Bobby Page, Dennis Ward, George Jarman, Jackie Cowan, Gary Wylie, John Flynn, and Bud Dempsey. Also joining the Sooners would be the quixotic and supremely talented Joe Don Looney. Only the second junior college transfer ever accepted by Bud Wilkinson (the first had been fullback Don Anderegg in 1947),[15] Looney had attended both the University of Texas and Texas Christian University for one semester each on track scholarships before transferring to Cameron Junior College in Lawton, Oklahoma. While at Cameron, Looney had led the Gold and Black to an undefeated season and a 28–20 victory over Bakersfield (California) Junior College in the "Little Rose Bowl."[16] Jay O'Neal, the Oklahoma assistant coach who discovered and brought Joe Don to Norman, reflects on recruiting Looney:

> Most of what I've read about Joe Don Looney is totally off the wall and doesn't make a lot of sense. He was not highly recruited by us; in fact, the chances that he would have ever been admitted to the University of Oklahoma were about ninety to one against. His grades coming out of the University of Texas and TCU had been poor, so he had to graduate from Cameron Junior College with nineteen hours of A or B over the spring and summer to even qualify. So it was just on a lark that I went by Cameron after they'd won the Little Rose Bowl. As a general rule, we didn't take junior college kids, so even in order to be considered the player would have had to have been outstanding, and Joe Don was. My goodness gracious, if you'd watched the film on him, here was a guy punting the ball out of sight, outrunning everybody and running over the people he couldn't outrun. He was fabulous. Under today's rules where we have scholarship limitations, we never would have taken a chance on him, but at that time, with no limitations, we were willing to take the risk. So I told him, "Joe Don, if you can graduate with the necessary grades we'd love to have you," but I never thought he'd ever do it. However, he was a smart kid and he made those grades.[17]

In the late spring of 1962, Wilkinson had good reason to be excited about the quarterback position. The Sooner varsity, led by sophomore signal caller Tommy Pannell, had beaten the alumni team in the annual spring teaser. Wilkinson had never started a season with a sophomore at quarterback before—Jimmy Harris had started most of 1954 as a sophomore, but only after Gene Calame was injured early on—but he was prepared to make an enthusiastic exception for Pannell, who could run, pass, and execute the Split-t to near perfection. But eight days prior to the season opener Pannell went down with a season-ending fractured ankle, and once again Wilkinson found his squad unsettled at its most critical position. Jay O'Neal comments on the state of the team without Pannell:

When Pannell went down with that broken ankle during two-a-days, it threw us. From that point on, who we selected to start at quarterback was pretty much determined by who was playing well that particular week. Not that the other quarterbacks weren't good in their own right, but the team had worked with Tommy, was conditioned to respond to his techniques, and had developed a great deal of confidence in him. Anytime you make a change at quarterback so close to the first game, there are bound to be problems and I believe that, as a result of his injury, we never had any real offensive consistency in the first part of 1962."[18]

⁚

Oklahoma opened the 1962 season with a highly anticipated game against head coach Ben Schwartzwalder's Syracuse Orangemen. Syracuse had captured the 1959 national title and had finished nineteenth in 1960 and fourteenth in 1961.

Neither the Sooners nor the Orangemen could establish a foothold in the first half, and, on the strength of a thirty-five-yard field goal, Syracuse took a hard-fought 3–0 lead into the locker room. After suffering through the past two seasons with a Sooner team that had struggled mightily on offense, Big Red partisans watching the game in Memorial Stadium or listening on the radio were experiencing unpleasant waves of déjà vu.

Both teams managed deep penetrations into the other's territory in the third period, but neither could produce points for their efforts. Late in the fourth period, Syracuse was sitting on the Sooners' twenty-eight-yard line with a fourth and one. Coach Schwartzwalder ordered a line plunge by fullback Jim Nance, but Johnny Tatum and Paul Lea were there to deny him, and Oklahoma took possession of the ball with four minutes left to play. The Big Red found themselves in a 3–0 hole from which, with their sputtering offense, they were unlikely to emerge. While on the sidelines, another drama was playing out.

Joe Don Looney had been pacing behind the coaching staff, impatiently pestering the coaches to put him into the game. As the Sooner offense began to take the field for what promised to be the final time, an exasperated Looney told Wilkinson that if allowed to play he would "win the game." Finally, Wilkinson shook his head in resignation and sent Joe Don onto the field. On Oklahoma's first carry, halfback Jackie Cowan skirted the right perimeter for eight yards. On the second play, fullback Looney followed a crushing block by Leon Cross for five yards and a first down at the Sooner forty-yard line. Back in the huddle, quarterback Monte Deere prepared to call the next play when Looney growled, "Just give me the damned ball and I'll score." Deere handed the ball to Looney on the next play, and, after gaining two tough yards inside, Looney was engulfed by Syracuse defenders. Suddenly, Looney emerged from the scrum, fighting, staggering, and finally regaining his balance as he flashed sixty yards down the left sideline for the touchdown. Oklahoma successfully converted the point after and held on for the victory. As stunning as Looney's feat was, it was no more important to the game's outcome than the Oklahoma defense had been. End Rick McCurdy recovered three Syracuse fumbles—one inside the Sooner ten-yard line—to preserve the victory. However, as is usually the case, the offense received the glory, and thus began the legend of Joe Don Looney.

The Sooners' euphoria over winning their first season opener in four years was short-lived as they lost their next two games, to Notre Dame in Norman and to Texas in Dallas. "Those losses were deflating because when you examine the scores, we could have won either game easily," reflects O'Neal.[19]

Although Oklahoma entered late October with a losing record for the third straight season, the pattern of the previous three years would be broken as Wilkinson led his team on a resolute march through the Big Eight Conference. The Big Red snapped Kansas Coach Jack Mitchell's three-game winning streak 13–7; walloped Kansas State, Colorado, Iowa State, and Missouri by the combined score of 162–0; downed first-year Nebraska head coach Bob Devaney's Cornhuskers 34–6; and wrapped up the season with a business-as-usual scuttling of Oklahoma State in Stillwater 37–6.

It has been suggested that Oklahoma's resurgence in 1962 could be attributed to a decline in fortunes of the other seven conference squads. However, a comparison of the records of those seven teams both during Oklahoma's down years of 1960 and 1961 and its return to respectability in 1962 belies this argument. In 1960, Oklahoma's conference partners amassed a combined win/loss record of 37–33–1, while in 1961 their mark was 37–32–3. In the year of Oklahoma's recovery, 1962, its conference foes posted a 34–35–3 record, not significantly divergent from the previous two seasons. Examining each team individually in 1962, only two teams performed markedly outside the curve of the previous year. Colorado dropped from 9–2–0 in 1961 to 2–8–0 in 1962 while Nebraska would rise from 1961's 3–6–1 record to 9–2–0 in 1962 under its new head coach Bob Devaney. Therefore, it may be concluded that the success enjoyed by Wilkinson in 1962 was a result of the team he laboriously coached and fielded and not from any decline in performance by his opponents.

At the end of the 1962 regular season, Leon Cross, Wayne Lee, and Joe Don Looney had earned All-American honors, the first Sooners to do so since Jerry Thompson in 1959. In late November, the Sooners had received an invitation to the twenty-eighth annual Orange Bowl game. Their opponent would be the Alabama Crimson Tide, coached by Paul "Bear" Bryant. Bryant, in his third year in Tuscaloosa, had won the national title in 1961 and was bringing a 9–1–0 team into the 1963 Orange Bowl. Jay O'Neal recalls a special visitor to the Oklahoma team in the pregame locker room prior to kickoff in the Orange Bowl:

> We had taken the team out on the field to warm up and then when we went back into the locker room, I suspected something unusual was happening. Unlike normal procedure, we weren't getting the guys ready to take the field for the opening kickoff; there was an air of anticipation. Then the doors opened and in came the Secret Service escorting President Kennedy. He shook each of our hands and then, as he looked around, he spotted Larry Vermillion. The president walked over to him, smiled, patted him on his protruding stomach and said "Hey Bud, you need to get this guy involved in our physical fitness program!"[20]

For as good as the Sooners were, Alabama was better. Their vicious defense was headlined by Lee Roy Jordan, and their versatile offense was made all the more dangerous by sophomore phenomenon, Joe Willie Namath. A Pennsylvania native, Namath had been rejected by the University of Maryland because

After his visit to the Sooner locker room, President Kennedy performs the opening coin toss for the 1963 Orange Bowl. Secret Service agents escorted both the Sooner captains and the Alabama captains up into the stands, where Kennedy was seated for the ceremony. Sooner captain Leon Cross can be seen in profile on the far left of the photo; Tide captain Lee Roy Jordan (usually #55, but wearing #54 for the Orange Bowl game) stands with his back to the camera facing JFK. Courtesy Leon Cross.

his college board scores were not high enough, so he headed south to play for the Bear. By 1962, most college football teams had incorporated passing plays into their routine, but few could throw the ball with Namath's dexterity, variety, accuracy, and strength. Years later, Bear Bryant called Namath "the best athlete I ever coached."[21]

Jordan made thirty-one tackles in the contest, and while Oklahoma effectively controlled the Tide running game, Namath passed his team to a 17–0 victory. "Namath killed us," remembers O'Neal. "Not many teams threw the ball very well in those days. Blocking rules didn't allow for much time in the pocket, and it really took a guy like Namath, who was a superb passer, to make it work. They just had a better team than we did."[22] Bud's son Jay Wilkinson provides interesting insights into Bryant and Wilkinson's relationship:

Bear Bryant was a phenomenal coach. He was one of those rare people who had the capacity to evolve with time. He was intelligent and flexible enough to adjust to social trends such as allowing his players to wear long hair while maintaining the same strong discipline and strict standards he'd always demanded from his team. In fact, after Oklahoma lost in the 1951 Sugar Bowl to Kentucky, dad and the Bear had agreed to meet every year and spend two or three days in a hotel suite with a blackboard and just talk football. My junior year at Duke, we had turned down an invitation to the Gator Bowl; this was the same year that Oklahoma lost to Coach Bryant's Alabama team in the Orange Bowl. Coach Bryant came to dad's suite that evening and I remember saying to him, "Coach, I believe that if we hadn't fumbled twice inside your ten-yard line it would have been a much different game." He looked at me and replied in that deep drawl of his, "Jay, I still think we're going to find a way to win that game."[23]

With 1962 behind him, Wilkinson could look forward to 1963 knowing that he would be welcoming back a seasoned, junior-laden squad. But issues still remained for the coach. Although the concerns he had expressed to Dr. Cross in the spring of 1962 regarding his waning lack of enthusiasm for the game appeared to have subsided with the excitement generated by a winning season, the seeds of political ambition that had been planted in 1960 were beginning to take root.

4 Bud's Last Hurrah

JANUARY 1963–JANUARY 1964

In early 1963, Sooner fans, although enjoying their team's 8–3 resurgence in 1962, were once again wringing their hands over the fate of Bud Wilkinson. The cleats and pads had barely been stored after the Orange Bowl loss when Stanford University began courting Wilkinson. In early January, officials from Stanford, anticipating a vacancy at their head coaching position, offered him the job. When informed of the development, President Cross discussed the opportunity at length with Wilkinson without attempting to dissuade him as he had done on two separate occasions in the early 1950s.[1]

Meanwhile, rumors of Wilkinson's political ambitions continued to swirl. Some suggested that he would either enter the gubernatorial race or pursue the senate seat left vacant by the passing of senate majority leader Robert S. Kerr on New Year's Day 1963. And Wilkinson, in an effort to avoid being dishonest, unintentionally added fuel to the fire by neither admitting strong interest nor denying either pursuit. "Although rumors were rife about dad's interest in entering the political arena," comments Jay Wilkinson, "I know for an absolute certainty that he was not even remotely considering either a gubernatorial or senatorial run in early 1963."[2]

In the final analysis, Wilkinson decided to remain in Norman. He felt that the legacy of success he had established and the insurmountable records his teams had set since 1947 would be tainted were he to depart on the heels of the past four years' 23–17–1 record. Plus, the prospect of returning for the 1963 season with a healthier, stronger team reignited a coaching fire inside of him that had been flickering.

In January 1963, Wilkinson also had to deal with major changes in his coaching staff. The Colorado head coaching position came open, and Bud's offensive coordinator, Eddie Crowder, was tapped to fill it. In the process of building his staff, Crowder selected Jay O'Neal, Rudy Feldman, and Chet Franklin, all from the Sooner staff, to join him in Boulder. Wilkinson gave his blessings to all except Jay O'Neal, whom he asked to remain in Norman; O'Neal and Crowder had comprised Bud's backfield staff, and losing both could have proven ruinous. Feldman, who had assisted Gomer Jones with the linemen, needed to be replaced, and Bud decided to contact Alabama line coach Bobby Drake Keith on Jakie Sandefer's recommendation. Keith recalls, "Bud called and asked if I'd come up and visit with him. I had planned to stay in coaching and I figured it'd be hard to beat a resumé with Bear Bryant and Bud Wilkinson on it. So I flew to Norman for an interview. After the visit I asked him, 'Coach, I'm very impressed but I've been hearing rumors that you might be thinking about retiring.' He told me, 'I can't quit, Drake, I've got one son in medical school and another in divinity school.' So although I was happy at Alabama, I decided to go to Oklahoma."[3] With Keith coming aboard, the Sooner staff consisted of Wilkinson, Jones, O'Neal, Keith, George Dickson (who had quarterbacked Notre Dame's 1949 national championship team), Jerry Thompson, Bob Cornell, Leon Cross, and graduate assistants John Tatum and Bill Battle.

And in Oklahoma's first game of the 1963 season, it appeared that things *had* changed. After losing their opening-day game in two of the last three seasons, the fourth-ranked Sooners took a strong Clemson team to task. The Tigers, picked by sports pundits to capture the ACC crown in 1963, jumped on a shocked Oklahoma team, taking an early 14–0 lead. As Mervin Hyman wrote in *Sports Illustrated:* "Clemson made the sorry mistake of scoring two second-quarter touchdowns. This infuriated proud Oklahoma. Its rangy linemen began to hit more purposefully, Jim Grisham ran 26 yards for a touchdown, Lance Rentzel raced 49 yards for another and Oklahoma won 31–14. For once, Clemson's Frank Howard, noted for his droll witticisms, was not funny. His lone, sad comment was: 'They've got big, tough bullies in that line.'"[4]

Up next on the schedule for the 1–0 Sooners was a road contest against John McKay's USC Trojans, the defending national champions. USC was in the midst of a twelve-game winning streak and had not lost at home since 1961. Assistant coach Bobby Drake Keith had scouted the Trojans for Oklahoma and, when asked the best way to defend their speed and balance, replied, "Pray for rain."[5] But it did not rain in Los Angeles on game day. The broiling sun had virtually rendered the playing field unbearable as the surface temperature in the Coliseum approached 120 degrees. McKay suggested to Wilkinson that the game be delayed until that evening to allow the field a chance to cool off, but Bud declined; he was confident that his team was better conditioned than USC.

"It was hotter than hell in the Coliseum," remembers O'Neal. "We had a great game plan; our quarterback would take the snap and, watching which way USC would stunt, use that to his advantage. But we weren't getting a consistently clean center snap and by the time our quarterback, Mike Ringer, managed to gain control of it the Trojans had already made their stunts so we were making big gains on what looked like quarterback sneaks."[6] The Sooners upended the favored Trojans, 17–12, and stepped up to the number one spot in the nation. *Sports Illustrated*'s Dan Jenkins wrote after the game:

> Admittedly, Oklahomans have had plenty of football teams to sing about in the past, but they have not had many victories as sweet or as important as the one over USC. On the fiery grid of the Memorial Coliseum, Bud Wilkinson's deep, brutal Sooners beat the Trojans man for man. Hammering away in Wilkinson's ball-control fashion, they provided the still-fresh 1963 season with a most astonishing statistic. On a day when the Coliseum floor scarcely gave off a wisp of air to breathe, when special bamboo canopies had been built to shade the players on the sidelines and men sat in the press box without shirts, the Sooners ran 100 plays.[7]

With a bye week between the Southern Cal triumph and the Red River Rivalry, the number one–ranked Sooners had two weeks to enjoy their view from the top. Not since September 29, 1958, had Oklahoma occupied the top position in the Associated Press poll. Wilkinson's teams had spent 261 weeks in the wilderness, and now, at long last, they appeared to have emerged stronger, quicker, and more resilient. But the revelry was to be short-lived. Although the quarterback position had been unsettled as late as the week prior to the opening game with Clemson, Mike Ringer had moved in and played well; the team was in sync and the offense was moving the ball. Then, the week prior to the Texas game, team cohesion took a hit when an injury Ringer had suffered prior to the USC game became infected, effectively sidelining him for the remainder of the season.

The 28–7 loss to the Texas Longhorns on October 12, 1963, brought the Sooners crashing back down to earth. Although Wilkinson had regained much of his coaching enthusiasm after winning the first two games and reaching the number one spot in the wire service polls, the setback to the Longhorns, his sixth straight loss to his friend and former pupil, Royal, was deflating. Although Texas was a far superior team to Oklahoma in 1963—it would finish the season with Royal's first national championship—Wilkinson once again sensed the nagging specter of defeat peering over his shoulder.

"We had a big psychological advantage in the OU game because we were scared to death after watching them beat Southern California on television," declared Royal. "Oklahoma deserved to beat USC, but they came out of that game with a problem."[8] The problem to which Royal was referring was Joe Don Looney. Bud knew before the Texas debacle that his team was a good one, and with Joe Don Looney performing at his best it was close to being a *very* good one. But Looney could also prove to be a source of tremendous disruption, and he had rankled Wilkinson tremendously with his petulant attitude since preseason training camp. After the Texas game, Bud's patience with Looney ran out.

"In 1962, Joe Don was a terrific player and had been easy to get along with," recounts O'Neal. "He was in a new, major college football environment and he was determined to prove himself. But we had no weight program at that time so he went to LSU the summer prior to the 1963 season and became involved in Alvin Roy's weight conditioning program; Alvin was a pioneer in weight training and later became the trainer for the San Diego Chargers. When Joe Don left for LSU he'd weighed 195 pounds; when he returned a few months later, he was at 225. He looked like Superman; he was bigger, faster, and tougher than he'd ever been before. But he was also more difficult."[9]

After the Texas game, the issue came to a head. John Tatum, a graduate assistant in 1963, relates the event:

There are very few stories about OU football history that haven't been written, but this is one of them. There aren't many people who know the real story of what happened regarding Joe Don Looney's expulsion. Over the years I've been asked by various writers what happened but I wouldn't tell them. Looney was an extremely difficult individual and one of the greatest wastes of talent that ever passed through Norman. When people would ask me about Joe Don, I'd reply, "No comment," and ask why they didn't write about someone who did something more redeeming with their lives than going off and taking care of some guru's elephant in India? Something happened to Joe Don after his first year in Norman. He returned to campus in the summer of '63 all muscled up, solid as a rock, he'd gained weight, and he had an attitude. We were in practice the Tuesday after OU had beaten Southern California in the Coliseum. Joe Don had had a great game against the Trojans, but when we took the practice field the next week and he found out that he was still listed on the alternate unit, he was mad as hell. Jay O'Neal was running the practice drill that day, and I was playing defensive end. I was decked out in shorts, tennis shoes, t-shirt, a cap, and a whistle, and I was using an air dummy. Jay told me to crash, float, box, drift—the things a defensive end normally does. Looney was in full gear except he had his helmet off because of his prima donna attitude. Anyway, when the ball was snapped, I crashed down with the air dummy on Joe Don, and it hit him in the ear and pissed him off. He used some choice words on me and I replied, "Joe, if you'd been wearing your helmet like everyone else you wouldn't have gotten your ear scraped." So he put his helmet on and goes back and gets in the line and soon it's his turn again. Here he comes and, once again, I float, and he throws a forearm over the top of the air dummy at my nose. I shoved the dummy up into his face, and he takes another swing at me, then I wrestle him to the ground. So here I am fighting a 225-pound guy in full armor and I have no protection on. He tore off my shirt and I pulled off his helmet. The other coaches jumped in and separated us, and that was it. We went back to practice. What happened on the practice field that day was no different than what had happened on the practice field innumerable times; football is a violent sport played at OU by highly competitive people. Tempers often flare which leads to fights on the field. Nobody ever thinks anything about it, and nobody thought anything about the scuffle he and I got into that day. In fact the coaches, Gomer especially, kidded me about picking on Joe Don. Everybody thinks Looney was released immediately after that incident but that wasn't the case. We had a week off after Southern Cal before we went to Dallas. During the Texas game, Bud wanted to send Joe Don in to play but he refused before finally relenting. And when he did go in, his effort was half-hearted. When we got back to campus, Bud called a team meeting without Joe Don present, and the decision was made to throw him off the team. I was driving back home from Oklahoma City when a news bulletin came on the radio that said Joe Don had been kicked off the team because he had been involved in a fight with assistant coach John Tatum. I was with two other people, and I was shocked that that was the reason they'd given the press, because the incident had happened two weeks earlier. Recently I read an article by Al Eschbach, and it provided an account of the incident. In his account, Looney had "knocked out the assistant coach." Well that's just wrong, I was never knocked out, not even close. But the fact that he had been involved in a fight with me during practice *may* have played some part in his dismissal.[10]

Jay O'Neal also believes that Looney had not given 100 percent against Texas. "After the Texas game, the dissension on the team was boiling over. If you watched the game film, Joe Don didn't seem to be himself and a lot of the guys resented it. It had gotten to the point where he was almost uncontrollable."[11]

As the season progressed, the Sooners overcame Jack Mitchell's Kansas team and Gayle Sayers's brilliance the following week in a heart-stopping 21–18 thriller followed by consecutive wins over Kansas State (34–9), Colorado (35–0), Iowa State (24–14), and Missouri (13–3), before heading to Nebraska on November 21, 1963. The next morning, Friday November 22, the team ate breakfast, meetings were conducted, players were taped, and everyone boarded the buses for the trip to Memorial Stadium for afternoon practice. As they drove to the stadium, they were struck by the uncharacteristic demeanor of the people on the streets of Lincoln. Rather than waving, or jeering, or simply walking along minding their business, people were milling about, talking, red-eyed, appearing shocked and upset. When the team arrived at the stadium, they were informed that President John F. Kennedy had been assassinated in Dallas. Bud, who was very close to the Kennedy brothers, wanted to cancel the game as so many other coaches had already done; however, he was dissuaded by a phone conversation with the president's brother Robert.

"Bud spoke with Bobby Kennedy, and Bobby told him that his brother would have wanted the game to be played," says Sooner lineman Jerry Thompson.[12] So a deflated Oklahoma team took the field that day before an uncharacteristically reserved crowd in Lincoln only to lose the game, 29–20. "Bud's heart just wasn't in the Nebraska game," comments Bobby Drake Keith.[13]

After defeating Oklahoma State in Norman on November 30, the team finished the year with a respectable 8–2–0 record and was ranked tenth in the final AP poll. "After the game, we received an invitation to play in a minor bowl but we voted to decline it," recalls Ralph Neely. "We didn't want to go to a runner-up bowl; we wanted the Orange Bowl. Back then, there were just a fistful of bowl games and the Orange was one of the best as it still is today."[14]

The loss to Nebraska was at least partly attributable to Bud Wilkinson's shock and disappointment over the loss of his friend and political mentor, but the Kennedy assassination had another effect on Bud; it pushed him ever closer to the inevitable decision to set coaching aside and enter the political arena. "The assistant coaches took turns hosting a get-together with the wives after road games," recounts Bobby Drake Keith, "and the night after the Nebraska game, we got together at my house. Bud was the last one to leave that evening. We sat and talked for a long while and the topics ranged from the practical to the philosophical. He finally left about 2:30 A.M. and I had a very strong feeling at that time that he was going to resign."[15]

Six weeks later to the day, speculation became reality as Bud Wilkinson tendered his resignation on January 11, 1964, as head football coach at the University of Oklahoma. Wilkinson retained his position as athletic director for one more week before resigning it as well on January 18.

∵

When evaluating the legacy that Bud Wilkinson left in the wake of his seventeen years in Norman, there are three separate and distinct points to be measured. The first issue generally considered is his success on the football field. When Wilkinson arrived with Jim Tatum in 1946, the Oklahoma Sooners had historically been a mediocre football team. From 1905 through 1926, Bennie Owen ushered in a period of football innovation and resulting success while posting a 122–54–16 record. But the success of the Owen years faded after 1926 as the program settled into eleven years of mediocrity before Tom Stidham led Oklahoma to its first bowl game and first national ranking in 1938. From 1939 through 1945, the Sooners once again struggled with mediocrity. In 1946, with Wilkinson's help, Tatum took Oklahoma to its second bowl, and, upon his departure, Bud Wilkinson ascended. Wilkinson lured the University of Nebraska's line coach, Gomer Thomas Jones, to Norman and began an assault on college football precedents leading to on-field records that have not and may never be broken. Bud Wilkinson's mechanical genius with the Split-t offense and his personal skills in dealing with his players elevated the University of Oklahoma to the pantheon of college football's historic powerhouses.

The second measure of Wilkinson's legacy must be the social and athletic strides he made in incorporating African American players into his program during a period of tremendous resistance to such matters. In 1946, the National Association for the Advancement of Colored People (NAACP) chose the University of Oklahoma as the target for testing the constitutionality of the Jim Crow laws, legislation designed to segregate African Americans from certain aspects of white society. On January 14 of that year, Ada Lois Sipuel Fisher, an African American from Chickasha, Oklahoma, and an honors graduate from Langston University, challenged the law preventing African Americans from matriculating at all-white state universities by petitioning for enrollment at the University of Oklahoma School of Law. Her application was denied, and a four-year court battle ensued before the U.S. Supreme Court finally ruled that such laws deprived citizens of their constitutional rights and were unconstitutional and unenforceable.[16]

Six years later, Bud Wilkinson recruited OU's first African American player, Prentice Gautt, an honors student and star running back from Oklahoma City's Douglass High School. Wilkinson could have easily avoided the controversy and its ensuing problems by denying Gautt but chose instead to accept the challenge. His motives were clearly more altruistic than practical given that when Gautt enrolled at the University of Oklahoma in 1956, the Sooner roster was still brimming with young talent; and although Gautt was a welcome addition, he was not critically needed. Far more common an occurrence in the social milieu of the time was the case of Charles Aaron "Bubba" Smith from Beaumont, Texas. Smith had grown up a dyed-in-the-wool Texas Longhorn fan and, although a difference-making high school player, was refused admission to the University of Texas in 1963 because of the color of his skin. Subsequently, Smith traveled north to play for Duffy Daugherty at Michigan State, where he earned All-American status in both his junior and senior seasons before going on to greater fame with the NFL's Baltimore Colts.

When Wilkinson smashed the athletic racial barrier at Oklahoma in 1956, sports integration had yet to form a discernable blip on the radar screens of southern sports programs. In 1959, when Alabama played an integrated Penn State in the Liberty Bowl, it created such a furor that a movement arose by 'Bama fans and administration to cancel the game, and in 1963, when Darryl Hill became the first African American player at the University of Maryland, Clemson and South Carolina threatened to secede from the ACC. While Gautt became the first black team member for the University of Oklahoma in 1956, the Southwest Conference would not break the color barrier for another ten years when SMU head coach Hayden Fry recruited Jerry LeVias in 1966, and Texas and Alabama, both conceding to social pressure—generally originating from outside the borders of those states—as well as the desire to upgrade the quality of their respective teams, accepted their first African American players in 1970.

The impact of early integration at the University of Oklahoma, both socially and athletically, cannot be underestimated. Wilkinson would go on to recruit other African Americans such as Wally Johnson, Eddie McQuarters, Nehemiah Flowers, and Ben Hart, all of whom would establish inroads for future minority students and players. The success of black athletes on the playing fields of Norman not only would give the University of Oklahoma a distinct athletic advantage in the years to come but would hasten the acceptance of African Americans into mainstream society. Wilkinson stated that accepting Prentice Gautt into the fold of Oklahoma football was "the most significant thing I did when I was coaching; there's no question in my mind."[17] And Wilkinson's courageous pursuit of black players paved the way for Chuck Fairbanks in 1967. Fairbanks, a native of Michigan and an alumnus of Michigan State (he had played on Duffy Daugherty's 1952 national championship team), had grown up color-blind in a social context. While at Houston as an assistant coach, Fairbanks played a role in recruiting their first black player, Warren McVea. And during Fairbanks's tenure and beyond in Norman, Barry Switzer's ability to relate to and lure black athletes to Norman revolutionized college football.

The third gauge of Wilkinson's legacy is closely linked to the first. By the end of the Second World War, the state of Oklahoma was emerging from the trauma of the Depression and the dust bowl. The state's postwar economy had been bolstered by the painful demise of the small-farm system that had been washed away by the drought of the 1930s and replaced by large corporate farmers, and by the emergence and proliferation of the petroleum industry. But despite the inroads being made into the state economy, the stigma of Stein-beck's *Grapes of Wrath* image remained.

Prior to hiring Jim Tatum and Bud Wilkinson, the University of Oklahoma's board of regents observed that the morale of the average state resident was so low that many of them actually felt apologetic about living in Oklahoma. Regent Lloyd Noble felt that the coaching vacancy created by Dewey Luster's resignation after the 1945 season offered an opportunity for the state to elevate its national image by hiring a coach who could field a winning college football program. As has already been noted, Jim Tatum became the twelfth head coach at the University of Oklahoma in 1946, and upon his departure for Maryland one year later, Bud Wilkinson took the throttle. Over the next ten seasons, Wilkinson's Sooners won three national titles and thirteen conference titles and embarked upon two winning streaks, one of thirty-one games and one of forty-seven games—a national record that still stands as of this writing. And although the overwhelming majority of Oklahomans had never set foot on campus, they identified with both the University of Oklahoma and with the accomplishments of Wilkinson's team—*their team*; they gloried as their Sooners dominated a sport made popular by Notre Dame's Rockne, Minnesota's Bierman, and Army's Blaik.

As a direct result of the accomplishments of Bud Wilkinson's Sooners, Oklahomans once again had just reason for pride and optimism.

5 Gomer

JANUARY 1964–DECEMBER 1965

Although Bud Wilkinson and Gomer Jones had worked closely together to build the Oklahoma football team for seventeen years, Jones's elevation to the helm after Wilkinson's departure was not a quick, easy, or unanimous decision for the board of regents. Some board members had long been unhappy with what they considered Wilkinson's interference in influencing policy—a bailiwick they felt was solely their own—and, consequently, bristled when he strongly endorsed his longtime assistant.

Although Jones enjoyed the full weight of Wilkinson's public endorsement, privately Bud had his concerns. It was common knowledge among those in Gomer's private circle that he neither aspired nor had ever aspired to a head coaching position, and Wilkinson also felt that a younger man might have been better able to withstand the rigorous demands of the job and deal with the accompanying stringent criticism. Wilkinson had privately spoken with Bobby Drake Keith and Jay O'Neal to gauge their interest in the position, but both were prohibitively young, and O'Neal had already given Jones his word that he would remain on the staff should Jones accept the job. Therefore, Wilkinson lobbied heavily for Gomer with the regents—so much so that they felt the need to resist his pressure.

A further complication in the process arose because after Wilkinson resigned as head coach, he retained his position as athletic director, giving the regents reason to suspect that he had done so to influence the hiring process. So, despite Wilkinson's urgings that the university take immediate action by offering the job to Jones, the regents began an independent search for their own candidate. Among those considered were Illinois backfield coach and Sooner alum Coleman "Buck" McPhail, University of Colorado head coach Eddie Crowder, University of Washington head coach Jim Owens, the Coast Guard Academy's Otto Graham, Doug Weaver of Kansas State, Ray Nagel of Utah, Pop Ivy of the Houston Oilers, Merrill Green of Texas Tech,

Ralph Neely and Gomer Jones. Courtesy Ralph Neely.

UCLA line coach Sam Boghosian, Texas head coach Darrell Royal, Nebraska backfield coach Mike Corgan, Sooner assistant coaches Jay O'Neal and Bobby Drake Keith, and Kansas head coach Jack Mitchell.[1]

As the process continued, a grassroots movement among the players in support of Jones's candidacy emerged. "They weren't going to offer Gomer the job," comments Ralph Neely, "so some of us got together including myself, Norman Smith, Jim Grisham, Lance Rentzel, and a few others, and requested a meeting with the regents. We presented them with a petition signed by members of the team requesting that Gomer be appointed coach. I found out several years later that Gomer hadn't wanted the job and that he had taken it because he knew we had wanted him to."[2] But in actuality, the players' petition was only part of the reason Jones openly expressed a desire for the job. He realized the importance of filling the vacancy quickly; even though Wilkinson had resigned in early January while stating that recruiting was well ahead of where it had been the previous year,[3] Jones realized that maintaining momentum on the recruiting trail as well as reassuring the players already on campus that the status quo would remain solid was of paramount importance. And although Jones finally did accept the position, he never intended to remain head coach for the long haul. He considered his role in replacing Bud Wilkinson merely a stopgap measure for the football program.

"I was sitting in Gomer's living room during that period," recalls Leon Cross, "and he told me over a couple of glasses of scotch that he didn't want the job. But he knew that the board of regents wasn't going to give it to Jay O'Neal or Bobby Drake Keith because they were too young. So he planned to take it for no more than two years, get it back on the winning track, and then turn it over to one of the younger guys. Gomer was also very concerned that his staff of assistants would lose their jobs were he not to step forward."[4]

On January 19, 1964, one day after Bud Wilkinson officially resigned as athletic director, Gomer Thomas Jones was offered and accepted the dual roles of athletic director and head football coach at the University of Oklahoma. Wilkinson had departed a position that paid him $22,400 per annum, and Jones was offered the same figure but demurred, insisting that he be paid no more than $18,000 until he had "proven himself."[5] Gomer was warmly received by both fans and press. The 1963 Sooners had performed well, and it was generally expected that the momentum generated by Oklahoma's 8–2 record would carry over into 1964. Jones was well liked by the fan base and loved by his players, and, while not as urbane as his predecessor had been with the politics and public relations aspects that the job required, he appeared to be up to the task. The only controversy that occurred before the 1964 season kicked off was caused by an ill-advised bumper sticker making the rounds in Oklahoma stating, "I am for Fred Harris and Gomer Jones." This was a particularly embarrassing situation for Jones because Harris was running for Oklahoma's vacated senate seat against his friend and former boss, Bud Wilkinson. Jones had not endorsed Harris and threatened to sue the Harris campaign committee over the issue.[6]

The Sooners departed for their opening game against the Maryland Terrapins on September 16, ranked second in the Associated Press's opening poll. On the Thursday prior to the game, Jones accepted an invitation to visit the

Sooners on White House tour, September 1964. Courtesy Ralph Neely.

White House. The team was welcomed graciously by President Lyndon Johnson, who wished them good luck in all but one game in the coming season.

On game day, September 19, 1964, Oklahoma found it necessary to rely on President Johnson's proffered luck. Installed as a two-touchdown favorite, Oklahoma found itself stranded on the short end of a 3–0 score as the fourth quarter wound down. Virtually punchless that afternoon, Oklahoma had gone through quarters two and three without a first down. But then, with only four minutes left in the game and on his first snap from center, Sooner quarterback John Hammond, who had been inserted into the game in place of Mike Ringer, uncorked a ninety-yard touchdown pass to Lance Rentzel, giving Oklahoma a 6–3 lead. The play also broke the existing distance record for a Sooner touchdown pass, overtaking the Buddy Leake–to–Max Boydston bomb in the 1954 opener against California by three yards.[7] Seconds later, an interception by Sooner John David Voiles at the Terp twenty-eight with 1:45 remaining set Oklahoma up for the final touchdown in its 13–3 victory. When asked for a comment after the game, Gomer wiped his brow, pointed skyward, and stated "Somebody got us through!"[8] Though Jones was flippantly referring to celestial intervention in the victory, he was blatantly aware of two realities as he headed toward the locker room—his defense had played better than expected, but his offense had displayed disturbing incompetence. While fullback Jim Grisham had taken the conference by storm in 1963 earning All-American honors, he would discover at College Park, Maryland, that defenses would be ready for him in 1964.

The next three weekends would foreshadow Jones's two seasons at the helm. Southern California traveled to Norman on September 26—exactly five years to the day since Northwestern's 1959 landslide victory over the Sooners—and inflicted a demoralizing 40–14 setback on the Sooners. The following week, Royal's Longhorns would place their seventh consecutive check in the win column in the fall classic, 28–7. After a short respite in Norman, the team embarked for Lawrence. The October 17 game represented what many considered to be the most discouraging loss of Gomer Jones's tenure.

Kansas star Gayle Sayers set the day off to a bad start for Oklahoma by returning the game's opening kickoff ninety-three yards for a touchdown. Later in the first quarter, Sooner Lance Rentzel's seventy-six-yard touchdown jaunt was nullified by a penalty, but early in the second quarter, Grisham bulled over the KU goal line for the equalizing touchdown. Minutes later, Rentzel entered the Jayhawk end zone for the second time, lifting Oklahoma to a 14–7 lead. Neither team would score in the third period, but in the final minute of the fourth quarter, Kansas sprang to life. With only fifty-eight seconds remaining in the game, Rentzel's punt had backed Kansas up on its nine-yard line. Making brilliant use of the sidelines, KU moved the ball inexorably to the Sooner twenty-six-yard line, and then, on the game's final play, Jayhawk quarterback Bob Skahan tossed a scoring pass. With no time remaining on the clock, Kansas took the ball on an end sweep around the right side for the two-pointer and the 15–14 victory. In the losing cause, Oklahoma had completely dominated the game from the second play until the Jayhawks' final drive, outdistancing its opponents 322–192 in total yardage and posting twenty first downs to KU's eleven.[9] The loss sent ripples of discord through the Sooner community. While the team took the setback particularly hard, the student body expressed their disapprobation of the 1–3 Sooners by hanging an effigy of Coach Jones on campus in front of Kaufman Hall. Jones laughed the incident off, quipping, "You're not a coach until you've been hanged twice and fired once."[10] As unsettling for Jones as the incident must have been, he had no idea that the harsh criticism had only just begun.

Jones's Sooners arched their backs and won the next three conference games against Kansas State, Colorado, and Iowa State before suffering a 14–14 tie with Missouri on November 14. The next weekend, Oklahoma welcomed a powerful and motivated Nebraska team to Norman. The Huskers, in Bob Devaney's second year at the helm, sported a 9–0 record, were riding a nation-leading sixteen-game winning streak, were ranked fourth in the AP poll (behind Notre Dame, Alabama, and Arkansas), and were approaching their first undefeated season since 1915. The Sooners, who entered the game as prohibitive underdogs, were tenuously grasping their 4–3–1 record.

But the script that had been prewritten by the national press would not stand. Oklahoma drew first blood with a twenty-three-yard Butch Metcalf field goal in the first stanza, only to have Nebraska roar back on the arm of Husker quarterback Robert Churchich to take a 7–3 lead. That score would hold until early in the fourth period when Oklahoma mounted a time-consuming drive covering eighty-eight yards to regain the lead 10–7. On the Sooners' next possession, halfback Larry Brown burst through the line for a forty-eight-yard touchdown gallop, giving OU a 17–7 victory. At game's end, Oklahoma fans screamed and embraced while filling the air with a shower of "Go Gomer Go" stadium cushions as the team hoisted an ebullient Jones off the field on their shoulders. It was to be the crowning moment of Gomer Jones's head coaching career. His Sooners had improved their record to 5–3–1 and, with their upset victory over Devaney's conference champion Huskers, had impressed the bowl representatives in attendance and given his team a shot at postseason action.

Oklahoma finished the regular season with a 21–16 triumph over Oklahoma State and accepted an offer to face Florida State in the twentieth Gator Bowl. In spite of the relatively close betting line established prior to the game, the Sooners did not match up well with the Seminoles. Florida State's high-octane passing attack driven by quarterback Steve Tensi and wide receiver Fred Biletnikoff, both headed to the NFL, would present an offense the likes of which the run-oriented OU defense had not seen in 1964.

Further compounding Oklahoma's problem with the Seminoles, hours before the game was to be played it was revealed that four Sooner seniors and key members of the team had signed undated contracts with professional teams (Ralph Neely had signed with the AFL's Houston Oilers while Lance Rentzel, Jim Grisham, and Wes Skidgel had inked with the NFL's Minnesota Vikings). The players had been told that the contracts would not be officially dated until after the bowl game and were led to believe that the process would then be acceptable under existing rules. When asked by Jones if the charges were true, the players told the truth, and Jones had no alternative but to dismiss them from the team. Partially as a result of the dismissals, the Sooners went down to defeat at the hands of Florida State, 36–19.

Initially, Jones was universally praised for his quick and correct actions regarding the four players. But after the Gator Bowl loss, the outcry across the Sooner nation grew loud and persistent. While Jones would take the disapprobation in stride, little did he realize that he was about to embark upon the most challenging and difficult twelve-month period of his coaching career.

∵

As the 1965 season approached, the Sooners prepared to take the field with only six seniors, nine juniors, and seven sophomores in the starting lineup.[11] Compounding the difficulties faced by their relatively young team were changes to the offensive scheme; Jones and his assistants had decided to incorporate more I-formation sets. Jay O'Neal discusses the offense used in 1965: "We began running a formation that was a sort of a precursor to the Wishbone. We would 'ride the fullback' by moving him up in the formation a step, which later became the Wishbone base play. But the coaches called the plays, our quarterback wasn't required to read the defense; it wasn't that we didn't have confidence in our quarterbacks, it was just that we hadn't figured that part of it out yet."[12]

But as the whistle blew signaling the start of the new college football season, Oklahoma faltered coming out of the gate. Opening on the road for the second straight season, the Sooners' five turnovers and multiple penalties spelled defeat in their 13–9 loss at Pittsburgh. The following week, Oklahoma returned home to host the Naval Academy, losing 10–0. In that game, Oklahoma reached a modern-era low point by picking up only seventy-seven yards of total offense (seventy-one on the ground and six through the air), managing only six first downs, and being forced to rely on two goal-line stands to prevent the score from becoming far worse. By the second quarter, the 57,000 in attendance had decidedly thinned out. *Tulsa World* writer Jay Cronley, son of the *Daily Oklahoman*'s sports editor John Cronley, was a student at the university and attended the Navy game. "Attendance was beginning to become a problem," explains Jay. "During that game the stadium was so empty you could have played Frisbee."[13]

After the Navy game, things went from bad to very bad indeed. The Sooners suffered their eighth straight loss to Texas, 19–0, before notching their first win of the season, a 21–7 payback victory over Kansas. The following two weeks witnessed Oklahoma lose to Colorado and post its final win of the season, a 24–20 victory over Iowa State in Norman.

Though the press remained relatively respectful of Coach Jones in spite of his record, speculation over his fate and whom his successor might be ran rampant. The game following the win over Iowa State was played in Columbia against a 5–2–1 Missouri team that was destined to defeat Florida in the Sugar Bowl and place sixth in the final AP poll. The contest started on an optimistic note for the Sooners as they stopped Missouri on downs inside their ten-yard line. But then their shaky house of cards collapsed as the Tigers dismantled them 30–0. Oklahoma's trip to Lincoln the following weekend had similar results. The Cornhuskers, finally feeling their oats under Bob Devaney, were undefeated and would finish fifth in the final AP poll and third in the final UPI poll. Although outmanned, the Sooners took an early 9–0 lead before finally succumbing 21–9.

On November 26, 1965, the Oklahoma football team was at low ebb. Its record stood at 3–6–0 including four shutouts. Jones, pilloried by constant public criticism and hardly without a moment's respite from the rumor mill grinding away with conjecture over his successor, was weighing the pros and cons of tendering his resignation. However, he realized that with a decisive season-ending victory over Oklahoma State in the Sooners' final game, he might be able to hold the wolves at bay and raise his team's morale in preparation for a successful resurgence in 1966.

Although spirits were low among stalwart Sooner fans, the thought of losing to Oklahoma State was never considered a possibility. Oklahoma had owned the team from Stillwater since 1946 when Tatum and Wilkinson were hired to achieve that very goal. Since then, the Sooners had posted nineteen straight wins over Oklahoma State and in so doing had outscored the hapless Pokes 659–138 (an average score of 35–7). And the 2–7 Cowboys were coming to Norman with a worse record than the Sooners'.

The game was, despite the dismal combined records of the participants, a tooth-and-nail, well-played bout that saw the lead change several times. Oklahoma State kicked the go-ahead (and subsequently winning) field goal with under two minutes left to play. Oklahoma fought back downfield in the game's waning moments but failed on a forty-one-yard field goal attempt. Bill Connors wrote that with one play before the final gun, the goalposts were already coming down, students were fighting on Owen Field, and "bedlam erupted," coining the term that would eventually come to represent the rivalry.[14] Bobby Warmack, a freshman on the '65 squad, recalls the events following the 17–16 loss to OSU:

After Oklahoma State beat us in the final game of the season, things got pretty bad. We had a jock dorm back then, Washington House, and all the freshmen stayed on the top floor while the varsity was on the bottom two floors. And the word went out after the OSU loss that as a freshman, you don't want to be caught in the dorm anytime that night by a varsity football player. They were angry and frustrated. You didn't want to be found in the hallway, or if somebody pounds on your door, you don't want to open it. It was like, if you know what's good for you, you'll go spend the night in Oklahoma City or go home.[15]

Gomer Jones resigned his position as head football coach at the University of Oklahoma on December 6, two days after the Oklahoma State debacle. He had been given a vote of confidence by the board of regents after the Sooners' loss to OSU; therefore, his resignation, which came so quickly on the heels of that loss, took everyone by surprise. "I just got tired of all the criticism and all the rumors," he said. "It didn't help the situation to have people saying 'So-and-so will be coaching next year,' but they were right. Now 'so-and-so' *is* going to be coaching."[16]

University president Dr. Cross wrote later that members of the Touch-down Club had presented him with an ultimatum in November, stating that unless Jones was removed from the helm, the organization would withdraw its financial support. Cross also stated that they had met with Jones as well, but, according to the coach, they did not issue any ultimatums.[17] However, despite being assured by Dr. Cross that his job was secure after the Oklahoma State game, Jones had clearly had enough. Later, he indicated that the thought of tendering his resignation began to germinate in late November.

"I don't think it was a surprise when Gomer resigned," continues Warmack. "As things progressed his final year it was somewhat anticipated that we'd be getting a new coach. We suspected that Gomer and his regime had run its course. He had some great years, but over the last two it had just gone downhill to the point that the program wasn't what it had once been. A change clearly needed to be made."[18]

∵

Gomer Jones was one of the most well-loved and respected coaches ever to blow a whistle on the sidelines of Owen Field. For seventeen years, he worked alongside Bud Wilkinson to raise the Sooners to elite status and helped them maintain that status. Jones took good players and made them great players, producing seventeen All-Americans (five of them two-time winners) and two Outland Trophy winners. Bud Wilkinson commented that Gomer Jones was the greatest football teacher he had ever known, an opinion shared by his for-mer players. "Gomer could criticize you and make you a better player without tearing you down as a person," recalls Sooner lineman Glen Condren.[19] Former Sooner and Miami Dolphins star Jim Riley reflects on Gomer's tenure:

> Gomer was as big a part of the dynasty as Bud because he was such a great defensive coach and a great line coach. We had a fairly good year my sophomore year but the down year was my junior year, in 1965. We

had some talent but we didn't have much offense. We went 3–7, and believe me, that was terrible—you get hate mail from your mother when you post a record like that at the University of Oklahoma. I have friends who played with me back then, especially the 1965 season, who are still embarrassed by it; some won't even attend reunions or functions. Sadly, my time at OU was a big disappointment. We went 15–15–1 in my three years, and that wasn't what I went there for. I went to OU because they had been winners and I'd been listening to "Boomer Sooner" as I was growing up and playing high school ball.[20]

Some have suggested that Jones's staff in 1964 and 1965 did not have the diversity of ideas or the willingness to adapt to opponents who had become increasingly familiar with the Split-t. Those who criticize Jones's staff point out that with the exception of Bobby Drake Keith and George Dickson, every one of his assistant coaches was a product of the Oklahoma environment. While it is true that Jay O'Neal, Carl Allison, Bob Cornell, Dick Heatley, Brewster Hobby, Joe Rector, and Jerry Thompson were all former Sooner players, most had filtered out of the system to gain experience elsewhere before gravitating back to Norman. Additionally, Keith had coached at Alabama for Bear Bryant, and Dickson had led the 1949 Fighting Irish to a national title as a quarterback and remained as an assistant coach in South Bend afterwards.

Jones's staff has also been compared to that of Wilkinson's preceding him and Jim Mackenzie's following him. Over the years, members of Wilkinson's staff moved into head coaching positions; Jack Mitchell, Jim Owens, Wade Walker, Darrell Royal, J. D. Roberts, Rudy Feldman, and Eddie Crowder each advanced to lead their own teams. Under Mackenzie, Chuck Fairbanks, Barry Switzer, Larry Lacewell, Galen Hall, and Homer Rice all distinguished themselves as head coaches. But it is disingenuous to conclude that since no one from Jones's staff moved on to lead a team after 1965, that they must not have had the talent and ability to do so. It is important to note that individuals from both Wilkinson's and Mackenzie's staffs who moved on to coach their own teams enjoyed an advantage that Jones's staff lacked—they came from programs that had, over the years, enjoyed significant success.

The coaching staff has also been suspect for appearing not to have adjusted adequately enough to allow Oklahoma's offensive players to succeed in 1964 and, to a greater extent, in 1965. "You run an offense long enough and people learn to defend it," comments former Sooner running back Ron Shotts. "I think that was the main problem in 1965. Even Bud's last year or two weren't as successful because I think people were catching up with his offense. We probably didn't make the changes needed to compete and time just caught up with us."[21] While there is some validity in Shotts's comment, it is an established fact that a coach is somewhat restricted in what scheme to run by the personnel at hand. The argument can be made that based on the *overall* talent available in 1965, the coaches were running what they considered to be the most effective offensive set available to them. "And I think other schools began to get better athletes," continues Shotts. "During the mid-fifties, Bud had the pick of the litter, but as time went on more schools began to recruit more and better athletes. Also, evaluation of personnel, a very important component, could well have been an issue. In my opinion, some of the people riding the bench were probably better than the starters in some instances."[22]

It is a given that the level and ability of athletes on campus at any university will fluctuate from year to year, but during the late 1940s and 1950s the talent bar was set so high in Norman that ensuing Sooner squads inevitably had difficulty measuring up. And while Sooner football from 1960 through 1965 saw a number of difference-making stars applying their trade between the hash marks, the level of talent across the board was not of the caliber that Wilkinson had brought to campus a decade earlier. As they had with Bud in his last five years, problems at the quarterback position continued to plague Jones. The Sooners had not known stability and productivity at the position since 1954–1956 when Jimmy Harris and Jay O'Neal ran the show to perfection. "We didn't have enough of the quality athletes needed to establish and maintain the kind of program we were accustomed to," reflects Jay O'Neal. "If you look at Bud's last few years, he was just so busy with everything; it wasn't that recruiting wasn't a top priority, but it shared time with other top priorities and as a result, it suffered."[23]

J. D. Roberts, Oklahoma's 1953 Outland Trophy winner shares O'Neal's opinion. "Gomer was sharp and could handle the position of head coach. The coaching staff was solid, too. The problem had to boil down to a question of talent. Although there were some great players and some good players on those teams, across the board they just weren't the quality they once had been."[24]

Glen Condren, standout Sooner player during the Jones years, suggests another problem during Gomer's years: a lack of on-field leadership. "We had some good players but I think we were underachievers; even though we turned out six or seven professional players we didn't excel in college as a team, partially because we didn't have the leadership that we should have had. You *could* blame Gomer for that but I don't think it would be fair. How does a head coach develop a leader? That sort of thing has to come from within the individual."[25]

The question of whether the team excelled at its highest and best potential begs another question. Was Gomer Jones the same level of motivator that Bud Wilkinson had been in his heyday? Jones had worked alongside his players for seventeen years as Bud's line coach and defensive coordinator. He had earned and maintained the respect, loyalty, and love of his men, but by all indications he was not the motivator that Wilkinson had been for two reasons—his basic temperament lent itself to an all-too-available compassionate side, and he did not maintain the aloof demeanor required to be an effective administrator. "When Gomer was the line coach, he was sort of 'one of the boys,' or, as much as you could be and still be an effective coach, which he certainly was," continues Condren. "But Bud was never one of our peers. He was elevated. In terms of being a motivator, Bud was the ultimate, the master. There was simply no comparison between Bud and Gomer. Gomer was the organizer."[26] Gomer's friend and former Sooner halfback Jack Ging weighs in on the subject:

I think Gomer was an excellent example of the Peter Principle in action. He was the best assistant coach in America, a great line and defensive coach, but he left all the politics to Bud who would talk to the alums and go on TV and promote. Gomer was a damned fine football coach; he had been an outstanding player at Ohio State and for seventeen years he was a perfect complement to Bud. You see, Gomer was like a *man*, like our father.

We could always take our troubles to him. But being a coach and being a head coach are two completely different things. Wilkinson was a step removed from us; I had so much respect for Bud that I didn't want him to know about all the crap I was doing off the field, so I went to Gomer.[27]

Jay Wilkinson stated that his father had always believed that there was a difference between being a head coach and being an assistant coach. "He pushed for Gomer's appointment to the head coaching position for a couple of reasons," remembers Jay. "He thought Gomer deserved a chance and he felt that it would be best for

Jack Ging. Courtesy Jim Terry.

the university. But he knew that there would be risks on both ends. He was very sympathetic towards Gomer, and what happened to him during 1964 and 1965 weighed heavily on my father."[28]

In the spring of 1964, graduate assistant John Tatum decided to leave the university and went to Jones's office to personally thank him for his help and support. Tatum recalls, "When we were about finished talking, he looked at me and asked 'What are you gonna do, Johnny?' I told him I was planning to become a high school football coach, and I asked him if he had any advice to give me. He replied, 'Yes, I do. Go find a place that hasn't won in a long time because you'll only have one way to go, and that's upward. You'll be able to build the program the way you want and look good in the process. Always remember this, Johnny—never follow a winner.'"[29]

When Bud Wilkinson resigned in January 1964, Gomer Jones had been faced with a two-pronged dilemma; he was worried about the livelihood of the assistant coaches, men who had loyally served the university, and he was deeply concerned about maintaining the quality football program that he and

Wilkinson had created and nurtured for almost two decades. And when he was finally offered the position and accepted, he knew that he had stepped into the very situation he had counseled against, that of following an iconic figure, a goal that no coach had ever successfully achieved. For Jones, it was the ultimate irony.

As he finished the 1965 season with the taunts and jeers of fans ringing in his ears, Jones could have taken the same path many other coaches had taken before him—that of tossing an assistant coach under the bus as a scapegoat offering in order to retain his job for yet another season; he had, after all, received a prima facie vote of confidence from the university president and the board of regents. But instead, he accepted full responsibility for the failings of the past two years and tendered his resignation, a course of action that he believed to be in the university's best interests.

Gomer Jones ended his career as a head coach without compromising the principles by which he had always lived. Perhaps Glen Condren serves as a conduit expressing the sentiment of Jones's players and friends through his observation, "Gomer Jones deserved better."[30]

6 Renaissance in Norman

JIM MACKENZIE, DECEMBER 1965–APRIL 1967

Although Jones relinquished his position as head coach, he retained the athletic directorship and by the second week of December was occupied, under the guidance of university president Cross, with the search for a new headmaster for the Sooner football team. Vince Dooley, who had taken over at Georgia in 1964 and led the once-moribund Bulldogs back to respectability, was considered as was Doug Dickey of Tennessee. Gentle overtures were once again extended to Darrell Royal, but well on his way to sainthood in the state of Texas, Royal had no desire to return to Oklahoma. So Jones decided to turn his attention to another highly successful program three hundred miles northeast of Norman.

Since taking the reins at the University of Arkansas in 1958, Frank Broyles had led the Hogs from obscurity to ascendancy. After a disappointing first year in Fayetteville, his teams rapidly developed into championship contenders as they finished in the AP top ten from 1959 through 1962. In 1963, their rivals to the southwest, the Texas Longhorns, took their first national title while Arkansas fell to 5–5–0, prompting Broyles to implement offensive changes.

"We made some good decisions after the 1963 season," recalls Merv Johnson, an assistant at Arkansas during that period. "We changed our offense in '64 and got lucky. We had a couple of really good running backs, a good quarterback, and we had speed and quickness on defense. Also, we went to Southern Cal and picked up the I-formation from John McKay."[1] The Hogs' resulting 11–0–0 record the very next season represented one of the greatest twelve-month turnarounds in college football history. The next year Arkansas's record stood at 10–0–0 in late November as it prepared to ride its twenty-two-game winning streak onto the floor of the Cotton Bowl for a bout with LSU.

An indispensible component of Arkansas's success during this time was its dynamic young defensive coordinator* and assistant head coach, Jim Mackenzie.

---

*The term "defensive coordinator" was not in the lexicon of the day but will be used by the author for contextual clarity.

After graduating from high school in Gary, Indiana, Mackenzie traveled south to Kentucky to play college ball for Bear Bryant. Bryant, who had arrived from Maryland in 1945, had, in one year on campus, taken the Terps from a 1–7–1 season in 1944 to 6–2–1. When young Mackenzie finally arrived in Lexington hoping to play for Bryant, he found himself competing with an influx of postwar players. "Jim was trying out on a team that literally had hundreds of service veterans vying for the same position and he was just out of high school. The tough ones who were good enough made it and Jim was one of them," recalls Barry Switzer.[2] Mackenzie became a two-time All-Southeastern Conference tackle at Kentucky and, along with teammates Vito "Babe" Parilli, Pat James, Bob Gain, and Charlie McClendon, played on the Wildcat team that upended an undefeated national championship Sooner squad in the 1951 Orange Bowl.

After the 1953 season, Bryant departed Kentucky for Texas A&M, and Mackenzie, who had just graduated, began his coaching career at Jenkins High School in Kentucky, where he remained for two years before becoming line coach at Allen Academy in Bryan, Texas. Meanwhile, in 1957 Frank Broyles left Georgia Tech, where he had been Bobby Dodd's offensive coordinator, to accept the head coaching position at the University of Missouri, and he hired Mackenzie as his defensive coordinator. "Jim came to Missouri from Allen Academy in 1957," remarks Johnson, a senior on the Missouri roster. "He was a tough, tough coach, a walking embodiment of the old Bear Bryant philosophy, and I didn't enjoy playing for him. But he had a bright football mind and taught hard-nosed football conditioning. It was quite an eye-opener for the players at Missouri when he, Frank, and Jerry Claiborne arrived."[3] But Broyles's tenure at Missouri lasted only one season before he was offered the job he had coveted above all others: the head coaching position at the University of Arkansas.

"Coach Bryant told me over cocktails that when he left Kentucky he had had the opportunity to go to Arkansas, and he declined," explains Switzer. "He said he'd always considered that to have been the biggest mistake he'd ever made in his life financially, because Arkansas was on the verge of an economic boom and he'd have been in on the ground floor."[4]

Former Tennessee and Pittsburgh head coach and 1956 Heisman trophy runner-up Johnny Majors came into contact with Mackenzie when he joined the Arkansas staff in 1964. "I've had some fine assistants and I've played under some pretty darned good coaches," reflects Majors, "but I thought Jim Mackenzie was in the top one-percent of them all. At Arkansas, I was the defensive backfield coach and he was the assistant head coach and defensive coordinator. He was extremely intelligent, confident, and he knew the game of football and what it took to win. Jim was a great motivator; he had learned how to extend players to their best ability from Bear Bryant."[5]

In Oklahoma, rumors were spreading like wildfire about the demanding Arkansas assistant coach coming to Norman. Gomer Jones had already reached the conclusion that bringing in a proven OU alumnus such as Jim Owens or Darrell Royal might not be the best path to follow; he had gone on record stating that "a new face might be a good idea."[6] After conducting an interview with Mackenzie in mid-December, Jones and the board of regents made the decision to offer him the head coaching job. Leon Cross recalls Jones telling him, "I think [Mackenzie] is one of the brightest, most dynamic young coaches I've ever met. He'll get the job done here at Oklahoma."[7]

So it became official; on December 22, 1966, James Alexander Mackenzie became the fifteenth head coach of the Oklahoma Sooners.

⁘

Mackenzie realized when he accepted the job that he was entering a situation in which he was already behind on at least two fronts; he was inheriting a team that was deficient in talent at a number of positions, and he knew that under his administration the university would be getting off to its third slow recruiting start in the past three seasons. A top immediate priority for him was to complete his staff as soon as possible and get it off and running on the recruiting trail with heavy emphasis on Texas.

"One thing that has really concerned me is that every year for three years there has been some incident right in the middle of the recruiting period," said Mackenzie, referring to Wilkinson's resignation in 1963, the dismissal of players prior to the bowl game in 1964, and Jones's resignation in 1965. "But I think Gomer got some good players despite the difficulties. I sure hope he did, anyway," added Jim with a laugh. "I only have a four-year contract." When a

Jim Mackenzie and his staff, 1966. *Left to right:* Galen Hall, Barry Switzer, Homer Rice, Jim Mackenzie, Pat James, Chuck Fairbanks, Swede Lee. Courtesy Homer Rice

reporter reminded him of the Sooners' loss to his Kentucky team in 1950, he commented, "That was a great thrill, but the thing to do now is to win some games *here*. I'm a Sooner now."[8] Upon the family's arrival in Norman, Jim's wife, Sue, was asked by an eager reporter how it affected her family life when Jim's team lost a game. She hesitated, smiled, and replied, "I don't know; I've never been married to a losing coach. Jim plays to win—every time."[9]

One of Mackenzie's first additions to his staff was Homer Rice. Although he was offered the offensive coordinator job, he had not been in a position to make an immediate decision; he had just rejected an offer to become head coach at the Citadel and expected to be asked to take the same position at Duke. Rice explains what happened:

I received a call on a Sunday evening telling me that Duke had selected someone else and literally ten minutes later, I got a call from Jim. To this day I still don't know how he found out so quickly that the Duke offer hadn't come through. The next morning, I flew to Norman and accepted the job. Jim's staff came together fairly quickly. Barry Switzer was the offensive line coach, Galen Hall was the receivers coach, and I coached the offense, quarterbacks, and running backs. Pat James ran the defense while Swede Lee had the linebackers and ends. Larry Lacewell and Billy Gray were the freshman coaches. After Jim finished assembling his staff, Darrell Royal made the comment that "Jim Mackenzie had hired the strongest staff in America."[10]

Barry Switzer, a star center and linebacker from the University of Arkansas, became a graduate assistant in Fayetteville in 1960. His brother Don, an attorney, had urged him to attend law school, but Barry had other plans; his heart was in football. But in 1961, his coaching career at Arkansas was interrupted by military service. He tells the story:

I joined Frank's staff in 1960 and coached freshman ball with Freddie Akers. Then I went into the Army in February, 1961 and was stationed at Fort Leonard Wood, Missouri. In January and February, they call Leonard Wood "Little Korea" because it's colder than hell up there. Then I was sent to Aberdeen Proving Ground on Chesapeake Bay where I was living in a barracks as a twenty-three year old college graduate with a bunch of eighteen and nineteen-year old guys, most of whom had lied about their age. But I enjoyed that post because I got to hitch-hike to Philadelphia, Washington, and New York and I got to see the Yankees play Baltimore when Maris, Mantle, and Brooks Robinson were playing. While I was stationed at Aberdeen, I got a phone call from Dixie White, the Arkansas offensive line coach, who told me that Coach Broyles wanted me back on the staff when two-a-days started. I told him I didn't get out of the service until the middle of September, so Dixie gave me the name of a person to write in order to petition for early release. I went to the company headquarters office, walked in, and told the master sergeant "Private Switzer requests an early release form." And the sergeant, who'd been in the Army for at least 30 years, looked at me and said, "Hell, all you six-monthers try to get out early and I ain't never seen a damned one of you do it yet." He tossed the papers across the desk and said, "here's your form. Good luck," and laughed at me as I left. So I went back to the barracks, filled it out, and addressed it to Congressman Wilbur Mills of Arkansas, Chairman of the House Ways and Means Committee. I explained to the Congressman that Coach Broyles had wanted me back in Fayetteville to help coach the Hogs. Then, about ten days later, I heard an announcement over the PA system declaring, "Private Switzer report to company headquarters!" When I got there, the same master sergeant has this pissed-off look on his face and tossed a manila envelope across the desk to me without saying a word. I just said, "Thank you, sir," took the envelope and walked back to the barracks. When I opened the envelope, I had my early release.[11]

Before the 1965 football season ended, members of the Sooner football team had suspected Coach Jones would be replaced, and rumors of the eminent hiring of Mackenzie were circulating. "I remember that it was anticipated that he might be coming," comments Bobby Warmack, "and the feeling among the players was that we didn't want 'that guy from Arkansas' because he was too tough."[12] As it turned out, Warmack and his teammates had good reason for trepidation. Shortly after Mackenzie moved himself, his family, and his staff to Norman, he implemented an arduous "voluntary-mandatory" conditioning program. Larry Lacewell describes the training program:

The training we put the players through in the winter of 1966 was like *Stalag 17*. At that time we had no indoor workout facilities so we conducted it at the old Army base on the outskirts of campus in what used to be a barracks. The building was long, narrow, had a wooden floor, no heat, and the roof always leaked when it rained, snowed, or threatened to do either. It was probably one of the most Spartan environments I've ever seen. Jim was big on conditioning and discipline, so we would have drills in fifteen stations within the building and each player would spend an allotted amount of time at each station before the whistle blew and they'd move to the next. They'd wrestle, they'd vault, they'd box, they'd lift weights—it was an extremely tough program and a lot of guys quit. Pat James and I had been at Alabama and we thought the Bear was pretty tough, but we'd never seen *anything* like the program Jim installed in Norman in the winter of '66. I was a freshman coach and I was absolutely in shock over the severity of it.[13]

Bobby Warmack also has recollections of the arduous regimen:

It was called "the fourth-quarter class," and it was designed to teach people endurance, stamina, and toughness—qualities it takes to win in the fourth quarter. Pat James, our defensive coach, had been on Bear Bryant's staff when he was at Texas A&M and had gone through the Junction City training program. He told us that what they had put those A&M guys through was nothing compared to what we went through. Unlike the Junction City program which only lasted about ten days, our fourth-quarter class lasted six weeks; I think our team lost an accumulative 1,400 pounds as a result of it. A lot of guys decided that playing football wasn't worth going through that ordeal and quit. It was one tough son-of-a-bitch and absolutely the most difficult workout we'd ever gone through in our lives.[14]

But for as rigorous and demanding as Mackenzie's training program was, the man himself, off the field, was gregarious, friendly, and likeable. He enjoyed life, friends, and family. "He would walk into a room and people would automatically love him," says Switzer. "But he could be intimidating to other coaches, especially if they didn't

Jim Mackenzie. Courtesy Jim Terry.

have a personal relationship with him like I did. I knew his demeanor, his inner soul."[15]

Mackenzie not only brought a contingent of coaches with him from Arkansas but also planned to implement the Arkansas I-formation at the University of Oklahoma. He told the alumni during a chamber of commerce meeting in Tulsa that his team would pass more, but how much more would be dictated by the abilities of the quarterbacks and receivers.[16]

As spring practice began, a slimmed-down roster sporting slimmed-down players took the practice field. The all-important position of quarterback ran seven deep, and the seventh man on the chart was Bobby Warmack; however, by the end of spring training, he had worked his way into the second position behind Jim Burgar. Future NFL star Jim Riley was in his final year as a Sooner and would play on a team buttressed by the likes of Granville Liggins, Bob Kalsu, Ed Hall, Gene Cagle, Ron Shotts, Mike and Gary Harper, Eddie Hinton, Ben Hart, John Titsworth, Mark Kosmos, Eugene Ross, Rodney Crosswhite, Ken Mendenhall, Steve Barrett, Bobby Stephenson, Mike Vachon, Tom Stidham, Richard Goodwin, John Koller, Rickey Burgess, Harry Hettsmansperger, Joe Poslick, and Randy Meacham.

Mackenzie's Sooners kicked off their season on September 17, 1966, when Oregon traveled to Norman. The Ducks had endured a 4–5–1 season in 1965 and were installed as significant underdogs for the contest. To the surprise of the 48,950 in attendance, both teams went into halftime with the score tied 0–0; the Sooners, with Burgar under center, had managed only sixty-six total yards, so Homer Rice convinced Mackenzie to play Bob Warmack in the second half.

Shortly after halftime, the deadlock was broken when wingback Eddie Hinton took an Oregon punt sixty-three yards home for a 7–0 Sooner lead. Mike Vachon would add a field goal later in the third quarter, and, after Oregon lost the ball on a jarring tackle by Mike Vachon on the ensuing kickoff, Bob Warmack engineered the final touchdown drive as Oklahoma and Jim Mackenzie took their opening game, 17–0. Afterwards, Mackenzie praised the punting of Tom Stidham while exclaiming that the team still had "too many busted plays and alignments."[17]

The following weekend, Mackenzie took his show on the road and scored a resounding victory over Iowa State in Ames. The Sooner offense took flight early in the game as Warmack's forty-one-yard run setup a two-yard touchdown line plunge by Ron Shotts. Oklahoma chalked up 342 yards of total offense in the 33–11 victory, and, more importantly, the Sooners began to build confidence and momentum for their annual game with Texas: a game Oklahoma had not won since 1957. The Sooners had not been competitive in the majority of their eight straight losses to the Longhorns. In five of those games, Texas dispatched the Oklahomans handily, winning by an average margin of twenty-one points. Mackenzie knew that he not only had to prepare his team physically but also had to help it overcome a tremendous psychological hurdle. The players on the Sooner roster in 1966 had been in elementary school when OU last left the Cotton Bowl Stadium victorious, and none of them had experienced anything but defeat at the hands of Darrell K. Royal and his Longhorns. Jim Mackenzie was determined to change that mindset.

With a week off to prepare, injuries were not an issue; Jim Riley suffered from an injured ankle, and Mark Kosmos was hampered by a locked knee, but both were expected to see playing time in Dallas. Although defensive minded himself, Mackenzie pushed the offense to its limits in the days prior to the showdown, honing its responses like his distant predecessor, Wilkinson, had once done. His players had to know precisely how to react to any given situation, and although Oklahoma was not there yet, it was making progress. For the first time in years, the Sooners would make the Dallas trip with the ability to pass the ball effectively, an attribute that had been a common denominator among the few teams that had defeated Texas in the 1960s. However, from an endurance standpoint, Mackenzie was concerned that the mild weather Oklahoma had experienced in the weeks leading up to the game had not prepared his players for the stifling Dallas heat. "We haven't had any Dallas weather," said Mackenzie. "In fact, we haven't had any hot weather since the first of August." To meet the problem, he ran his team through a grueling series of sprints after each practice.[18]

On game day, Oklahoma and Texas took the Cotton Bowl field early to warm up. As Mackenzie paced back and forth on the sidelines, he noticed Longhorn placekicker David Conway making one of every two field goals he attempted from the fifty-yard line. Walking out toward the middle of the field, Mackenzie yelled across to Texas assistant Russell Coffee, "What are you trying to do, intimidate us?"[19] But the intimidation the Texans had been dishing out since 1958 was about to end.

On their opening drive, the Horns took the ball to the Oklahoma three-yard line but were forced to settle for a field goal. On the Sooners' next drive, Bobby Warmack scooted into the Texas end zone for Oklahoma's go-ahead score; Mike Vachon, in what would *not* be a harbinger of things to come this day, missed the extra point, and the Sooners led 6–3. The Crimson and Cream defense held Texas scoreless the remainder of the half, and Vachon notched his first field goal of the afternoon seconds before halftime to boost the Sooner lead to 9–3.

On the opening drive of the second half, Oklahoma moved the ball to the Texas sixteen before Vachon was called upon to kick his second three-pointer, increasing Oklahoma's lead, 12–3. On the Longhorns' next possession, Sooner Bob Stephenson intercepted the ball and returned it to the Texas six. Three plays yielded only three yards, and once again, Mike Vachon came on. His third field goal of the day bumped Oklahoma's lead to 15–3. Midway through the final quarter, the Longhorns mounted a substantial drive that culminated in their first—and only—touchdown of the day, but their two-point conversion pass attempt was batted down by Rod Crosswhite. With 2:19 remaining, Vachon kicked a school-record fourth field goal to give Oklahoma an 18–9 victory. Bob Warmack, who had been sharing quarterbacking duties with Jim Burgar, ran roughshod over the Texas defense for 280 total yards (220 rushing and 60 passing). As a result of his performance, Warmack had solidified his position as the Sooners' starting signal caller and would hold onto it for the next two years. Moments after the game ended, the goalposts came down, classes were canceled in Norman on Monday, and Jim Mackenzie became only the second head coach of the Oklahoma Sooners—Bennie Owens had been the first in 1905—to beat Texas in his inaugural year. After the game, Mackenzie quipped, "If anyone had told me we would out-kick Texas, I would have said they'd been smoking marijuana."[20]

The following Thursday evening, Jim Mackenzie went on his weekly television program and stated that in spite of the victory over Texas, he was concerned. When asked by host Howard Newman why this was, Mackenzie replied that his concern was centered around "three fast backs, two good lines, and one good punter," referring to their next opponent, Kansas.[21] But his worries were one week premature as his Sooners raided Lawrence like Quantrill had done 104 years earlier, downing the Jayhawks 35–0. Oklahoma, standing at 4–0 for the first time since 1957, had finally cracked the 1966 Associated Press poll, checking in at number ten.

But there was trouble on the horizon. Notre Dame, long the nemesis of the Sooners, would be visiting Norman the following weekend. The number-one ranked Irish were widely regarded as the most formidable team in the nation, having defeated their first four opponents—Purdue, Northwestern, Army, and North Carolina—by a combined score of 128–21. The game played by the Irish and the Sooners on October 22, 1966, reflected a similar mismatch as Notre Dame outpaced the rebuilding Sooners 38–0. "We just couldn't match up against Notre Dame," comments Homer Rice. "They were too strong, too deep."[22] The Notre Dame game was followed by a difficult loss to Colorado in Boulder the following weekend. The next two games brought a victory (Oklahoma 37, Kansas State 6) and a loss (Missouri 10, Oklahoma 7).

Next on Oklahoma's agenda was its annual nationally televised Thanksgiving Day game with Nebraska. The Huskers, ranked fourth in the nation, were undefeated, were Big Eight champions, and had already received a bid to play Alabama in the Sugar Bowl. Two years earlier, Nebraska had faced a similar scenario as it headed to Norman; Devaney's 1964 Huskers had also been undefeated, were ranked fourth in the nation, and were striving for their first undefeated season since 1915 only to see their dreams and aspirations crushed in a 17–7 loss to Oklahoma.

The first quarter, peppered by turnovers committed by both teams, ended in a scoreless stalemate. With five minutes gone in the second period, a Nebraska drive stalled at the Sooner twenty-one-yard line, forcing them to settle for a field goal and a 3–0 lead. And then, on Oklahoma's last drive of the first half, Warmack's fifty-two-yard pass led Eddie Hinton into the NU end zone for a 7–3 halftime lead.

The third quarter produced a standoff until the Huskers crossed the Sooner goal line late in the period. "That's when Bobby Stephenson, with his great speed, came around the corner and blocked the extra point," recalls Barry Switzer. "And that turned out to be the difference in the ball game."[23]

"Jim was the kind of coach who was completely involved in every play of every game," continues Switzer. "Having been a defensive coordinator all his life, he would occasionally make play suggestions to his defensive coach, Pat James, because he felt like it was the right alignment, and most of the time he was very successful when doing it. He was super at anticipating what the other team's offense would do but he would normally not involve himself in our offensive calls."[24] However, on one occasion when he *did* become involved, he finally acquiesced to the judgment of his offensive coordinator, and the result paid big dividends. With minutes remaining in the Nebraska game, Warmack and the Sooners moved the ball from deep in their own territory to the Husker forty-five before stalling. Down by two points and facing third and long, the next offensive call would be crucial. Homer Rice recalls the event:

Pat James and I were in the booth together, he was calling defense and I was calling offense. While our team had been on defense I had had time to go back and study the Husker defensive formations. I noticed that on third-and-long situations—every single one of them—they'd line up in an even front. Now, we were behind 9–7 with just a couple of minutes to play, we had moved the ball across midfield and we were in a third-and-long situation. We hadn't called a draw play the entire game so I called one down to Barry who signaled it into the huddle. Jim heard the call, grabbed the headset, and yelled at me "What in the hell are you doing, Homer?!? We've got to throw the damned football to get into field goal range!" I calmly replied, "Coach, *trust me*." So, my whole football career was riding on this one play. Had it not worked, I was just going to walk out of the stadium, get on a bus and leave. But Warmack gave the handoff to Gary Harper who busted through the line, ran downfield, and got us into field goal range. We lined up, kicked the field goal, and won 10–9. Jim was elated. After the game, Tom Osborne, the Husker offensive coach, congratulated me on the call.[25]

Six days later, Jim Mackenzie was named the Big Eight Coach of the Year, narrowly edging out Bob Devaney. "The award surprised me because we didn't win the Big Eight. I'm quite honored," said Mackenzie.[26]

The Sooners found themselves sitting nicely at 6–3–0 and in contention for a bowl berth if they won their final game against Oklahoma State in Stillwater. Though the Cowboys came into the contest sporting a deceptive 3–5–1 record, they had not lost a home game since November 1965. A victory would put the Sooners into a tie for second place in the conference; a loss would drop them to fifth. "When I stop and think about this game I get sick to my stomach," said Mackenzie on Wednesday before the game. "It's one of those games where nothing that's gone before means the same, no matter if one of the teams has won 30 in a row. You have to disregard everything."[27]

The game was played on a cold, blustery, overcast afternoon. After a scoreless first period in which OU's Mike Vachon suffered two blocked field goals, Oklahoma State scored early in the second period and successfully converted for two points on an improvised play following a botched center snap. The Cowboys took an 8–0 lead into the halftime locker room.

The Sooners, behind the running of Ron Shotts, took the opening kickoff of the second half forty-eight yards for a touchdown. Warmack's two-point conversion pass to Bob Kalsu on a tackle-eligible play rounded off the score at 8–8. The next twelve minutes remained scoreless until Oklahoma State tallied late in the third period for a 15–8 lead. And then, minutes into the fourth quarter, Oklahoma was positioned on the OSU one-yard line with a first and goal, but four cracks into the line produced nothing. With five minutes remaining in the game, a short Cowboy punt put the Sooners on the OSU thirty. A series of grueling, punishing runs by Shotts consumed over three minutes of clock time before the home team finally broke the plane of the goal line. With the score standing at 15–14, Mackenzie decided to go for the two-pointer. The play called for the quarterback to take the snap, roll to his left, and then throw back across the field to Ben Hart; but as soon as he began to roll out, Warmack was converged upon by Cowboy defenders. Looking for an outlet, he tossed the ball to Shotts, who made the catch at the five-yard line only to be tackled at the two. Oklahoma State recovered the on-side kick, quickly ran through the remaining time, and took its second consecutive victory over the Sooners.

Jim Mackenzie and his team had finished the season with a 6–4–0 record. Although the Sooners had the opportunity to play in the Liberty Bowl against Miami, Mackenzie decided that their future would be better served by foregoing the bowl game in order to get a quick start on recruiting. If Jim lost a recruit he wanted, it would not be from lack of effort; no one outworked Jim Mackenzie. A sign atop his desk proclaimed: "The harder I work, the luckier I get."

In February 1967, offensive coordinator Homer Rice accepted the position as head coach at the University of Cincinnati. Jim then promoted Chuck Fairbanks to replace Rice and Billy Gray to defensive secondary coach. The following month, Rice invited Mackenzie to speak at a coaching clinic. "While Jim was in Cincinnati, he complained of numbness in his arms and accompanying weakness," recounts Rice.[28] Barry Switzer, who also had been concerned about Mackenzie's health and had noticed troubling signs, recalls, "He saw a cardiologist frequently; Jim knew he had a problem. We'd play pickup basketball at lunchtime, and afterwards he'd have to go lie down. Shortly before his death, I walked by his office one day and noticed that he just had a blank look on his face, just staring off into space. And I just knew as I stood there not far from his desk that he was in deep thought, concentration, and didn't even realize I was there; so I just walked on. That wasn't a football moment, it was deeply personal."[29]

Mackenzie continued his rigorous routine into April, even though the symptoms of imminent heart failure became increasingly pronounced. On April 27, Jim announced to his staff that he was "going to go get us a quarterback," and hopped onto a private plane headed for Texas. Leon Cross had been lured from West Point back to the University of Oklahoma by Mackenzie in the winter of 1966 to take over the recruiting program. He recalls Mackenzie's last recruiting trip:

I had arranged for Paul Finefrock to fly him to Amarillo to talk with Monty Johnson, a top quarterback prospect. Marshall York picked Jim up at the airport and dropped him off at Monty's house. Mackenzie left the meeting with the Johnsons and went to the York home before flying back to Norman. While at the Yorks, he expressed discomfort thought to be caused by heartburn and was given a glass of iced tea. Later, Marshall took him to the airport that evening to board the plane. On the flight home, Finefrock, who owned a gypsum mine near Lawton, flew Jim over the excavations so he could have a look at them in the moonlight and then dropped him off in Norman.[30]

Finefrock and Mackenzie landed shortly after nine o'clock that evening. "Jim said to me, 'Don't shut down the engines, I'll just hop out,'" recalled Finefrock. "And he did. He had a bounce in his step even then. There was no evidence of anything wrong."[31]

"Around midnight," continues Cross, "Jim began suffering from chest pain and phoned his doctor to discuss the medication. Shortly after he'd gone to bed, he got up to go to the bathroom and suffered a massive heart attack."[32] Galen Hall lived right across the street from the Mackenzies and was the first to the scene. "About 11:30 that night we got a knock on the door," he recalls. "It was Jim's eight-year-old daughter who told us something had happened to her dad. So I ran across the street and found Jim was lying unconscious on the floor. I tried to revive him but wasn't able to; it was evident to me he was already gone."[33]

Mackenzie's single speed in life had been overdrive; he coached, played, ate, and recruited in high gear. Having been a lineman, he had always been predisposed toward weight gain and always seemed to be struggling with it. "He was the kind of guy who would fast for five days and when he finished, he'd make a chocolate cake and eat the entire thing," says Merv Johnson. And Jim was a chain smoker. "I roomed with him on the road a couple of years," continues Johnson, "and he would wake up very early, 4:30 or 5:00 A.M., and would have his first cigarette of the day before his feet hit the floor. There was very little moderation with Jim, and it caught up with him way too soon."[34]

The sudden, shocking loss of a man who had so strongly affected the renaissance that was sorely needed on the playing fields of Norman, a man who had endeared himself to friends, family, colleagues, and on-field foes, and a man who had so strongly affected his players both personally and professionally, was both painful and numbing.

And Jim Mackenzie had been a visionary as well as a coach. Shocked at the state of facilities at the University of Oklahoma upon his arrival, he had been determined to do something to improve them. Leon Cross tells of Mackenzie's plans and contributions:

> Coach Wilkinson had not been a facility guy. Bud was concerned about over-emphasizing the program and the image that might project to the faculty and general public. He didn't want sports to be perceived as more important than scholastics, so very few upgrades were made during his tenure. In fact, Old Jeff House, the athletic dorm, was without air-conditioning and had not been renovated since it had been used as a WAC barracks during World War II. Jim hired me as recruiting coordinator but he also wanted us to implement a plan to eventually form "Sooner Clubs" in major cities around the nation. Back in Arkansas, they had formed "Razorback Clubs" designed to promote Razorback football and raise funds to build facilities. But then when Jim died, Chuck's priority was, as it should have been, building the football team so the Sooner Clubs went on the back burner although we did manage to start them in Norman, Oklahoma City, and Tulsa in 1968. Since then they've spread and now the Caravan travels from club to club, city to city in late summer to get everyone ready for the season.[35]

Jim Mackenzie was taken back to Gary, Indiana, his hometown, for burial; Switzer, Fairbanks, and James were among the pallbearers. While Mackenzie's friends and family had suffered a tragedy, the Sooner nation, reeling from the impact of the loss, grieved not only for Mackenzie but for the future of the team that had shown such promise during the coach's 476 days on campus. "Jim Mackenzie, had he lived," reflects Homer Rice, "would have been recognized as one of the greatest coaches in college football. He would have been in the same category as Bobby Dodd, Bear Bryant, Bud Wilkinson, and Frank Broyles. He had great leadership ability, was tough, and yet was a very likeable person."[36] Barry Switzer, who had been a close friend as well as a colleague, often reflects on what might have been. "I've often thought how tragic it was to lose him because had Jim Mackenzie not died April 28, 1967, he would have won 300 games at the University of Oklahoma."[37]

In the first seven decades of the twentieth century, four men had been instrumental in establishing a great football legacy at the University of Oklahoma: Benny Owen, Jim Tatum, Bud Wilkinson, and Jim Mackenzie. And now, although James Alexander Mackenzie was gone, the foundation he had laid in one brief year was solid; the torch he had lit would be passed.

7 Changing of the Guard

Jim Mackenzie was gone, and the University of Oklahoma was faced with the time-critical problem of finding his replacement. Shortly after Mackenzie's funeral on Friday, April 29, George Lynn Cross made a presidential appointment, promoting Chuck Fairbanks to head football coach; there had been no search committee. In his press statement, Fairbanks said, "Although it has always been my ambition to become a head coach, I wish it had been realized under different circumstances." And in a team meeting on May 2, he told his players, "The eyes of the whole United States will be on us to see what we're made of." Fairbanks further stated that he would continue to use the offensive and defensive systems installed by Mackenzie, adding, "We hope to have a more varied offense. It's necessary to make some changes this year because defenses are catching up with the offense."[1]

Although Mackenzie's coaches remained on staff with the exception of Swede Lee, who had left for Cincinnati with Homer Rice (Rice had also been approached by Dr. Cross to gauge his interest in the head coaching position but was committed to the University of Cincinnati),[2] some changes in assignments were made. Barry Switzer, concerned that he was too young to accept the role of offensive coordinator, was nevertheless finally persuaded by Fairbanks to do so; Pat James, in addition to his duties as defensive coordinator, was elevated to assistant head coach; Galen Hall would continue to coach receivers; Billy Gray would coach the defensive secondary; Buck Nystrom was brought aboard to coach the offensive line; Warren Harper was hired as Swede Lee's replacement as linebackers coach; Don Jimerson and Jerry Pettibone would coach the freshman team; and Port Robertson would continue to serve as the team's academic advisor. Leon Cross still coordinated the overall recruiting efforts, aided by Don Jimerson and Jerry Pettibone.

As Oklahoma prepared for the opener on September 23, the team was itching to go. The returning players had completed their second excruciating "fourth quarter class" in the spring and had endured a rigorous early September training regimen that raised their conditioning and training levels to a peak.

In the fall of 1967, the Sooners finally had the right set of coaches ready to lead the right group of players against the usual challenging schedule. With Bobby Warmack returning at quarterback, Oklahoma dispatched Washington State in its opening game with relative ease, 21–0. The game also saw the debut of a player whom Bill Connors of the *Tulsa World* referred to as a "reserve tailback": Steve Owens.[3] Though playing in only his first game as a Sooner, Owens led all rushers on the afternoon with seventy-four yards.

When asked by reporters after the game whether it felt good to notch his first victory, Fairbanks replied, "You bet your life! I've got that one forever; it's in the record books." When also asked if he had exhausted an entire pack of gum while pacing the sidelines during the game, he dug into his pockets, smiled, and said, "Nope—I've got two sticks left."[4]

The following weekend, Maryland fell 35–0, and then Oklahoma began serious preparations for Texas. The Longhorns, sporting an uncharacteristic 1–2 record, entered the game as five-point favorites despite the Sooners having been unbeaten and unscored upon. The first half of the classic saw Oklahoma dominate as it took the ball on its first possession seventy-eight yards for a touchdown. Three more Oklahoma deep threats misfired before halftime as it clung to a slim 7–0 lead. In the third quarter, Texas posted a field goal after a fumble recovery, cutting Oklahoma's lead to 7–3. Later in the third, the Longhorns scored their lone touchdown but failed to convert. At the game's end, the Sooners found themselves on the short end of a 9–7 score despite having outplayed the Longhorns for more than three quarters.[5] But unlike past Sooner teams, this squad did not fade when faced with a setback. The next four opponents, Kansas State, Missouri, Colorado, and Iowa State, fell beneath the Sooner onslaught, setting the stage for a showdown in Norman with the conference-leading Kansas Jayhawks. Former Sooner quarterback Jack Mitchell had recently retired after nine years at the Jayhawk helm, and Franklin C. "Pepper" Rodgers had taken over. Kansas came to Norman with only one conference loss and, by beating the Sooners, could clinch the Big Eight title and earn a berth in the Orange Bowl. Oklahoma found itself in a similar position; the Orange Bowl Committee had assured the Sooners that with victories over Kansas, Nebraska, and Oklahoma State, they would be Miami bound.

Though favored by as many as three touchdowns, Oklahoma was decisively outplayed in the first half; the Sooners crossed midfield only once and never penetrated beyond the Kansas forty-six-yard line. However, the defense did its job, holding the Jayhawks to a single field goal, the margin of KU's halftime lead.

The situation continued to deteriorate for the Sooners in the third quarter as Kansas bumped its lead to what seemed to be an insurmountable 10–0 margin. And then, in the fading moments of the third quarter, the Sooners awakened. Spearheaded by Owens and Warmack, Oklahoma went on a seventy-seven-yard march to the Kansas end zone. Mike Vachon tacked on the extra point, the deficit was reduced to three points and, to Pepper Rodgers's obvious consternation, Sooner fans began tossing the first oranges onto Owen Field. Both teams traded fruitless drives for the first eight minutes of the fourth quarter and then, with 6:37 remaining in the game, the Sooners found themselves pinned deep in their own territory, at the four-yard line.[6] At this point, Switzer called for a pass to Steve Zabel in the right flat; the pass went for eleven yards and a first down. Zabel recalls what happened next:

> Warmack threw it to me and it got us out of the shadow of our own goalposts. Then we ran Owens, and we ran Owens, and we ran Owens, overcoming a couple of fourth down situations, until we finally reached the Kansas thirty. And then Coach Switzer called a "24 pass," which required me to run downfield and beat my coverage. Luckily, I got past the defender, Tommy Ball, and just as I ran past him, I heard him yell, "*Oh shit!*" and then, I saw the ball on a high arc in the air and *I* was saying, "*Oh shit!*" but I made the catch in the end zone and we won the game 14–10.[7]

The field was showered by oranges tossed by ecstatic fans, and the Sooners had the inside track to Miami. Future Sooner quarterback Steve Davis was in the stands that afternoon and recalls his reaction to the winning touchdown:

"I can remember sitting in the stands the day Oklahoma beat Kansas in 1967. I'm in the north end zone sitting with my friends and when Bob Warmack hit Steve Zabel with that winning touchdown pass I literally cried and sat down in my seat. And right there at that moment in time I said, 'Someday I'm going to be in *this* stadium playing down on *that* field.' I made that commitment that very day."[8]

And on a less dignified note, one hundred yards away in the south end zone, as perennial Sooner fan Charlie Northcott leapt to his feet, one of tens of thousands celebrating Zabel's touchdown, he accidentally spat a wad of gum into the hair of the lady sitting in front of him.

The 7–1 Sooners climbed from seventh to fifth in the November 20 AP poll, but they had work to do before their Miami Beach invitation became an actual reservation. Bob Devaney's Cornhuskers, although sporting a 5–3 mark, always posed a serious threat in Lincoln, and if that hurdle could be cleared, Oklahoma State loomed. Although recent Oklahoma teams had experienced trouble maintaining momentum, the 1967 edition was a different species, reminiscent of some of Bud Wilkinson's 1950s squads. The inertia generated by their five-game winning streak continued unabated as Oklahoma handled Nebraska 24–14 on November 23, and nine days later placed the Big Eight universe back into its proper alignment with a 38–14 pasting of Oklahoma State. During this late season run, the Sooner offense had seldom played better as Bob Kalsu, Bob Craig, Byron Bigby, Eddie Lancaster, Ken Mendenhall, Steve Zabel, and punter Gordon Wheeler each made enormous contributions to the team's success.

The Big Eight Conference champion Sooners—it was their first league championship since 1962—also garnered individual honors at the end of the regular season. Sophomore Steve Owens won the conference rushing and scoring crowns, gaining 808 yards while tallying 72 points,[9] Ron Shotts, Owens's gifted backfield companion, had placed second in conference rushing with 726 yards, and teammate Bob Warmack set a new total yardage record at the University of Oklahoma with his 2,523 yards.[10] And though it may not have merited national honors, Owens and Shotts carried the ball a combined 366 times without a single fumble in 1967.[11]

The Unstoppable Steve Owens. Courtesy Steve Owens.

In defeating the Cowboys, the Sooners had provided a semisweet departing gift to their most loyal and avid supporter; effective on July 1, 1968, Dr. George Lynn Cross planned to retire. The OU-OSU game had been his last in Memorial Stadium in the capacity of university president, a position he had held since 1943. After twenty-five years at the helm, Cross was ready to fade into the background at the University of Oklahoma, retreating to his quiet office in the Botany Department to enjoy his emeritus status.

Fairbanks allowed his team a week off before preparing for the Orange Bowl. The Sooners would then return to practice for ten days before flying to Miami on Christmas Day to prepare to meet Tennessee.[12] The Volunteers, coached by Doug Dickey, were also a team in ascent, having just wrapped up their first SEC championship since 1956. Dickey, like Mackenzie and many members of the OU staff, had learned their trade at the knee of Frank Broyles in Fayetteville. Dickey considered the Sooners and Volunteers similar teams in many ways. "Both teams are comparable in personnel, both have great team speed and both run the I-formation although ours doesn't rely quite as heavily on the tailback."[13] Similarities and differences notwithstanding, the entire country was looking forward to the showdown between the second- and third-ranked teams in the nation, the Southeastern Conference champs versus the Big Eight champs.

Tennessee took the opening kickoff and drove into Oklahoma territory but lost the ball on a fumble. The Sooners accepted the gift ungraciously as they moved sixty-eight yards for their first touchdown. Late in the first quarter and into the second, Oklahoma mounted an eighty-seven-yard drive finished off by a twenty-one-yard Warmack-to-Hinton touchdown pass. Vachon failed to convert, and Oklahoma led 13–0. After stifling a Tennessee drive, OU once again marched seventy-four yards, scoring on a Steve Owens line plunge seconds before the half expired. The Sooners' two-point attempt fell short, and Oklahoma held a 19–0 halftime lead. But in the second half, momentum took a nasty shift. Bob Warmack recalls, "We had a great first half. Everything we did—running, throwing, defense—was working perfectly. I had one of the best halves I've ever played in the first half and then turned around and had one of the worst. When we came out in the second half, it was as if a different team was wearing our jerseys; we just couldn't seem to do anything right. I threw a couple of short passes and the defense was right there to pick them off. That changed the momentum and really shook my confidence. Tennessee had made some very effective halftime adjustments."[14]

The Volunteers scored touchdowns off those two interceptions and within a two-and-a-half minute span in the third quarter the game was back on. With five minutes remaining in the third period, Tennessee put a field goal through the uprights to reduce Oklahoma's lead to 19–17. But then, Sooner Magic made a timely reappearance when, early in the fourth quarter, Oklahoma safety Bob Stephenson intercepted a Tennessee pass and took it home, increasing Oklahoma's lead to 26–17 with nine minutes remaining in the game.

But it was not over yet. Tennessee, not to be denied, mounted a twelve-play, seventy-seven-yard scoring drive to trim Oklahoma's lead to 26–24. And then, with under two minutes remaining, Oklahoma faced a fourth and less than a yard at its own forty-four-yard line. After pondering the decision on the sideline, Fairbanks decided to go for the down, but Owens's dive over tackle failed and Tennessee took over in Oklahoma territory. "Owens had been very effective all day," recalls Warmack, "but when we tried to run it in there to pick up the first down on that critical fourth and inches, they just stuffed us."[15] Later, Fairbanks stood by his decision. "I thought it was the right thing to do," he said. "The way Tennessee was moving the ball, I didn't want to give it back to them."[16] With seven seconds remaining, the Vols moved the ball to the OU twenty-seven-yard line and were set to attempt a game-winning field goal. Their kicker, Karl Kremser, got a good strike on the ball, it had the distance, but at the last second it sailed wide by inches; Oklahoma's 26–24 victory had been preserved.

Chuck Fairbanks had completed his first season in grand form; although the Sooners were officially ranked third in the final AP poll, they had defeated the second-ranked team, making them de facto runners-up to the national champion USC Trojans.

The 1967 Sooners were an undersized club and lacked a preponderance of blue-chip athletes, but they possessed other elements fundamentally more important to the success of a football team: cohesive leadership and commitment. Bob Warmack stated, "The spirit of that team was insurmountable. Every single man pulled for everyone else. We didn't have many stars, but a team like that went a lot further than a team with six or seven stars who aren't pulling together."[17]

The foundation that had been laid by Jim Mackenzie in the spring of 1966 had paid off in two short years. Conditioning, personnel placement, and coaching had been key factors in the turnaround. In the two years before Mackenzie's arrival, the Sooners had posted a 9–11–1 record; in the two seasons following his arrival, Oklahoma had achieved a 16–5–0 record, had attained a number-two national ranking, and had defeated Texas for the first time since the Eisenhower administration. Chuck Fairbanks had been the right choice to lead the Sooners after Mackenzie's untimely passing. He had provided strong leadership, intelligent guidance, and the prescience to realize that the path the team had embarked upon under Big Jim had been the correct one.

8 Stability, Decline, and Crisis

FEBRUARY 1968–OCTOBER 1970

Not since 1958 had Oklahoma performed as brilliantly as had the 1967 team. The Crimson and Cream posted a 10–1–0 record, placed third nationally in the final Associated Press poll, won the Orange Bowl by defeating the second-ranked Tennessee Volunteers, and laid claim to two players who had established team and conference records: Bob Warmack and Steve Owens. Additionally, the Associated Press had declared the Oklahoma Sooners "The 25 Year Champions of College Football." In its press release, the AP noted that from 1943 through 1968, Oklahoma had averaged 26.1 points per game, leading the nation. Army placed second, Mississippi and Notre Dame tied for third, and Texas and Michigan State tied for fifth.[1]

Sooner fans exuded excitement as they entertained fresh memories of a brilliantly diverse Sooner offense led by Bobby "The Worm" Warmack with his dangerous combination of running and passing; Eddie Hinton, who possessed quick and elusive wideout talents; and Steve Owens, a big, powerful, relentless runner who no defense seemed able to stop at the point of contact. The fans were also counting on a repeat performance by a stingy Oklahoma defense.

But Fairbanks had serious concerns. "We have a chance to be a good football team," he said, "but we lack quality depth throughout the squad." While Fairbanks expected his offense to be good, with the absence of defensive linchpins Granville Liggins, Bobby Stephenson, John Koller, and Rick Goodwin—all of whom had graduated—he feared there would be gaping holes in his defense.[2] He realized that his linebacker corps would only be average, prompting him to experiment in the spring with moving Steve Zabel from tight end to linebacker. Also, Fairbanks decided to drop the "monster" defense that had been imported by Mackenzie in 1966 and install the 4–3–4 "Missouri" defense in its place. "The defense we were playing in '68 through '70 was bullshit," comments Barry Switzer. "And if we'd gone to the seven-man front four deep in '71 we would have dominated everyone—we really would have been something. Our offense was so super it enabled us to keep the ball away from people, but we weren't that good on defense; we were just a little above average."[3]

Fifth-ranked Oklahoma opened the year in South Bend, Indiana, against the third-ranked Fighting Irish. The matchup between the two teams was far from even, with the Irish linemen heavily outweighing their Sooner counterparts. Oklahoma's defensive backfield was also comprised of relatively light athletes. "I knew we had small defensive backs," recalls Eddie Hinton. "I used to tease them all the time telling them they couldn't guard my mother."[4]

On the opening drive, the Irish pushed the Sooners downfield, taking a quick 7–0 lead. And then, Hinton and Warmack went to work. Hinton explains how the first Sooner score developed:

> I always played well in televised games, so when I saw Notre Dame on our schedule I went to Switzer in the spring and said, "Coach, you know that three-yard look-in pass that we only use every now and then? If we throw that pass on the first play of the game, I can score from anyplace on the field." Switzer replied, "Eddie, that play's not designed to score; it's designed to pick up five or six yards." I told him, "It'll be a surprise attack, coach. I'll even go down to Ada so Warmack and I can work on it during the off-season."
>
> Then, on the first play of the Notre Dame game I went over to Warmack and said, "Worm, you've *got* to throw the ball and hit me right on the money, you've got to catch me in stride. If you get it to me, I can run between the linebackers and the safeties. The defense will just be standing there watching me because they won't expect us to pass on first down."[5]

True to his word, on the Sooners' first play from scrimmage, Hinton took Warmack's pass seventy-five yards for the tying touchdown. With the score knotted at seven, the Irish were threatening when Hinton struck again:

> I had been watching their big wide receiver, Jim Seymour; he was 6'3" and around 240 and I'm 6'1" and 190, but I'm thinking I can cover him. So I go over to Switzer on the sideline and say, "Hey coach, I can guard that

tight end; he can't match my speed, he can't get away from me." Switzer looked at me and said, "Eddie, you've never played a *down* of defense." And I just repeated, "I can stop him, coach!" So he just shakes his head, says, "Good God, Eddie," and walks over to Fairbanks who listens to him, pulls his cap off, scratches his head, and says to Barry, "He told us he would catch that pass and score, and he did; let's put him out there." So they put me on Seymour and when Notre Dame came out of the huddle, (Irish quarterback Terry) Hanratty looked at me like "Well, *he's* not supposed to be over there," and he called a time-out to confer with his Coach, Ara Parseghian. Ara told him, "Just throw it; he's no defensive back." So they snap the ball and Seymour runs a curl right in front of me; I slip, but regain my footing, snatch the ball out of his hands, and take it thirty-four yards upfield.[6]

After Hinton's interception, Oklahoma continued to move the ball effectively downfield against the Notre Dame defense until Warmack hit a leaping Steve Zabel with a pass in the end zone for a 14–7 Sooner lead as the first quarter expired.

As the game wore on, the Sooners began to relent to the bigger, stronger Irish. "One of the lies the coaches told us," chuckles Hinton, "was that these bigger players would tire out late. We *knew* that if we could take the game into the fourth quarter, our level of conditioning would allow us to wear down our opponent and we'd win. And I'll be honest with you, the only time that didn't happen was against Notre Dame in 1968. The Irish didn't wear down; they got stronger."[7] When the final seconds of the game clock died, so had the Sooners, 45–21. The 1968 Notre Dame loss would represent a turning point at the University of Oklahoma; having watched their players tossed around like leaves in the Indiana wind, the coaches came to realize that it was not necessary to sacrifice size and muscle for quickness and speed; they discovered that in order to compete at the top of the college football pyramid, Oklahoma would have to use bigger, stronger players not only on the line of scrimmage but also in other positions. "We weren't big enough to hang with the Irish who outweighed us on average forty pounds per man," reflects recruiting coordinator Leon Cross.

"After that game, Fairbanks told me to go out west and scour the junior colleges to find some bigger players."[8]

The forty-five points scored by the Irish against Oklahoma were not entirely attributable to an imbalance of size, according to Sooner All-American Ken Mendenhall. He reflects, "We had lost key players from our defense after 1967 and we simply couldn't replace them. And the guys we'd lost also represented much of our defensive leadership. I believe that was the biggest reason for our drop-off in 1968. Plus, the players the coaches had hoped could step up and fill in couldn't, a fact that became painfully obvious during our game in South Bend. The Irish ran up and down the field on us. That got us off to a bad start and we had some disappointing games later in the season. We also had some players quit, which made us even thinner."[9]

Oklahoma would flip-flop losses and wins for the first six games of the season. After the loss to Notre Dame, the Sooners defeated North Carolina State in Norman to raise their record to 1–1; an off week was followed by another loss to Royal's Texans (OU held a thin 20–19 lead only to watch it slip away on a seven-yard Steve Worster touchdown run in the game's final seconds), followed by a victory over beleaguered Iowa State, once again pulling Oklahoma's record to .500. The 2–2 Sooners lost their next bout, a 41–27 defeat at the hands of Colorado in Boulder, and then Fairbanks made a change that would affect the rest of the season; he called Steve Zabel into his office and asked him to play linebacker as well as tight end. Zabel recounts, "Coach Fairbanks told me, 'Steve, we've proven that we can't outscore people, so we need you to play defensive end as well as tight end.'"[10] Zabel, a natural athlete who had excelled as a linebacker in high school, made an immediate impact on defense. *Sports Illustrated* commented, "What transformed the Sooners—they lost three of their first five games and gave up 133 points—into winners was not the development of their backfield, but the switching by Coach Chuck Fairbanks of 217-pound end Steve Zabel from offense to defense. With Zabel on defense, the Sooners allowed only 64 points in their last five games, all of them victories."[11] The Sooners had, indeed, beaten their last five regular season foes including undefeated league-leading Kansas, once-beaten Missouri, up-and-coming Nebraska, and Oklahoma State. Oklahoma finished the season with a respectable 7–3 record and accepted an invitation to play SMU in the Astro-Bluebonnet Bowl.

"Some considered 1968 a down year after the success we had in 1967, but it wasn't; we were successful," says Switzer. "We shared the conference championship with Kansas and we had beaten them in Lawrence."[12] Switzer was correct. By December, the '68 Sooners *were* a good team, made better by the continuing emergence of sophomore tailback Steve Owens. Owens, who won the Big Eight rushing title with 808 yards as a sophomore in 1967, toted the ball seventeen times for sixty-six yards in the Sooners' first game against Notre Dame; but from the second game through the remainder of the regular season, he averaged thirty-six carries per game and never gained fewer than one hundred yards per contest. By the sixth game of 1968, Owens had surpassed his 1967 rushing total, and by his eighth game he had established a new school single-season rushing record, 1,244 yards, eclipsing Billy Vessels's record of 1,072 set in 1952.[13] On the day before Thanksgiving, Owens ran wild against Devaney's Nebraskans, scoring five touchdowns while breaking the conference season rushing record by gaining 172 yards; additionally, in the same game, Bobby Warmack became the conference's all-time offensive leader with 4,289 career total yards.[14] At the conclusion of the regular season, Owens had rushed for 1,536 yards and had become recognized as a serious Heisman Trophy candidate for 1969.

Oklahoma entered the Astro-Bluebonnet bowl as marginal favorites against Hayden Fry's 7–3–0 Mustangs. The Sooners began the game showing flashes of the brilliance they had displayed during their five-game winning streak. Scoring on its first possession and threatening on its second, OU appeared to have the Mustangs' number. And although the Sooners held onto a slight 7–0 lead at halftime, the team's spirit was dampened when both Warmack and Zabel suffered knee injuries on consecutive plays late in the second quarter. Bobby Warmack, a senior, had ended his brilliant career as a Sooner on the floor of the Astrodome in Houston.

While the first half had been a study in defensive football, the second half was a donnybrook, with both teams posting a total of forty-eight points. Mickey Ripley performed well in Warmack's stead, but SMU prevailed, 28–27, as Sooner Bruce Derr's field goal attempt from the Mustang eighteen-yard line with nineteen seconds remaining missed.

Although 1968 had ended on a sour note, Steve Owens had been named a consensus All-American, while Owens, Warmack, Hinton, Mendenhall, and Zabel were each appointed to the All–Big Eight Conference first team. Eddie Hinton had established new Sooner records with most receptions in one season, 60, and most career receptions, 114. To ice the cake, the Sooners had just completed their third winning season, Fairbanks had compiled a 17–5 record in his first two years, and he appeared to have things moving in the right direction.

∵

On August 16, 1968, the Oklahoma All-Stars squared off against the Texas All-Stars in the annual Oil Bowl game in Wichita Falls, Texas. The Oklahomans had not won since 1964 when future Sooners Ron Shotts and Jim Burgar helped propel their state to a 21–16 victory. Although the Oklahomans would lose 39–7 in 1968, they had good reason for jubilation; the quarterback who ran and passed the Texans for 241 yards while playing only three quarters, Jack Mildren from Abilene Cooper High School, was headed for Norman.

Initially, Mildren, the top high school prospect in the state of Texas in 1967, had not planned to attend the University of Oklahoma. In early 1968, Texas A&M head coach Gene Stallings had been putting a full-court press on Mildren in an effort to make the young man an Aggie. Mildren was impressed with A&M and leaning in their direction, when Barry Switzer entered the picture. "The year I recruited Jack, the Southwest Conference had placed a restriction on the number of times a school could visit a recruit in the state of Texas," explains Switzer.[15] While each SWC school was limited to two visits, other conferences were not bound by this restriction, a rule disparity that had a great impact on Texas, Texas A&M, and other schools in their conference. Barry Switzer used that edge to full advantage while pursuing Jack Mildren.

During the critical recruiting months of January and February, Switzer virtually lived in Abilene and grew very close to the Mildren family. Switzer relates an incident that occurred while recruiting the young player:

> I got to know Jack's parents, Larry and Mary Glynn, very well. I spent a lot of time at their home. We used to eat our meals together and then we'd go into the living room to watch television—we were big fans of

The Porter Wagner Show. One Thursday night, I was at their house in the kitchen helping his mother wash dishes after dinner when Texas A&M arrived for their visit. The doorbell rang at 7:00 P.M. and there stood Stallings and six or seven members of his staff; they already knew I was there because my car was parked out front. As the coaches were walking in the front door and I was walking out, I couldn't resist turning and shouting from the sidewalk, "Mary Glynn . . . I'll be back around 10:00 and help you finish those dishes!"[16]

Several weeks later, Jack Mildren signed a binding letter of intent to attend the University of Oklahoma, and the Southwest Conference changed its visitation rule the very next year.

As the Sooners entered spring practice in early April 1969, all eyes were on the three-man quarterback competition between Mildren, Mike Jones, and Mickey Ripley. In the first spring scrimmage, Mildren got off to an inauspicious start by being sacked five times and by throwing one interception and one incompletion. But as the spring progressed so did Mildren, and by the time the Varsity-Alumni game was played on May 10, he was hitting his stride. In the game, won by the Varsity 17–8, Mildren drove his team for their first score in the second quarter, and their second touchdown after an eighty-yard drive in the third quarter. But it was a non-scoring drive engineered by Mildren that impressed the most. Starting inside his own five-yard line, Mildren led the team on a cross-country, ninety-four-yard drive before fumbling a few feet from the Alumni goal line.[17]

As the Sooners prepared for their opening game against Wisconsin in Madison, Fairbanks and Switzer had devised a new offensive set that they hoped would allow more versatility in their attack: the Diamond-t. The offense placed two halfbacks, side by side two yards behind the quarterback with the tailback lined up several yards directly behind the signal caller. "The Wishbone had enjoyed great success at Texas the previous year," explains Switzer, "and Chuck was trying to figure out a way to keep Owens back there along with our other fast backs. We had some speed—we'd just recruited Roy Bell—and we wanted to become an effective three-back offense like Texas. But the Diamond-t wasn't very effective and we eventually dumped it."[18]

The team also continued to run the Missouri defense, which caused some dissension within the coaching staff. Lacewell explains, "Chuck had us playing a man-to-man defense that we weren't equipped to run—he could be awfully stubborn and he didn't want to give it up. Pat James, our defensive coordinator, was particularly annoyed because he was made to use the man-to-man even though he felt we weren't well-suited for it—he wanted to go back to the 'monster' defense that Mackenzie used in '66, but Chuck insisted that we stick with Missouri's 'check' defense, the 4–3. And as a result, in '69, we got blistered by several good passing teams and in 1970 it nearly got us fired."[19]

Mildren, who got the starting nod as a sophomore, led the sixth-ranked Sooners to a season-opening 48–21 victory over Wisconsin in Madison. His first collegiate pass, a sixty-seven-yard touchdown to Joe Killingsworth, marked Oklahoma's first score of the young season. Shortly thereafter, the Abilene sophomore tossed another touchdown strike, a twenty-eight-yarder to Roy Bell, before finishing the scoring with a sixteen-yard scramble for his third score. Steve Owens scored four touchdowns while gaining 189 yards. It was Owens's tenth consecutive regular season game to rush for over one hundred yards, breaking the national record set by the University of San Francisco's Ollie Matson in 1951.[20] That the Badgers entered the game on a fifteen-game losing streak (their record over the past two seasons had been 0–19–1) was of little consequence; the game still represented a valuable scrimmage in a loud, unfriendly environment, the perfect petri dish to develop the new Sooner squad and their young, promising quarterback.

Their next game would be against the Pittsburgh Panthers, winners of two or their last twenty-one games. The Panthers' dismal ways continued as Mildren, Owens, and company dispatched them 37–8. In the game, Mildren was the leading ground gainer with 135 yards on 15 carries (a 9-yard average per tote), while passing for another 71 yards. Owens, suffering from a painful Charlie horse, still ran for 104 yards on 29 attempts and crossed the Pitt goal line three times; his national record-setting string of consecutive games rushing over 100 yards grew to 11.[21]

Then came the off week prior to the Texas brawl. Texas, a team that had finished the previous season ranked third in the nation, would end the year as national champions. Powered by James Street, Cotton Speyrer, Steve Worster, and Jim Bertelsen, the Texas Wishbone attack was picking up momentum every week. Darrell Royal, after viewing film of Oklahoma's first two games, declared that he believed the 1969 Sooners to be a better team than the 1968 edition, a squad his Longhorns had barely beaten.[22]

The Sooners got off to a promising start, scoring back-to-back touchdowns in the first quarter, but Texas rallied, and in the final minute of the period Street's pass to Speyrer cut OU's lead to 14–7. The Longhorns' second score came in the final two minutes of the second quarter, as Bertelsen barreled over the Sooner goal line to tie the game at halftime. The third quarter saw Oklahoma's Bruce Derr and Texas's Happy Feller trade field goals until, again, Texas posted a second three-pointer late in the third quarter to take a 20–17 lead. With the game still up for grabs, the Sooners mishandled a Texas punt with less than five minutes remaining in the game, giving the Horns the ball at the OU twenty-three-yard line. Five plays later, Worster scored once again, and once again the game ended badly for Oklahoma. Going into the contest, the Sooner coaching staff had planned to stack the line of scrimmage in an effort to force Texas to pass the ball, a strategy at which the Longhorns had not been known to excel. But excel they did on this day as Texas quarterback James Street went to the air eighteen times and completed 9 for 215 yards and one touchdown.[23]

As Oklahoma prepared for its next test against visiting Colorado, the coaching staff decided to deemphasize the Diamond-t and return to the I-formation, an offense Mildren had run throughout his high school career.[24] Buffalo head coach Eddie Crowder brought a team to Norman ready to play, and although the final score was Oklahoma 42, Colorado 30, the game was teetering on a 35–30 precipice with just over two minutes remaining. As the Sooners began their final possession of the game, Owens, who had only gained seventy-four yards against a stiff Colorado defensive front, appeared to be in danger of having his twelve-game one-hundred-yard rushing streak broken. Mildren systematically fed Owens the ball, moving his team downfield, until, with only nine seconds left, Colorado called a time-out. When play resumed, Owens took the ball on a sweep right and, behind a block from Roy Bell, rolled out of bounds at the Buffalo one-yard line; Big Steve would score on the next play. The final Sooner drive allowed Owens to exceed the one-hundred-yard mark, extending his nation-leading record to thirteen games.

Next, the Sooners traveled to Manhattan to face a Kansas State team unlike any Wildcat team Oklahoma had ever faced before. KSU entered the game with a 3–1 record (its only loss had been to an undefeated Penn State team by three points) and ranked eighteenth in the nation. Its quarterback, Lynn Dickey, was averaging over 175 passing yards per game and was destined for the NFL; his 6,208 career passing yards at Kansas State remained a school record until it was broken by Josh Freeman in 2008. "It's going to be a real tough game," said Fairbanks.[25] He had no idea.

The Wildcats jumped quickly to a 14–0 lead before the Sooners got their bearings. But less than a minute following the second KSU score, Mildren tossed a seventy-seven-yard scoring strike to Killingsworth to bisect the lead. The 'Cats came right back on the next possession to build a 21–7 lead, only to see it sliced into once again by Mildren with a sixty-six-yard touchdown pass to Everett Marshall. Kansas State held a 28–14 lead at intermission.[26]

And then the dam broke. The Wildcats scored three unanswered touchdowns in the third period and never looked back. Aided by Sooner turnovers in their own red zone, whatever chance Oklahoma possessed had vanished on the Kansas plains before the fourth quarter began. When the game ended, Oklahoma had been vanquished 59–21. It was the most points ever scored on a Sooner team; Dickey had completed more passes against OU than any other quarterback in history (28) and set a new conference single-game passing mark (380 yards) in the process. And it was the first Kansas State victory against Oklahoma since 1934 when the Wildcats eked out an 8–7 decision.[27] "We were absolutely blown out at KSU," remembers Mendenhall. "It was a tremendous embarrassment. They had a legitimate team, Lynn Dickey was an NFL caliber quarterback, and they ran from a pro-set offense using five receivers."[28]

The Sooners would flounder for the rest of the season, posting victories over Iowa State, Kansas, and Oklahoma State while losing in decisive fashion to Missouri and Nebraska. The Tigers, ranked ninth in the AP poll when they defeated Oklahoma, would go on to win the Big Eight Conference; the Huskers would finish eleventh in the AP poll with a team that was gearing up for national championship performances the following two seasons. Ken Mendenhall sums up the season:

> We got killed by Missouri and Nebraska, two teams we'd handled with relative ease the year before. Frankly, 1969 was an embarrassment. We'd won the conference in '67, finished third in the nation while beating the second-ranked team in the Orange Bowl and in 1968 we finished eleventh nationally while sharing the conference championship with Kansas, a team we'd beaten in Lawrence. Then in 1969, we went 6–4 and it was a bitter pill to swallow. We didn't play that great on offense in '69, either. I don't buy into the idea of team "chemistry" as a general rule, but in 1969 we didn't click. It ended up as a disappointing year for me as a senior. I had gone into the year hoping we would have a shot at the national title.[29]

Switzer has also been critical of his performance that season. "I did a terrible job in '69," he says.[30] But Switzer was the offensive coordinator, and his offense, while not performing up to the standards it would realize in years to come, performed admirably, scoring 285 points, an offensive output second only in the decade to the 343 points scored by the '68 Sooners. Switzer's offense had only scored less than fourteen points once, in the 44–10 loss to conference champion Missouri. The problem with the Sooners had clearly been on defense; opponents tallied 289 points against Oklahoma in 1969, the highest total number of points allowed by any Sooner team of the decade.

Though the '69 Sooners would finish the year fourth in conference play, Steve Owens would be rewarded for three years of bruising accomplishment by becoming the second Sooner to win the Heisman Trophy. Owens had set NCAA records for consecutive one-hundred-yard games with twenty-three and for most carries in one game and one season and took home the national rushing and scoring titles.[31]

A year before, Oklahoma had suffered a debacle loss to Colorado, 41–27, and the first "Chuck Chuck" bumper stickers popped up around the state. However, the naysayers had been quieted by the ensuing five-game winning streak and near miss against SMU in the Astro-Bluebonnet Bowl. The slaughter in Manhattan, Kansas, six days before Halloween in 1969 would signal the beginning of a crisis for the Sooner coaching staff; they found themselves more heavily scrutinized, criticized, and analyzed than any staff in Norman since 1965.

And it was to get worse before it got better.

Spirits in the Sooner nation were dampened in late July 1970 by the news of Bob Kalsu's death in Vietnam. Kalsu, who had earned All-American honors at OU in 1967 and had been named rookie of the year with the Buffalo Bills the following season, had enlisted in the army and was serving with an artillery spotting detachment in one of the hottest fire zones in South Vietnam, the A Shau Valley. On July 21, Lieutenant Kalsu and his friend, Pfc. Nick Fotias, had emerged from their dugout to avoid tear gas fumes when Kalsu was killed by an incoming mortar round. Kalsu's commander, Colonel Philip Machaud, said of him, "[He was] a fearless guy, smart, brave and respected by his troops."[32] Kalsu died days before his wife, Jan, gave birth to their second child in Oklahoma City. Kalsu's passing created a tidal wave of sorrow among his family, friends, and teammates, who had suddenly, tragically, and irrevocably had the game of football put back into its proper perspective.

In September, the 1970 Oklahoma Sooners adopted the Houston Veer offense; it would be the third offense Jack Mildren had been asked to learn and execute in his two years under center in Norman. Behind and supporting Mildren were Roy Bell, Joe Wylie, Everett Marshall, and Leon Crosswhite. On the outside snagging Mildren's passes would be Jon Harrison, Greg Pruitt, and Albert Chandler. The offensive line welcomed back only two starters, Steve Tarlton and Darryl Emmert. The 4–3–4 defensive alignment, so erratic the year before, would return. The stopping unit would consist of Rick Mason, Bruce DeLoney and Albert Qualls at end and Kevin Grady and Derland Moore at tackle; the rear was protected by Steve Casteel, Steve Aycock, and Forb Phillips at linebacker, with Monty Johnson, Glenn King, Geoffrey Nordgren, John Shelley, Steve O'Shaughnessy, Dan Ruster, Larry Roach, Vic Kearney, and Steve Shotts manning the secondary.

Though hugely criticized the year before, the defense played lights-out ball against SMU in the opening game. Seeking payback from the 1968 Asto-Blue-bonnet Bowl loss, Mildren and company played relentlessly on offense while the Sooner defense gave Mustang quarterback Chuck Hixson no respite in the 28–11 victory. In the contest, Oklahoma amassed an impressive 405 yards of total offense as the Veer appeared to be alive and well in Norman.

On September 19, the Wisconsin Badgers paid the Sooners a visit, bent upon exacting some measure of revenge for the previous season's embarrassment at the hands of Mildren and company, and by halftime they led OU 7–0. In the third quarter, Fairbanks's halftime elocutions spurred the Sooners to three touchdowns in their first three possessions as they posted their second victory of the season, 21–7.

But all was not well in Norman; the Veer had begun to misfire. Although known for his dangerous running, Mildren was held to minus nine yards rushing against the Badgers and had been forced to rely on Wylie, Bell, Marshall, and Crosswhite to move the ball on the turf.

Next on the schedule was an early fall bout with Oregon State. The Beavers made the 1,500-mile trip southeast toting a 1–1 record; they had lost their opening game to UCLA but had rebounded by defeating Iowa. Oregon State was coached by Demosthenes Konstandies Andrecopoulos, better known to Sooners as Dee Andros; Dee, along with his brother Plato, had been players under Bud Wilkinson in the years following World War II.

The Beavers gave the Sooners all they could handle in the first half, taking a 13–0 lead before finally falling behind OU 14–13 at intermission. In the second half, Oregon State took command, shutting down all aspects of the Oklahoma attack while posting ten unanswered points en route to a 23–14 upset. The Sooners had been held to 103 yards rushing; Mildren, frustrated for the second week in a row, was held to minus yardage rushing while Beaver running back Dave Schilling nearly matched Oklahoma's team rushing production with ninety-six yards. *Daily Oklahoman* writer Bob Hurt commented that Oklahoma "showed so little offense that they were in danger of having their deodorant confiscated."[33] Fairbanks commented after the game, "I am embarrassed by the ineptness of our offensive team. Maybe it's our coaching philosophy; maybe we don't have the right players at the right positions."[34]

Fairbanks was correct on both counts. Oklahoma football was on a downward spiral, and a contest with the Sooners' biggest rival—Texas—was just fourteen days away. The second-ranked Longhorns were defending national champions, had defeated their first three opponents—California, UCLA, and Texas Tech—by the combined score of 111–45, and had beaten the Sooners eleven of the past twelve years. As the Red River Rivalry drew nearer, the Oklahoma landscape was ablaze with fall colors accented sharply by a proliferation of "Chuck Chuck" banners, signs, and bumper stickers. To save the season as well as their jobs, the Sooner coaching staff knew that something drastic had to be done, and quickly.

9 The Magnificent 'Bone

OCTOBER 1970

One of the great ironies in the storied history of college football is that Darrell K. Royal, the iconic head coach of the University of Texas, was from Hollis, Oklahoma, had been a star player for the University of Oklahoma from 1946 through 1949, and remained a close friend of his former head coach, Bud Wilkinson. While a Sooner, Royal set interception records as a defensive back, set punting records, and, as a quarterback, led the 1949 Sooners to their first undefeated and untied season since 1918. In 1953, Royal accepted his first head coaching job with the Canadian Football League's Edmonton Eskimos and after one season migrated back to the United States for head coaching stints at Mississippi State and Washington before settling into the position with which he would forever be associated: head coach of the Texas Longhorns.

In Austin, Royal's teams became known for being stocked with blue-chip players who were supremely conditioned and sublimely coached, a practice he had learned from Wilkinson. And finally, after laboring seven years with a Texas team that had fallen into severe disrepair during the 1950s, he led the Longhorns to their first national championship in 1963. But in 1964, Royal had to contend with a rising star in the east: Frank Broyles's Arkansas Razorbacks. Broyles became head coach in Fayetteville in 1958 and, during the next six seasons, only defeated Royal on one occasion. However, in 1964, the year after Texas brought home its first national title, Broyles's Razorbacks embarked upon a three-game winning streak over the Longhorns, a trend that directly coincided with three consecutive 6–4 seasons in Austin.

In his inaugural year at Texas, Royal implemented the Wing-t offense, which his teams ran with dangerous perfection through their 1963 national title season. But in 1965, as wins declined and losses mounted, the Longhorns traded the Wing-t for the I-formation, an alignment that failed to bring the success Royal sought.[1] Asked by sportswriters what had happened to the vicious tackling and ferocious offense usually associated with his Texas squads, Royal quipped, "We

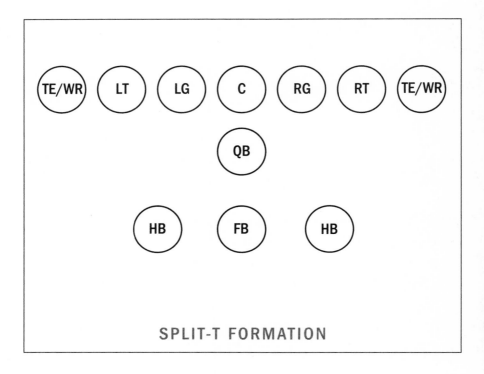

SPLIT-T FORMATION

graduated it."[2] But graduation notwithstanding, after losing to the Hogs for the third straight year in 1967, Royal knew that changes were in order.

In the spring of 1967, Royal added Emory Bellard to the Texas staff. While a high school head coach in Texas, Bellard had conceived a new offense while tinkering with the Split-t; by leaving the blocking patterns the same and moving the fullback a couple of steps ahead of the halfbacks, he had produced a dangerous multifaceted formation resembling a Y, which quickly became labeled "the Wishbone." "I'd been experimenting with it since 1954," recalls Bellard, "and when I moved on to Breckenridge High School we used some of its concepts in the state playoffs in 1958 and 1959. What we ran at Breckenridge closely resembled the offense we eventually installed at Texas in 1968."[3] Barry Switzer is quick to attribute the provenance of the Wishbone offense to Bellard. "There were some high school coaches that were running the 'Bone in the sixties, but Emory Bellard is the one who invented it; he should get credit for it."[4]

∵

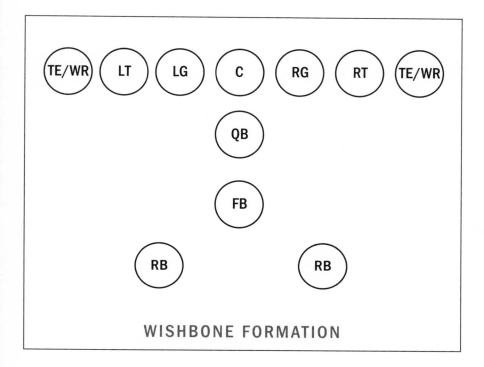

WISHBONE FORMATION

The Wishbone offense was a gifted child of a gifted parent: the Split-t formation. Conceived by Donald Faurot while he was head coach at the University of Missouri in 1941, the Tigers' rugged Split-t led them to an 8–2–0 season and a seventh-place national ranking. Faurot would pass his knowledge of the Split-t on to Bud Wilkinson and Jim Tatum while coaching at Iowa Pre-Flight in 1943, and Wilkinson employed it with deadly efficiency at the University of Oklahoma throughout the 1950s. Jay O'Neal, who both ran the early precursor of the Wishbone at Oklahoma and coached it on the high school level in Colorado, explains the operational difference between the Split-t and the Wishbone:

> The Split-t was not a triple-option offense because you didn't option the halfback; you either called the handoff *before* the snap and gave him the ball, or you faked it and ran the option on the end. The Wishbone was a true triple-option offense; the quarterback could hand the ball off to the fullback, keep it himself, or pitch it out to his trailing halfback.

In the Split-t, the belly play was the dive handoff to the near halfback and the fullback would always be the lead blocker; in the Wishbone, the belly play was always the handoff to the fullback, who was positioned a couple of yards closer to the quarterback than he had been in the Split-t. The lead blocker in the Wishbone was the near halfback, a position very critical to its success. That guy *had* to take care of the cornerback. What was so great about the way OU ran it was that those lead blockers were phenomenal. If you watch the film of Switzer's Wishbone, you can see how critical that lead block is to the success of the play.[5]

After Texas's '67 season ended, Royal promoted Bellard from linebackers coach to offensive coordinator and spoke with him about making changes to the Longhorns' offense. "In the summer of '68, Emory and I discussed the idea of using the Wishbone offense," says Royal. "I thought his idea was great because it was a triple option, an offense I had been very familiar with from my days with the Split-t in Norman. The variations Emory came up with intrigued me because it added another dimension to the original Split-t."[6] At the conclusion of the 1967 season, Royal asked Bellard if the things he had done with the Breckenridge offense would be effective on the college level. "I told him, 'Darned right they would be,'" recounts Bellard. "So we decided to use the Wishbone and it completely revolutionized college football."[7] Bellard was correct; after installing his Wishbone in 1968, Texas posted a remarkable 30–2–1 record over the next three seasons while winning back-to-back national titles in 1969 and 1970. "Emory wrote one hell of a sweet song with that offense," reflects Royal.[8]

As Texas's success with its new offense grew, Bellard's "song" caught on elsewhere. Woody Hayes, the hard-nosed Big Ten coach whose power football philosophy had been etched in granite since the 1950s, contacted Royal in December 1970 before his undefeated and second-ranked Ohio State team was scheduled to play Stanford in the 1971 Rose Bowl.[9] "Woody always liked to surprise other teams," comments Ohio State quarterback Rex Kern. "We were sitting in a quarterback meeting several weeks before the Rose Bowl game when Woody walked in and announced, 'We're going to surprise Stanford. We're going to run the Wishbone. We've bought Darrell Royal's triple-option tutorial cassette, it's on its way, and we're going to incorporate it.'" Kern recalls that the Buckeyes abandoned the offense they had used the previous three years—"the same offense we'd used to go 27–1"—and went to the triple option. "Even though we didn't beat Stanford in the Rose Bowl," he continues, "the offense was still effective."[10] And although Ohio State reverted back to the I-formation the following season, the Buckeyes kept the Wishbone in their repertoire. "Woody kept the Wishbone as a change-up in certain situations, at least until *I* arrived," comments Archie Griffin with a smile.[11]

Although Royal and his staff occasionally shared the new formation with other schools, a most remarkable example of collegial magnanimity occurred in mid-October 1970 when Royal extended assistance to the coaching staff at the University of Oklahoma. Bellard explains what happened:

> One day, Darrell comes into my office—and this is the gospel truth—and said, "Chuck Fairbanks and his coaches are in bad shape up in Oklahoma; they're fixin' to get fired. I want to help him. Barry Switzer will be calling you to learn about the Wishbone." I was stunned for a moment and then managed to reply, "You've got to be *joking*." But he wasn't. So Barry called me on several occasions and I gave them all of our knowledge about the formation. And within a year or so, we couldn't catch 'em; they had too much speed and talent. In retrospect, I doubt Darrell would be nearly as benevolent if he had it to do over again.[12]

Switzer was amazed that Bellard and Royal would talk to the Sooner staff about putting in the new offense. "Chuck and I spent a lot of time with Emory on the phone going over it," recalls Barry. But it was not as though Switzer was starting out from scratch. "On a one-to-ten scale, we were starting out at about seven. We had film of every game they'd played," he says, "and I wore that film out watching it and studying it. What I *had* needed from Bellard were rules of execution for quarterbacks, methods for attacking defenses, and other questions of a much more detailed technical nature. I also implemented some blocking schemes that were different from what Texas was doing."[13]

Switzer had been particularly impressed by how cooperative Bellard and

Royal had been. "Emory was terrific," he recalls. "When you consider the nature of the situation, here was Texas, a blood rival, helping us out. It was an incredible thing for them to do. Ford would never give Chevrolet ideas on how to beat them at production or marketing, but Darrell and Emory, to their credit, helped us. And from that point on," chuckles Switzer, "we killed them."[14]

Since September 1970, the Sooners had been running the Houston Veer, an offense Fairbanks was familiar with from his days as an assistant coach in Houston. But the results had been disappointing; after three games, Oklahoma stood at 2–1, including a disappointing home loss to Oregon State. Switzer describes how the decision was reached to adopt the Wishbone:

> After the Oregon State loss we had an open date before Texas. I had talked to the other assistant coaches about making the change to the Wishbone and received unanimous support. Then I told Chuck that we were going to get our asses fired if we didn't adopt the Wishbone; he had been depressed about the situation so I figured he was probably about ready to listen to any damned fool idea I might come up with—including changing our whole offense within a few days before playing our biggest rival. He heard us out and then said he would think it over and give us an answer the next day. I was concerned that Chuck wouldn't make the change because I knew he would call Duffy Daugherty and Biggie Munn and all his Michigan State friends and they would advise him to stick with what he believed in. But these guys weren't living in the house we were living in and they weren't looking at the problems we were looking at. The next day, he gathered the staff together and said, "Well, hell, let's give it a shot; nothing much depends on it except our futures." I have to give Chuck credit because in order to make that change he had to go against the advice of his mentors; that took guts. The peer pressure on him had to have been tremendous. In retrospect, I would have preferred to have installed it back in the sixties but I wasn't the head coach and it wouldn't have suited Steve Owens's running style anyway. We realized what we had in Owens and it would have been counter productive to have installed any defense that might have reduced his

role. But if we had installed the 'Bone in the spring of 1970, we would have been far more effective our first year. If we'd had the time to practice, for our staff to put in the preparation, we would have dominated 1970 like we did in 1971.[15]

Although the Sooner coaching staff had supported Switzer's idea, they knew it was risky; but in early October 1970, it was painfully obvious to them that a risk was necessary. "Barry was totally committed to it and spearheaded the idea," says Galen Hall. "But as coaches, we knew it was a gamble."[16] The first time Larry Lacewell saw Texas execute the Wishbone, he was aghast. "Frankly, I didn't know how in the world we were ever going to stop it," he reflects. "It was just devastating. And then, in the last game we played using the Veer, Oregon State beat us, and we knew something had to be done. Hell, I was afraid the entire coaching staff was going to get run out of Norman. We were desperate; it was time to change."[17]

Switzer was also aware of an advantage Oklahoma would have over Texas with the 'Bone—the Sooners had more quickness and speed. With Pruitt, Wylie, Bell, and Mildren in the backfield, he realized the Sooners would more closely represent a track team than a football backfield. Greg Pruitt was a remarkable talent and had been recruited and used as a wide receiver in 1969, but it had been his eventual move to Wishbone running back that spurred him to fame and helped spark the success of the new formation. "They were having difficulty getting the ball to me," Pruitt recalls, "so they told me that in the Wishbone they could just *hand* the ball to me since they were having problems *throwing* it to me from the Veer. So I said, 'Okay, fine.'" But the move dropped Pruitt from starting receiver to backup running back overnight. "I even thought about quitting," he says. But Pruitt knew the Wishbone would work. "The thing that fascinated me about it was that when it was diagramed on the chalkboard, it appeared to be very easy to defend. You put Os down and Xs to defend them and it looks pretty simple." But Oklahoma, he explains, took the Wishbone one step further than Texas by adding speed. "And that made a huge difference," says Greg, "because even if that X looked like it could cover the O on the chalkboard, when the O runs a 4.3 and the X runs a 4.7, it isn't quite so easy."[18]

From September 27 to October 9, 1970, the Sooners had thirteen days to install, practice, and perfect their new offense. It would be the fourth and final offensive alignment Jack Mildren would be asked to run during his years at the University of Oklahoma.

The Wishbone, a formation that brought glory to the Texas Longhorns, an offense born of the Split-t formation so brilliantly and successfully used by Bud Wilkinson and Oklahoma in the 1950s, had finally come full circle.

It had come home to Norman.

10 Ascent

OCTOBER 1970–JANUARY 1972

On October 10, 1970, the Oklahoma Sooners took the field with their nascent Wishbone against the team that had spent the past two years developing, honing, and dominating the college football world with theirs—the Texas Longhorns.

"I would like to tell you that we went to Dallas and dazzled Texas with our new Oklahoma Wishbone, but the fact is that we didn't impress Texas one bit," said Switzer.[1] That anyone might have expected a different result than the 41–9 shellacking the Longhorns dealt the Sooners that day was a tribute to naïveté. Although the Sooners' adaptation to the Wishbone might have surprised Royal, the lopsided score had not. "It's the same offense we've been defending through spring practice and through two-a-days for the past three years," said Royal after the game. "If we don't know how to line up against it by now, we're in trouble."[2]

At the game's conclusion, the Sooner nation fumed at both their team's 41–9 embarrassment and their 2–2 record, and concerns for the future of the program—both long-term and short-term—abounded. But Switzer and Fairbanks did not share the fans' disenchantment. Oklahoma had nearly matched Texas in first down production and had churned out 222 yards of total offense compared to the Longhorns' 335. Additionally, the Longhorns' victory could be at least partially attributed to the five turnovers Oklahoma gift wrapped that afternoon.

"I felt good about the game," said Switzer. "We had moved the ball against a great Texas defense in our first try at the Wishbone."[3] Royal had also been impressed. "I was surprised when they won the toss and elected to receive," he said. "But then they took the ball and *drove* against us."[4] The game had also allowed the Sooner coaching staff to make adjustments. A. G. Perryman had started the game at fullback but, by the fourth quarter, had given way to sophomore Leon Crosswhite; late in the game, Crosswhite scored Oklahoma's only touchdown against Texas that day, and its first touchdown of the Wishbone era.

"The Monday after the Texas game," recalls Crosswhite, "Switzer called me up to his office and said, 'I've been talking with Darrell Royal all morning and I asked him if he were me, who he'd start at fullback. And he told me he'd play 'that Crosswhite kid.' Then Coach Switzer said I was going to be the starting fullback for the Colorado game. Now, I tried to act like I wasn't too excited when I was in his office, but after I went out the door I could have jumped to the moon! It was a turning point for me."[5]

Next up for the Sooners was a trip to Boulder to play the Colorado Buffaloes, the thirteenth-ranked team in the nation. Oklahoma ceded the game's first touchdown to Colorado before scoring twenty-three unanswered points to upset the Buffs 23–15. "We went to Colorado installed as three-touchdown underdogs, and we beat the shit out of them," recounts Switzer.[6] But his recently acquired confidence in the new formation would take a hit when Vince Gibson brought his Kansas State team to Norman the next weekend. The Wildcats, led by quarterback Lynn Dickey, had blasted Oklahoma the previous year in Manhattan, and the Sooner nation was anxious for revenge. After once again allowing its opponents to score first, Oklahoma fought to a 14–7 lead and held it into the fourth quarter. But with four minutes remaining in the game, the Wildcats finished an eighty-three-yard drive to tighten the score to 14–13; the KSU extra point attempt was blocked and Oklahoma maintained a nervous one-point lead. Then lightning struck the Sooners when Jack Mildren's pass was intercepted, and two plays later, Dickey tossed a third-down twenty-eight-yard touchdown pass, giving the Wildcats a 19–14 victory. The Sooners had gained 235 yards for the day while Kansas State had managed 463, with 384 of them yielded off Dickey's arm. With the season halfway done, Oklahoma was 1–2 with its new offense and clutching to a 3–3 record. Although the coaching staff believed they were on the right path, their confidence that they would be allowed enough time to right the Sooner ship before losing their jobs was shaken.

The next stop for the Sooners was Ames, Iowa, a venue that had historically been very kind to them; the Cyclones left the Missouri Valley Conference to join the Big Six Conference after the 1927 season, defeated Oklahoma 13–0 in Ames in 1928, and only managed one other victory—a 10–6 scuffle in 1960—since. But the Cyclones were not ready to concede anything to the Sooners in 1970. In the first quarter, Iowa State's first three possessions produced three touchdowns. Oklahoma, realizing the severity of the situation, went to work and by the fourth quarter had tied the score at 21–21. With just over four minutes remaining in the game, Iowa State scored on a seventy-yard touchdown pass to take a 28–21 lead. On the Sooners' final drive, Greg Pruitt sparked the comeback with an eleven-yard dash on the first play. Two plays later from the Oklahoma forty-eight, Mildren pitched the ball to Willie Franklin, who tossed a downfield strike to Albert Chandler at the Cyclone fifteen. Three plays later, Joe Wylie punched into the Iowa State end zone, bringing the Sooners within a single point, 28–27. After a time-out, Fairbanks sent his team onto the field to try a two-point conversion. Mildren took the ball from center, rolled right, and pitched the ball to Pruitt, who scored behind Crosswhite's block.[7] Oklahoma had eked out a 29–28 victory in the nick of time. Lacewell describes the game's importance:

> We took a big chance by changing our offense to the Wishbone in the middle of a season. We rolled our Wishbone out in Dallas and had it shoved right back down our throats by the Longhorns. Then, we beat Colorado and the next weekend we were beaten by Lynn Dickey and Kansas State, 19–14, on our own field. Things were getting pretty ugly and I was truly afraid for my job. Our coaching staff was in crisis mode. Then we played Iowa State at Ames and had to come from behind to win. Let me tell you, to a man, the coaches knew that winning that game probably saved our asses.[8]

The Sooner Schooner saw plenty of action as Oklahoma bounded by Missouri (28–13) and Kansas (28–24) before traveling to Lincoln for a showdown with undefeated and third-ranked Nebraska. The Huskers were headed toward their first national championship, a title they would share with Darrell Royal's Longhorns. Despite entering the game as sixteen-point underdogs, the Sooners led three times before finally succumbing 28–21. Following the Nebraska game, the Sooners gave their fans a preview of the performance they might expect from the next year's team as they buried Oklahoma State beneath an avalanche of 592 yards and 66 points in a 66–6 exhibition. At halftime, the score stood at Oklahoma 45, OSU 0, and, adding insult to injury, the Pride of Oklahoma Band started its halftime show with the tune "Mercy, Mercy."[9] At the game's end, fans and players alike hoisted Fairbanks onto their shoulders and carried him off the turf. On the other side of Lewis Field, Oklahoma State head coach Floyd Gass was sitting quietly in the locker room. As reporters began to gather around him, he responded to any and all questions they might be pondering with one brief statement: although the Cowboys had played the Sooners in Stillwater, Gass said, "We should have stayed home today."[10]

The Sooner offense had begun to come together as a cohesive unit in the second half in Ames when it produced a mind-boggling 386 yards in two quarters alone. The only loss Oklahoma suffered the rest of the year had been to national champion Nebraska in Lincoln, and even that game had been in contention until the last moment. By the conclusion of the regular season, Fairbanks's Sooners felt anything but humble. They were standing atop a respectable 7–4–0 record, their new offense was beginning to fire on all cylinders, and they were imbued with momentum and self-confidence. Most importantly, they had received an invitation to play Bear Bryant's Alabama Crimson Tide in the Astro-Bluebonnet Bowl in Houston on New Year's Eve.

The Sooners spent the weekend prior to the Thursday night game going through two-a-days at Rice Stadium. A buffet was held on Monday, December 28, attended by the Alabama and Oklahoma coaches and staff. The Astro-Bluebonnet Bowl had arranged for two aides wearing animal costumes to be present for entertainment; one wore a bear costume, the other a bunny. Everyone knew that the bear was supposed to represent Coach Bryant, but when asked what the bunny stood for, Astrodome publicist Orland Sims replied, "That's the only other costume we had on hand."[11]

The game began on a sour note for Oklahoma as Alabama mounted an eight-play, fifty-four-yard drive on its second possession to take a 7–0 lead. But the Sooners came blazing back, aided by fifty-eight-yard and twenty-five-yard touchdown runs by Pruitt, and a two-yard score by Joe Wylie. At the half, Oklahoma led 21–14.

Alabama posted the lone third-quarter score with a twenty-one yard field goal, and then, with just over seven minutes remaining in the fourth period, the Tide scored the go-ahead touchdown to take a 24–21 lead. Oklahoma took the ball back on its own twenty and, in five plays, moved the ball to the Alabama twenty-six-yard line, when Bruce Derr was sent in to attempt the tying field goal. The kick was good, and the score was tied. A last minute drive by the Tide culminated in a missed field goal, and the 1970 "kissing-your-sister" Astro-Bluebonnet bowl ended in a 24–24 tie. Pruitt, Mildren, Wylie, and Crosswhite had combined for 349 rushing yards—the highest ever for OU in a bowl game, eclipsing the previous record of 286 against LSU in the 1951 Sugar Bowl.[12]

Oklahoma's 7–4–1 season-ending record had earned it the twentieth position in the final Associated Press poll; Alabama had not been ranked. Fairbanks, his coaches, and his team could afford to be optimistic about the future. The midseason transition to the Wishbone formation appeared to have been a success, and with a talented and experienced team returning in 1971, Oklahoma would once again entertain national aspirations.

The "Chuck Chuck" days had finally come to an end.

∵

In March 1971, John MacLeod's Oklahoma Sooners basketball squad earned their second consecutive berth in the National Invitational Tournament in New York City. A contingent from the University of Oklahoma traveled to New York City the week before the Sooners' first round game, a Monday afternoon affair against the University of Hawaii. On Sunday evening, March 10, while returning to his hotel, athletic director Gomer Jones collapsed on the subway platform at 34th Street and the Avenue of the Americas. With Jones at the time were his wife, Jeannette, John MacLeod, trainer Ken Rawlinson and his wife, assistant basketball coach Dennis Price along with his wife and parents, and five members of the Sooner basketball team—John Yule, Paul Crowell, Kirby Jones, John Gorman, and Ron Lynch. "We were standing there talking," said MacLeod, "and all of a sudden we heard someone yell 'Gomer!' as he fell against my leg and landed at my feet."[13] Both MacLeod and Price attempted mouth-to-mouth resuscitation and external heart massage, to no avail. Gomer Thomas Jones, so instrumental in the post–World War II success of the University of Oklahoma and so dear to all who had known him, had succumbed to a heart attack at the age of fifty-seven.

"I had had dinner with Gomer and Ken Rawlinson in New York City on Saturday evening," recalls Homer Rice. "I had to fly to Houston for an NCAA meeting the next day and when I picked up the paper the next morning I read that Gomer had been stricken with a heart attack and died."[14]

Services for Jones were held on Wednesday, March 24, at the First Presbyterian Church in Norman. Official pallbearers were Leon Cross, Brewster Hobby, Frank "Pop" Ivy, Bobby Drake Keith, and Joe Rector. The enormous crowd attending the service provided a warm, telling tribute to Jones's years of dedication to his university, his friends, and his players. Bud Wilkinson, Chuck Fairbanks, Colorado head coach Eddie Crowder, Big Eight commissioner Wayne Duke, Texas head coach Darrell Royal, Missouri athletic director Sparky Stalcup, Nebraska athletic director Don Bryant, Oklahoma State's Floyd Gass, former OU coaching assistant Pete Elliot, and former OU players Billy Vessels, Steve Owens, J. D. Roberts, Jerry Tubbs, Jimmy Harris, Max Boydston, Stan West, Bobby Goad, Leon "Willie" Manley, and George Brewer were among the former stars and dignitaries in attendance. In his eulogy, Pastor E. Kenneth Feaver extolled Gomer's honesty and his "stubbornness born of it" while describing Jones as a gentle man with "a kindness which tempered the discipline he knew he had to impose."[15]

The man who had worked side by side with Jones for seventeen years, Bud Wilkinson, found that he had temporarily lost his characteristic eloquence. "This has left me speechless. Gomer was a great friend and a great man." Overcome by nostalgia, Darrell Royal remarked, "Every time I think of Gomer I see him leaning on the door by the locker room as we'd run out on the field saying, 'Stay loose, kid.'"[16]

And as spring turned to summer and summer to fall, Gomer would have been proud of just how loose his kids *had* become. With a strong contingent of returning players running a deadly-effective offense, Chuck Fairbanks was preparing to unleash a team that would return Oklahoma to the elite level of college football—a pinnacle it had once taken for granted under Bud Wilkinson.

∵

Jack Mildren had not been happy when Barry Switzer informed him of the decision to adopt the Wishbone formation in October 1970; Jack loved to pass and realized that in the Wishbone his opportunities to air out the ball would be marginalized. "You could tell Jack was frustrated at first," remembers Crosswhite. "He was irritable, and although he didn't voice his frustration to most of the guys, it wasn't hard to see."[17] But in addition to being a fine passing quarterback, Mildren was imbued with other qualities that made him the perfect Wishbone operative. He was smart and nanosecond-quick at the point of attack; the entire process, from center snap to decision on the corner, generally occurred in a matter of seconds, and Jack Mildren was masterful in its execution.

But even though Fairbanks's figurative gun was loaded in the fall of 1971, he was still careful not to project too much public optimism. "Fundamentals were a problem in 1970," said the coach. "We didn't have the time to thoroughly teach the foundations of the offense. Now we've had the time; we've studied the theories and we're going to see if they work."[18] Oklahoma would be better in 1971, and the coaches knew it. The Sooners welcomed back thirty-nine lettermen and sixteen starters from the previous campaign, nine on offense and seven on defense. With each passing day of practice, both Fairbanks and Switzer had watched Mildren and his backfield become quicker and deadlier in their execution. In addition to Mildren, Pruitt, Crosswhite, and Wylie returning, the line promised to be formidable with Tom Brahaney, Ken Jones, Dean Unruh, Eddie Foster, Robert Jensen, Darryl Emmert, and Ron Stacy onboard. The wide receiver position would also be solid with Willie Franklin, Albert Chandler, and Jon Harrison.

The defense also promised to improve in '71. Although All-American linebacker Gary Baccus had been lost for the year with an arm injury, Fairbanks expected the more experienced secondary and linebacking corps to step up. He had fretted over the defensive line's inability to mount a consistently intimidating pass rush in 1970 and hoped that with experience, it would improve. Returning were Raymond "Sugar Bear" Hamilton, Derland Moore, Steve Aycock, Steve O'Shaughnessy, Mark Driscoll, Glenn King, John Shelley, Geoffrey Nordgren, Dan Ruster, Albert Qualls, Bruce DeLoney, and Lionell Day. Backing up Derland Moore was a player whose skills and lineage the Sooner nation would get to know intimately in the coming years: sophomore Lucious Selmon. The solid kicking of John Carroll put the icing on the Sooner cake.

Mildren, Aycock, and King were elected team tri-captains as the Sooners geared up for their opening-day game against Hayden Fry's Southern Methodist Mustangs. The two teams slugged it out on a rainy afternoon with Oklahoma prevailing 30–0. It was the Sooners' first shutout since blanking Nebraska 47–0 in 1968, and their most decisive opening victory since 1958 when they banished West Virginia from Norman, 47–14.[19] Although the Sooners had entered the game ranked tenth in the 1971 preseason AP poll, they dropped one position after their opening-day win.

Next, Oklahoma traveled east to play the Pittsburgh Panthers, a team that had just dealt fifteenth-ranked UCLA a 29–25 defeat in Los Angeles. After giving up a field goal to the Panthers, Joe Wylie returned the following kick-off eighty-five yards for the go-ahead—and stay-ahead—touchdown. Then Mildren and company began to operate in workmanlike fashion as they dismantled Pitt, 55–29. The Sooners were beginning to play with confidence and abandon. Against the Panthers, they ran only 59 plays while gaining 569 total yards, a 9.6-yard-per-snap average. In addition to his proven rushing ability, Mildren completed six of nine tosses for 149 yards while Pruitt touched the ball nine times for 118 yards, an average of 13 yards per carry.

Next on the Sooners' dance card was the University of Southern California. The Trojans had dropped their home opener to Alabama—Bear Bryant, after experiencing firsthand what a Wishbone offense could do when he played Oklahoma in the Blue Bonnet Bowl nine months earlier, had switched the Tide's offense to the 'Bone. Following their loss to 'Bama, the Trojans shut out their next two opponents, Rice and Illinois, by the combined score of 52–0, before traveling to Norman. Switzer called Greg Pruitt to his office during the week of the game and asked him to wear a specially made t-shirt emblazoned with "Hello" on the chest and "Goodbye" on the back. Pruitt donned the shirt and went to class. Later in the afternoon, he found his way to Campus Corner, where he encountered local television and radio station crews doing a live feed. Pruitt was interviewed, and his shirt made headlines. "Later on that day at practice," recounts Pruitt, "Barry announced to the team that he had given me that shirt and he was pretty sure a picture of it was already hanging in the USC locker room. And he told me it'd damned sure *better* be 'Hello Goodbye' on game day because the Trojans weren't going to be happy about me wearing that shirt."[20] Pruitt wore the t-shirt beneath his jersey on game day as he lacerated the Southern California defense with 205 yards rushing, including scoring dashes of 75, 42, and 7 yards while averaging 13 yards each time he touched the ball. Oklahoma led 33–14 and, after allowing the Trojans an "oh-by-the-way"

Greg Pruitt in Cleveland Stadium, 2010. Courtesy Greg Pruitt.

touchdown on the game's final play, defeated Southern California, 33–20. Greg Pruitt earned National Back of the Week honors from *Sports Illustrated* magazine and was well on his way to stardom.[21]

The Sooners had lost twelve of the past thirteen games to Texas by a combined score of 282 points to 124, and as they crossed the Red River heading south in October 1971, they were determined not only to break their habit of losing to the Longhorns but to make a clear, unambiguous statement in the process. Both Oklahoma and Texas entered the game with identical 3–0 records. Texas, defending national champs, had beaten UCLA in Los Angeles, Texas Tech, and Oregon by a combined sore of 91–17 and was ranked third nationally while the Sooners weighed in at number eight.

Both teams scored furiously in the first quarter as the Longhorns twice held touchdown leads before Oklahoma pulled even. In the second quarter, Pruitt's forty-one-yard jaunt fueled OU to a 21–14 lead. Shortly thereafter, Pruitt scored on another long run, upping Oklahoma's advantage to 28–14 before a Longhorn touchdown tightened the game 28–21. John Carroll booted a field goal with one second remaining to give Oklahoma a 31–21 halftime lead. "Later," laughs Switzer, "Darrell Royal said, 'Every time Oklahoma had the damned ball on offense it looked like they were running downhill!'"[22]

When the dust cleared, Oklahoma was the last team standing, with a 48–27 victory in hand. Oklahoma had outgained Texas 435 yards to 231. "The game boiled down to them lining up the way they were supposed to," said Mildren, "and us lining up the way we were supposed to in order to find out who had the best players. As it turned out, we did. We knocked a lot of people down and had another great day running."[23] And Pruitt had led them all with 216 yards.

When Greg Pruitt made the decision to attend the University of Oklahoma after high school instead of the University of Houston—his hometown school—he was forced to endure brutal verbal abuse from family and friends. He explains why beating Texas had become paramount to him:

I had an uncle named A. V. Philpot, my mother's brother, and when I left Houston to go to OU he called me a traitor. Every summer I went back home and had to work for him doing carpentry, and he used to stick it to me constantly, saying things like "Yeah, you're going to Oklahoma and we're gonna kick your butts." In 1970, my first year to play, they beat us 41–9 and I had to go back home and listen to that *all . . . summer . . . long*. That was one of my incentives to do well because I wanted him to stop messing with me. And after the 1971 game, he did.[24]

The victory over Texas boosted the Sooners to the second position in the AP poll, behind fellow conference mate Nebraska. In the process, Oklahoma had leapfrogged its next opponent, Colorado, who had fallen from fifth to sixth place nationally on the strength of a lackluster 24–14 victory over lightly regarded Iowa. In his ninth season as head coach at Colorado, Eddie Crowder had performed what amounted to coaching magic in Boulder in 1971; the Buffs had only won six games the previous season, but they would travel to Norman on October 16, 1971, with a 5–0 record in tow, including victories over LSU, coached by Charlie McClendon, and Ohio State, led by Wayne Woodrow Hayes. But the momentum Colorado had built over the first five games rapidly evaporated into the thicker Norman atmosphere as Pruitt, who would gain 190 yards on the afternoon, took complete advantage of Crowder's plan to stop the Sooners at the corners by barging over left tackle for a sixty-six-yard touchdown run on Oklahoma's first possession. On the Sooners' next possession, it took Mildren just one play to tally the second OU score of the day on a fifty-four-yard pass to Jon Harrison. Just like that, Oklahoma led Colorado 14–0. After a John Carroll field goal and an eighty-nine-yard drive sparked by another of Pruitt's lightning-fast sprints—this one for fifty-nine yards—the Sooners led 24–0 at the break.

Hal Brown, sports editor of the *Lincoln Star*, had traveled to Norman because he was "tired of watching runaway games," referring to the Husker landslides he had been witnessing all year. At halftime, he proclaimed, "Tell Chuck if he's doing this to impress the Nebraska writer, he can call 'em off. The Nebraska writer is duly impressed."[25] Oklahoma finished the afternoon with a pedestrian 45–17 victory.

The following weekend, Oklahoma found itself in an unusual position—that of exacting revenge against a Kansas State team that held a two-game winning streak in the woefully unbalanced series. The Wildcats had butchered the Sooners 59–21 in 1969, and it had unsettled Fairbanks's generally calm demeanor. Although he had not said so, he had felt that KSU coach Vince Gibson had run the score up needlessly. In 1970, the Sooners had had the game seemingly under control only to watch it slip away in the waning minutes of the fourth quarter.[26] On October 23, 1971, Oklahoma vanquished Kansas State in much the same way the Roman legions vanquished Carthage in 148 BC. The game was never in question as the Sooners romped to touchdowns in eleven of their twelve possessions en route to a 75–28 victory. Oklahoma blasted the Wildcats for 785 total yards (711 of those on the ground) while Pruitt accounted for 294 of those yards by himself—187 of them in the first half alone. His production against K-State set a new conference record, topping Gale Sayers's 283-yard mark. Roy Bell contributed four touchdowns in the contest while Jack Mildren rushed for an additional 156 yards. On the other side of the line of scrimmage, Kansas State rushed for 245 yards, making the combined rushing total for the two teams, 956 yards, a new NCAA single-game record.[27]

The following three opponents—Iowa State, Missouri, and Kansas—fell like dominoes by a combined score of 119 to 25. And as the college football nation began preparations for an annual Thanksgiving feast, Oklahoma and Nebraska began preparing for a showdown. In 1970, after decades of struggle, Nebraska had finally grabbed college football's golden ring by ending the season ranked number one in the AP poll. The 1971 edition of the Nebraska Cornhuskers had been every bit as impressive as the team from Norman; through ten games, the undefeated Huskers waylaid their foes by a combined score of 389 points to 64, a 33-point average margin of victory. They had shut out Kansas, Iowa State, and Missouri while holding Oregon, Minnesota, Texas A&M, and Utah State to a touchdown or less.

The Oklahoma-Nebraska game on Thanksgiving Day, November 25, 1971, has long been considered one of the greatest football contests ever played. The sportsmanship, crowd intensity, and quality of play achieved levels seldom seen before or since. Nebraska's electrifying wingback, Johnny Rodgers, stunned the home crowd by returning Oklahoma's first punt seventy-four yards for a touchdown. The Huskers built a 14–3 lead in the second quarter, but Mildren scrambled for a touchdown with five minutes remaining and tossed a scoring pass to Harrison with five seconds remaining to give Oklahoma a 17–14 advantage at intermission. By halftime, the Sooners had amassed 311 total yards to Nebraska's 91.

In the third quarter, Husker tailback Jeff Kinney muscled over the Oklahoma goal line for two scores, giving Nebraska a 28–17 lead. But, in the fading moments of the period, Jon Harrison tossed a fifty-one-yard halfback pass to Albert Chandler, who was finally wrestled down at the Nebraska sixteen. Four plays later, Mildren scored and Oklahoma tightened the gap to 28–24. In the middle of the fourth period, Lucious Selmon recovered a Nebraska fumble in Sooner territory, and, with only seven minutes remaining, Oklahoma moved sixty-nine yards to take the lead 31–28. However, the lead was fleeting as Nebraska, on its next series, mounted a seventy-four-yard, time-draining drive culminating in Kinney's fourth touchdown of the day. The Cornhuskers held on to a 35–31 lead for the victory and their second national championship in as many years. After the loss, the quality of the Sooner squad was recognized by the pollsters as the team only dropped one spot, to number three, in the AP poll.

In its last regular season game, Oklahoma would throttle Oklahoma State 58–14 before packing for New Orleans to play fifth-ranked Auburn in the Sugar Bowl. The 8–1 Tigers, led by their Heisman-winning quarterback Pat Sullivan, were no match for Oklahoma's power as the Sooners rolled to a 31–0 halftime lead. In the third quarter, John Carroll set a Sugar Bowl record (also a school and Big Eight Conference record) by kicking a fifty-three-yard field goal. Leading comfortably 40–7, the Sooners gave up two consolation touchdowns in the last four minutes of the game before winning 40–22. Additionally, Oklahoma's total rushing yardage, 439, and total number of first downs also set new Sugar Bowl records.[28] Jack Mildren became the first player in Sugar Bowl history to score three touchdowns in the game. As he was walking off the turf with his teammates at Tulane Stadium, Mildren was summoned to join a group of coaches and officials in the middle of the field where he was informed that he had been named the Player of the Game. Bill Connors of the *Tulsa World* wrote, "In what amounted to a salute that reflected their respect for Mildren, the laughing, sweating bodies who had mauled Auburn 40–22 stood and watched. 'Let's see Jack get it,' shouted offensive tackle Dean Unruh. In a moment, Mildren came running with his trophy and received perhaps the most appreciated applause he has ever known. Those who knew him best were acting like fans. 'This is great!' blushed Mildren."[29]

The 1971 Sooners were an offensive throwback to a time fifteen years earlier when Wilkinson's 1956 team—considered by some to have been the best Sooner squad of all time—had led the nation with a 481.7 total yards per game average, with 391 yards per game in rushing, and with 46.6 yards per game in scoring.[30] The 1971 Sooners established a new NCAA rushing record by averaging 472.4 yards per game and a new total yards per game average of 566.5 while averaging 44.9 points per contest; Pruitt averaged 9.4 yards per carry alone, and the team 7.1 yards per snap. Switzer comments on the Sooners' rushing performance: "We averaged 472.4 yards per game rushing in 1971. That still stands as an NCAA record thirty-nine years later. With most teams today leaning towards passing offenses, no one rushes for 400 yards per game anymore. They say records were made to be broken, but you can quote me on this one: That record will *never* be broken."[31]

Additionally, John Carroll led the nation as a kicker by averaging 7.3 points per game. Pruitt and Mildren, much like McDonald and Thomas had in 1956, vied with each other for superlatives. Pruitt gained 1,760 yards rushing while Mildren had rambled for 1,289, becoming the first pair of Sooners to exceed the 1,000 yard mark in the same year. Both players also ranked in the top-ten vote recipients in the Heisman balloting, with Pruitt placing third and Mildren sixth. Mildren was also named the Chevrolet Offensive Player of the Year by ABC.

"For four weeks in a row," says Switzer, "Pruitt had incredible rushing totals: against Southern Cal he had 205 yards, 216 against Texas, close to 200 against Colorado, and damned near 300 against K-State. And he only carried 10 or 12 times each game. He led the nation rushing, averaging 9.4 yards per carry, a record that still stands. Mildren, Wylie, Bell, Crosswhite, were all spectacular talents on an exceptional team."[32]

In spite of the loss to Nebraska, the Oklahoma Sooners had reclaimed their position as a perennial power in college football. With their Wishbone in full array, with recruiting at its peak, and with competing defenses still struggling to cope with the irresistible combination of brain, brawn, coordination, and speed that were the salient characteristics of Oklahoma's Wishbone, the future was bright.

11 Conference Champions!

Although the offense returned eight starters in 1972, the loss of Jack Mildren gave pause to Sooner loyalists. Mildren, who had not come into his own under center until the Sooners adopted the Wishbone in mid-fall of 1970, had developed into the linchpin of the versatile and explosive Oklahoma offense; whether Pruitt was turning the corner on a cross-country run, Crosswhite was scattering defensive linemen in his wake, or Jon Harrison was hauling in a touchdown pass, it all started with Jack Mildren. The competition to claim the vacated quarterback spot was limited to Dave Robertson, James Stokely, and a number of underclassmen including the highly recruited Kerry Jackson from Galveston, Texas, and Steve Davis, from Sallisaw, Oklahoma.

In the spring of 1972 Fairbanks had assigned Leon Cross the task of finding a replacement for Jack Mildren. His search had taken him to Los Angeles, where future film star Mark Harmon had earned a reputation as a junior college quarterback. Harmon loved the Sooners, could operate the Wishbone, and had aspired to play for Fairbanks, but pressure from his parents kept him in Los Angeles, where he eventually enrolled at UCLA.[1] However, by the time spring practice had ended, Dave Robertson, a senior from Garden Grove, California, had won the job. Although Robertson was a smart, sophisticated passer who had fit perfectly into the Sooners' I-formation scheme when he was recruited in 1968, the coaching staff had doubts about his ability to operate the Wishbone offense four years later. "You go into a circumstance like that just wanting to compete to play," reflects Robertson. "That's what college athletes do regardless of whether they've sat for two years or not. I think other people had far greater concerns about my ability than I did, but I was just excited about the opportunity to play. I felt like I could get the job done even though I would never be Jack Mildren."[2]

Robertson would be operating behind a seasoned line consisting of Tom Brahaney, Dean Unruh, Ken Jones, Eddie Foster, and tight end Albert Chandler.

Robertson's job of revving the offensive engine would be made easier by running backs Greg Pruitt, Joe Wylie, and Grant Burget, fullbacks Leon Crosswhite and Tim Welch, and receivers John Carroll and Albert Chandler. The Sooners faced an unlikely "problem" in the fall of 1972; according to assistant coach Wendell Mosley, the influx of freshman talent would create issues for Oklahoma. Mosley, a top-notch recruiter, told Barry Switzer that the biggest problem the Sooners might face in '72 would be deciding *where* to play left halfback Greg Pruitt. When the incredulous Switzer asked Mosley to explain, he replied, "I'm about to sign a kid from Port Arthur, Texas, who is better than Pruitt." The kid's name was Joe Washington.

Having been dazzled by Pruitt's performances the past two seasons, Switzer was justifiably skeptical. He said of Washington's first scrimmage at OU:

The first scrimmage we held before the 1972 season was a three-hour session under the lights. Finally, we called for Joe Washington. As he ran over to us, his shoulder pads were too big for him and he looked small and kind of cute, like a Pop Warner player and we just couldn't believe he was going to make us move Greg from left halfback. We put our first defense on the field and we sent Washington into the huddle to see what he could do against them. The ball was on the twenty-yard line, going north to south. Then I sent word into the huddle to run a counter play. Our quarterback took the ball, spun, and handed it to Joe and—zip, zag, zip, zag, zip—Joe went north, east, south, and west all at the same time, and the defenders broke their knees and ankles reaching for him. He put skid marks and turf burns on our All-Americans. He ran 80 yards right through our entire first-team defense and nobody laid a hand on him; I mean, nobody touched him! I looked over at Chuck who was standing ten yards away. We didn't exchange a word—we just stared at each other. We both knew what we had seen.[3]

The Sooner defense had not been treated kindly by graduation. Although seven starters had been lost after 1971, optimism was not. Starters Derland Moore, Raymond Hamilton, Garry Baccus, and Lucious Selmon would return, bolstered by Steve Dodd, Kenith Pope, Pete Halfman, Dan Ruster, Jon Milstead, Larry Roach, Clyde Powers, Gary Rhynes, and Vic Kearney. The defense was further strengthened by an exceptionally talented group of underclassmen, including Randy Hughes, Rod Shoate, Pat Hussey, and Rick Gambrell. In the wings, two freshmen loomed who would play a tremendous role in the Sooners' success in coming years: Dewey and Lee Roy Selmon.

The sixth-ranked Sooners opened the year by hosting Utah State. The game was a total mismatch as the Sooners breezed to a 28–0 lead in the first seventeen minutes before wrapping up the game 49–0. Dave Robertson was a perfect 5–5 passing for 155 yards, and Pruitt scored three times before the second string made its appearance in the second half. Oklahoma held the Aggies to

Dave Robertson draws a crowd, 1972. Courtesy Dave Robertson.

59 total yards (–55 rushing, 114 passing), while posting 617 total yards themselves (412 rushing, 205 passing). If there was a cloud on this silver-lining day, it came in the form of eleven Sooner fumbles. After the game, Utah State coach Chuck Mills said of the Sooners, "The weakest part of this OU team is their warm-up drill."[4]

The next two weekends saw Oklahoma grow stronger and more devastating as it steamrolled Oregon 68–3 and Clemson 52–3. After the first three weeks of play, the Sooners had outscored their first trio of opponents 169–6, had gained 1,863 total yards, including 1,496 rushing yards, and had jumped from sixth in the Associated Press poll to second.

Next stop for the Sooner Express: Dallas. The Longhorns began 1972 ranked fourteenth in the preseason poll but had climbed to ninth nationally after their second game, a 25–20 victory over Texas Tech. Standing at 3–0 as they prepared to play Oklahoma, they were coming off of an unimpressive win in their third contest, a 27–12 victory over Utah State in Austin—the same team Oklahoma had taken to the woodshed three weeks earlier, and the unimpressive showing had dropped them to tenth in the AP poll. Still, in spite of Oklahoma's impressive displays of power and Texas's halting, sporadic performances, as the two unbeatens prepared to square off the second weekend in October, everyone expected a rip-roaring, bare-knuckles contest. One of the oldest and most vitriolic rivalries in sports, the Oklahoma-Texas game is also one of the most difficult to predict. No matter the strengths of one side or the weaknesses of the other, the contest had been decided by fewer than ten points thirteen times since 1945.

The Sooners dominated the game as their opportunistic offense took full advantage of turnovers forced by the Sooner defense on their way to a 27–0 victory. In the first quarter, Derland Moore stopped a Texas drive by forcing Longhorn quarterback Alan Lowry to mishandle a pitchout, resulting in a fumble recovered by OU. The Sooners drove to the Horn six-yard line before fumbling the ball back to Texas. Rick Fulcher's field goal midway through quarter one gave Oklahoma a 3–0 lead. Late in the first half, the Longhorns began a drive at their own two-yard line and moved the ball to the Sooner seventeen, where they found themselves in a fourth-and-two situation. Royal decided to go for the down but, fortunately, the Sooner coaches had done their homework; they knew Texas was fond of using a belly play in such situations and had installed a special defense for such a situation. Longhorn Roosevelt Leaks was stuffed for no gain, and the Sooners took over possession. The first half ended with Oklahoma holding a white-knuckled 3–0 lead.

Late in the third period at its own twenty-five-yard line, Texas, on a third down and long yardage situation, called for a quick kick. Derland Moore explains what happened next:

> At practice on the Friday before the game Larry Lacewell walked by and adjusted my position on the defensive line; we had been warned that Texas might try a quick kick and we were preparing for it. During the game, it was about 120 degrees on that field and when Texas broke the huddle on that third down and *sprinted* back to the line, everyone on our side of the ball knew what was about to happen, so we began yelling, "quick kick!" up and down the line. After the snap, I was able to shoot through untouched and block the kick which careened into the end zone where Lucious Selmon smothered it for a touchdown.[5]

Oklahoma added another touchdown early in the fourth quarter after Joe Wylie returned a punt forty-four yards to set up the score. Fulcher added another field goal minutes later, and then, on their next possession from their own twenty, Longhorn quarterback Lowry attempted a pitchout to trailing halfback Roosevelt Leaks. "On that play," continues Moore, "Texas was using wide splits between their linemen so I was able to get through their line and into their backfield. I grabbed Lowry, who tried to pitch the ball over to Leaks, but Gary Baccus batted it towards the end zone. The ball was bouncing all over the place before I got to it, and when I did get to it, I fumbled it around before finally getting control of it; in fact, my own teammate—Ray Hamilton—tackled *me* and nearly made me lose the ball—I think he wanted it for himself," laughed Moore.[6] Moore's fumble recovery in the Texas end zone completed Oklahoma's scoring in the 27–0 rout. Larry Lacewell's defense, having just gone twelve quarters without allowing a touchdown, had been aided by a stellar Sooner kicking game; on seventeen of their possessions, the Longhorns were forced to start inside their own thirty-yard line fifteen times, and on five possessions they started inside their own fifteen, thanks to Rick Fulcher's booming kickoffs and John Carroll's towering punts.[7] Oklahoma rolled up 245 rushing yards to Texas's 73, the lowest ground-game total of any Royal-coached Longhorn team. It was the first time Texas had been shut out in 101 games and the first time Oklahoma had shut them out since 1956. The Sooners maintained a firm grasp on the number two spot in the AP poll and shaved number one USC's voting lead from fifty-two points to eighteen. Oklahoma had not allowed a touchdown in four games and had outscored its opponents 196–6.

But the jubilation experienced by the Sooners and their fans was to be short-lived. Colorado, sporting a 3–1 record, was primed and ready to avenge the previous season's 45–17 embarrassment in Norman—and what better place to do it than in the thin air of Boulder. As the two teams prepared to play, the field had been undergoing constant rain for better than forty-eight hours. Leon Crosswhite describes the scene:

> At Colorado, Switzer was looking out the dressing room window watching the grounds crew running a tractor with a squeegee blade trying to clear the water from the field. But they were driving the tractor from end zone to end zone and were having little effect removing the water. Switzer, realizing how ineffective their technique was and how it would affect his offense, started hollering, "The crazy fools; they're not taking any water off the field! They need to be going *across* the field, sideline to sideline!" But Coach Crowder knew the water would slow our offense down and I don't blame him one bit for using it to his advantage.[8]

The rain-soaked, slick field combined with the fervor and enthusiasm of a highly motivated Buffalo team playing before the largest crowd to ever attend a sporting event in the state of Colorado—52,022—spelled disaster for Oklahoma in the 20–14 loss. The Sooners only tallied two first downs in the first quarter and none in the third while rushing for a season-low 163 yards. Colorado coach Eddie Crowder attributed his team's victory to a balanced attack that "hadn't been tried on Oklahoma yet this season." The Buffs gained 172 yards on the ground and 151 in the air on the afternoon.[9]

To the Sooners and their fans, the loss in Boulder was a bitter pill. Aspirations of an undefeated season and a national title seemed to have been scorched on the same pyre that consumed their team's illusion of invincibility. Also temporarily lost in the Boulder conflagration seemed to have been the knowledge that Oklahoma, since going to the Wishbone in October 1970, had posted a 20–5–1 record and was still a powerful team abounding with talented young players.

Seven days following their loss to Colorado, the Sooners began their onslaught on the remainder of their conference opponents. In rapid succession, Oklahoma defeated Kansas State (52–0), Iowa State (20–6), Missouri (17–6), and Kansas (31–7) before packing their bags for their showdown with Nebraska in Lincoln. The Huskers had just won their second consecutive national title in 1971 and was the odds-on favorite to repeat in 1972. With Husker head coach Bob Devaney having announced in February that he would retire after the '72 season, it was expected that the wave of emotion accompanying his departure would provide enough momentum to take Nebraska to its third straight crown despite the loss of key personnel.

As Oklahoma and Nebraska prepared to clash on November 23, they both brought top-ten rankings along with them—Oklahoma fourth and Nebraska fifth. But the Sooners were hobbled; their All-World running back Greg Pruitt was injured. In the four games following the Colorado loss, Pruitt had scorched the turf for 553 yards and was running neck-to-neck with Nebraska's Johnny Rodgers in the race for the Heisman Trophy. Pruitt had twisted his ankle badly against Kansas the week before Thanksgiving, was suffering greatly, and displayed a pronounced limp when deplaning in Lincoln. Never having missed a game in high school or college due to injury, Pruitt was asked by reporters what his chances were of playing against the Huskers. "If it wasn't below here," he said, drawing a horizontal line along his waist, "it would be different."[10]

The game began auspiciously for Oklahoma when, with barely one minute gone, receiver John Carroll left with an injured knee. He was replaced by true freshman Charles Wayne "Tinker" Owens. Owens, brother of Sooner Heisman Trophy winner Steve Owens, had been promoted to the varsity in mid-September by Galen Hall. Recruiting Owens in February 1971 had not been an easy task for Leon Cross. He recounts, "When we recruited Tinker, Coach Fairbanks made me justify it. We sat in his office and he asked me why I wanted to offer a scholarship to a 145-pound guy; he might have thought we were going after him just because he was Steve's brother. But I told Chuck that Tinker was a track star, had been the state low hurdle champion, and averaged about twenty-eight points per game on the basketball court."[11]

The Cornhuskers would open the scoring midway through the first quarter when they recovered a fumbled punt at the Oklahoma forty-nine-yard line. Nine plays later, Husker fullback Bill Olds barreled fourteen yards through the heart of the Oklahoma line, giving Nebraska a 7–0 lead. Then Greg Pruitt's injury finally forced him to leave the game with seconds remaining in the first quarter. "I was hurting something awful," Pruitt said. "I knew I could play the whole game if I was lucky and if I could avoid any contact, but I just couldn't figure how to do that."[12] Pruitt was replaced by sophomore Grant Burget. Neither team scored in the second period as Nebraska hung on to what appeared to be a safe 7–0 lead at halftime.

With the third quarter in its ninth minute, Joe Wylie was stripped of the football at OU's twenty-four-yard line, and six plays later Nebraska scored its second touchdown. Suddenly the Sooners, with their two offensive stars sidelined and only six minutes remaining in the third period, found themselves in a fourteen-point hole.

Starting at the twenty-four-yard line on its next possession, Oklahoma floundered on its first two plays but on third and ten, Dave Robertson completed a thirty-eight-yard pass to Tinker Owens, setting the Sooners up at the Nebraska thirty-eight. Earlier in the game, an incomplete pass had created an opportunity for Owens; he had gotten open behind the Nebraska secondary when the ball sailed over his head. "I found out *then* that I could get open," said Owens. "He [Nebraska defender Zaven Yaralian] was laying off me nine yards or so, afraid of the deep route. I figured I could go one way, pull up, and get him turned around. I knew I could get around that guy all day."[13]

The Sooners continued the drive behind the hard-running of Leon Crosswhite until Joe Washington crossed the Husker goal with 2:15 left in the third period. Rick Fulcher's conversion kick made the score Nebraska 14, Oklahoma 7. On their next offensive series, the Sooners found themselves with a first down at the Nebraska thirty-six. The first two plays garnered four yards, and on third and six, Robertson once again pegged Tinker Owens for a twenty-two-yard

Leon Crosswhite. Courtesy Leon Crosswhite.

gain to the Nebraska ten-yard line. "I was guessing with him (Owens)," said Husker defender Yaralian, "but I was guessing wrong. I had been studying film on John Carroll all week and I didn't know a thing about number 11."[14] On the next play, Robertson found Owens weaving through the Nebraska end zone, but the play was disrupted when Yaralian was flagged for pass interference. The penalty gave Oklahoma a first and goal from the one-yard line, and Grant Burget scored on the next play. Three minutes later, Lucious Selmon recovered a fumble by Nebraska quarterback Dave Humm, and Rick Fulcher put the Sooners out in front to stay, 17–14.

One of the greatest come-from-behind victories in Oklahoma history had been accomplished by a strong, determined Sooner defense—a unit that had only allowed six touchdowns all season long—and an equally strong offense augmented by freshmen stars Joe Washington and Tinker Owens. In the exceptionally well-played game, the only penalty flag seen on the day had been the critical fourth-quarter pass interference call against Nebraska.[15] "One of the keys to that game was that people stepped up," explains Dave Robertson. "When John Carroll and Greg Pruitt went out of the game early on, Grant Burget, Joe Washington, and Tinker Owens stepped up. That's the benefit of playing at a place like Oklahoma; you've always got a lot of talent around you."[16]

The loss had been deflating for Husker head coach Bob Devaney. In his final appearance on the sidelines in Memorial Stadium, he had not only lost but had seen both his streak of twenty-six-straight conference wins and twenty-four-straight home victories busted. Additionally, the event was not without a certain amount of irony. Devaney did not believe in playing true freshmen and had not taken advantage of the 1972 rule change allowing them to play, yet he had seen two of them play instrumental roles in defeating his Huskers.[17] Joe Washington had played well, and Tinker Owens had caught five critical passes for 108 yards. When asked to comment about Tinker's performance after the game, Fairbanks smiled and commented, "He has good bloodlines."[18] The victory over Nebraska had not only set the Sooners on the right path for the future but also instilled in the team a confidence that would guide them through the next few seasons. "That game set us up for a three-year run where we thought we were going to win . . . *believed* we would win every game," says Galen Hall.[19]

The only thing standing in the way of the Sooners earning their first conference title since 1968 was Oklahoma State. But the Cowboys proved no match for their in-state rivals as Oklahoma prevailed 38–15. On the same day the Sooners were beating Oklahoma State, Auburn was torpedoing number two Alabama 17–16, allowing Oklahoma to slip comfortably into the number two spot in the AP poll.

In early December, the Sooners were invited to New Orleans to play once-beaten, fifth-ranked Penn State in the thirty-ninth Sugar Bowl—it was the first Sugar Bowl ever played at night and on New Year's Eve rather than New Year's Day, a practice that would continue through the 1975 season. The Nittany Lions were led by their All-American quarterback John Coleman Hufnagel and running back John Cappelletti; Hufnagel had become the first Penn State quarterback to pass for more than 2,000 yards in one season, and Cappelletti would win the Heisman Trophy the following year.

In the game, Oklahoma's defense would hold the Nittany Lions—a team that had averaged over 400 yards per game in 1972—to a total of 49 yards rushing and 147 passing in the 14–0 Sooner triumph. It was the first time Penn State had been shut out in sixty-eight games. Tinker Owens topped off his phenomenal freshman season by being named the Sugar Bowl MVP. He had scored OU's first touchdown and set up the second. It was the first and only time the honor would be bestowed on a freshman.

When evaluating his team's performance in 1972, Chuck Fairbanks stated, "It was a great team effort, all season long. But if I had to single out one person who was responsible for our success, it would be Dave Robertson. The job he's done leading our team at quarterback has been outstanding."[20] During a press conference held at the hotel on Friday before the game, coach Joe Paterno had been asked to comment on rumors that he had been contacted by NFL teams interested in luring him away from University Park. He had replied that he had not been approached. When asked the same question, Chuck Fairbanks replied, "I don't think right now I'd be interested in that. But you don't know what the future is going to bring."[21] His cryptic reply left the situation open to speculation.

But not for long.

12 Switzer-Land

JANUARY 1973–DECEMBER 1973

Southern California wrapped up the national title in 1972 with Oklahoma at a close second, setting the stage for a showdown on September 29, 1973, to be played at the Coliseum in Los Angeles. It was a certainty that head coach John McKay would have his top-ranked team stoked and ready to vent its fury on the Sooners; he had not forgotten the humiliation suffered by his Trojans during their 1971 trip to Norman.

Oklahoma suffered heavy losses to graduation after the 1972 season; quarterback Dave Robertson would make the change from quarterback to graduate assistant coach, and Kerry Jackson prepared to step into the vacated spot under center. Gone as well were Greg Pruitt, Leon Crosswhite, and Joe Wylie, and from the offensive line only John Roush and Eddie Foster returned. Joe Washington stepped into the left halfback spot, and Tim Welch took over at fullback. Kyle Davis would receive the nod at center while Mike Vaughan and Terry Webb stepped into line positions. On defense, the three Selmon brothers, Lucious, Lee Roy, and Dewey, would man the line at both tackles and noseguard; Rod Shoate—who had led the team with 139 tackles in 1972—returned at linebacker, along with Gary Gibbs and David Smith. Kenny Pope and Clyde Powers provided the coverage at cornerback, Gary Baccus and Mike Struck filled in at end, Randy Hughes and Durwood Keeton manned the safety positions, and Rick Fulcher and Jimmy Littrell performed punting and placekicking duties, respectively.[1]

But before the coaches had time to sign a bevy of new high school talent, a bomb dropped in Norman. On January 26, Chuck Fairbanks announced his resignation to become head coach for the National Football League's New England Patriots. Emotions in the OU camp were largely supportive of Fairbanks's move although public opinion in the state was by no means all positive. Dave Robertson addressed the segment of Sooner fans who lashed out at Fairbanks, by saying, "I don't think Chuck Fairbanks owes the people of Oklahoma anything (because of) the way they treated him in past seasons when he was going through some rough times. This is a big step forward for him." Dewey Selmon stated, "Some of the players I've been talking with feel a bit down about it. Personally, I hope Barry Switzer stays on; he knows our system."[2] Selmon wasn't alone in his predilection for Switzer. According to fullback Tim Welch, over 98 percent of the team supported Barry Switzer's promotion to head coach and had prepared, signed, and presented a petition supporting Switzer to athletic director Wade Walker. The players were in perfect alignment with the coaching staff as well. Larry Lacewell observed that it was the only situation he had ever seen where no one else on the staff was even *applying* for the position. "We've got total confidence that Barry can get the job done," said Lacewell. "I've got a great sense of loyalty to Barry; heck, I even named my kid after him."[3]

Athletic Director Wade Walker.
Courtesy Wade Walker.

Although Switzer's elevation to head coach appeared to be a fait accompli, on the same day Fairbanks resigned, university president Paul Sharp appointed a special search committee charged with determining a suitable candidate for the position. The search committee—headed by David A. Burr and comprised of regents Jack Santee and Huston Huffman; professor of English Dr. Alan R. Velie; senior journalism student Virginia Sue Apple; and Wade Walker—had been asked to report their findings to Dr. Sharp and the board of regents while working independently of the Athletic Council, an organization that had already unanimously recommended Switzer for the position twenty-four hours after Fairbanks's resignation.[4] Three days after forming the search committee, President Sharp received its statement of unanimous support for Switzer and appointed him de facto head coach; the de jure pronouncement by the board of regents would follow on February 9. Switzer's salary would be $24,000 with an annual expense account of $3,000.[5]

Switzer's promotion was met with enthusiastic approval from the locker room to the board room to the general public. Arkansas head coach Frank Broyles said he was "flattered and pleased" to hear the news and commented, "It's the first time one of my players has become a head coach. He [Switzer] had been a freshman coach here for only one year before everyone wanted to lure him away and I had to elevate him to the varsity. He was one of the most respected assistant coaches in America and I predict that he will be an outstanding head coach."[6] Former Sooner star Steve Owens, delighted to hear of Switzer's promotion, commented,

Barry Switzer, 1968. Courtesy Jim Terry.

"That's great! When I saw that Chuck had left for Boston I told my wife that there was no way they could let Switzer get away. I couldn't think of a better man for the job."[7] Owens's supposition that Switzer might "get away" was not as far-fetched at the time as it sounds in retrospect. Switzer stated that had he not been elevated to head coach he would have accepted Fairbanks's offer to join him at New England as backfield coach.[8] "I had a job for sure," he said, "I just wasn't sure if it would be at the University of Oklahoma."[9]

The brief three-day delay in replacing Fairbanks had not affected recruiting as Switzer and his staff pushed ahead in a seamless effort to reassure any high schoolers who had been unsettled by Fairbanks's departure. Scott Hill, who had himself been a highly recruited high school quarterback, went on record with a prescient comment. Hill remarked, "Coach Fairbanks will have New England in the Super Bowl and Coach Switzer will have us number one in the country."[10] Hill was close in his prediction regarding Chuck and the Patriots;

although never making it to the Super Bowl, Fairbanks took a Patriots team that had posted only one winning record in the previous eight seasons and led them to AFC East titles in both 1976 and 1978. But, unlike Patriot fans, the Sooner nation would not have to wait three years to see Hill's prediction about Barry Switzer fulfilled.

❖

Spring practice under the Switzer regime began on April 5. The process of training and grooming a supremely talented group of underclassmen expecting to become starters at many positions was publicly overshadowed by the competition at quarterback; sophomores Kerry Jackson and Steve Davis led the contenders, including true freshmen Scott Hill and Joe McReynolds. But in reality, Jackson had wrapped up the job while serving an apprenticeship to Dave Robertson the previous year. A blue-chip quarterback from Galveston Ball High School, Jackson had been at the top of every major college's wish list in February 1972. An excellent passer with a strong arm, Jackson was also an option magician blessed with intelligence, quickness, strength, and speed.

Jackson also represented the first African American not only to play quarterback at the University of Oklahoma but also to play the position at any major university south of the 36th parallel—the demarcation line used in the Missouri Compromise of 1820 to divide free and slave states. The presence of African American athletes had grown steadily on campus during the 1960s, and under Switzer's new management promised to flourish profoundly. Switzer reflects on the transition:

> When I became head coach, at my first staff meeting I told all my coaches that we were going to recruit the very best players at every position regardless of color and the best players would take the field on game day. We were not going to rely on the quota system like some other schools, and we weren't going to be recruiting black athletes only for the positions they were so widely used—running back and wide receiver. I told my staff that if anyone had a problem with that policy they needed to see me after the meeting, or they needed to find another place to coach. We were most certainly forerunners in promoting the black athlete.[11]

Strengthening his coaching staff, on April 16 Switzer lured coach Bobby Proctor away from Vanderbilt to assume the role of defensive backfield coach. When asked by the press why he was making the move, Proctor replied, "Heck, I'm leaving because it's *Oklahoma*."[12] Donnie Duncan was also brought aboard to coach the receivers while defensive line coach Jimmy Johnson left Norman to become defensive coordinator on Frank Broyles's staff in Fayetteville.[13] Additionally, Galen Hall was promoted to offensive coordinator.

As spring practice became more intense, gifted underclassmen were beginning to step forward and impress their coaches. In addition to other talented young players, Switzer expressed excitement about a family of defensive linemen who would soon become like a nuclear family to all Oklahoma fans: Lucious, Dewey, and Lee Roy Selmon.[14] But a week before spring practice began, Lee Roy was diagnosed and hospitalized with pericarditis, a circulatory viral infection, and, because the ailment had a tendency to run in families, Lucious and Dewey were also sidelined and examined. The Selmons' situation forced the coaches to reconsider their decision to redshirt Jimbo Elrod. Mike Struck, scheduled to play defensive end, was moved to tackle, and Elrod was forced to learn to play end—a new position for him—in a matter of days. Lucious had been cleared and played the first three games of the season without his brothers, but when Lee Roy and Dewey were finally cleared to play against Texas, all three brothers took the field in the Cotton Bowl side by side, becoming the first and only time that three brothers had ever started for Oklahoma in the same season.[15]

The decision by the gifted Selmon brothers to export their talents from Eufaula, Oklahoma, to Norman nearly did not happen. In 1969, Lucious Selmon had all but decided to sign with Eddie Crowder and the University of Colorado, and, had Lucious headed to Boulder, his two brothers would have certainly followed. Larry Lacewell tells the story:

> Lucious's parents really wanted him to go to Oklahoma, but he was leaning strongly towards Colorado. He had played fullback and linebacker at Eufaula, and we really hadn't been recruiting him solidly. However, on the day before national signing day, we lost Barry Price, the top lineman in the state of Oklahoma, to Oklahoma State. So, I was out on the road

recruiting, and I called Chuck and told him I thought we ought to go ahead and offer Selmon the scholarship. Well, lo and behold, when I got to Eufaula, Colorado head coach Eddie Crowder's car was already parked in front of the Selmon home. I was just a defensive coordinator, and I couldn't believe that I would be going up against the Colorado head coach on the day before national signing day. And Fairbanks had never set foot inside the Selmons' home; not once. But since Crowder was already in the house, I went on into town and waited in the diner. A little later, Eddie came in and told me I could go on out to the Selmons' house. But before I left the diner I stepped into the bathroom, and Crowder went to the pay phone on the wall back by where the bathroom was and called Lucious; and from the bathroom I could hear Eddie as clear as a bell. He kept telling Lucious, "Don't let 'em talk you out of it." And when I went back to the Selmons' house, I was able to use everything Crowder had said to my advantage. I told them, "I'll bet you Eddie Crowder said this and I'll bet you Eddie Crowder said that." And Lucious's eyes got big and his parents' eyes got big. We sat in their living room after dinner and talked until pretty late; in fact Lee Roy and Dewey went to sleep on the couch while Lucious, his parents, and I were talking; they'd eaten a big dinner and all that recruiting talk just knocked 'em out. I emphasized to Mr. and Mrs. Selmon that Oklahoma was just ninety-nine miles from Eufaula while Boulder was over six-hundred miles away; I also took the blame for *not* recruiting Lucious earlier and for not placing heavier importance on him. And you know how the story ends—Lucious, Lee Roy, and Dewey all ended up at OU and made history. Getting those guys to sign with the Sooners ended up being one of the greatest recruiting coups of all time.[16]

As momentum and confidence were beginning to grow during spring training, the second shoe fell on Switzer and his young team when an article in the *Galveston County Daily News* appeared accusing the Sooners of accepting doctored high school transcripts from Galveston Ball High School players Kerry Jackson and Mike Phillips. The article stated that OU faculty representative David Swank, upon learning of the breaking news, conducted his own investigation at Galveston Ball and determined that the transcripts had been manipulated to reflect that both players were eligible to enroll at university level. While nothing was stated as fact, it was speculated as being highly likely that the NCAA had been alerted to the problem by either Darrell Royal of Texas or head coach Rod Paige of Texas Southern University. Royal commented, "I did not turn OU in, but if I had seen the transcript and known that it had been altered, I would have turned them in."[17] Paige also denied blowing the whistle while stating that he had been certain at one point that both Jackson and Phillips would be playing for him at Texas Southern but he had known that they probably would not qualify under existing scholastic guidelines. "So their decision to go to Oklahoma came as quite a surprise."[18] Sooner assistant coach Bill Michaels, the man who had recruited the two players in question, also became implicated when it was discovered that he had helped the Galveston Ball football staff install the Wishbone offense in 1971.

After completing its internal investigation, the University of Oklahoma, in a mea culpa acknowledgment of its role in the violation, informed the NCAA that it would voluntarily forfeit eight games in which either of the two players had participated; the NCAA, in turn, announced that it would await a recommendation from the Big Eight Conference after its May 19 meeting prior to handing down its final decision on the matter. In that meeting, the conference decided to defer its decision until after a special two-day meeting in Chicago on August 6. The Sooners would effectively remain in limbo for the next three months. In the meantime, practice continued.[19]

With Kerry Jackson sidelined, Steve Davis stepped into the starting lineup, thus becoming the only Sooner quarterback ever to go from scout team one year to starter the next. "In my freshman year, 1971," recalls Davis, "I had worked my way up the depth chart and the next year they redshirted me. I gained a lot of weight, became frustrated and wanted to quit. I was also tired of getting knocked around by the Selmons while running the scout team. But then we were put on probation and I worked my way into the starting job by default."[20] But Davis's promotion to starting signal caller was far from by default. Switzer and his offensive coordinator, Galen Hall, had recognized the promise in Davis as a redshirt and had watched it develop during the spring of

1973. In his second scrimmage, Davis drew Switzer's praise, along with comparisons to Jack Mildren, by leading all rushers with 101 yards rushing.[21]

Oklahoma had not initially been interested in bringing Davis to Norman. "Steve was the last guy we offered a scholarship to in 1971," recalls Leon Cross. "He wasn't the biggest or fastest guy around, but his high school coach told me, 'The one thing Steve Davis will do for you is win football games.'"[22] Steve Davis describes what happened:

> When Oklahoma recruited me, Coach Fairbanks didn't want me. It was Leon Cross who was my biggest supporter. Very late in the recruiting process Leon called and told me that Clyde Crutchmer had declined OU's scholarship offer and was going to Colorado and Leon wanted to know if I wanted the scholarship. Well hell yeah, I wanted it! I dreamed about it as a pre-teen and as a teenager; I had literally *always* wanted to be where I eventually found myself for those four years in Norman. I lived out a dream at the University of Oklahoma. But when I arrived in 1972, they had recruited eight quarterbacks to replace Jack Mildren. On the first day, a depth chart was posted and freshman Coach Don Jimerson told us not to worry about where we were on it, that it really didn't matter. He said they were just trying to get everybody listed, and I was okay with that. But when that depth chart finally came out I was number eight—Larry McBroom, my roommate, was number seven, and he was wearing a cast from breaking his shoulder in the All-State game. But heck, I was *happy* to be number eight.[23]

⋱

In early August, the Big Eight Conference submitted its findings to the NCAA, and on August 9 the final ruling was published. Oklahoma had been handed a two-year probation, which would render the team ineligible for postseason competition and which prohibited it from appearing on television during the 1974 and 1975 regular seasons. Television contracts for the 1973 season, which had been previously arranged, were unaffected, and the Sooners would be eligible for bowl participation at the conclusion of the 1975 regular season. Quarterback

Kerry Jackson was ruled ineligible in 1973 while Mike Phillips was totally exonerated.[24] When he heard the ruling, Nebraska's Bob Devaney added a note of levity by quipping that he would "like for his team to be good enough to be investigated, but not good enough to be put on probation."[25]

The problem was no laughing matter in Oklahoma. Although facing a daunting situation, new head coach Barry Switzer was not about to toss in the towel. The day after the official announcement of OU's probation was issued, Switzer held a press conference. During the event, he removed his jacket, unbuttoned his cuffs, and said, "The only thing to do now is fight. I don't mean to fight the Big Eight or the NCAA, but now is the time to really get in there and dig; to rise and face the challenge." Switzer had made it clear that his team would not give up; Switzer's Sooners were going to arch their backs and attack.[26]

Several days later, the preseason Associated Press poll made its appearance, and Oklahoma found itself ranked eleventh nationally; in addition, most pundits—both regional and national—placed the Sooners no higher than fourth in the Big Eight Conference, trailing Nebraska, Colorado, and Missouri.

"When I took the head coaching job," recounts Switzer, "of course, I hadn't anticipated the probation. But in spite of it, we knew we would be a strong team. The better defensive players were returning—Lucious, Lee Roy and Dewey Selmon, Jimbo Elrod, Clyde Powers, Randy Hughes, Durwood Keeton, Rod Shoate—and we were getting Tony Peters from junior college. We were returning some great, great players. And we also used the probation to our advantage; we used it for motivation."[27]

The Sooners' first game under new management would be in Waco, Texas, against the Baylor Bears, operating under second-year head coach Grant Teaff. The Wishbone with Davis at the controls ran smoothly as Oklahoma breezed to a 35–0 halftime lead before finishing the game with a 42–14 victory. A Sooner record—one of many to come—was established as both Joe Washington and junior college fullback Waymon Clark gathered in 113 yards each while Steve Davis earned 110, making it the first time in Oklahoma football history that three players in the same backfield rushed for over 100 yards in the same game. But the victory had not been without a price. Halfback Grant Burget injured his knee at the end of a twenty-three-yard run; the injury would end Burget's season.

Following the Baylor game, Switzer's crew had a bye week to prepare for its next clash, a road trip to Los Angeles to play defending national champion and number one–ranked Southern California. The Trojans had run the table with a 12–0 record in 1972 on their way to the national title. In 1973, USC returned most of its key players from the previous season's team and was firmly installed in the number one spot in the polls. After defeating Arkansas 17–0 and Georgia Tech 23–6, the team was riding a fourteen-game winning streak.

The two teams played the game at night beneath the stars and stadium lights. The contest was not televised, so Sooner fans were forced to rely on a masterful radio broadcast by first-year play-by-play announcer Mike Treps.

The defense allowed Oklahoma to survive its first two offensive series, both of which ended in lost fumbles; however, on OU's third possession, when Sooner Clyde Powers fumbled the ball away on a punt return, Trojan quarterback Pat Haden finally made Oklahoma pay for the mistake by tossing a fifteen-yard touchdown pass to split end J. K. McKay (Coach John McKay's son), and Southern California took a 7–0 lead. Although the Sooners moved the ball consistently in the first half, fumbles and a missed field goal prevented them from scoring.

Then, seconds before halftime, the Trojans punted to Joe Washington. Washington fielded the ball at the Sooner forty-eight-yard line and embarked upon one of the most electrifying plays in modern Oklahoma football history. The fans—who would not see the play until it was shown on television the following day—listened while announcer Mike Treps attempted to described a play that defied description. After Washington caught the ball, he danced backwards to his own twenty-eight-yard line, twisting, juking, and turning in a choreographed syncopation of movement while never taking his eyes off of the oncoming wave of Trojan defenders. Breaking his first tackle, he continued to retreat to the Sooner seventeen-yard line with four defenders in tow, where he pivoted and, taking advantage of a crushing block from a teammate, headed back up the right sideline. Washington's gridiron ballet continued as he avoided three pursuers while gliding seven yards up the right sideline, where he suddenly disappeared from sight into a scrum of six cardinal and gold jerseys only to shock both Trojans and Sooner teammates alike by emerging from the cloister. Spinning and dropping to one supporting hand to steady himself, he headed back upfield, hurdled a USC tackler at his own thirty-five-yard line, and slipped a tackle at the forty before finally being brought down at the Sooner forty-five. Yards run on the play? Fifty-nine. Time elapsed? Thirty-two seconds. Net result of the play? A three-yard loss.

While Joe Washington's run stirred the hopes and imaginations of a hopeful Sooner nation, it had been more than an elusive marathon scramble culminating in a three-yard loss. The play also stood as a metaphor for the Switzer-led Oklahoma Sooners during the crucible of probation, representing determination and achievement in the face of overwhelming odds. After the punt return, Barry Switzer and Washington's father awaited him as he hurried to the sideline. "When I came off the field, Coach Switzer was laughing and shaking his head. Then he said as I passed him, 'Goddamn it, Joe, don't you *ever* do that again.' That was probably the first thing that endeared him to me," smiles Washington. "And I've never told anyone this before, but when I got to the sidelines, I grinned, shook my head from side to side, and said to no one in particular, *'Damn!'*"[28]

On its first possession of the third quarter, Oklahoma scored the equalizing touchdown on a two-yard Steve Davis run following a seventy-six-yard drive. Although Oklahoma would outplay Southern California decisively that evening, the game ended in a 7–7 deadlock. The eighth-ranked Sooners, a team that had entered the game a double-digit underdog, had beaten the Trojans in every conceivable category but the final score. USC tailbacks Anthony Davis and Rod McNeill had been stifled by the Sooner defense, gaining only eighty-nine combined yards. Trojan wide receiver and future NFL and College Football Hall of Famer Lynn Swann was not allowed a catch all evening thanks to the tight, error-free coverage of Tony Peters. The Sooner offense won the night with 389 total yards including 102 by Steve Davis, 126 from Waymon Clark, and 82 from Washington.[29] Oklahoma picked up eighteen first downs to Southern Cal's nine, and the Big Red had run sixty-nine offensive plays to USC's fifty-three. Additionally, the tie also put an end to USC's nation-leading fourteen-game winning streak and knocked the Trojans out of first place in the AP poll while the Sooners climbed two spots to sixth. In his postgame comments, McKay offered a rare compliment to the Sooners, stating that their defense was "One of the best I've ever seen."[30]

Although the team was momentarily deflated after the game, Switzer's enthusiasm for its effort, reflected in his postgame locker room speech, lifted spirits and put the game into its proper perspective. "I know how you feel, men," said Switzer. "I've got an empty feeling inside, too. But we're a hell of a football team. A great football team. We whipped them everywhere but on the scoreboard. We can hold our heads high—and they can't. Men, I'm damned proud of you. Damned proud. Hell of a job, men. Super!" But Steve Davis was inconsolable. Sitting slumped in a blue chair with tears in his eyes, Davis was blaming himself for the tie. "It's so disappointing," he lamented.[31]

The following weekend, Oklahoma faced seventeenth-ranked Miami in Norman. The Sooners, flushed with excitement after their performance in Los Angeles, failed to recognize how dangerous the Hurricanes could be. Sporting a 2–0 record, Miami had sprung into the AP poll from nowhere by defeating Texas 20–15 in its opening game and then followed that performance with a 14–10 decision over Florida State in Tallahassee.

It looked like the game would be business as usual as Steve Davis drew first blood for the Sooners with a first-quarter touchdown run; however, Miami answered with its own score moments before the period ended. But the worm seriously began to turn as Miami shocked Oklahoma in the second period when Davis, while attempting a pitchout to Tim Welch on third and four at the Miami twenty, was intercepted by Hurricane Eldridge Mitchell, who went eighty yards for the go-ahead score. A third Miami touchdown late in the first half sent Oklahoma to the locker room down 20–7. Once again, the shocked Sooners were losing a game that they had dominated statistically; after two quarters, OU had gained 234 yards to Miami's 79. "So now it's halftime, we've got only thirty minutes left to win the game, and we've spotted 'em a couple of touchdowns," recalls Switzer. "We put ourselves into a hole."[32] But Barry Switzer understood the first law of holes: when you find yourself in one, stop digging.

The Sooners began to battle their way out of their thirteen-point deficit in the third quarter when Davis cut into the Hurricane lead with a thirteen-yard touchdown jaunt, cutting the margin to 20–14. The Sooner defense stifled the

Hurricanes on their next series, forcing them to punt the ball to the Oklahoma forty-seven. Clark carried for a yard, and on second down Steve Davis uncorked a fifty-two-yard bomb to Tinker Owens, who brought the ball in at the Miami seventeen before scurrying into the end zone. Score: OU 21, Miami 20. "Tinker made a one-handed grab on a post-route down the middle late in the third quarter to win that ball game," recounts Switzer enthusiastically. "He just reached up and brought it in with one hand and never broke stride. That was one critical play not only for that game, but for the season."[33]

With the Sooners clutching to a one-point lead, Miami moved the ball to the OU twenty-one-yard line early in the fourth period only to miss a field goal. However, Oklahoma's Rick Fulcher would make good on his attempt with four minutes remaining in the game to give the Sooners a 24–20 victory. Davis had sparked the effort with his team-leading 144 yards rushing and 123 yards passing. When asked after the game what his game plan had been, former Sooner assistant and Miami head coach Pete Elliott responded sarcastically, "Our plan was to have Mitchell steal a bunch of pitchouts and go for touchdowns. I think we fell short by one."[34]

Oklahoma held steady at number six in the AP poll as the team began preparations to face the Longhorns. The only game Texas had lost in 1972 had been to the Sooners, and it had finished that year ranked third in the Associated Press poll, right behind OU. Darrell Royal's team entered the '73 Red River Rivalry ranked thirteenth nationally and owning a 2–1 record. Royal was eager to avenge the Horns' previous year's embarrassment at the hands of the Sooners.

The game kicked off at noon on Saturday, October 13, before a sellout crowd of 72,204 wildly partisan fans evenly divided into groups of crimson and cream and orange and white. It did not take the Sooners long to mark their territory when, on their first possession, they hit pay dirt on a forty-yard Washington-to-Owens halfback pass. Later, Washington told Owens that he had been trying to throw the ball out of bounds and could not believe that Owens had caught it, stayed in bounds, and scored. After Texas reduced the deficit with a pair of second-period field goals, Oklahoma struck again for a touchdown, this time on a sixty-three-yard Davis-to-Owens missile. Owens remembers, "In the second quarter, I scored on a sixty-three-yard post-pattern pass from Steve Davis. How

Tinker Owens punishes Texas, 1973. Courtesy Tinker Owens.

that happened was Jimmy Helms came to OU from the Texas staff and he told our staff how Texas read the run and pass; if they were playing run their safeties normally sucked up, so we would run play action on them and that left us wide open down the field. Consequently, it wasn't so much us running great patterns as it was our taking advantage of their defensive tendencies."[35] Then, with thirty seconds remaining in the half and Oklahoma sitting on the Texas forty-seven-yard line, Davis hit junior college transfer Billy Brooks with a coup-de-grâce pass. The Sooners had totally dominated their southern foes as they went into the halftime locker room leading 21–6.

At the Oklahoma-Texas game, October 13, 1973. The photographer caught Rex Norris as he was telling the Selmon brothers, "Remember this moment for the rest of your lives because it will remain one of your all-time finest memories." The Sooners won the game 52–13. Courtesy Rex Norris.

It would only get worse for the Longhorns after intermission. A pair of interceptions by Clyde Powers led to two more six-pointers for the Sooners before Oklahoma switched from its deadly-effective passing game to the more clock-consuming ground game on its way to a stunning 52–13 victory. The game, far from the furious defensive struggle predicted, had turned into a Sooner blowout. It had been a true team effort for Oklahoma; the defense had been bulletproof, the kicking game led by Jim Littrell's punting and Rick Fulcher's placekicking—by the end of the game he had kicked fifty-three-straight extra points—had been stellar. The offense had been not only near-perfect but perfectly balanced; its 508 total yards were divided into 283 passing and 225 rushing, including 117 yards from Washington and four receptions for 163 yards from Tinker Owens. Steve Davis had placed reservations for his place in the pantheon of Sooner quarterbacks by engineering one of the greatest Oklahoma offensive shows south of the Red River since 1956. *Daily Oklahoman* writer Frank Boggs described the 52–13 Sooner victory most succinctly when he wrote, "It was more one-sided than a hanging."[36]

The surprising youth-laden '73 Sooners had done the improbable; they had decisively outplayed the defending national champion USC Trojans in the Coliseum, they had spotted the seventeenth-ranked Miami Hurricanes a 20–7 halftime lead and had still prevailed, and they had delivered a knockout blow to archrival Texas while delivering Royal his worst defeat ever as head coach at Texas. Oklahoma advanced to third place in the Associated Press poll after its fourth game and possessed all the momentum of a runaway downhill-bound eighteen-wheeler.

Over the next six weeks, the Sooners would slice through conference opponents Colorado (34–7), Kansas State (56–14), Iowa State (34–17), Missouri (31–3), and Kansas (48–20) before facing what was expected to be their final true test of the regular season when Nebraska, led by first-year coach Tom Osborne, would come calling. The tenth-ranked Huskers had blasted through their November conference slate of Colorado, Iowa State, and Kansas State by the combined score of 109–44 and were headed to Dallas to face Texas.

In what was to be its final television appearance until January 1976, Oklahoma manhandled the Huskers as no other team had done since 1968 as the Sooners took them to task in a 47–0 rout. Holding a 14–0 halftime lead, Barry Switzer whipped his team into a halftime fervor with his locker room exhortation: "People, let me tell you what's happening here. You have just played the greatest defensive half any college team has ever played. Right now you have a chance to really do something; to play like that in the second half and show the whole country how a really great team plays. Let's give 'em something to remember you by for the next two years!"[37]

The Sooners did precisely what Switzer asked them to do by pitching a 27–0 shutout over the frustrated Huskers. Nebraska managed only 174 total yards and ten first downs in the game while the Sooners generated 358 yards. In the game's full course of sixty minutes, the Sooner defense allowed Nebraska to snap the ball only once on the Oklahoma side of midfield, and that play resulted in a fumble. In the locker room after the game, Switzer told his team, "We're champions! You guys are great . . . super . . . every one of you! That's a great way to go out, people! They didn't think we could do it but we did. People, it's OU 2, Cotton Bowl zero! Let me tell you what I'm gonna do. Today we give everyone on the varsity a game ball. You're Big Eight Champions . . . every one of you!"[38] While addressing the press after leaving the locker room meeting, his enthusiasm had not subsided. "Let me ask you something," Switzer began. "Have you ever seen a finer defensive team playing college football?" Receiving nothing but silence in reply, he continued. "I've coached fifteen years and this is the finest I've seen, much less had the opportunity to coach. They do so many things well . . . pass defense, rush the passer, great pursuit, run, great attitude, great quickness, intelligent. "And," he added with a smile, "great coaching."[39]

The final game of the year, the annual bedlam game with Oklahoma State, was just what everyone expected as Oklahoma bested its in-state rivals with ease, 45–18.

The 1973 Sooners had overcome adversity like few teams had ever done. They succeeded on the field in spite of a crippling probation and the loss of a star quarterback. They were undefeated Big Eight Conference champs and finished the season ranked third in the Associated Press poll. In October 2006 when Barry Switzer was asked if the '73 team might have been his most gratifying coaching experience, he replied:

Absolutely. Just picture it—we were on probation and people picked us fourth or fifth in the Big Eight, which was a joke; our staff and players all laughed when they heard that. We knew how good we were and that we'd probably be the team to beat; and we also knew that whoever represented our conference in the bowl game would be the second best team in the Big Eight because they were going to lose to us. So yeah, it was satisfying. But at the same time we couldn't have accomplished it without the talent base and the coaching we had. We knew we were going to be awfully good and we were.[40]

And they were only getting started.

13 Playing in the Dark: Part One

JANUARY 1974–JANUARY 1975

By posting a 10–0–1 record in 1973, Barry Switzer became the first first-year head coach at the University of Oklahoma to go undefeated in modern times and only the second in its history; the first, Vernon Louis Parrington, namesake of the university's campus oval, led his team to a 2–0–0 record in 1897.

The 1973 Sooners reawakened a spirit that had been dormant within the Sooner nation since the late fifties. Switzer fielded a team his first year that not only had gone undefeated for the first time since the forty-seven-game winning streak of 1953–1957 but also had completely outclassed most of its opponents in the process. With the single exception of the 1967 team, Oklahoma had run a bloody gauntlet in the 1960s that had left a large portion of its fan base jaded and cautious in its support. In Fairbanks's last two seasons, 1971 and 1972, the coalescence of power and finesse that was characteristic of the Wishbone offense rejuvenated and revitalized the fan base, providing solid justification for the emotional investment required for identifying with a team while at the same time minimizing the risk. But with Fairbanks, even during his best years at the Sooner helm, there was baggage. The glory and hope generated by his '67 team was followed by an anticlimactic 7–4–0 record in 1968, and the pride and excitement surrounding Steve Owens's winning the Heisman Trophy in 1969 was tempered by the disappointment of that season's 6–4–0 record with its blowout losses to Kansas State, Missouri, and Nebraska. With Switzer's red-hot performance in 1973—a feat accomplished with a cast comprised largely of talented underclassmen—came unhindered joy and unabated optimism. While Fairbanks's quiet, restrained personality had promoted a cautious loyalty in Sooner fans, Switzer's ebullience and confidence in both himself and his team were precisely the tonic necessary to cure the ills contributing to tentative fan allegiance.

However, as pleased as Switzer was with his first team's performance, he had been unhappy with their final ranking in the Associated Press poll. The Sooners had finished the season ranked third behind Notre Dame and Ohio

State.[1] Switzer, who had just returned from Dallas in early January where he had watched Nebraska beat Texas 19–3 in the Cotton Bowl Classic, expressed his feelings about his team's third-place finish. "Notre Dame beat the number one team, Alabama, so I felt like they'd move up," he said. This is the best team we've had since I've been here and we're ranked the lowest. But we won the Players' poll, anyway. The Southern California players said we were the best and so did Miami's. They took a poll of the Miami players and we got thirty-four votes to two for Alabama and three for Notre Dame. Players for both Texas and Nebraska also thought we should have been number one."[2]

However, John McKay, coming off the heels of a 42–21 Rose Bowl drubbing by Woody Hayes, said of the Buckeyes, "They're better than Oklahoma or Notre Dame."[3] But McKay's comment hinted of sour grapes; both his 1971 and 1973 teams had been humbled by the Sooners. The Trojans had trailed Oklahoma in the AP poll since October 1973 and would never again, under John McKay's leadership, be ranked above the Sooners.

Going into the 1974 season, the Big Eight Skywriters Tour polled the league coaches and found unanimous support for the Sooners to win not only the conference but the national title as well. Journalist Charlie Smith wrote, "If Oklahoma loses so much as a game, a saliva test ought to be given the winners and an investigating committee set up. . . . If that's pressure, then every coach in the country would like to have it. The Sooners are that good."[4] Smith's assessment was correct. The Sooners *were* that good, and not just on paper. The offensive line was, to a man, stocked with blue-chippers. The starters included Jerry Arnold, John Roush, Kyle Davis, Terry Webb, and Drake Andarakes, with Tinker Owens on the end and Wayne Hoffman at tight end. Andarakes, who had been sidelined with knee surgery, was replaced by sophomore Mike Vaughan of whom a seemingly prescient coach Gene Hochevar said, "He could be a great one before he's through." After evaluating the line in late August, Switzer commented, "We could have one of the strongest offensive lines ever at the University of Oklahoma."[5] Operating behind the front wall were junior quarterback Steve Davis, Joe Washington, and Grant Burget at halfback, and Jim Littrell at fullback following Waymon Clark's disciplinary dismissal.

But Switzer, aware that his loaded offense would need to reload in the coming seasons, had lured a player to Norman in February who would help ensure future successes: Elvis Peacock. Peacock, who had played halfback in the Wishbone formation his junior year in high school in Miami, had become a Sooners fan while watching them play their annually broadcast Thanksgiving Day games against Nebraska. One of the most highly sought-after high school athletes in the nation, Peacock had been courted by most major college programs, including

Elvis Peacock, 2010. Courtesy Elvis Peacock.

USC, Michigan, Ohio State, Miami, Florida State, Florida, and Georgia. Prior to taking his recruiting visit to Oklahoma, Peacock discovered that he had made a potentially career-altering mistake. He describes his experience on the road to Norman and afterward:

The weekend I thought I was scheduled to go to Oklahoma, I was actually going to Oklahoma State. The coach from OSU had called me and arranged for me to visit them, and I agreed because at that time I hadn't realized that there was a difference between Oklahoma University and Oklahoma State University. But OU coach [Gene] Hochevar explained the difference to me, so I told him that even though I was scheduled to visit Oklahoma State on the weekend he wanted me to come to Norman, if he'd meet me at the airport *before* the coach from OSU got there, I'd go to OU instead. And of course, that's what happened. I flew to Oklahoma and Joe Washington, Kerry Jackson, Mike Phillips, and Anthony Bryant met me at the airport. They decided to take the back roads on the return drive to Norman and on the way, we stopped at a convenience store to get some cokes; when we went back out to the car, there were about ten patrol cars hemming us in and we were surrounded by police with weapons drawn. Evidently, the skull cap I was wearing was the same one that was being worn by a guy who'd been robbing stores in the area. It was actually pretty funny to me. After I got to campus, I was truly impressed with the way blacks and whites got along together. The racial harmony on the team was excellent, and I think a lot of it had to do with Coach Switzer. He grew up around blacks, even lived on their side of the tracks. He never looked at a person's color; he just looked at the person. We had Native American players, Hispanic players, African American players, and white players, and everyone was the same. We hung out together, mingled in one another's dorm rooms, and developed friendships based on personalities, not on color. It was just the way it should have been. Race was never an issue at the University of Oklahoma.[6]

By early September, the Sooners were primed and ready—or so they believed—to welcome the Baylor Bears to Norman. Baylor, a team the Sooners had shellacked the previous season—a team that had finished 1973 firmly entrenched in the Southwest Conference's cellar—was expected to finish last again in 1974. The Bears had been installed as forty-two-point underdogs versus OU or, as one Baylor fan put it while standing in the lobby of Oklahoma City's Skirvin Hotel on game day, "by 42 points or by whatever margin Barry Switzer wants to make it."[7] But the Sooners had not anticipated the determined and well-coached Baylor team that made the trip to Norman. Head coach Grant Teaff and his Bears were embarking upon a season that would become known in Waco as "The Miracle on the Brazos," a year that would result in Baylor victories over Oklahoma State, Florida State, Arkansas, and Texas and would culminate in their first Southwest Conference championship since 1924.

"The 1974 Baylor game was a total surprise," recalls Tinker Owens. "In the old days, before the season started you could just glance through your schedule and you could pretty much check off the ones you knew you would win for sure, and normally the two games we couldn't count on winning every year were Texas and Nebraska. But Baylor wasn't thought to be in that category."[8]

The Sooners led the Bears by a slim 7–5 halftime margin—a far cry from the 35–0 pasting Oklahoma had dealt Baylor in the first half just twelve months earlier. The Bears, an I-formation team throughout 1973, had taken the field against Oklahoma with split backs running the pro-set offense, which, according to Sooner linebacker coach Warren Harper, "Really caused us problems."[9]

"College football is, in a way, a copycat game," says defensive end Jimbo Elrod. "You have to keep changing up what you're doing to keep people off guard. Baylor was just changing up what they'd been doing and they surprised us by doing something we hadn't expected."[10] Baylor continued to match the Sooners blow for blow into the third quarter. When Steve Davis was knocked into semiconsciousness and pulled from the game, Kerry Jackson, having satisfied the terms of his NCAA probation, substituted at quarterback and, although he performed well, was unable to penetrate the Baylor end zone. A revived Davis reentered the game late in the third quarter and, in the first three seconds of the fourth, led Oklahoma to its second touchdown of the afternoon. On their next series, the Sooners drove sixty-three-yards for an insurance touchdown.[11]

But the Bears were not finished. Capitalizing on true freshman Elvis Peacock's fumble, Baylor tallied its second—and final—touchdown of the afternoon and, after failing to convert, trailed 21–11. Any doubt about the final outcome was extinguished when Oklahoma scored on its next possession from a Tinker Owens end reverse, giving the Sooners a 28–11 final victory. "Baylor was just tough, offensively and defensively," continues Elrod. "Our team was strong and had a lot of confidence, but you can't expect it to fire on all cylinders every week."[12]

Even though Oklahoma dropped out of first place in the AP poll after the game, Switzer was more concerned about his team's on-field errors. "We definitely need to worry about not beating ourselves," he said. "We had too many missed tackles. Three guys made most of the tackles against Baylor . . . the Selmons and Shoate."[13]

Following the Baylor game, the Sooners held what amounted to two consecutive weekend scrimmages as they buried Utah State (72–3) and Wake Forest (63–0). A phalanx of seventeen Sooners carried the football against Utah State as eighty-two OU players saw action that day.[14]

As the 3–0 Sooners began preparations for their trip to Dallas, the coaches closed the practices, and the intensity increased dramatically. As Greg Pruitt observed from his playing days, "Practices held on Texas week were much different than normal practices. 'You can't do *this* against Texas!' the coaches would shout. 'You can't do *that* against Texas!' They built Texas up to be this huge monster down in the southwest."[15] And not without good reason. The coaches realized that when the warriors from Norman strapped on their helmets to play their rivals from Austin, all prognostications, opinions, odds, and logic went flying out the window. As one of the greatest rivalries in college football, the annual fistfight between Oklahoma and Texas was generally anyone's game right down to the final gun. But in 1974, the majority of fans north of the Red River were not buying it. They had seen their Sooners run off three straight laughers against Texas by a combined score of 127 to 40, and they had noticed the 23-point spread by which Oklahoma was favored.[16] To make matters worse (or better, depending on which side of the Red River one happened to live), over the past twenty-four months—since October 1971— the Longhorns had only managed one touchdown and two field goals against Oklahoma. However, those fans who had lived through Sooner football for the past two decades, *were* buying into the doubt; this seasoned band of loyalists knew the Red River Rivalry scenario and had seen it before many times. They had watched Darrell Royal have his way with Oklahoma throughout the 1960s, had seen him win on more than one occasion when he should not have, and held a begrudging respect for what their fellow Oklahoman had accomplished in Austin. They knew what Royal was capable of achieving with his team; after all, it had come at their expense.

On game day, as the Sooners awaited their turn to run down the 150-foot Cotton Bowl ramp leading from the locker rooms to the field, placekicker Tony DiRienzo—who had come to the United States as a foreign exchange student from São Paolo, Brazil, in 1971—was full of nervous energy. He describes his Cotton Bowl Stadium experience:

The Cotton Bowl was definitely the loudest, biggest crowd I've ever seen. As I'm walking down the ramp next to Coach Switzer, I have my helmet off; I'm like a little kid in a candy store for the first time. I'm looking here, I'm looking there, taking in all the sights and sounds, and then Coach

Switzer looks at me and says, "Tony, put your helmet on." And I said, "Ah c'mon, coach . . ." because back then we all had the long hair, so I'm looking good and enjoying the feeling. And he repeated *put your helmet on, Tony.* So I did, and as soon as we walked down the ramp the fans started throwing bottles and everything you can imagine at us . . . and oh my God! We were covered with beer and they were cussing at us and I thought, "now I know why he had me put that helmet on."[17]

The Sooners owned the first quarter statistically, but fumbles cost them excellent scoring opportunities. In the second quarter, DiRienzo uncharacteristically missed a thirty-nine-yard attempt, but, with three minutes left in the first half, Steve Davis scored on a keeper from the Texas twenty-two-yard line. Not to be denied, Texas returned the ensuing kickoff fifty-five yards to the OU thirty-eight, and with sixteen seconds left in the first half, the Longhorns' Bill Schott booted a forty-one-yard field goal to tighten the halftime score, 7–3.

The third quarter started auspiciously for Oklahoma as John Carroll's thirteen-yard punt gave the Longhorns possession at the OU thirty-three-yard line. Six plays later, Earl Campbell blasted twelve yards through the Sooner line for the touchdown. With the conversion, Texas led 10–7. Early in the fourth quarter, a thirty-eight-yard field goal increased Texas's lead to 13–7. On their next possession, Oklahoma faced a third and seven at the Horns' forty-yard line, and on the next play Steve Davis pitched to Austin native Billy Brooks, who circled right and ran to the end zone, tying the score. And then the unthinkable happened; John Carroll's PAT attempt careened just right of the goalposts.

DiRienzo, the first player in the history of Oklahoma football to have been recruited exclusively to placekick, had been handling kickoffs and sharing field goal responsibilities with John Carroll. After Carroll missed the critical point after kick, Switzer sought DiRienzo out on the sideline. Tony tells what happened:

John was doing the punting, short field goals and extra points, so I'm on the sidelines during the game, really not a lot of pressure, doing long field goals and kickoffs. I'm just pretty much watching the game and enjoying the atmosphere. Then John missed a crucial extra point late in the game, and Coach Switzer comes over to me and says, "from now on, you're doing all the kicking." All of a sudden, I went from observer to key player; it sort of hit me right between the eyes. The game was pretty tight, and so instead of me just sitting on my helmet the rest of the game I was pacing the sidelines hoping for a shot.[18]

DiRienzo got his shot six minutes later as he lifted a thirty-seven-yard field goal through the Texas uprights to give the Sooners a 16–13 triumph, their fourth consecutive victory over Royal and his Horns. "Kickers want to be part of the team, part of the game," says DiRienzo. "We want to contribute and do a good job. I needed to prove myself to my teammates."[19]

While the crimson-and-cream-clad fans in the stadium were celebrating, linebacker Rod Shoate was receiving congratulations from his teammates. Shoate, playing with a painful shoulder injury that limited the use of one arm, led the defensive effort with an incredible twenty-five tackles—two for losses of twelve yards—broke up two passes, caused a fumble, and recovered another that led to DiRienzo's game-winning field goal. For his efforts, Shoate was named the Associated Press National Lineman of the Week, the third time he had garnered the award.[20]

The dogfight that normally accompanied a trip to Boulder, Colorado, never materialized the next weekend. "It was Bill Mallory's first year as head coach at Colorado," recalls Switzer, "and he'd made some comments about Oklahoma being an undisciplined team and how we'd let Little Joe wear his silver shoes. Joe was concerned about the publicity so he came to me before the game and asked me, 'Coach, what do you want me to do about this? I don't want it to cause you any problems. Do you want me to wear the shoes?' And I told him that what I wanted him to do was to wear 'em and to put 200 yards on Colorado's ass. And he had 198 yards by halftime."[21] As the dust settled after the game, Oklahoma found itself on the winning end of a 49–14 score. After watching his defense surrender 641 yards to the Sooners, Mallory commented, "If [the Sooners] continue to play the way they did today, they won't lose a conference game." The Colorado players were virtually unanimous in their praise of Joe Washington and declared that Oklahoma had been "the best team they'd ever seen."[22]

Kansas State followed Colorado on the Sooners' schedule, and, although the Wildcats entered the fray with determination, they fared less well than Colorado in a 63–0 losing effort. OU's blowout victory had enabled them to close in on top-ranked Ohio State. The Sooners were riding a seventeen-game winning streak and appeared to be unstoppable; but as they rolled into Ames, Iowa, on Thursday, October 31, they had no idea that Iowa State head coach Earle Bruce had planned an unpleasant Halloween trick for them. In preparation for the Sooners, Bruce had taken a page from Oklahoma's 1970 playbook. The Cyclones had secretly scrapped their I-formation and converted to the Wishbone. Taking advantage of a rain-soaked field, Iowa State eschewed the outside running game, opting instead to go to their strength and attack OU's line with their big, bruising running back Mike Strachan. The wet field helped to neutralize Oklahoma's speed, and at the conclusion of the first half they were clinging to a 7–0 lead. But momentum shifted decisively for the Sooners as they scored two touchdowns off of Iowa State fumbles in the first sixteen seconds of the second half on their way to a 28–10 victory. While Joe Washington led all rushers with 86 yards—well below his average of 136 per game—Iowa State had managed to burn the Sooner defense for 349 yards, the most allowed by an OU team in over two years.[23]

Practices the following week leading up to the Missouri game had disappointed Switzer. He felt that his team was too loose and was making too many mistakes due to lack of concentration. But his concerns were allayed by his team's performance as it whitewashed the 5–3–0 Tigers 37–0.[24] The victory was a timely one because while Oklahoma was dispatching Missouri, number-one ranked Ohio State was being upset 16–13 by Michigan State in East Lansing. Oklahoma would inherit the top spot in the Associated Press poll and, by so doing, would continue a Sooner tradition. In each of their national title years—1950, 1955, and 1956—when the Sooners either gained or regained the top spot in the wire services polls, they had done so after a victory over the Tigers.[25]

With Oklahoma, Alabama, and Michigan remaining undefeated, the national title became a three-horse race. Although the Sooners were once again number one, Switzer realized that without the benefit of a season-ending bowl game appearance his team was at a disadvantage. With both the Crimson Tide and the Wolverines—both of whom would be displaying their considerable talents in bowl games—nipping at Oklahoma's heels in the polls, it would be critical for the Sooners to perform impressively in their final three games in order to have any chance to grab the golden ring. But Oklahoma's next game, versus the Kansas Jayhawks, was not the cakewalk that Switzer and his Sooners had needed. Kansas quarterback Scott McMichael stunned the Sooners by running seventy-three yards early in the opening quarter for the game's first points. Steve Davis retaliated in the second stanza with a seventy-two-yard touchdown pass to Billy Brooks to tie the game. Oklahoma added two more six-pointers and Kansas added one to give the game a dangerously close 21–14 feel at halftime. The third quarter was scoreless as Oklahoma held onto their white-knuckled single touchdown lead going into the fourth quarter. Three Sooner touchdowns later followed by a Tony DiRienzo boot capped the final score at Oklahoma 45, KU 14.[26]

The nerve-wracking victory over the Jayhawks had little effect on Oklahoma's standing in the November 18 AP poll. Alabama, ranked second, had failed to impress with their 28–7 victory over Miami, and third-ranked Michigan's 51–0 buggy-whipping of hapless Purdue had not provided them with the upward mobility they had needed to gain significant ground. The Sooners were still number one, but their greatest challenge of 1974 was on the horizon.

The Cornhuskers had opened 1974 ranked seventh in the AP poll and over the next ten weeks had bounced around within the top-ten penthouse like a ping-pong ball. After dropping their second game of the season—a heart-stopping 21–20 loss to Wisconsin in Madison—the Huskers dropped to tenth, climbed the ladder once again to sixth, before again dropping to ninth after their surprising 21–10 home loss to Missouri on October 12. By the time the Cornhuskers were preparing to host Oklahoma on Thanksgiving weekend, they were on a five-game winning streak, had returned to number six in the charts, and were eager to have their shot at top-ranked Oklahoma. The Huskers, having lost their last two outings to the Sooners, yearned for a convincing payback. Plus, a victory would give Nebraska an official tie with Oklahoma for the Big Eight crown, while a victory for the Sooners would make them conference champs.

After a scoreless first quarter, Steve Davis stilled the crowd in Lincoln with a ten-yard touchdown in the second stanza. Minutes later, Nebraska posted the equalizer on a thirty-eight-yard Dave Humm–to–Chuck Malito touchdown pass. At halftime, the teams were tied at seven.

In the third quarter, Nebraska mounted a seventy-six-yard drive to take a 14–7 lead. On the next possession, lady luck continued to smile on the Huskers when OU's Elvis Peacock fumbled the ball back to Nebraska on OU's fifteen-yard line. But the Oklahoma defense stiffened, forcing the Huskers to attempt—and miss—a twenty-three-yard field goal. The Sooners then moved the ball methodically to the Nebraska thirty-eight-yard line, where they found themselves facing a third-and-sixteen situation. "Steve rolled out to pass—he didn't complete one all day—and instead ran for 19 yards," said Switzer. "Later he called it his best run of the year."[27] While it may have been Davis's best run of the year, it was certainly the Sooners' most fortuitous one. The ensuing first down at the Nebraska twenty-one-yard line set the stage for a Joe Washington touchdown, drawing Oklahoma and Nebraska into their second tie of the game. Early in the fourth quarter, a fifty-seven-yard Sooner drive sparked by double-digit runs by Davis and Littrell put OU on top 21–14. The Huskers then found themselves with their backs to the wall, and the Oklahoma defense made sure they stayed there. Nebraska was unable to mount another scoring drive while Oklahoma salted the game away with a final score—a three-yard touchdown run by Davis—giving the Sooners a 28–14 victory. Three Sooners—Davis, Washington, and Littrell—had eclipsed the 100-yard mark in the game as the team rolled for 482 yards rushing; Davis had not needed to attempt a single pass on the afternoon.

All that now stood between the Sooners and their first perfect season since 1956 was Oklahoma State. Head coach Jim Stanley, in his second year in Stillwater, had raised the hopes of the Cowboys and their fans with victories over Arkansas and Missouri, and with a 7–6 near-upset in Lincoln, Nebraska. And, following a script the Sooners had seen too many times in 1974, they found themselves tied at halftime with an inferior foe. But late in the third quarter, Jimbo Elrod knocked the ball loose from Cowboy quarterback Charlie Weatherbie and the rout was on. The Sooners scored on their next possession, again on a fifty-seven-yard punt return by Joe Washington, again after a mishandled OSU punt was recovered at the Cowboy five-yard line, and again moments later when an Oklahoma State player "forgot" to field the kickoff, which was recovered by Oklahoma. When the fiasco ended, Oklahoma stood atop a 44–13 score, atop the AP poll, and atop a twenty-game winning streak (twenty-nine games without a loss).[28]

The picture became complete on January 1, 1975, when second-ranked Alabama—the only other undefeated major college team in the nation—suffered a 13–11 Orange Bowl loss to Notre Dame, leaving the Sooners the undisputed, undefeated national champions.

Barry Switzer was king. He had led the Sooners for two seasons without a loss—a feat that had only been accomplished in Norman before him by Bud Wilkinson. In two years, his Sooners had faced and defeated seven teams ranked in the top twenty and four in the top ten. His '74 team had led the nation in scoring, averaging forty-three points per game. At the season's conclusion, Joe Washington, Rod Shoate, Lee Roy Selmon, Dewey Selmon, Tinker Owens, John Roush, Randy Hughes, and Kyle Davis had earned All-American honors, while Washington, Shoate, the Selmons brothers, Owens, Roush, Hughes, Wayne Hoffman, Jimbo Elrod, Jerry Arnold, and Terry Webb were selected as All–Big Eight Conference players. Joe Washington finished third in the Heisman Trophy balloting and was named Player of the Year by the Touchdown Club of Washington, D.C.

The probation handed down to Oklahoma in 1973, so daunting at the time, continued to work to Oklahoma's advantage. A team of players innocent of any wrongdoing had been forced to bear the burden of transgressions committed by others. The players had been forced to play without benefit of the national television exposure each of them had sought when agreeing to play for the Sooners, they were prohibited from enjoying a postseason bowl trip, and they had been banned from winning a national title in one of the major wire service polls. But instead of transferring to other schools or losing motivation, they had come together as a team with one common purpose—to prove that, from coast to coast, they were the best college football team in America. "I think the '74 team was the most cohesive team that we had in the four years I was there," reflects Tinker Owens. "We knew we couldn't go to a bowl game so our mission became to win the national championship and prove to everyone that we were the best team in the country."[29]

Mission accomplished.

14 Playing in the Dark: Part Two

JANUARY 1975–NOVEMBER 1975

The Sooners reaped tremendous benefits from their resurgence in the early 1970s. Switzer and his recruiting coordinator, Jerry Pettibone—the only coach to have worked under both Barry Switzer and Tom Osborne—signed some of the greatest high school athletic talent seen on any campus at any one time. Billy Sims, Greg Roberts, Reggie Mathis, Kenny King, Phil and Paul Tabor, Victor Hicks, Daryl Hunt, Thomas Lott, George Cumby, Reggie Kinlaw, Mike Babb, Bud Hebert, Woodie Shepard, Uwe von Schamann, and junior college transfer Bobby Kimball were all ensnared in the same golden net.

In addition to the inundation of talent brought to Norman, the university also enjoyed a windfall from the fund-raising efforts of athletic director Wade Walker and associate athletic director Leon Cross. Beginning in the spring of 1973, the pair began touring the state in an effort to raise funds to improve Oklahoma's woefully outdated athletic facilities. "From the forties to the seventies, the facilities had remained pretty much the same," says Leon Cross. "We used to call the training track under the stadium 'Pneumonia Downs' because it was so dark and damp."[1] Athletic director Wade Walker reflects on his and Cross's efforts:

Shortly after I began serving as athletic director, along comes Barry Switzer, and within three years, that man has won two national championships. During that time, Leon and I wore out two brand-new cars crisscrossing the state of Oklahoma to raise money for the university. Anywhere there was alumni to be found, that's where we'd go. During my administration, the economy was terrific and our football team was winning. Let me tell you something: if Barry Switzer had not been the outstanding coach that he was, we couldn't have done any of this because football paid for all of those improvements; it is absolutely golden. And there were so many improvements that needed to be made. As a result of the success of our program under Switzer, we were able to renovate the south end zone, build a new upper deck, a new press box, a new track, a new swimming pool, we renovated the north end zone with football offices and dressing rooms, added a new equipment room, training facilities, and a meeting room. We also built Wilkinson Center, renovated Jeff House and Washington House [currently Gomer Jones dorm], L. Dale Mitchell baseball field and stadium and Mosier Center indoor track and funds were raised for the Sam Viersen gymnastics center.[2]

But 1975 was not without its concerns. In the spring, the Kansas City Chiefs began looking for a new head coach to replace Hank Stram. The Chief's general manager, Jack Steadman, contacted Switzer to gauge his interest. Switzer recalls being approached by the Chiefs:

They were going to send their private jet to pick me up and take me to Kansas City to talk about the job. I told them that first, I needed to make some arrangements but actually I just wanted to think it over. I didn't want to decline right off the bat, you just don't do that. Then I started thinking about all the players I'd recruited and all the hard work I'd put into the program. I had guys coming in like Billy Sims, Kenny King, Reggie Kinlaw, Daryl Hunt, George Cumby, the Tabor twins, and Victor Hicks, just a great class; and I thought, "Hell, I've got more first round draft choices in Norman than they have in Kansas City," so I called them and declined.[3]

As early as March, football fever began to grip the state of Oklahoma. Advertisements made their first appearances in newspapers, offering absurdly premature bookings to the 1976 Orange Bowl:

Yea Oklahoma!
Orange Bowl—Miami, Florida
January 1, 1976
The Sooners Will Be There!
Make your plans now and have all year to dream.
Write for our package tours.[4]

Oklahoma *was*, in fact, a good bet to earn an Orange Bowl berth as the Big Eight Conference champ, but a second national title was a long shot—not because the Sooners were not talented and experienced, but because the odds of every factor in an extremely complex situation falling into place at the same time as it had in 1974 was problematic at best. "For a team to go undefeated like we did in '74," said Switzer, "you have to be just plain lucky."[5] Indeed, in the thirty-nine years that the Associated Press had been polling college football (the service began in 1936), only seven teams had managed to win consecutive national titles: Minnesota (1940–41), Army (1944–45), Notre Dame (1946–47), Oklahoma (1955–56), Alabama (1964–65), Texas (1969–70), and Nebraska (1970–71). And since the UPI poll made its first appearance in 1950, only one team had managed to emerge as the unanimous champion in both the AP and UPI polls for two consecutive years—the Oklahoma Sooners.

The recruiting success Oklahoma had enjoyed in Texas appeared to have taken a hit in August when the NCAA handed down new legislation stipulating that recruits could only be visited by university representatives on three specified occasions.[6] The Southwest Conference had previously limited itself to visiting recruits only at the end of a season while the Big Eight Conference had no such regulation. Royal stated that he did not believe it would affect Oklahoma's recruiting south of the Red River; Switzer disagreed. The suspicion was that Royal had been the driving force behind the new regulations, that he was tired of being out-recruited in Texas and then losing to players from his own state the second weekend in October. This opinion was predominant throughout the state of Oklahoma, including in Royal's hometown of Hollis, a scant four miles from the Texas border. Fairly or unfairly, it seemed that one of the few voices speaking up in support of Royal in Hollis at the time was that of his father, B. R. Royal. When asked if his son was picking on Oklahoma, B. R. replied, "No sir, not a bit. It's just that Darrell is fair and he wants everyone else to be the same way."[7]

As the Sooners drew near their opening game, concerns within the coaching staff began to arise. Thirty-five lettermen and ten starters from the 1974 squad had departed, and although the nucleus remained strong there were still frayed edges. Wayne Hoffman's graduation left a gaping hole at tight end, which Switzer plugged by promoting true freshman Victor Hicks. A dominating athlete from Lubbock, Texas, Hicks, had been pursued by every major college program in the country. After he had made a preliminary decision to follow his girlfriend to the University of Texas, his mother suggested that perhaps he should still take his visit to Oklahoma.

> During my visit, Elvis Peacock was the guy assigned to show me around campus. He and I attended an OU basketball game—it was Alvin Adams's senior year. We just happened to be sitting behind Terry Webb, a senior guard, who was there with his recruit. Peacock said, "Tee-Dub (that's what we called Terry), I want you to meet Victor Hicks from Lubbock. He's got his choice narrowed down to us and Texas." Webb looked over at me, looked back at Elvis, put some popcorn in his mouth, chews on it for a bit, and then says to me, "Well hell, that's easy. You can either go down there and take an ass whippin', or you can up here and dish out an ass whippin'."[8]

Hicks decided it was far better to dish it out than to take it and committed to the University of Oklahoma.

With Gary Gibbs and Rod Shoate gone, the linebacker position was also unsettled, spurring coach Warren Harper, in charge of the position, to promote freshman Daryl Hunt to the first team alongside senior Jamie Thomas, whose promotion had come when starter Bill Dalke suffered a neck injury in fall practice.[9]

Once the season got under way, it did not take long for the surprises to start rolling in. Five days before the Sooners' season opener, twenty-one-point underdog Missouri traveled to Birmingham on Monday evening and defeated second-ranked Alabama 20–7, handing the Tide its worst regular season loss in fifty games. With its upset victory, Missouri had sent a message to the college football world: in the age of scholarship limitations, designed to prevent the major college powers from drawing too deeply from the well of available high school talent, no team was safe.

But parity notwithstanding, the Sooners' greatest obstacle in 1975 would come from another source: complacency. For the past two years, Oklahoma had been a team on a mission. Suffering from the restrictions of probation—restrictions that most felt were draconian and undeserved—Oklahoma set out to prove that it was the best college football team in the nation. Once this goal had been reached in 1974, there was elation and celebration accompanied by an unavoidable anticlimax. In September 1975, as they prepared to host the Oregon Ducks, the Sooners were riding a twenty-game winning streak and had not lost a game since October 1972; there were juniors on the squad who had never tasted defeat, seniors who had never lost to Texas. With the single exception of the 1973 tie with USC, winning had been status quo in Norman for two and a half years, and, ironically, with the national title in 1974 crept the onset of dispassion and a correlative state of mind leading the Sooners to overestimate their own abilities and underestimate those of their opponents.

"In 1975, we were struggling," recalls Steve Davis. "Even though we rose to the occasion and played fairly well against Pittsburgh and Texas, we had real problems with apathy."[10] Davis's opinion was shared by Tinker Owens. "We just didn't quite come together in 1975 like we had the previous year," comments Owens.[11] Nevertheless, Oklahoma was still *Oklahoma*—a team replete with enough blue-chip talent to easily handle most opponents—and when Oregon made its southeastern trek to Norman on September 12, the defending national champs skewered the Ducks 62–7. However, the easy victory revealed another burgeoning problem. Fullback Jim Littrell had been doing the punting, and the taxing combination of running the ball on offense and punting when it was necessary took a toll on his leg strength. So Switzer sent out a casting call for a punter. Tinker Owens relates what happened:

Coach Switzer called everyone together and said, "I want anyone who has ever punted in his life—I don't care if it was in Pop Warner, Junior High, or High School—to try out for the punting job." I had punted in high school, and when I tried out for Switzer, I punted really well. I was hitting long, high spirals, great punts—I mean, I was trying my ass off to win that job. I didn't realize until later that I was the only one who *had* wanted it. Years later, Joe Washington said to me, "Tinker, do you remember when you got that punting job our senior year? Did you know that nobody else wanted it—nobody was really trying except you?" The reason was that our deep snapper was unpredictable, largely because we never practiced punting much because we normally scored touchdowns or field goals. So I ended up with the job. My first punt in a game, against Pittsburgh, went about forty-five yards, was perfect, and the fans were going crazy because of it. But unfortunately, it was all downhill from there. My average kept dropping every time I kicked. Typically, I had to grab the ball off of the turf and as soon as I got it, I only had time to take one step before I kicked it.[12]

When Johnny Majors's Pittsburgh Panthers came to Norman on September 20, they brought two impressive assets along with them: the fifteenth position in the Associated Press poll and a running back destined to become the first in Division-1A history to eclipse 6,000 career rushing yards and to earn the Heisman Trophy the following year: Tony Dorsett. The game was touted nationally as a showdown between Dorsett and Washington; but neither the Panthers nor Dorsett proved worthy of the challenge as both fell flat—Pittsburgh to the Sooners, 46–10, and Dorsett to Washington, 166 yards to 17. On a fourth down play in the first half, Dorsett made the mistake of his college career by trying to run the ball into defensive back Scott Hill's territory. Hill met Dorsett three yards behind the line of scrimmage and delivered what Switzer would describe as a "slobber-knocker." The impact of the hit sent Dorsett into another realm of consciousness, left an indentation on Hill's cheek, and sent shock waves through Memorial Stadium. The Sooners took possession of the ball and the game, and Dorsett was done for the day. It would be the only time in his college career that he would fail to gain one hundred yards in a game. "When I eventually met Dorsett years later," recounts Scott Hill, "he didn't remember me, but he did remember my number and he *sure* remembered Elrod and the Selmons."[13]

The following weekend, Oklahoma prevailed for the second time in three years against a determined Miami team. After leading 20–7, Oklahoma held on in the face of a ten-point Hurricane fourth-quarter surge for the 20–17 victory. The Sooners barely had time to wipe the sweat from their collective brow before they found themselves in the middle of another fight for survival the next weekend when Colorado visited Norman. The Buffaloes sported the nation's top offense, a 3–0 record, and an ace in the hole—the league's best placekicker in Tom Mackenzie. Mackenzie was a perfect sixteen for sixteen in extra point attempts and in his two years kicking for Colorado had made forty-one of forty-three field goal attempts. The first half was all Joe Washington as he zipped eleven yards for the Sooners' first score and returned a punt seventy-four-yards for the second. Oklahoma held onto a 14–7 lead at halftime, but Colorado tied the score after a Sooner fumble in the third quarter. Early in the fourth period, an eighty-yard drive put Oklahoma back in the lead, 21–14, but with 8:35 remaining in the game, the Buffaloes took the ball at their own thirty-two-yard line. Then, consuming over seven minutes from the clock, Colorado methodically drove the length of the field and, with slightly over a minute left to play, scored on a twenty-two-yard pass. In a heartbeat, it appeared that Oklahoma's twenty-three-game winning streak was over. When all appeared lost, salvation appeared for the Sooners in the form of Colorado head coach Bill Mallory. Eschewing what would have been the winning two-point conversion, Mallory sent Mackenzie to the three-yard line to attempt the tying conversion kick. Mackenzie had already missed two field goals in the game but was still a perfect eighteen for eighteen on conversions. The ball was set and snapped, the kick was up, and it sailed wide left. The Sooners took the ball at their own twenty-yard line and ran out the clock. Their winning streak stood at twenty-four and their unbeaten streak at thirty-three, but their close brush with disaster against the Buffs had cost them the top spot in the Associated Press poll. Ohio State ascended to number one on the strength of a 41–20 drubbing of UCLA. Jimbo Elrod had been graded in superlatives during the Colorado game with nineteen tackles—twelve unassisted and three resulting in losses of sixteen yards. For his efforts, he was unanimously voted Big Eight Conference Defensive Player of the Week.[14]

While the Sooners were heading south in the national polls, Texas had been busy climbing. The Longhorns debuted at number twelve in the AP preseason poll and, following victories over Colorado State, Washington, Texas Tech, and Utah State, had gradually moved up to fifth. Regarding the upcoming joust with Texas, Sooner quarterback Joe McReynolds commented, "Everybody favored us to beat Miami and Colorado by a whole mess of points. We may go down to Dallas as a favorite but not everybody's saying OU will win by thirty."[15] However, McReynolds's view was not shared by the oddsmakers, who, undaunted by their gaffe the previous season when they had installed Texas as massive underdogs, were still favoring the Sooners, this time by a whopping nineteen points. Switzer was having none of it. "I don't expect to take the ball and rip Texas," he said, "and I don't expect them to take the ball and rip us."[16] While Royal, in his pregame press conference, stressed the quality of the Sooner team as a whole, he specifically singled out Joe Washington as his major concern. "He's phenomenal," commented Royal. "You can't believe his runs. He has the greatest reactions I've ever seen in football. He puts your heart in your throat every time he touches the ball."[17] Switzer's reservations about a Sooner victory were also tempered by fullback Jim Littrell's ankle injury, forcing Jim Culbreath to move to fullback with Horace Ivory backing him up. Unbeknownst to Switzer, the serendipitous appointment of Ivory—a junior college transfer—to fullback would be revolutionary; although Ivory did not possess the size normally associated with the position, he would transform it by adding speed and quickness to the repertoire of the basic triple-option belly play.[18]

Early on, the game appeared to be going Oklahoma's way as it jumped to an early 10–0 lead. Behind Earl Campbell's relentless rushing, Texas upped the ante with a touchdown in the second quarter, making the halftime score Oklahoma 10, Texas 7. In the third quarter, Steve Davis connected with Billy Brooks on a fifty-two-yard pass to set up an eleven-yard Washington touchdown run as Oklahoma increased its advantage to 17–7. Then, in the fourth period, Texas blocked a Sooner punt, which led to a touchdown, reducing the Longhorns' deficit to three points. Appearing to own both the final quarter and the momentum, Texas stormed to a 17–17 tie before, on a third-and-four situation at the Sooner twenty-seven-yard line, Peacock's plunge for no gain was nullified by a facemask penalty, giving Oklahoma new life at its own forty-two. The Sooners then methodically moved the ball to the Texas thirty-three-yard line, where, on first down, Davis noticed the Texas defense slanting heavily to one side of the line and called an audible handoff to Ivory, who took the ball, blasted forward, cut left, and followed the sideline to the end zone. Tony DiRienzo converted, and Oklahoma held a thin seven-point lead. Late in the game, Texas had the Sooners pinned at their own eight-yard line when Switzer ordered Joe Washington to quick kick on third down; the ensuing kick sent the football past the unsuspecting Longhorns on a seventy-four-yard journey to the Texas eighteen-yard line. From that point on, the Sooner defense took control to preserve the 24–17 victory. The winning streak was twenty-five, the unbeaten streak was thirty-four, and Oklahoma remained number two nationally.

Kansas State, Iowa State, and Oklahoma State fell in succession, but against Iowa State OU's offense would revert to its careless ways by putting the ball on the ground an alarming thirteen times, losing seven. Still, Oklahoma had won twenty-eight straight games, and the unbeaten streak was thirty-seven.

Then came Kansas. The Sooners had found themselves running a gauntlet in 1975, with every team rising to the occasion of its game with Oklahoma and knowing that by taking the Sooners' scalp its season would be affirmed. Alabama offensive coordinator Bud Moore had been brought to Lawrence in 1975 to turn the moribund Jayhawk football program around and, after losing his opener to Washington State, had converted to the Wishbone offense and put Nolan Cromwell behind center to run the show. After the transition, Moore's Kansas squad won five games while losing only two on their way to Norman. Installed as decided underdogs, the Jayhawks took a page out of Switzer's 1973 playbook by using the disrespect they were receiving as motivation.

The first quarter gave all indications of another Sooner victory. On Oklahoma's second possession, DiRienzo drew first blood with a perfectly aimed fifty-two-yard field goal. The Jayhawks were stifled on their next series, and on OU's ensuing possession the Sooners drove to the Kansas one-yard line. On the next play, as Peacock was fighting to cross the goal line, the ball was knocked from his grasp and sputtered out of bounds at the Jayhawk seven. On fourth down, DiRienzo got into position for a field goal, but the kick was blocked and the worm had irrevocably turned. "That was the most disappointing thing that happened in the game," said Switzer. "Right there, the momentum changed."[19] Late in the second quarter it appeared that the score would remain 3–0 in Oklahoma's favor at halftime when a Kansas ten-man rush snuffed a Tinker Owens punt, giving the Red and Blue a first down deep in Sooner territory. Jayhawk quarterback

Cromwell—who had entered the game leading the conference in rushing—evaded Daryl Hunt's pursuit to score and gave Kansas a 7–3 halftime advantage. It was the first time that the Sooners had trailed at halftime since October 6, 1973, when they had overcome a 20–7 deficit to defeat Miami; but there would be no such Sooner resurgence against Kansas in November 1975.

In the second half, everything that could go wrong for the Sooners did go wrong. Kansas built their 7–3 lead to 10–3 after recovering an Oklahoma fumble and to 16–3 after recovering another fumble, before finally completing the ambush by the score of 23–3. It was all over; the winning streak had ended at twenty-eight games and the undefeated streak at thirty-seven, and it was the first time in ninety-nine games that the Sooners had failed to score a touchdown. The national title aspirations appeared to have died on the Memorial Stadium turf.

Scott Hill gave credit to the Jayhawks. "Kansas had a terrific team that year," he reflects. "Nolan Cromwell and Laverne Smith were phenomenal. In fact, that's the one and only time I remember getting run over in my career in Norman."[20] Tinker Owens considered the game an offensive disaster. "I don't remember how many turnovers we had that day," he explains, "but I think it was eight or nine."[21] It was nine. The Sooners had taken possession of the football fourteen times on the afternoon, and eleven of those opportunities ended in bad fortune. When Kansas linebacker Rick Kovatch was asked after the game where the Jayhawk defense was primarily looking for the football, he had replied with a slight smile, "On the ground."[22] Steve Davis reflects on the loss:

> When Kansas came to Norman, they were determined not to be beaten by our speed burners, Joe Washington and Elvis Peacock. With our offense, we simply must take what the defense gives us; if they stop the run and force you to pass, you need to pass, and we struggled with passing that afternoon. Instead, we tried to force the defense to take what *we* wanted to use. Kansas decided that they were going to make us use the slower guys, the quarterback and the fullback, if we were going to beat them. And I think we pressed, made some mistakes, and didn't play well. There was no single player that was responsible for that loss; it was

the perfect storm at just the wrong time for us. Even though we were a senior-laden team in 1975, at that point we still hadn't quite figured out who we were.[23]

The loss had been equally painful to Joe Washington. He recalls, "It was probably the lowest point for me in my four years in Norman. But Kansas was good. Cromwell was a big, strong, athletic quarterback and Smith was fast. However, even though Kansas had a lot of speed, our defense handled them. What really hurt was that our offense continually put our defense in the hole. We fumbled so many times in that game and it was the first time I ever saw Tinker Owens drop a pass. I always thought that there might have been something more I could have done to prevent the loss; I took it awfully hard personally."[24]

After the game, Switzer radiated praise for his men. "I'm proud of our team," he exclaimed. "They fought their guts out today. We've come a long way together and I'm just proud."[25] And then, he became pensive. "But I think that if we'd played an error-free ball game, Kansas still might have won."[26]

Difficult though it may have been, the loss to Kansas provided renewed motivation for the Sooners. Davis, Owens, and Washington believed that before November 8, 1975, Oklahoma had not truly come together as a single unit with a common purpose. But after the loss, as the season's ultimate goal—a second consecutive national title—appeared to have been dashed from the realm of possibility, the Sooners realized a newly discovered sense of resolve. The complacency and anticlimax from which the team had suffered prior to the opening game had vanished, replaced by a sense of renewed dedication and immediacy. The Sooners had dropped precipitously from second to sixth in the wire service poll, and the coaching staff and the team now realized that there was no longer any margin for error. They knew that the final two games of the season, against Missouri in Columbia and Nebraska in Norman, would be a proving ground for the defending national champions.

15 Back to the Summit

The loss to Kansas shocked Sooner loyalists. It was an event surreal in its nature and yet all too tangible in its ramifications. Aspirations of bringing a second consecutive national title home to Oklahoma seemed dashed, yet in the Sooner locker room Switzer was already rebuilding. He pointed out to his players that all had not been lost; the conference title—and along with it a berth in the Orange Bowl—was still on the table, and, while a long shot, the national title was still a possibility. All it would take, like Switzer had said, was a little luck.

Historically, playing Missouri in Columbia had not presented major problems for Oklahoma. Though the Sooners occasionally departed Columbia with slim victories, they had only suffered two losses on the Tigers' home field since World War II and lost there only twelve times since René-Robert Cavelier, Sieur de La Salle claimed Missouri for France in 1678. But the team from Norman that made the trek to Columbia in November 1975 was very much "whistling past the graveyard"; they may have been defending national champions, but their confidence, so unflappable over the past five years, was shaken.

Missouri had been ranked fifth in the AP poll before losing in early October to Michigan in Ann Arbor, 31–7, but by mid-November the Tigers were sporting a 6–3 record and were ranked eighteenth in the wire service polls. They had only lost one game at home that season, and that was to the third-ranked Nebraska Cornhuskers. Head coach Al Onofrio was using a wide-open offensive formation not drastically dissimilar to the spread formation that would come into vogue twenty-five years later. Quarterback Steve Pisarkiewicz, a talented passer, ran the show with strong support from running back Tony Galbreath, and wide receiver Henry Marshall made it too dangerous for defenses to load the box.

The first half of the game appeared to be just the tonic the Sooners needed to heal their wounded self-confidence as the offense accounted for twenty points and the defense held the prolific Tiger offense scoreless. But when the second half started, things changed. Slowly and methodically, Pisarkiewicz and Galbreath brought Missouri back into the game until finally, late in the fourth quarter, the Tigers had pulled ahead 27–20. Oklahoma fans, who had been listening to Sooner Radio Network's Mike Treps's broadcast of the game, were having uncomfortable roilings of déjà vu and feared a second straight defeat was in the offing. Referring to Missouri's third period comeback, Scott Hill remarks, "It was extremely frustrating; they scored twenty-seven unanswered points on us in fifteen minutes."[1] Jimbo Elrod comments on the situation, "Did our defense let down in the second half? Absolutely not. Our offense had pretty much controlled the ball in the first half so Missouri hadn't had much of a chance to put anything together. But they made some offensive adjustments at halftime; they put three or four receivers on one side of the field and we hadn't seen much of that. And we couldn't just ignore the run because they had two excellent running backs. But the defense *never* let down."[2]

On OU's next possession after the Tigers had grabbed the lead, three plays netted the Sooners only nine yards as they faced a critical fourth and one from their own twenty-nine-yard line. The clock was now their enemy, and a punt to Missouri would have been tantamount to capitulation. The game was on the line, the atmosphere in Columbia was electric, and Sooner fans tuning in on their radios had long since left their seats to pace the floor. Mike Treps describes the fourth down play: "The Sooners broke the huddle and moved to the line of scrimmage. Steve Davis takes the ball and, on a simple option, tosses it to Joe Washington, who cuts through a hole on the right side of the line . . . and suddenly he's in the open field! I was screaming, '*Run Joe, Run!!*' into the microphone; I couldn't have been more excited. And Joe took it seventy-one yards for the score. Even now, after all these years, that's still the one play people remember me calling on the radio."[3] Washington's heroics brought the Sooners to within one point of Missouri. Switzer knew that with a loss or a tie, Oklahoma would be out of contention for the conference title, so he called for a two-point conversion. Once again, Davis handed Washington the football on the same play they had run moments earlier; as he followed Victor Hicks to the Missouri goal line, Washington was hit but, struggling, landed facing backwards on the goal line. The play was close, but the officials counted it, and the Sooners had taken a one-point lead. "Being in Columbia, I can't believe they gave it to us," says Owens. "It was just that close."[4] Missouri, regaining possession with seconds remaining, moved the ball dangerously deep into Sooner territory, but a last-gasp field goal missed the mark, and Oklahoma prevailed, 28–27.

"That was a big play for us, without a doubt," recalls Washington. "Coming back and winning against Missouri got us out of that mental valley we'd been in since the Kansas loss. Winning that game was huge."[5] But the victory, so desperately needed by the Sooners, still failed to help them in the AP poll as they fell from sixth to seventh.

Meanwhile up north, Nebraska was enjoying its first undefeated season under Tom Osborne. The Huskers had just dispatched Iowa State 52–0 to solidify their hold on the number two spot in the nation, and with only one weekend remaining in the regular season, they had a choke hold on the Big Eight Conference title. The oddsmakers had listed Nebraska and Oklahoma as almost dead even, with a slight three-point nod going to the Sooners' home field advantage. But when a poll was taken asking Big Eight Conference players who they believed would win the showdown, the overwhelming majority had picked Nebraska; only three players—Colorado's Dave Logan, Oklahoma State's Gary Irions, and Kansas's Waddell Smith—picked the Sooners.[6]

Throughout the second half of the season, both Oklahoma and Nebraska had been courted by the Sugar Bowl. Although the Big Eight Conference champion was contractually consigned to the Orange Bowl, the Sugar Bowl had sent representatives to virtually every game the Sooners and Cornhuskers had played since late October and had made it perfectly clear—although not legally binding—that the loser of their matchup would be welcomed to New Orleans on December 31, 1975. But two weeks before the OU-NU game, rumors began to reach Switzer and Osborne hinting that the loser of their game would not, in fact, be invited to New Orleans. The Sunday prior to the Huskers' trip to Norman, Switzer learned the truth. The Sugar Bowl was no longer interested in the Big Eight Conference runner-up. It was revealed that Alabama's Bear Bryant had lobbied the Sugar Bowl selection committee enthusiastically for tenth-ranked Penn State—a team with two losses—to play his Crimson Tide. Bryant, who made no secret of the fact that he had used his influence in the selection process, was pilloried by press and fans alike for openly hand-selecting what was considered to be a weaker opponent to compete against his team in New Orleans.[7] On Monday, Switzer informed the Sooners that if they were to lose to Nebraska, the Sugar Bowl was no longer an option, but the relatively young Fiesta Bowl would be awaiting them with open arms. The team reacted favorably to the Fiesta Bowl news, partly because they welcomed the opportunity to go to any postseason bowl after staying home for two years, and partly because no one on the team expected to *lose* to the Huskers. However, when told of the Sugar Bowl development, Nebraska's team voted to decline the Fiesta Bowl; for the Huskers, it would be Miami or nothing.

Oklahoma started the game as if determined to give it away. After Nebraska's first possession culminated in a sixty-seven-yard drive and a missed field goal, the Sooners gave them a second chance by fumbling the ball. But on third down, Husker quarterback Vince Ferragamo's pass was intercepted by Mike Phillips, and OU was back in business—but not for long, as Jim Littrell turned the ball over at the Sooner thirty-two. Nebraska moved the ball to Oklahoma's six-yard line before settling for a twenty-three-yard field goal and a 3–0 lead. After failing to move the ball, the Sooners punted and Nebraska set up shop at midfield. Several plays into the Nebraska drive, Ferragamo was hit by Scott Hill, the ball came loose, and Lee Roy Selmon recovered for the Sooners at the NU forty-two. Oklahoma secured the ball and began to drive downfield as the first period ended with Nebraska on top, 3–0.

Four minutes into the second quarter, Davis scored, and Oklahoma took a 7–3 lead. The rest of the half saw both teams struggling offensively until the Huskers' final possession. Ferragamo completed a forty-four-yard pass to Chuck Malito deep into Sooner territory, and on the ensuing play a pass interference call put the ball on the Oklahoma one-yard line. But with only seconds remaining and no time-outs, the Husker threat was thwarted by the Sooner defensive line, and both the drive and half ended with Oklahoma nursing a tentative 7–3 lead.[8]

Another Sooner fumble early in the third quarter allowed Nebraska to take a 10–7 lead, but soon afterwards Lee Roy Selmon jarred the ball loose from Ferragamo, and Oklahoma was back in business at the Nebraska forty-seven. Noticing that the Husker defense was overloading the opposite side of the line from where Tinker Owens was set, Davis started running toward the split end side, beginning a drive that ended in the Nebraska end zone, giving the Sooners a four-point lead.

Then the Husker offense, so brutally efficient and effective all year, began to implode. Shortly after the Sooner touchdown, Nebraska mishandled a punt, which was smothered by OU's Lee Hover at the Husker thirteen. Several plays later, Peacock slashed through for Oklahoma's third touchdown of the afternoon. With the score now sitting at 21–10, the Sooner defense quickly snuffed out what remained of Nebraska's rushing game (the Huskers would gain only nine yards on the ground in the second half), and Ferragamo was forced to go to the air. The Nebraska drive was once again frustrated when OU's Jerry Anderson intercepted to set up another Sooner score. A late touchdown run by freshman Billy Sims produced the final points of the day, and Oklahoma took a decisive 35–10 victory to the locker room.[9]

As the Sooners were celebrating, number one Ohio State was upending fourth-ranked Michigan. Second-ranked Texas A&M, idle that Saturday, would solidify their poll standing by defeating archrival Texas the following weekend. Oklahoma, on the strength of their strong showing against the Huskers, catapulted from seventh to third in the AP poll, and the national title once again seemed a remote possibility. Ohio State was scheduled to play UCLA in the Rose Bowl—a team they had massacred 41–20 in Los Angeles two months earlier, and undefeated Texas A&M had one regular season game remaining against the Arkansas Razorbacks before heading to the Liberty Bowl in Memphis to play unranked Southern California. Any scenario putting the Sooners back on top of the college football world on New Year's Day would depend upon a very unlikely series of upsets.

Since 1947, the Rose Bowl had been the exclusive venue of the Big Ten and Pac-10 conferences, with their champions appearing in a head-to-head matchup every New Year's Day. Other members of those conferences had been left out in the cold, contractually forbidden to appear in other bowl games. In 1975, the rules were changed; runners-up from both conferences were allowed to appear in other bowls, and the University of Michigan had hit the jackpot. In December, they were invited to the Orange Bowl to play Oklahoma. The fifth-ranked

Wolverines, led by true freshman quarterback Rick Leach and running back Gordon Bell, were a relentless team with a rugged defense that had only permitted an average of eleven points per game that season.

The Sooners departed a snow-blanketed Norman and flew to sunny Miami on Christmas Day. There was a spirit of quiet anticipation beneath the celebration; Texas A&M had been ambushed by Arkansas on December 6, clearing the way for Oklahoma's ascent to the number two position in the AP poll. The Sooners were now just one unlikely Ohio State stumble away from having their fate placed back into their own hands.

Four teams from the Big Eight Conference had earned invitations to bowl games in 1975. Besides Oklahoma, Colorado, Kansas, and Nebraska (having reconsidered their earlier decision to stay home after losing to the Sooners) had all gone to bowls. By December 27, Kansas had lost to Pittsburgh in the Sun Bowl, Colorado had been spanked by Texas in the Bluebonnet Bowl, and Nebraska went down to defeat at the hands of Arizona State in the Fiesta Bowl. Oklahoma was the last Big Eight team standing. At dinner on Christmas night, Switzer surprised the team by reading the riot act, telling them that any players arriving late for busses, meals, or meetings or slacking off in practice would find themselves on the first plane back home. He also announced that there would be no facial hair tolerated except for neatly trimmed moustaches. He then followed up on his statement by taking the team through a two-hour and twenty-minute drill the next day, culminating with a ten-minute head-on-head scrimmage—the toughest drill the team had experienced since preseason two-a-day practices. Switzer realized that what had happened to three other very sound Big Eight Conference teams could very well happen to his team too.[10]

Prior to kickoff, Steve Davis, an ordained Baptist minister, was invited to recite the pregame prayer. He recalls the event:

> I had just completed my warm-ups when they took me down to the center of the field where Billy Vessels was standing, waiting to introduce me. Billy was on the Orange Bowl Committee and was so proud that Oklahoma had been invited because we had been off television and out of bowl games for the past couple of years. We hadn't made a visit to the Orange Bowl

since 1968, so it was a big deal for him. Billy stepped up to the microphone, introduced me, and I had just started speaking when the PA announcer, unaware that I was already in the middle of my brief prayer, broke in to give the score from the Rose Bowl, informing everyone that Ohio State had been upset by UCLA, 23–10, which opened the door for us to win the national title. Well, the crowd just went nuts, and Billy, upset that they'd interrupted my prayer, was furious. I think he was embarrassed for me but heck, *I* wasn't embarrassed. I think I said something like, "well this is great news, let's try it again" and I started the prayer over. He took me aside afterwards and apologized, but I told him not to worry about it. When I walked back into the dressing room, Galen Hall grabbed me, shook my hand, and said, "this game just became very important."[11]

But 2,700 miles west of Miami, there was no celebration in the Ohio State locker room. The Buckeyes had fallen to a team they had defeated with relative ease two months before. Arguably one of the best teams to ever fail to win a national title in the decade, Ohio State, led by two-time Heisman Trophy–winning tailback Archie Griffin, had been poised to win it all in 1973, 1974, and 1975, only to finish second, fourth, and fourth in the national polls. Griffin reflects on the Buckeyes' 1976 Rose Bowl loss, which played such a large role in the Sooners fate:

We had beaten UCLA pretty solidly earlier in the year, and I think we might have taken the rematch a bit for granted, plus, we had over five weeks between our last game and the bowl game. We actually played well against the Bruins in the first half, moved the ball up and down the field, but it seemed like something always happened to frustrate our drives. And in the second half, UCLA made some key plays when they had to. We had a great team that year—I love those guys to this day. And you know, I think there was a good chance that if Coach Hayes *had* won that Rose Bowl, he might have retired.[12]

As Oklahoma prepared to take the field, Steve Davis put things into perspective. "After spending three great seasons together," he recounts, "we realized that the Orange Bowl would be the last game we'd ever play together as a team. I was fortunate enough to be a captain at Oklahoma for two seasons, and I just felt this tremendous responsibility to go out and represent our state and university and play well."[13]

Although no scoring occurred in the first fifteen minutes of the Orange Bowl, Michigan controlled the flow of the game. The Wolverines earned five first downs to Oklahoma's one, which came in the final minute of the quarter. Behind the running of Leach, Bell, and fullback Rob Lytle, the Wolverines produced seventy-eight yards to the Sooners' twenty-five. "I remember how hard-hitting and physical the game was and how respectful the Michigan team was," recalls Davis. "And they were tough; the first three plays of the game, they slammed our fullback, Jimmy Littrell, then they hit Joe incredibly hard, and then they hit me hard enough to give me a headache for the rest of the game."[14]

In the second quarter, the Oklahoma offense awakened. On its third possession of the period, Joe Washington opened the action with a nine-yard scamper, and then Davis untracked the Sooner passing game with a thirty-nine-yard aerial to Owens, taking Oklahoma to the Michigan thirty-nine-yard line. On the very next play, Davis optioned left and flipped the ball to a hard-charging Billy Brooks on an end around. Brooks evaded a defender, cut back inside, and took the ball to the end zone. NBC announcer Jim Simpson commented on the touchdown, saying, "Michigan wasn't as fooled as they were out-executed."[15] With just over a minute remaining in the half, Wolverine quarterback Leach, scrambling on third and fifteen, was hammered by Jerry Anderson and Jimbo Elrod. "We high-lowed Leach," recounts Elrod. "I took him out underneath and Jerry took his head off. It was a legal play, but a tough one."[16] The play occurred by the Michigan bench and infuriated coach Bo Schembechler, who complained vociferously to the officials, to no avail. Leach suffered a mild concussion and would not return to the game until the fourth quarter. The first half ended with Oklahoma in the lead, 7–0.

Oklahoma's miscues continued in the second half as they gift wrapped another fumble, giving the Wolverines new life at the Sooner twenty-six-yard line. Subbing for Leach, quarterback Mark Elzinga moved the Wolverines to a first down at the OU sixteen, but then, on third down, Gordon Bell took a pitchout, rolled right, and tossed a pass into the end zone, which was intercepted by Sidney Brown. Later in the third period, Steve Davis started a drive from the Sooner thirty-six and on first down rolled out and appeared to be destined for a huge loss, but scrambled for an eight-yard gain. Two plays later, Davis kept the ball for another significant gain—this time for fifteen yards—before pitching back to Peacock for three more yards. Several plays later, Davis rolled out and ran for eleven and another first down. With less than three minutes left in the quarter and facing a third-and-twenty situation, fullback Jim Culbreath split the center of the Michigan line for twenty-one yards and another first down. As the quarter ended, Davis and the Sooners were sitting on the Michigan ten-yard line. In the third quarter alone, Oklahoma had posted seven first downs to Michigan's one and had rushed for ninety-three yards to the Wolverine's nine; and Michigan had still not completed a pass.

On the first play of the fourth period, Davis scored Oklahoma's second and deciding touchdown. Rick Leach returned to the game but would prove to be largely ineffective against the Sooner defense. Gordon Bell would score the lone Wolverine touchdown after yet another Sooner fumble gave Michigan the ball on the OU two-yard line. Leach, trying a quarterback keeper on the two-point conversion attempt, was manhandled by the Selmons. Each team was stymied on their final possession, and the game ended with the Sooners on top, 14–6. After the game, the Michigan team was rife with praise for the Sooners. Rick Leach said he believed Oklahoma should be voted number one, and Bo Schembechler stated, "Oklahoma is a fine football team, one of the best Michigan has ever played."[17]

Two days later, on January 3, the final wire service polls were issued, and Oklahoma once again reigned supreme, becoming the first college football team to win two consecutive national championships twice, in 1955–56 and 1974–75. "In retrospect, that game we lost to Kansas was responsible for our winning the national championship," reflects Davis. "After we lost—and it was the only loss we experienced in our years at OU—we came back as a challenged football team with a purpose; we wanted to set things right, and we played at the top of our potential the rest of the season and through the bowl game."[18]

With his 73 yards in the Orange Bowl, Joe Washington had become Oklahoma's all-time leading career rusher with 4,071 yards.[19] As postseason honors were bestowed, an unprecedented acknowledgment of talent over production occurred when wide receivers Billy Brooks and Tinker Owens were named All-Americans. "That'll never happen again," comments Owens. "We only caught nineteen passes between us all year."[20] Joining Brooks and Owens on the long list of Sooner All-Americans for 1975 were Lee Roy and Dewey Selmon, Terry Webb, Mike Vaughan, Jimbo Elrod, and Joe Washington. But the Sooners' graduation losses were professional football's gain as Lee Roy and Dewey Selmon, Washington, Elrod, Brooks, Owens, and DiRienzo were taken in the 1976 National Football League draft. Since the inception of that draft in 1936, fourteen Sooners had been selected in the elite first round; in the 1976 draft alone, three Oklahomans were taken—Lee Roy Selmon, Joe Washington, and Billy Brooks. Prior to 1976, the highest draft position that a player from Oklahoma had achieved in round one was second: Billy Vessels in 1952 and Max Boydston in 1955. In 1976, Lee Roy Selmon became the first Sooner ever selected with the first pick in the first round; it would happen again four years later when Billy Sims was chosen first by the Detroit Lions.

The Sooners were no longer on probation; their days of playing in the dark were at an end. "The probation hurt our national image, yes," said Switzer. "And it certainly hurt our recruiting in 1973. But no, it didn't hurt the way we played on Saturdays and no, it didn't hurt our morale at all. Adversity draws people together."[21] As in bygone days when Americans sought entertainment and news from their radios, Oklahoma fans everywhere had been forced to follow the Sooners through a more interactive medium. There was a certain mystique involved in listening to a game by radio, and through that experience the fans grew uniquely closer to their team. "There were certainly pros and cons to the situation," remarks Jimbo Elrod. "The radio provided a certain mystery to the event and to the team. Everybody had to listen to the radio to figure out who we were. In that regard, it became a special time for many Oklahoma fans who got to know us more intimately."[22]

The nucleus of talent that had led the Sooners through the transitory period from Fairbanks to Switzer, through the dark tunnel of house arrest back into the light of day, had departed. A new transition now faced Oklahoma, and there was a new collection of talent ready to step forward.

16 Transition and Resurrection

JANUARY 1976–JANUARY 1979

While Oklahoma's back-to-back championships in 1974 and 1975 were the result of a coordinated effort orchestrated by a dedicated staff and talented, equally dedicated teams, they could also be partially attributed to an action taken by Bud Wilkinson nearly twenty seasons earlier. The seed Wilkinson planted in 1956 when he shattered the racial barrier by offering Prentice Gautt a scholarship had taken deep root and had begun to bear fruit during the 1960s, and by the 1970s the Sooners were reaping a rich harvest of talent. In 1960 and 1961, Wallace Johnson had been the only African American represented on Oklahoma's roster. In 1962, Ed McQuarters became the only black player, and in 1963 Nehemiah Flowers would join him. But from 1964 through the end of the decade, the Sooner roster began to prosper from the recognition and recruiting of black student athletes. Ben Hart, Granville Liggins, Jim Jackson, Eddie Hinton, SanToi Debose, Bobby Thompson, and Eugene Ross—who would become the first African American team captain—would illuminate the way for other black players to follow on their own personal journeys to Norman. By 1971—the Sooners' breakout year with their Wishbone offense—ten African Americans graced the roster, seven of whom were either starters or alternate players. And by the mid-seventies, the composition of the team had dramatically altered; nearly 25 percent of the 1975 national title team's 130-man roster consisted of African American players, half of whom were either starters or alternates at their positions. The racial harmony among the black and white players, both on the field and off, had not only drawn many young blacks to Norman but had provided them with a welcoming and nurturing environment promoting their success as both students and players.

❖

At the conclusion of the 1975 season, the Big Red of Oklahoma could justifiably lay claim to dominance in the first half of the decade. From 1971 through 1975—forfeited games from 1972 notwithstanding—the Sooners had won fifty-four games, lost three, and tied one, and had garnered four consecutive conference crowns and two consecutive national championships. Switzer's first three years had been reminiscent of Sooner glory from the 1950s, and the valleys of the 1960s became but a vague memory effortlessly repressed.

In January 1976, one of the greatest classes to ever trod Parrington Oval had departed, many to play their games professionally on different fields in different cities across the nation. Lee Roy and Dewey Selmon left for Tampa Bay, Joe Washington and Tony DiRienzo for San Diego, Billy Brooks for Cincinnati, Tinker Owens for New Orleans, and Jimbo Elrod for Kansas City. The loss of so many highly skilled players would be enough to relegate any other team to rebuilding status, but Oklahoma was not any other team; when it was suggested to him that the Sooners would be rebuilding in 1976, Oklahoma State head coach Jim Stanley snorted in disdain and commented, "They aren't rebuilding; they're in transition."[1] Stanley's point was well made, but when a team loses as many All-Americans and supporting starters as did the Sooners after the 1975 season, whether it is called "rebuilding" or "transition" simply becomes an exercise in semantics.

With the departure of the heroes of 1973–1975, the transition started with experienced players such as Dean Blevins, Jim Culbreath, Elvis Peacock, Horace Ivory, Mike Vaughan, Chez Evans, Jaime Melendez, Karl Baldischwiler, Lee Hover, Daryl Hunt, Victor Hicks, Mike Phillips, Obie Moore, and Myron Shoate. A strong supporting cast of underclassmen also standing in the wings awaiting their chance to perform consisted of Thomas Lott, Billy Sims, Kenny King, Freddie Nixon, Jimmy Rogers, Woodie Shepard, George Cumby, Reggie Kinlaw, Phil and Paul Tabor, Kent Bradford, Mike Babb, Greg Roberts, Jody Farthing, Bud Hebert, Victor Brown, Uwe von Schamann, Greg Sellmyer, and Sherwood Taylor. And, as Tinker Owens had done in 1972, another incoming receiver, Steve Rhodes, was destined to make an indelible mark on Sooner history as a freshman.

The defensive secondary with Zac Henderson, Scott Hill, Sidney Brown, Jerry Anderson, and Jerry Reese all returning would be formidable. "When I came back to school in the fall," recounts Hill, "I brought ball caps that had 'Murder Inc.' printed on them, and I gave them to all the defensive backs. We became known as 'Murder Inc.' that year. Our coach, Bobby Proctor, loved it and it became our nickname."[2] True freshman Steve Rhodes claimed to have been "terrified" of his own secondary in practice. "They were very, very physical," he states. "But they helped me tremendously because I knew I wouldn't be playing against anyone all year with their level of talent."[3]

But in the spring of 1976, Oklahoma nearly lost three future impact players. Having declined the opportunity to redshirt in 1975, sophomores Thomas Lott, Kenny King, and George Cumby, seeing no possibility of gaining significant playing time in 1976, decided to transfer. King tells why he came to Oklahoma and why he nearly left:

> When I left Texas, there were two things I was looking for: I wanted a chance to play football, and I wanted to find a non-prejudiced environment. When I went to Oklahoma on my visit and Larry Briggs took me to the Blue Onion, I saw Jaime Melendez, Zac Henderson, and Elvis Peacock partying *together*. I knew that if they partied together, they were going to play together. The only time I ever considered leaving was in my freshman year in the spring of 1976. I was first team left halfback going into spring ball when I caught the flu and went into the infirmary for four days. When I got out I was *fourth* team right halfback—that's how competitive the talent was. Thomas knew Dean would be playing quarterback for the next two years, George was a backup fullback at the time behind Jim Culbreath, and we didn't think we'd be playing anytime soon. So we were going to transfer down to Texas Southern where Wendell Mosley had just become head coach. But Coach Switzer got wind of the situation and, being the visionary that he was, pulled us aside and told us that all three of us were going to become key players at the University of Oklahoma. He asked us to be patient and not to give up. Only Barry Switzer and the three of us knew about this.[4]

Dean Blevins, Oklahoma High School Player of the Year in 1974 and Steve Davis's backup for the past two seasons, would be taking over at quarterback for the opening game of the season. Peacock and Ivory complemented Blevins at halfback, and although King had been bumped down the depth chart due to illness, he suddenly found himself thrust into the spotlight at fullback. "George Cumby, who by this time was our first team fullback, separated his shoulder for the second time in his career and Jim Culbreath, the second team fullback, had hurt his knee," says King. "So Switzer comes to me and barks, 'Kenny King! Let me see you in a four-point stance!' And I thought, 'I'm going to show this cocky S.O.B. something he hasn't seen at fullback . . . quickness.' The first play we ran was a straight-ahead dive

Kenny King, 2010. Courtesy Kenny King.

handoff over right tackle. Dean took the snap, and I was already through the line of scrimmage as he was reaching for my back with the ball . . . *I was gone.*"[5]

The fifth-ranked Sooners opened the season in Nashville against Vanderbilt. A comment made by Lacewell reflects just how seriously the team took the Commodores: "I was more worried about finding time to visit the Grand Ole Opry than I was about the game."[6] But Lacewell and his fellow coaches should have been more concerned because by halftime Oklahoma was clinging to a precarious 7–3 lead in a game that had been characterized by careless mistakes. Blevins had gone 0–6 passing in the first half, Oklahoma managed only one first down in the first quarter, and the defense had to fend off two deep penetrations by Vanderbilt. Although the Sooners emerged with a 24–3 victory, they had lost seven of eleven fumbles, and the two late touchdowns they scored were launched from deep inside Vandy territory. The Sooners had floundered. Although they had performed as might have been expected of a newly assembled team behind an inexperienced quarterback, the expectations brought down upon them as a result of the success of prior seasons was tremendous, and the pressure on the talented but untested young Blevins—after all, he had not taken a snap under game conditions in two years—caused problems. "They lined up in a variety of defensive formations," he said, "and I didn't recognize them early in the game."[7] Realizing that Blevins had been nervous, Switzer tried to calm him down on the sidelines between possessions. "Dean puts too much pressure on himself," said Switzer. "There was too much to think about—decisions on the corners, audibles, changing the blocking."[8] Although the offense struggled, the defense rose to the occasion. The Sooner stoppers held Vanderbilt to nine first downs and eighty-eight total yards.

After the game, Switzer tried to take solace from the fact that although his team had struggled to wipe their cleats on a Southeastern Conference door-mat, Texas, Notre Dame, Alabama, and Southern California had all lost while Nebraska had suffered a 6–6 tie with LSU. Temporarily assuaging though it may have been, the misfortunes of other top-notch programs did little to hide the fact that his team, in its first game, had displayed an alarming lack of offensive poise. Switzer realized that although the 1976 Sooners were loaded with talent from top to bottom, learning to play together, to function as a single entity, would take time.

Against California the next weekend, the first half saw Oklahoma display flashes of brilliance. Blevins passed for one score and ran for another, and wide receiver Lee Hover picked a fumble out of midair and returned it fifty-eight yards, giving the Sooners a 21–0 halftime cushion. When the game ended, Oklahoma had amassed 562 yards in the 28–17 victory, promoting new optimism. The following weekend, first-year head coach Bobby Bowden brought his Florida State Seminoles to Norman. The winless Seminoles had been installed as five-touchdown underdogs, and the Sooner fans packing Memorial Stadium, resembling Romans in the Coliseum, fully expected a blood sacrifice. The fans had not been pleased by their team's performances thus far; although Oklahoma was 2–0 and ranked fourth nationally, simply winning was no longer enough. And for their offense—which had operated to such perfection over the past five years—to sputter was unacceptable. Even though Oklahoma took the day with a 24–9 score while piling up 455 rushing yards and another 58 passing, the defense managed to add more worry lines to Switzer's brow. The Seminole offense—a unit that had only managed twelve points against Memphis and had been shut out in a 47–0 embarrassment against Miami—had mounted an eighty-yard cross-country scoring drive against the Sooner defense and another sixty-yard drive that had ended without points. "Not many teams have driven that far on us to score," said Switzer after the game. "And certainly not a team that lacked the talent Florida State does. I really don't know where we are as a football team right now."[9]

Third-ranked Oklahoma's next opponent, Iowa State, had been posting extremely unlikely figures in 1976. ISU was 3–0 and was ranked second nationally in scoring and third in total offense. Although their first three games had been played against Drake, Air Force, and Kent State, the Cyclones had still pummeled them by a combined score of 146–27, and hope sprang eternal as they prepared to entertain their visitors from Norman. A victory for the Cyclones would be of monumental importance to their program, and a well-played loss would provide a substantial morale boost. They would gain one and nearly gain the other.

For the fourth time in 1976, the Sooners found themselves fighting for their lives against an inferior but determined foe. At halftime, Oklahoma led 10–3 only to have the Cyclones tie the game 10–10 in the third quarter. With a scant four minutes to go in the fourth period, after appearing to be stopped, Ivory broke through a scrum of tacklers on third down and raced sixty-two yards to break the tie. And then with 1:36 remaining, Jerry Anderson intercepted a Cyclone pass at the Sooner thirty-one and took it back for a game-clinching touchdown. Oklahoma had only managed to tally four first downs in the first half and ended the game with eight while its 215 total yards was eclipsed by ISU's 315.[10] Unable to mount and sustain either rhythm or consistency, the Oklahoma offense appeared to be on life support.

The situation was compounded when starting quarterback Dean Blevins was checked into the infirmary the week before the Texas game with a non-football related illness. "We always lived in mortal fear of the quarterback going down, because it created potential problems with coordination," recounts offensive line coach Gene Hochevar. "When you make changes at quarterback, it changes the tempo of the entire offense."[11] The offense behind Blevins may not have fired on all cylinders every game, but there was no disputing that as a starter, he had not yet lost a game. "I found out while I was in the infirmary that I wouldn't be out in time to play against Texas," says Blevins. "That was crushing to me; it had been my dream to play against and beat the Longhorns."[12]

Lott, King, and Ivory in action. Courtesy Thomas Lott.

In Blevins's absence, sophomore Thomas Lott would be tossed into the fray. Lott, a talented athlete, had been moved from his preferred position—running back—and pressed into service at quarterback his junior year to run his high school's Wishbone offense. Promised that the move would only last until his coach could "find another quarterback," Lott grew into the role, and in the fall of his senior year he was informed by his head coach that he would be "stuck" with the position. "So I played quarterback my senior year," recalls Lott. "Although we did run the Wishbone, there wasn't a lot of optioning that occurred; I mostly just kept the ball."[13] Lott's performance was good enough to make him a blue-chip recruit and afford him the option of attending any university he chose; he chose Oklahoma.

Entering the 1976 Red River Rivalry, Oklahoma had not lost to Texas in five seasons. From 1971 through 1973, Texas had not been competitive against the Sooners, but in 1974 and 1975 the games had been in question well into the fourth quarter. In the 1976 game, Oklahoma was forced to keep its offense simple because of Lott's inexperience and, consequently, the game became a defensive struggle. With Texas holding a 6–0 lead late in the fourth period, Sooner David Hudgens recovered a Texas fumble, and ten plays later Ivory crossed the goal line. But Oklahoma's revelry soon turned to shock and disappointment when a high snap from center doomed the point after kick, leaving the game deadlocked 6–6 as the final ticks ran off of the clock. The Longhorns had outgained the Sooners 182 yards to 133 and had managed six first downs to Oklahoma's five.[14]

With Blevins still hospitalized, Oklahoma traveled to Lawrence to exact a measure of revenge for the previous season's shocking upset. Once again, Lott started under center but was allowed more flexibility in his play calling. He recalls the experience:

> It was my coming out party. I showed the coaches and my teammates that this was my job and I wasn't giving it up. Early in the game we ran a play where I pitched to Elvis on a sweep right, and meanwhile, I sneak over to the left side and he throws it back to me. It was thrown slightly behind me but was nothing I shouldn't have been able to catch. I had my hands on it, and as I turned to run downfield and score a touchdown, I dropped the ball. I cannot tell you how angry that made me; but it turned out to be a good thing because it pissed me off to the point where I took it out on the other team—I went after them like they had *stolen* something from me.[15]

What the Jayhawks had "stolen" was Oklahoma's winning streak in 1975, and the Sooners made them pay dearly in their 28–10 victory. In the game, King rushed for 85 yards, Ivory 91, and Lott, who had proven himself a quick and savvy triple-option operator, gathered in 104. Blevins, listening to the game on the radio from his hospital bed, saw the handwriting on the wall; he realized that the sporadic performance of the offense during the first four games of the season combined with Lott's systematic execution of the Jayhawks, had cost him his starting position. As noted by King, missing practice for any length of time could prove deadly to a career in Norman; the players referred to it as "the eye in the sky." Any time out of the huddle, any loss of visibility, could afford another talented player his opportunity to fill the vacuum and impress.[16]

The offense was improving week by week, but the defense was suffering; the secondary—one of the strong suits of the team in early September—had been decimated by injuries. Scott Hill sustained a knee injury against Kansas and was wearing a splint, Jerry Anderson suffered a separated shoulder in Lawrence and was lost for the year, and Sidney Brown had also injured his shoulder earlier in the season. Only Zac Henderson remained.[17] "All three team captains were hurt in the KU game," remembers Hill. "That really affected our team."[18] Oklahoma's next two opponents, Oklahoma State in Norman and Colorado in Boulder, would take full advantage of the Sooners' vulnerability in the secondary. Despite the Oklahoma offense grinding out a total of 55 points and nearly 700 yards total in the two games, OU would not be able to overcome its defensive problems, losing to the Cowboys 31–24 and to Colorado 42–31. After the Colorado game, a reporter naively asked Switzer if he had some players playing out of position in the secondary. Switzer managed a short, painful laugh before rattling off the names of Jerry Anderson, Scott Hill, Reggie Kinlaw, Tony Peters, Mike Babb, Mike Birks, Zac Henderson, and Jerome Harris, all of whom either missed the game, played at an unfamiliar position, or played hurt.[19] Thomas Lott reflects on the two losses:

> We scored twenty-four points against Oklahoma State and when we do that, we should win the game. Then we go to Colorado and score thirty-one points, and their passing beats us. Losing those defensive players really hurt. I remember getting on the bus after the game in Boulder; I was pissed off and I yelled at the team. I told them I didn't give a damn if we had to score one hundred points, we weren't losing another game! We came to the University of Oklahoma, a team that had only lost one game in three years, and we've already lost two friggin' games in a row! I refused to lose another game.[20]

Lott was as good as his vow. With the bandana-clad quarterback at the controls, the Sooners dismantled Kansas State (49–20) and overcame eleventh-ranked Missouri (27–20), once again setting the stage for a showdown in Lincoln.

But things were different in 1976. Nebraska, after tying its opening game with LSU, won its next five contests before losing to Missouri in late October. Kansas fell next followed by Oklahoma State—a team that gave the Huskers everything they wanted before losing 14–10 in Lincoln. By the time the Cornhuskers hosted the Sooners on November 26, they sported a 4–2 conference record, and with a victory over OU would finish the season in a three-way tie for the conference crown with Oklahoma State and Colorado, each with 5–2 conference marks. Also, should the Huskers beat the Sooners, they would earn the automatic Big Eight berth in the Orange Bowl by virtue of their victories over the other two tri-champions. With their 4–2 conference mark, the Sooners were still in the unlikely position of sharing the three-way Big Eight title with a victory over Nebraska; but since they had already lost to the other two tri-champions, the Orange Bowl would not be an option for them.

Nebraska had been *Playboy* magazine's preseason pick to win the national championship, and Tom Osborne was picked as its preseason coach of the year. The previous season, the magazine had selected Oklahoma to win it all, and it was the first time its prediction had come true. For four straight years Nebraska had lost to Oklahoma, and in 1972 and 1974, while playing in Lincoln, it had been necessary for the Sooners to come from behind to win. When Nebraska athletic director and former head coach Bob Devaney was asked if his team had developed a mental block against beating Oklahoma, he replied, "Nah, no mental block. We'll beat 'em this year." Then he paused and chuckled before adding, "but if we don't catch 'em this year, there *will* be a mental block."[21]

As Oklahoma and Nebraska prepared to take the field on an overcast, cold, and windy afternoon, Barry Switzer addressed his team in the locker room. When he had finished, he asked team captain Scott Hill to give the pregame prayer; Hill, knowing that the Nebraska team was a more experienced group, recited, "Please, dear Lord, don't allow injury or harm to come to any player. And please, please, dear Lord, *please* don't let the best team win!"[22]

The game started well for Oklahoma as it drove cross-country to take a 7–0 lead early in the opening stanza. Nebraska replied with a field goal and trailed 7–3 at the break. But fickle momentum moved to the Husker sideline, and by the six minute mark in the third quarter NU led 17–7 and had effectively rendered the Sooner offense powerless. Then, on OU's first possession of the fourth quarter, Elvis Peacock solved the Husker defense as he raced fifty-one yards for a touchdown. The two-point try failed, and with just over two minutes gone in the final period Nebraska's lead was cut to 17–13. Both teams continued to go nowhere on offense until, with under five minutes left, the Huskers drove the ball inside the Oklahoma thirty-five-yard line. Lacewell tells what happened on the Sooners' key defensive stand: "They were just out of field goal range, and they had a fourth down with a long yard to go. I'd coached against Tom so many times, that I had a good feel for what he might do, and I didn't think he had the confidence to try running the ball. Ordinarily in that situation, I'd go with an eight-man front, but if they switched off and threw the pass, we would have been dead in the water. I had a feeling he was going to throw it, so I had our defense back off at the last second; Humm attempted a pass and we ate him up."[23]

The Sooners took over on downs at their sixteen-yard line, facing a strong north wind, a dwindling clock, and a Nebraska defense bound and determined to protect its four-point lead. Oklahoma gained only four yards on their first two downs, and then the magic started. Switzer inserted backup halfback Woodie Shepard into the lineup with Lott, King, and Peacock and Steve Rhodes split wide on the right side. Earlier in the game, in an effort to warm his feet from the unforgiving cold, Shepard had been standing with his back next to a heater on the sideline. As he alternately held the sole of each foot close to the heat, his right shoe suddenly burst into flames and was quickly extinguished. Soon afterward, he was sent into the game. Rhodes relates the story:

It was the coldest game I've ever played in. Woodie Shepard hadn't gotten into too many games; he would usually play during mop-up time, but when we practiced the halfback pass there was no doubt Woodie would be in that huddle. He was picked for that desperation play in Lincoln because he would be throwing into the wind and he could really zing it out there. When they called that play in the huddle, I knew my job was to sell the idea to the defense that I was going to run block; I had to take my time with it and not hurry because if I hurried, it would trigger a defensive response. So after I faked, I ran downfield and cut back in, looked over my shoulder and there was the ball, a beautiful throw. We completed that halfback pass on third down, against a great defense, with our backs to the wall, into the wind—probably the toughest set of circumstances to pull off a trick play.[24]

Shepard's completion set the Sooners up at the Husker thirty-seven-yard line. After two plays lost nine yards, Switzer sent his best passer, Dean Blevins, into the huddle to execute the critical flea-flicker play. Blevins relates what happened next:

I had been standing on the sideline for three-and-a-half hours, and I was just completely frozen when they sent me in. It was third and long, and I remember the play because Nebraska busted an assignment; it was the one play that day when they had lined up wrong defensively. So when I went to the line of scrimmage and looked at the secondary and saw that they were in a "sky" formation, I *knew* our play would work if we could just execute it. The play was called "317 stop and lateral." So I took the snap, hit Steve between the numbers, and his pitchout to the trailing halfback, Elvis Peacock, was perfect. You would have thought it was a play we practiced ten times a day, it went so smoothly. And as Elvis flew down the sideline, the crowd, so passionate and wild moments before, went silent; it was a great moment.[25]

The play took the Sooners to the Nebraska two-yard line, and on the next play Peacock scored his second touchdown of the afternoon. Von Schamann's point after kick was perfect, and Oklahoma had earned a 20–17 victory and a Big Eight Championship for the fifth straight season. Days later, the Sooners received an invitation to play in the sixth Fiesta Bowl; their opponent would be Western Athletic Conference Co-Champion Wyoming. Fred Akers, the head coach of the Cowboys, had already agreed to move to Austin to succeed Darrell Royal—who had announced his retirement—when he led his team to Tempe; ex-Sooner quarterback Bob Warmack also served as an assistant coach for Wyoming.

The game was played on Christmas Day under balmy skies. Oklahoma took the fight to Wyoming early as the Sooners scored on their first two drives and built a 20–0 halftime lead before finishing the Cowboys, 41–7. Lott—who was named Fiesta Bowl Player of the Game—gained seventy-nine yards; Peacock, seventy-seven; Ivory, fifty-four; and King, forty-eight. But the most revealing statistic resided in the fact that the leading rusher in the game was a Sooner backup, Woodie Shepard, who picked up eighty-five yards on only seven carries. Before the game, all signs had pointed to a monumental mismatch. Oklahoma was bigger, stronger, and faster than Wyoming, and there was little doubt that the Sooners would handle the Cowboys' Wishbone offense. Indeed, Oklahoma's starting defense held the Cowboys to only two first downs, one of which came by penalty. Innuendoes arising after the game suggesting that Switzer and the coaching staff had intentionally "run up the score" on Wyoming were ludicrous. Oklahoma's role in the bowl game was so dominant that its starters were finished for the afternoon after the first drive of the second half, and seventy-two Sooner players saw action in the game.[26] Peacock comments, "Coach Switzer always liked to make sure that all his players got a chance to play in front of their families and friends. One of the misconceptions people always had about him was that he would run up the score on weaker opponents. When he'd say, 'let's go hang a half-a-hundred on someone,' he wasn't trying to *embarrass* anyone; he just wanted to give everybody down the depth chart an opportunity to play."[27]

At the end of 1976, the Sooners had evolved into a cohesive unit playing with a singularity of purpose. With a strong nucleus of experienced players returning the next season, excitement abounded both in the locker room and across the state.

As the Sooners were finishing their season with an exclamation point against the Wyoming Cowboys in December 1976, another watershed event was in its nascent stages. The fledgling College Football Association was holding its first organizational meeting. Rule changes that had been implemented at the NCAA Economic Convention in 1973 had shaken the foundation of college football's elite institutions. The founding father of the CFA and Big Eight Conference commissioner, Chuck Neinas, discusses the development:

The 1973 NCAA Economic Convention established limits controlling the number of grants-in-aids a university could have for all sports as well as the number of coaches you could employ for all sports. At that time, there was no distinction made between voting member institutions in the NCAA; therefore, in essence, Colorado College had the same vote as the University of Colorado, and Wabash College had the same vote as Notre Dame. The result was that those conferences not considered major conferences would always vote for the lower limits because of their own limited resources; this gave berth to the forty-eight-man travel squad limit in college football. I'll never forget when, after that rule was implemented, USC Coach John McKay was interviewed before his game against Notre Dame in South Bend. When the announcer asked him if he was ready to play, he replied, "You bet . . . I brought my 48 players and my 210 band members."[28]

In December 1976 the first CFA Constitutional Convention convened. All major independents and conferences with the exception of the Big Ten and the PAC-10 were represented. "We decided that we needed to form a unified group to act together in order to protect our programs and advance our cause," explains Neinas. In 1977, the CFA followed their 1976 Convention with its first de jure meeting, at which time those in attendance voted on bylaws and structure. The new organization had only begun to create ripples in the NCAA pond, but within five years its effect would become revolutionary.[29]

By August 1977, it appeared to everyone—including the national pundits—that Oklahoma would be the team to beat both in the Big Eight Conference and the nation as the Sooners found themselves sitting comfortably atop the Associated Press preseason poll for the third time in the past four years. And with eighteen returning starters evenly divided from offense to defense, the coaches in Norman had to be wringing their hands in eager anticipation. Though the average fan had been counting the days since January until the first ball would be launched into the warm September sky, they were more excited about a game scheduled to be played September 24 when Oklahoma would travel to Columbus, Ohio, for their first meeting with Woody Hayes's Ohio State Buckeyes.

In the 1970s, the only team that had rivaled Oklahoma in performance and achievement was Ohio State. Led by their bellicose and demanding head coach, the Buckeyes' record since 1972, 49–7–2, had been second only to that of the Sooners' 52–4–2, and as OU hotly pursued national titles from 1973 through 1975, Ohio State more often than not had been its primary impediment. When the schedule for the 1977 season was announced early in the decade, September 24, 1977, had been circled in red ink not only by Sooner and Buckeye fans but also by all true followers of the game.

In the final scrimmage before the home opener against Vanderbilt, Thomas Lott suffered a leg injury. "I missed the first two games that year," says Lott. "I could have played in the second game against Utah, but they held me out so I could regain my form for the big game against Ohio State the following weekend."[30]

On September 10, the Sooners with Dean Blevins under center took the field against Vanderbilt in a game played in Norman. Although a thirty-point favorite, the error-prone Sooners found themselves trailing the Commodores 15–0 in the second quarter and 15–11 at the half. Problems continued to plague Oklahoma in the third quarter until, in the fourth period, freshman quarterback Jay Jimerson—son of Oklahoma freshman coach Don Jimerson—entered the game and sparked the Sooners to an 18–15 lead. The drama continued until Vanderbilt, trailing 25–23, missed a last-gasp field goal. The slim victory dropped OU to number five nationally and dismayed Switzer, who called the error-filled game, "the sorriest exhibition of football in my coaching career."[31] But Blevins and the Sooners got back on track the following weekend with a 62–24 blasting of Utah in a final tune-up for the marquee game with Ohio State.

As the Sooners rolled into Columbus, the eyes of the college football world were upon them. Third-ranked, undefeated Oklahoma pitted against fourth-ranked, undefeated Ohio State on a cold, windy, overcast Ohio afternoon—the Goodyear blimp hovering over the stadium was battling 15–20 mile-per-hour winds—seemed a match made in college football heaven. As the two teams were warming up on the field, Oklahoma offensive line coach Gene Hochevar had an interesting encounter with Hayes. He recounts, "I had spent three days in Columbus with my wife in 1976 interviewing with Coach Hayes who had offered me a coaching job. We spent time with Woody and his wife and had truly enjoyed their company. I seriously considered taking the job, but I eventually turned it down. While we were warming up on the field before kickoff, I walked over to say hello to Woody, but when I went up to him to shake his hand, he wouldn't shake hands with me; he just turned his back and walked away without saying a word."[32]

Additionally, Hochevar had his offensive line honed to near perfection. He describes his training regimen:

Going into that Ohio State game we had a great line comprised of Carl Baldischwiler, Jaime Melendez, Paul Tabor, Greg Roberts, and Sammy Jack Claphan; they were one of the best o-lines I've ever coached. I don't think anyone realized how important they were to the success of our Wishbone offense. I put those guys through hell every day in practice; they came in earlier and stayed later than anyone else on the team. After afternoon practice on Tuesdays and Wednesdays, I used to call meetings in the dressing room at 9 o'clock at night after study hall. Orin of Orin's Pizza in Norman was a good friend, so I'd call him, he'd send over a stack of pizzas, and we'd raid Jack Baer's Coke machine. We used that time to go over that day's practice film; we talked about it with the team and made adjustments. So we were way ahead of everybody the by next day, and by the time Thursday rolled around, our guys were prepared for the weekend's opponent. I don't think anyone else on our team realized the kind of time and work we put into preparing for our position. That line was agile, hostile, mobile, mad, and they would come off the ball like seven speeding bullets. And they were really great kids too—I love every one of them to this day. I called them, "My beer-drinking 'C' students" although there wasn't a bad student in the bunch; they were a sharp group of guys.[33]

Shortly after kickoff, Oklahoma went to work. With the ball inside the Buckeye thirty, Lott handed the ball to Kenny King, who, while diving through the line, fumbled. But on this day, Sooner Magic was alive and well in Columbus—the

Oklahoma offensive line in Ohio Stadium on the eve of the Sooner-Buckeye Showdown. *Left to right:* Karl Baldischwiler, Jaime Melendez, Paul Tabor, Greg Roberts, Sammy Jack Claphan, Victor Hicks. Courtesy Gene Hochevar.

ball fell from King's hands, hit the ground, and careened back up into the arms of a forward-charging Elvis Peacock, who did not stop until he had crossed the Ohio State goal line. "I'm the guy who fumbled the ball that popped up into Peacock's hands," recounts King. "I deserve an assist."[34] On OSU's next possession, the brutal Sooner defense forced a fumble, recovering the ball inside the Buckeye red zone. On third down, sophomore Billy Sims shot through the line of scrimmage, dancing between tacklers on his way to the end zone. With only minutes gone in the first quarter, Oklahoma had stilled the crowd in the Horseshoe by taking a 14–0 lead. Von Schamann would add a field goal late in the first period and early in the second, boosting the Sooners' lead to 20–0. But the tires went flat on the Sooner Schooner as Sims, suffering from a strained tendon, left the game. "I've never been hit as hard in my life as I was in that game," reflects Sims. "It was without doubt the toughest football game I'd ever played in."[35] Shortly after Sims departed, Lott injured his leg and also left the lineup. With Lott sidelined, the coaches decided to send Jay Jimerson into the fray. Jimerson, a quick but small player, had been the Sooners' savior against Vanderbilt; but with Lott out and a freshman quarterback entering the game, the Ohio State defense smelled blood. Jimerson was quickly set upon by the Buckeyes, and Oklahoma began to falter. Observing the situation from the sideline, Lott recalls:

> There are games where coaches have to overcome players and players have to overcome coaching, and I believe one of those times happened in Columbus. Our coaching staff made a mistake that allowed Ohio State to climb back into the game when they put Jay, a true freshman, into the game. It wasn't fair to him. Dean was older and more experienced; had they put him in, we were up twenty to nothing, we were in their territory, and even if he'd just handed the ball off to one of the guys we've got in the backfield I guarantee you we're going to take the ball and go score. That would have made it 27–0, and we would have taken their hearts out of it. But Jay made some mistakes, pitched the ball on the ground, and it cost us. And let me tell you, I've never seen a quarterback so brutally assaulted as he was that afternoon; I'm standing on the sideline and I'm feeling terrible for him.[36]

Although they had not managed a first down until early in the second quarter, the Buckeyes began to regain their confidence late in the half, and by intermission the Sooners lead had been whittled down to 20–14.

The Buckeye Express continued to roll in the third period. Woody's boys scored twice more, and as the fourth quarter got under way Oklahoma was staring into a 28–20 deficit with an offense that had not moved the ball since the first quarter. The two teams traded possessions until, with just over four minutes remaining, Reggie Kinlaw caused a Buckeye fumble and the Sooners were back in business at the OSU forty-three-yard line. Dean Blevins, who had been inserted at quarterback earlier, describes what happened next:

> We were down by eight points with around three minutes to go, but once we recovered that fumble, I felt an overwhelming confidence that had a great deal to do with Switzer's persona. Barry had an air about him that

people on the outside perceived as arrogance but the players recognized as supreme confidence. We were never coached in a negative way, and I always felt like that was one of the keys to Switzer's success. He was the kind of guy that when he went down the ramp, you *wanted* to follow him. He made us feel good about ourselves, and that translated into play-making on the field. And that aura surrounded us when we recovered their fumble late in the fourth quarter. We were able to complete some passes, move down the field, put Ohio State on their heels, and score. I believe that it was our confidence which made winning seem, at least to us, inevitable.[37]

The Sooners had scored, tightening both the game and 80,000 partisan throats in Ohio Stadium. But their two-point conversion attempt was stopped short of the goal line, and the score remained Ohio State 28, Oklahoma 26. With the clock running down, the Sooners had no choice but to try an onside kick, a play that would come as no surprise to Woody or his players. There was little arc on Von Schamann's kick as the ball bounced into the waiting hands of Ohio State's Ricardo Volley, who mishandled it. When the intertwined pile of Sooners and Buckeyes was finally disassembled at the fifty-yard line, Oklahoma's Mike Babb held the ball victoriously over his head—and the Sooners were still alive. On the first play, Blevins fired a dart to Steve Rhodes, who fought his way to the OSU thirty-three-yard line. Next, King busted through the heart of the Buckeye line for seven yards, and with six seconds remaining Oklahoma called a time-out and sent von Schamann onto the field. Hebert got into position to receive and hold the ball, and von Schamann poised himself off at an angle when Ohio State called a time-out. As the Sooners stood on the field awaiting resumption of the game, a chant began to arise from the 80,000 in attendance at Ohio Stadium: "Block that kick! Block that kick!" over and over, in perfect cadence. Von Schamann tells the story:

I've never told anyone this before. My friend and roommate was Bud Hebert. Now everyone else refers to that field goal as "the Kick," but Bud calls it "the Hold" because he was holding the ball for me. When we woke up the morning of the game, he said he'd had a dream the night before and he'd dreamed I was going to win the game. So right before I went out onto the field to make that winning field goal, I went over to Bud and I told him I was going to make his dream come true. And then, after Woody Hayes called their time-out, I went into the huddle and straight over to my buddy Sammy Jack Claphan, shook his hand, and said, "don't worry about it . . . I've got it." Then I walked back out of the huddle—and that's when I heard the crowd chanting, "Block that kick!" My helmet was off at the time, but I put it on, raised my arms, and began leading the chant. After that game, I never did it again. If I'd missed that kick, I would have had to move back to Germany.[38]

Uwe did not miss; the forty-one-yard kick had plenty of distance and bisected the goalposts perfectly. With three seconds remaining, Oklahoma had regained the lead 29–28. The field was covered with prostrate Buckeyes, the crowd was in shock, and the Sooners—staff and players alike—stormed the field in celebration. "When Uwe made that kick," remembers Billy Sims, "you could've heard a rat kissing cotton in that stadium. And when the game ended, we got the hell off that field, too."[39] After a final Buckeye desperation pass, the game ended, and Ohio State went down to defeat. "After the way Hayes had snubbed me before the game, you can just imagine how sweet that victory was for me!" recalls Hochevar. He continues:

Uwe calls it "the Kick," Bud calls it "the Hold," but it should be referred to as "the Protection," because without the offensive line protecting them, neither would have happened. Our line blocked their asses off to get the ball down into field goal range late in that game. And with all the talk about that play, I've never heard our offensive line given any credit for the job they did against a great Buckeye defensive front. But that's just the way it goes with the offensive line; if you block your asses off, the backs get the credit and if you don't, then it's the offensive line's fault if they get their butts kicked. I always told our guys, "It's amazing what you can accomplish if no one cares who gets the credit," so our guys never expected any credit.[40]

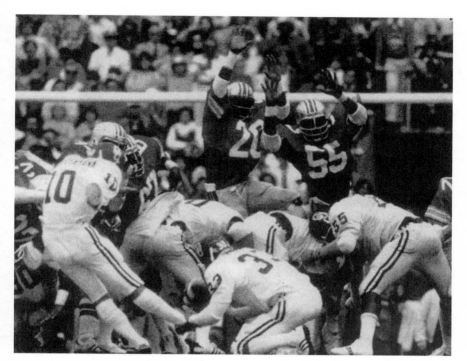

"The Kick." Courtesy Uwe von Schamann.

In the postgame locker room, a reporter told King that Hayes had commented, "We may have lost the game but at least we shut up that cocky little fullback." "My response," recounts King, "was, 'He may have shut up this cocky little fullback, but the outcome of the game was still 'we win, you lose.'"[41] Switzer awarded game balls to the entire defense. "Von Schamann," he beamed, "gets a kiss."[42] When the October 3, 1977, issue of *Sports Illustrated* hit the stands the following week, an airborne Billy Sims was featured on the cover. "But Uwe should have been on it instead of me," he reflects.[43]

The game had been one for the record books, one for eternity. Dan Lauck of *Newsday Long Island* wrote, "Oklahoma's football team can be down by eight, have its quarterback in plaster-of-paris, stuck in a hole, the clock inside of one minute, and still every Oklahoman from the panhandle east expects them to win."[44] So impressive in its display and result, the victory had vaulted the Sooners from third to first in the national polls.

But they would not have long to bask in the sun. After dealing Kansas a

24–9 loss in Norman, Oklahoma would fall to the Longhorns for the first time in seven years, 13–6. Texas's Russell Erxleben and Uwe von Schamann played one another to a tie, each kicking two field goals, but Longhorn Earl Campbell—who would win the Heisman Trophy that season—pounded the Sooner defense for 124 yards and scored Texas's only touchdown. The loss dropped the Sooners to seventh nationally, but they immediately began their climb back up the national ladder, rung by rung, by running the Big Eight Conference table, defeating Missouri (21–17), Iowa State (35–16), Kansas State (42–7), Oklahoma State (61–28), Colorado (52–14), and Nebraska (38–7). By the end of the regular season, Oklahoma was checking in at number two in the AP poll, hot on the heels of top-ranked and undefeated Texas. As winners of the Big Eight—their sixth consecutive conference crown—the Sooners had once again earned a berth in the Orange Bowl where they would play sixth-ranked Arkansas.

The Razorbacks had just wrapped up a 10–1 season under first-year head coach Louis Leo "Lou" Holtz. Already installed as an underdog in the New Year's Day classic, the line moved from seven to seventeen points after Holtz dismissed four offensive starters from his squad the week prior to the game. And as difficult as it was for the fans to consider Arkansas a viable opponent for mighty Oklahoma, it was even harder for the Sooners themselves to bring their "A" game to the table. The result was a fiasco. Even though Oklahoma learned prior to the game that the number one team in the land, Texas, had fallen and the door to the national title lay wide open, the Razorbacks razor-strapped Oklahoma that evening 31–6. Sooner fumbles in their own end of the field early in the game had set the stage for an Arkansas offensive onslaught. Larry Lacewell discusses the game:

> Arkansas had played Texas as tough as we did that year; they lost 13–9, and we lost 13–6, which should tell you that both Oklahoma and Arkansas were comparable. Late in the season we had beaten Colorado and Nebraska badly, but you have to bear in mind that both of these teams were not up to their usual standards. And all of a sudden, we look great but we actually weren't any better than we'd been all year, which was good . . . but not great. And then Arkansas suspends two running backs

who are as average as the day is long, but that's relatively inconsequential because their football team has been built around a good quarterback, a great kicker, and a great defense. We usually held light practices for bowl games before leaving home but, hell, that wasn't anything new; that was always the way we handled it. We had prepared for Michigan that way. But when we got to the site, we always busted our asses. We practiced harder than most bowl teams do. However, before the Arkansas game, we had the damndest time getting our players' attention; it didn't matter what we tried—we could've told them we were playing the Green Bay Packers, we could have threatened them with a baseball bat—it wouldn't have mattered. We could *not* make our players understand what they were facing; they were totally convinced that it would be a walk-over.[45]

But Kenny King had a different take on the game. He explains:

Did we take Arkansas for granted? No. We'd been to the Orange Bowl two years earlier; we knew the stakes and realized that it was a big, big deal. You don't take anything for granted in a game like that. It's been over thirty years, and there's been much speculation about what happened, and I hate to fan the flames of controversy, but I will make one comment about it: we broke the Wishbone and put Peacock at a wing position, and we ran a reverse. Now, we've never used that formation before or run that play ever before . . . *ever!!* When Dan Hampton, defensive tackle for Arkansas, sees Peacock going out on the wing he stands up and shouts, "Reverse Peacock reverse!" So yeah, I believe they knew our game plan. We were told that our game plan was left lying on a table specifically for the Arkansas coaches to pick up. After my playing days were done, I was coaching alongside a guy who'd been on the Arkansas staff, and he confirmed that that had happened. Otherwise, how in the hell do you explain Roland Sales—who hadn't done anything before then and hasn't done anything since—getting 205 yards against the Oklahoma defense?[46]

King's evaluation of Sales was accurate. Leading up to the bowl game in 1977,

Sales, a sophomore, had gained only 399 yards, had virtually disappeared from the record books his junior year, and rushed for only 625 yards his senior year.[47] But whatever the reason for Sales's Orange Bowl success, the suggestion that an Oklahoma playbook might have been intentionally provided to the Arkansas staff and played a key role in the loss is disturbing. Lacewell responds to the allegation:

Did they have our playbook? They could have—I had playbooks for lots of other teams. But I'll tell you what they *did* have that was more valuable than a playbook; they'd already played two great Wishbone teams that season, Monte Kiffin knew our offense from his days at Nebraska, and they had a month to prepare for us. But even though Kiffin was a great defensive coach, in all the years he'd played against us at Nebraska he always had a hard time stopping our Wishbone. So then he takes the same job at Arkansas under Holtz. Now, in the spring of 1977—eight months prior to that bowl game—Monte and I got together to compare defensive notes; our collaboration was simply a courtesy that college teams extend to one another. I couldn't wait to visit with him about his defense, and he couldn't wait to visit with me to learn how to stop the Wishbone because at Arkansas, he knew he would be playing Texas and Texas A&M—both Wishbone teams. Now at that time, we never *dreamed* that we'd be playing Arkansas in a bowl; it'd never happened before. So, I taught them every nuance about the Wishbone. And then, lo and behold, in December we find out we've got to play 'em! I remember going into the meeting at halftime during the Orange Bowl game and Galen Hall said to me, "Thanks a lot, Lace." Think what you want, but the bottom line is this: what was responsible for us getting our asses whipped was that they were a very well-prepared football team, they had a great defensive scheme, I called a shitty defensive game, and we got beat.[48]

The loss on New Year's Day 1978 was a difficult pill to swallow for the people of Oklahoma. After finding their team on the threshold of a sixth national title with only lowly Arkansas—a seventeen-point underdog—blocking the way, the game had been considered a foregone conclusion. But the Sooners had not only lost, but had lost badly. The offense had been unable to coordinate any sustained attack, and the defense had been unable to stop the Hogs from running wild. Gene Hochevar recounts his feelings about the game:

> That Arkansas game was the worst defeat I've ever been associated with in my life. It affected me more than any other setback I ever suffered. I mean, after that game for months . . . years . . . every time I thought about it I'd just want to vomit. I consider Lou Holtz to be the master of deceit; he came into that game with his card tricks and his bullshit and lulled everybody to sleep. He kicked four players off of the team the week before the game, and all he did was whine and cry, and our team fell for it; the players believed we were just going to go into that game and kick their asses with ease. After that game, I was absolutely physically sick; I went back to the hotel and didn't sleep all night. The next night we were committed to attending a country club celebration; I didn't eat, dance, or smile once, and this feeling stuck with me. No single event in the game of football has ever affected me more, before or since.[49]

1977 had been an unusual year for Oklahoma football. Getting off to a rough start against Vanderbilt, coming back to look like world-beaters in Columbus, and then losing to Texas had instilled in the Sooners a melodramatic sense of uncertainty. Then coming back to decisively sweep the Big Eight Conference had given them a misleading sense of accomplishment that had nudged them ever closer to the same overconfidence that had plagued the 1975 Sooners before their epiphanous loss to Kansas. In 1977, Oklahoma had begun the season number one and had finished ranked seventh, a result that would have pleased most college football teams. But Oklahoma was not most college football teams.

∵

Early in 1978, Larry Lacewell, Jerry Pettibone, and Gene Hochevar left the staff. To fill the positions, Switzer promoted Rex Norris, Gary Gibbs, Lucious Selmon, and Donnie Duncan.[50] When the Sooners began spring practice, Thomas Lott was firmly entrenched at quarterback, and sophomore Julius Caesar "J. C."

Watts was backing him up. Although Dean Blevins had lost his job after a tentative start in 1976 followed by an incapacitating illness, he was able to graduate knowing that his record as a starter was unblemished; he had run a 7–0 table, and, more importantly, he had stepped in and helped his team win two classic contests with his clutch passing: the 1976 Nebraska game and the 1977 Ohio State game.

On offense, the Sooners returned Greg Roberts, Paul Tabor, Sam Claphan, Louis Oubre, Victor Hicks, Steve Rhodes, Bobby Kimball, Kent Bradford, Mark Lucky, and Jody Farthing. On defense, the cast included George Cumby, Daryl Hunt, Phil Tabor, Tony Antone, Basil Banks, Sherwood Taylor, Greg Sellmyer, Darrol Ray, Mike Babb, Barry Burget, Jay Jimerson, Reggie Mathis, Bruce Taton, Bud Hebert, Barry Dittman, Rusty Griffis, and Reggie Kinlaw. The sophomore season of the quick and strong Kinlaw had ended when he tore ligaments in his knee during the Colorado game, and in the season opener with Vanderbilt his junior year he reinjured the same knee. He was advised to have more surgery but elected to play with the pain, knowing that it could cost him permanent injury. With the start of the 1978 season, he had declared himself 100 percent and was ready to enjoy his first season free from injury.[51] The iron-nerved Uwe von Schamann was on hand to do the placekicking. With Lott in the backfield were Kenny King, David Overstreet, Freddie Nixon, Jimmy Rogers, and Vickey Ray Anderson. "After the loss in the Orange Bowl," remembers Kenny King, "the seniors on our team felt like 1978 was going to be our year and that this team would be our team."[52]

At long last healthy after battling several debilitating injuries, Billy Sims finally returned to the field. As a high schooler, Sims had been the top-rated running back in the state of Texas, having gaining an astonishing 7,000 career yards. Born and raised in St. Louis, Sims grew up more a baseball fan than a football fan, playing sandlot ball with his friends under the shadow of the Arch. He talks about his plans to attend Baylor after high school:

I loved baseball; I dreamed of being the next Bob Gibson. Growing up in St. Louis, that's all we played. And then, when I was in eighth grade, I moved to Hooks, Texas, and lived with my grandparents. I didn't even *begin* playing football until the ninth grade. But I had a great high school career and in my senior year, my grandmother became very close to Baylor head coach Grant Teaff; she was a Baptist, she attended a Baptist Church, and Baylor was a Baptist University, so that's where she wanted me to go and that's where I had planned to go.[53]

But that was before Switzer went to work on him. He spent time with Sims, spoke with him as often as prevailing rules would allow, and eventually persuaded him—and his grandmother, Miss Sadie—that if Sims wanted to play on a championship team and have an opportunity to realize his full potential, Baylor could not compete with Oklahoma. "At Oklahoma," explains Switzer, "we had the supporting cast to give him the opportunity to achieve his goals." Barry relates an incident that happened when he was recruiting Sims:

Billy worked at C. J.'s Conoco Service Station out on I-30 [outside of Hooks, Texas], and he was working on the Saturday we were playing up in Boulder. We had a pretty good lead on Colorado at halftime, so I went into the locker room and used the pay phone to call him. C. J. answered, and I told him I needed to talk with Billy, so he went outside where Billy was pumping gas, and I could hear him yell, "Hey, Billy, Coach wants to talk to you!" Well, Billy knew I'd be in Colorado with the team, so he comes to the phone to see if it was really me and I told him I was calling him from the locker room in Boulder at halftime—that was how much I wanted him to come to Oklahoma. We talked through halftime until he finally heard the official come up, tap me on the shoulder, and say, "Coach, you've only got five minutes to get your team back on the field." So I said to him, "Billy, I've got to go finish this ass-kicking." He knew I couldn't have been talking to anyone else during halftime, that he was top priority. But when signing day rolled around, I had a problem; Billy chose Oklahoma, and he wanted me to be at his high school on signing day to sign him first . . . and so did Kenny King down in Clarendon, Texas. So I told Billy that if he'd hide out and not sign on the first day, it would build interest and anticipation and when he *did* sign, he'd have everyone's attention focused on him. He agreed, so I signed Kenny on national signing day and Billy two days later.[54]

On September 7, the fourth-ranked Sooners packed their bags for Palo Alto for their season opener with Stanford. The Cardinals, coached by Bill Walsh, was fresh off of a 9–3 season and a Sun Bowl victory over LSU. Although a fourteen-point favorite, Oklahoma had to scramble to preserve the 35–29 victory. The Sooners moved up to third in the nation, and, after back-to-back shellackings of West Virginia and Rice combined with number one Alabama's loss to Southern Cal, Oklahoma found itself occupying the top spot in the AP poll. The next weekend's 45–23 blasting of Missouri in Norman set the stage for the latest showdown with Texas in Dallas. The undefeated Longhorns were ranked sixth in the nation with victories over Rice, Wyoming, and Texas Tech.

On the Sooners' second play of the afternoon, King busted free for fifty-five yards behind a devastating block by Paul Tabor. Three plays later, Sims scurried eighteen yards for the game's first touchdown.[55] Behind Lott's precision quarterbacking, Oklahoma never allowed the game's outcome to fall into doubt, and when Lott's injured ankle forced him from the game with ten minutes remaining J. C. Watts filled in beautifully with a thirty-seven-yard touchdown drive of his own. OU prevailed 31–10, solidifying its grip on the top spot in the AP poll while Texas, now 3–1, fell to twelfth. Sims, who had entered the game with 420 yards rushing, gathered another 131 against the Horns and was beginning to attract national attention. But the victory was not without its price; Lott, King, Rhodes, and Hicks suffered injuries that threatened to sideline them indefinitely.

The next weekend, Oklahoma traveled to Lawrence to play 1–4 Kansas. J. C. Watts started in place of Lott, and Fred Nixon subbed for the injured Rhodes. What should have been a routine game turned into a donnybrook as penalties, fumbles, and mental errors led to a near disaster for the Sooners. In the final fifteen seconds of the game, Jayhawk quarterback Harry Sydney beat the Sooner defense with a pass to the end zone, bringing Kansas to within one point, 17–16. The ensuing point after attempt turned into a gut-wrenching comedy of errors. KU coach Bud Moore elected to go for the win with a two-point conversion, but the Jayhawks' first attempt took too much time and they were penalized. With the ball now at the eight-yard line, Kansas decided to take the kick and the tie, but the Sooners jumped before the snap, causing the kick to go awry. Oklahoma was penalized for being offsides, and the ball went back to the three where, once again, Moore decided to go for two points. The pass sailed over the head of the Jayhawk receiver, and OU escaped with a 17–16 victory.[56]

As the Sooners prepared for their game with Iowa State, Billy Sims found himself running neck-to-neck with USC's Charles White in the Heisman Trophy race. Taking a rushing total of 743 yards (a 7.1 yards per tote average) into Ames, Sims did little to damage his shot at the Heisman as he ran roughshod through the Cyclones defense for 231 yards while his team—with Lott and King back in the lineup—took home a 34–6 victory. The following two weekends, Oklahoma downed Kansas State (56–19) and Colorado (28–7) with Sims gathering in another 423 total yards. The undefeated top-ranked Sooners were on a collision course with 8–1, fourth-ranked Nebraska.

Entering the 1978 game with the Huskers, Oklahoma had not lost in Lincoln since 1970, but the last three games played in Lancaster County had been nail-biters for Sooner players and fans alike. The 1978 game would be no different in nature but would differ in result. Although Oklahoma outrushed the Huskers, the difference in the game would be errors; the Sooners put the ball on the turf a staggering ten times, losing six. Nebraska's unheralded quarterback, Tom Sorley, would complete eight passes while the Sooners would only attempt two and complete none. While the Husker defense played a heavy role in Oklahoma's fumbles and subsequent loss, Sorley's play against a tough Oklahoma defense—he overcame five third-and-long situations in the Huskers' three scoring drives—made the difference in the game. And with the clock rapidly bleeding late in the game and the Sooners trailing 17–14, Sims took a pitchout from Lott and skirted right end for thirteen yards before losing the ball to the Huskers at the NU three. Sims comments, "Even after I fumbled on the three-yard line with three minutes left in the game, we've still got them pinned deep in their own territory. We had a chance to hold them and get the ball back. But on their second offensive play, one of our defensive backs commits a personal foul that gave 'em fifteen yards and a first down. That lets them run the clock out.

But that day, I sure made a lot of fans in Nebraska."[57]

"People always remember that fumble of Billy's late in the game," reflects Lott. "But there were nine more that people don't seem to remember; I fumbled twice, 'Street fumbled twice, Billy fumbled twice, Jimmy Rodgers fumbled once, and we lost six of the ten. Any team that loses six fumbles to us will have half-a-hundred laid on them. But then, even after all those fumbles, we're *still* moving in to win the game in the final minutes."[58] As difficult as the number of turnovers were to accept for the Sooners and their fans, King looked upon the situation as a natural by-product of the high-risk, dangerous Wishbone. He considered the risk entailed by the rapid-fire ball exchange between quarterback and running back as a sort of "live by the sword, die by the sword" proposition. "At Oklahoma, we were going to put the ball on the ground at least five or six times a game. I caused a lot of those fumbles because while Thomas was riding me into the line I was yanking and tugging at that ball, all the while shouting at him, 'I can get ten, I can get fifteen!' Hell, I wanted the damned ball!" laughs King.[59]

King would get the ball enough the following weekend to gain 120 yards against Oklahoma State; but his numbers paled in comparison to the overall team figure of 629 yards rushing, 63 passing in the 62–7 gullywasher. Lott and Overstreet also had their numbers, but Sims outdid himself as he broke the conference rushing record set by Terry Miller in 1977 midway through the second quarter on his way to 209 yards for the day; in the first half alone, Billy gained 156 yards and scored four touchdowns. (Miller's record, 1,680 yards, had required 314 carries while Sims's new record, 1,762, was accomplished on only 231 touches.) Other records set in the game were most interceptions for a season—seven—by Darrol Ray (tying Huel Hamm in 1942, Darrell Royal in 1949, Steve Barrett in 1967, and Zac Henderson in 1977) and most first downs—thirty-six—for a Sooner team in one game. Von Schamann set an NCAA record with most consecutive successful career point after touchdown conversion kicks with 125.

As the Sooners were busy taking Oklahoma State to the woodshed, second-ranked Nebraska was being upended by Missouri, 35–31. The upset added new options to Oklahoma's bowl picture. The Sooners had planned to accept a Cotton Bowl invitation to play Houston, but after Nebraska's loss to Missouri, OU was once again in the Orange Bowl picture—not as the Big Eight champion but as the visiting team. After receiving the invitation from the Orange Bowl committee at 5:00 P.M., Switzer allowed the team to pick its bowl of choice, and the Orange Bowl—and another shot at Nebraska—was the unanimous choice. The ebullient Sims jumped onto a dressing room bench and shouted, "That's the one I want! I can't believe it!"[60] To Nebraska, the matchup was a bitter pill to swallow; after five straight losses to Oklahoma, Tom Osborne, having just notched his first victory in the series, had insult added to injury when he was notified within hours of his loss to Missouri that he would be tasked with playing his nemesis from Norman again. But the Sooners were delighted at the turn of events. "As we looked ahead to the Orange Bowl," recalls King, "we knew what was going to happen, and so did Nebraska."[61] It was the first time—and remains the last time—that a rematch would be played in the Orange Bowl.

Before the bowl game, there was other business with which to attend. Just after Thanksgiving, Billy Sims became the third Oklahoma Sooner to win the Heisman Trophy. The award was a personal triumph for Sims who—despondent over nagging injuries—had quit school in 1976. He reflects on the situation:

I was injured and out of the lineup, and I was ready to go back to Hooks. The coaches weren't talking to me, and I didn't know how to handle it. But Coach Switzer saw something in me that I didn't realize at the time. He had a lot of faith in me, and he stuck by me. In my first year to see playing time, 1977, I only had about 400 yards rushing, so nobody in their wildest dreams thought I would win the Heisman in 1978, except for Barry Switzer; he told me when he recruited me that I would win it. Of course, he told Kenny King and Thomas Lott the same thing.[62]

The Sooners, so fumble prone in their November 11 loss to the Huskers, did not put the ball on the ground a single time in the Orange Bowl. Oklahoma's relentless offense and stiff defense made the game a foregone conclusion early on in the 31–24 victory. And the game had not been nearly as close as the final score implied; with nine minutes remaining in the game, Nebraska trailed 31–10 and added its last two scores in garbage time. "The only conclusion you can draw is that Nebraska got lucky in Lincoln," comments King. "We beat them 31–24 in the bowl, and we could've beaten them worse if Barry hadn't called off the dogs. From start to finish, we went out and took control of that football game."[63] In the postgame locker room, Switzer awarded everyone on the team a game ball and declared, "You're the best team in the nation. You are the only team that can say you've beaten every team on your schedule."[64]

The 1978 Sooners had occupied the number one position in the Associated Press poll from September 25 through their late-season loss to the Huskers. It had been the best performance by an Oklahoma team since 1975. "In our three years, I honestly don't believe our team became completely cohesive until 1978," reflects King.[65] Billy Sims and Greg Roberts were consensus All-Americans; Reggie Kinlaw and Daryl Hunt were All-Americans; Sims, Roberts, Hunt, and Kinlaw made All Big Eight Conference along with Thomas Lott, Uwe von Schamann, Reggie Mathis, Phil Tabor, Darrol Ray, and George Cumby. Additionally, Greg Roberts became the fourth Sooner to win the Outland Trophy. Sims was named the Helms and Citizens Savings Athletic Foundation Player of the Year, won the Davey O'Brien Award, and became the third Sooner to win the Walter Camp Trophy. And Uwe von Schamann, although not receiving any official awards, had not missed a point after attempt since the Ford administration.

Thomas Lott, 2010. Courtesy Thomas Lott.

In 2010, Billy Sims still good-naturedly recalls his last-minute fumble on the three-yard line in Lincoln. "Thirty years later, people still remember that fumble!"[66] he remembers, laughing and shaking his head. What he does not consider is that there is one thing Sooner fans will remember far longer than that fumble: the forty-fourth John Heisman Memorial Trophy and the man who won it.

17 Julius Caesar and the Sooner Empire

JANUARY 1979–JANUARY 1981

The glow had hardly subsided from the Orange Bowl victory when assistant head coach Donnie Duncan announced that he had accepted the head coaching job at Iowa State. Cyclone head coach Earle Bruce had resigned five days earlier to fill the vacancy left in Columbus by the departure of the venerable and cantankerous Woody Hayes. To replace Duncan, Switzer enticed friend and former Arkansas staff member Merv Johnson to leave his position at Notre Dame and come to Norman, where he would assume Duncan's duties as offensive line coach and assistant head coach. The rest of the coaching staff remained relatively static. Galen Hall—with Switzer, the last holdover from Mackenzie's 1966 staff—continued to coach the offense; Bill Shimek and part-time coach Wendell Mosley helped with the offensive backfield; Mike Jones coached the wide receivers and headed recruiting; Rex Norris continued as defensive coordinator assisted by Lucious Selmon, who handled the defensive line; Warren Harper, Gary Gibbs, and Bobby Proctor tutored the secondary and linebackers; and part-time coach Scott Hill assisted with the defensive backs.[1]

As is the norm in college football every few years, the coaches once again found themselves in the position of replacing a nucleus of talented, experienced players. Thomas Lott, Kenny King, Greg Roberts, Sammy Jack Claphan, Reggie Kinlaw, Uwe von Schamann, Victor Hicks, Daryl Hunt, Bobby Kimball, Reggie Mathis, and Phil Tabor had cast their last long shadow on the afternoon turf in Memorial Stadium, and new talent found their way onto the playing field. Terry Crouch and Louis Oubre, both battle-tested linemen, would take over starting position in the offensive line; Forrest Valora replaced Hicks at tight end; Barry Joyner and Stanley Wilson would vie for the fullback position; and Steve Rhodes returned at wide receiver alongside Freddie Nixon. Cumby was back at linebacker, and Barry Dittman assumed the spot vacated by the peerless Daryl Hunt; John Goodman and Richard Turner were positioned at defensive tackle; Johnnie Lewis replaced Reggie Kinlaw at noseguard; Darrol Ray and Sherwood Taylor returned at safety; Basil Banks covered the corner; John Hoge and Mike Keeling were competing for placekicking duties; and Darrol Ray would be punting. Running back appeared more than solid with David Overstreet returning, supported by a group of talented freshmen including Chet Winters, Jay McKim, and Weldon Ledbetter. Although the returning cast was talented, the Sooners nearly lost their "crown jewel." Sims, after spending four years on campus including a medical redshirt year in 1976, had decided to forego his final year of college and enter the NFL draft. Billy had become more than a player to his head coach; Switzer nurtured the young man, even standing for him at his wedding officiated by Dean Blevins's father, Dexter. Switzer talks about what he calls the "Re-recruiting of Billy Sims":

Billy came to me after 1978 to talk about getting an agent and going pro; he told me that it was purely a monetary issue. He said, "Coach, I'm in debt. I'm married, my car's in the shop, Brenda's laid off work, and I've got this and this and this." When I asked him how much he needed to stabilize his situation, he told me $1,500. The players that leave school today to go pro sign multimillion-dollar deals, and if he'd been getting that kind of signing bonus I would have encouraged him to leave; but back then, it wasn't anything remotely close to that kind of money. So we talked about his situation and I told him two things he should consider; he could come back to school for his senior year and win a second Heisman, but whether he won it again or not he would still be the number one pick when he did enter the draft. And I also told him I'd promised Miss Sadie—his grandmother who'd cared for him in Hooks, Texas, and had recently passed away—that he would finish college. She had cared about only two things—Billy himself and his college degree; she had wanted him to be the first one in the family to finish his education. I reminded him that we had both made her that promise. I knew that if he left school he would never return to fulfill that vow; very few kids ever do. I hadn't given him a penny to come to Oklahoma, but I did help him out; I told him I'd take care of it, and I gave him the $1,500 and that settled it. He was able to remain in school and graduate.[2]

With Wishbone perfectionist Thomas Lott gone, the Sooners turned to a young man with an unusual name to pick up the slack: Julius Caesar "J. C." Watts. The first black quarterback to play for Eufaula High School, Watts led them to an 11–2 season and the state playoffs his senior season, earning him High School Player of the Year honors from both the *Daily Oklahoman* and the *Tulsa World*. The Sooners, always on the lookout for talented multifaceted quarterbacks, had J. C. affixed squarely in their crosshairs in the spring of 1976; Switzer had seen the young man play and realized that he not only could operate a triple option but also could add a viable fourth option to the offense: the pass.

After casting his lot with Oklahoma, Watts found the transition difficult, quitting school and returning twice before settling in and performing admirably in a backup role to Thomas Lott in 1978. In 1979, he became the starting quarterback with sophomores Kelly Phelps and Rod Pegues in support. Highly regarded quarterback Darrell Shepard, who had transferred to Oklahoma from the University of Houston in the wake of a recruiting scandal that resulted in probation for the Cougars, had to sit out the 1979 season in compliance with NCAA regulations.[3] Future Sooner star player and head coach John Blake—a highly touted freshman on the '79 team—was given the opportunity to try out at fullback. "But the coaches convinced me I wasn't a fullback," said Blake. "And they kept complimenting me in the drills at nose guard, so I guess nose guard's best for me."[4] Also unique among those seeking fame as walk-ons were university president William Banowsky's son Britton and thirty-eight-year old George McQuire—who had last tried to qualify for Wilkinson's team in 1957; neither would make the cut.[5]

"Anytime you start a season with a new quarterback, it can get a little tricky," explains Watts. "We had lost Lott who was a Wishbone wizard. But in '79 we had a good defense, and we had, of course, Billy Sims; so if I don't screw up the snap I knew we'd be okay."[6]

Oklahoma prevailed 21–6 in its season opener against Hayden Fry's Iowa Hawkeyes. Although the Sooners reverted to their careless ways during the game, losing five of seven fumbles, Sims rushed for 106 yards and Watts passed for 183. But errant pitchouts were not the most important loss suffered by Oklahoma on the afternoon. Steve Rhodes explains what happened:

We were trying to get into field goal position late in the first half. I was lined up on the Iowa sideline when I heard one of their coaches screaming to his safety, "Come over! Come over!" to where I was; he was calling out the exact route I was going to run. And I'm shaking my head and thinking, "Oh, man!" I knew I was going to get hit hard on the play. Then when J. C. threw the ball, it sailed on him, and I could see it was going to go about eight feet over my head. Now, I knew the safety was charging in on me, and I'm thinking, "I know I can't possibly catch it, but should I jump for it?" I knew if I *didn't* jump for it I might be perceived as not trying hard enough, so I jumped, and when I did the defensive back hit me right above the ankle with his helmet and flipped me over: That defensive back was Bob Stoops. I had broken my fibula, so I was granted a medical hardship and came back in 1980 for my fifth season.[7]

Hawkeye Bob Stoops hurdles over the line in pursuit of Billy Sims. Courtesy Jim Terry.

The Sooners had little trouble with their next three opponents, dropping Tulsa (49–13), Rice (63–21), and first-year Colorado head coach Chuck Fairbanks's Buffaloes (49–24) in short order. The next opponent, Texas, had already beaten 25 percent of the Big Eight Conference in 1979 by defeating Iowa State (17–9) and Missouri (21–0). Oklahoma would enter the game ranked third, and Texas would come in fourth; it would be the third straight year that both teams entered October with perfect records and the nineteenth time since the series became year-to-year in 1929. The Sooners were confident of their ability to move the football. In their first four games, they had averaged over 400 yards per contest. But the Texas defense, using an unpredictable combination of tricks and stunts, held the Sooners to 158 total yards in the 16–7 Longhorn victory. Texas had run eighty plays to OU's forty-nine, had used thirty-nine precious minutes of time to the Sooners' twenty-one, and had allowed Oklahoma to cross midfield but four times, and only one of those—a forty-seven-yard gallop by freshman Stanley Wilson—resulted in a scoring opportunity. "There were two major contributing factors to that loss," comments Watts. "First of all, they were as good as we were, and, secondly, we had at least seven turnovers, and I was probably responsible for some of those."[8] Further compounding the situation against Texas, the Sooners attempted to install complicated variations on their Wishbone offense. "We probably should have beaten them," reflects Merv Johnson, "but we outsmarted ourselves; we believed that Texas had our basic Wishbone attack down so well that we had to change it, so we tried to do some things that we weren't able to execute very well. We might have been better off just running a plain vanilla Wishbone."[9]

Despite dropping to eighth nationally after the loss, Oklahoma immediately picked up a head of steam for its charge through the Big Eight Conference. Sims, with his 579 total yards and a set of seriously bruised ribs, prepared for the stretch run in his Heisman-defending senior season. In the ensuing four weekends, Oklahoma would roll over Kansas State (38–6), Iowa State (38–9), Oklahoma State (38–7), and Kansas (38–0). Against Oklahoma State, a controversy had erupted the week leading up to the game. First-year Cowboy head coach Jimmy Johnson had suggested that Switzer, while visiting Lewis Field for OSU's season opener, had violated an NCAA rule by speaking with recruits attending the game at the invitation of the Cowboys, a charge Switzer vehemently denied. On game day, Oklahoma exacted a measure of revenge by scoring twenty-four unanswered points before the first half expired.

The Sooners staved off a determined Missouri team (24–22) the following weekend and found themselves hurtling headlong toward another showdown with Nebraska. Since 1964, the Huskers had traveled to Norman unbeaten on four occasions—1964, 1966, 1971, and 1975—and had left with losses every year except 1971. Norman had truly become the burial ground for Husker dreams. Sims entered the game with an accumulated rushing total for the season of 1,047; although having rushed for over 100 yards in six of ten games and over 200 in two, the low numbers he had posted against Texas (73), Kansas State (67), and Oklahoma State (71) had put him at a disadvantage in his race against Charles White of Southern California for the 1979 Heisman Trophy. Against the Huskers, Sims and the Sooners would be taking the field against a team that led the nation against the rush, allowing an average of only 67.2 yards per game and 1.6 yards per carry.[10] An emotional Switzer describes an encounter with Sims the week of the Nebraska game:

I'll never forget this. We were getting ready to play Nebraska for the Big Eight Championship, and on Thursday before the game Billy was trailing Charles White for the national rushing title and in the Heisman race. But then Billy exploded for 282 yards against Missouri on national television, and we needed every yard of it to win that game. So I went down and sat by him on the bench, and I told him how much I loved him and what a great career he'd had and what a pleasure it had been to recruit him and have him as a player. I told him that what he'd done the previous weekend had been unbelievable, but the team we were getting ready to play, Nebraska, led the nation in rushing defense, only giving up sixty-eight yards per game. I told him that beating them would take a hell of a performance by him and asked him if he had another one in him. He looked at me and said, "Coach, I saved the best for last." And by God, he had. The first time he touched the ball against Nebraska he went seventy yards for a touchdown, and it was called back. He rushed for 247 yards in that game, and to this day that's the most yards ever gained against Nebraska.[11]

Neither team had been able to score in the first quarter, but Oklahoma tallied in the second as Michael Keeling, who had won the placekicking job after the Texas game, booted a thirty-one-yard field goal, giving the Sooners a 3–0 edge. Not to be denied, the Huskers responded with a cross-country fifty-nine-yard drive to take a 7–3 lead at the half. In the third period, Watts found Valora with a fifty-eight-yard aerial to give the Sooners a 10–7 lead. Then, in the fourth quarter, OU mounted a giant-killing ninety-four-yard drive sparked by Sims's seventy-one-yard run. The next three plays netted only five yards, but on fourth down Watts kept the ball and ran left, shifted back to his right, and cut into the end zone. The Sooners held the 17–7 lead until Husker coach Tom Osborne unveiled his fumblerooski play, a feint borrowed from the playbook of Henry Frnka, an assistant on Vanderbilt's 1937 staff. On the play, the quarterback took the snap and immediately set the ball on the ground at the center's foot, where it was scooped up by Nebraska's right guard, Randy Schleusener, who ran it into the end zone.[12] Trick plays notwithstanding, the Huskers still went down to defeat, and Oklahoma, with its 17–14 victory, was Orange Bowl–bound.

Nine days following the Nebraska game, Charles White of USC became the forty-fifth Heisman Trophy winner. By season's end, White had averaged 6.2 yards per carry while amassing 1,803 yards and 18 touchdowns compared to Sims's 6.7 yards per carry with 1,506 yards and 22 six-pointers. Had the majority of Heisman voters not recorded their ballots prior to the Nebraska game, had they seen the full thrust of Sims's incredible performances against both Missouri and Nebraska, he might have won his second trophy. The news of White's selection was not popular in Oklahoma. J. C. Watts mirrored the predominant opinion by stating that the difference between Sims and White was like "the difference between steak and bologna." And although it was initially reported that Sims himself had reacted with anger at the news of White's selection, both Billy and his wife, Brenda, denied it. "He isn't upset," laughed Brenda. And a cheerful Sims told reporters, "My vote went to Charles White before the season was over. I think they made a good choice."[13]

Florida State had blown through their schedule like an ill wind in 1979, defeating iconic coach Charlie McClendon's LSU Tigers, Howard Schnellenberger's Miami Hurricane, and Charlie Pell's Florida Gators en route to their

Orange Bowl showdown with the fifth-ranked Sooners. In his fourth season in Tallahassee, Bobby Bowden had taken the bedraggled Seminoles from door-mats (they had won only one game in the two seasons prior to his arrival) to winners; since 1976, his teams had accrued a record of 34–11–0 and had not lost a game since mid-October 1978.

The game began badly for Oklahoma. In the first quarter, Basil Banks's dazzling fifty-nine-yard punt return ended when he was tackled from behind at the Florida State ten-yard line, where he fumbled the football through the end zone, resulting in a touchback. On its ensuing drive, FSU mounted an eighty-yard drive to take a 7–0 lead. On OU's next possession, Keeling's punt was blocked, giving Florida State the ball in the Sooner red zone. But Okla-homa's defense held, and the FSU field goal attempt was squashed when the hold was fumbled and the ball recovered by George Cumby. Florida State had dominated the first fifteen minutes, completing six of eleven passes, posting eight first downs to OU's one, and scoring the game's only touchdown. How-ever, from the botched field goal attempt through the remainder of the game, Florida State would manage only four first downs, would complete only two passes for twenty-four yards, and would not score again.

Starting with their first possession of the second quarter, the game belonged to Oklahoma. On two carries, Sims bulled his way to the FSU thirty-nine-yard line, and on the next play Watts broke free for a sixty-one-yard gallop to pay dirt. Thirty-six seconds later, with the score knotted at seven, Seminole quarterback Jimmy Jordan's pass was picked off by Bud Hebert—who personally made a shambles of the FSU air assault by intercepting three passes on the evening—setting OU up for its next strike, a five-yard run by Stanley Wilson. Keeling would add a field goal with three minutes remain-ing in the half to give OU a 17–7 lead at the break. The Sooners were equally relentless in the second half as they finished the game 24–7. Oklahoma had outgained the Seminoles 447 yards to 182 with Watts personally having his best day as a Sooner while rushing for 127 yards, earning him the Orange Bowl MVP award. "We had our way with FSU that day," recalls Watts. "I don't think they'd seen the kind of speed we had before. Our offensive line was terrific, and we dominated."[14]

After a disappointing loss to Texas, Oklahoma completed 1979 with a sweep of the Big Eight Conference, season-ending victories over the third- and fourth-ranked teams in the nation—both of whom were undefeated—an 11–1–0 record, and a third place finish in the AP poll. Switzer referred to 1979 as "one of my most satisfying seasons."[15] But with only three defensive starters returning the following September, 1980 promised to be one of his most challenging.

⁚

With nine offensive starters back in the fold in 1980, the Sooner attack promised to be strong and dangerous. Although Sims had departed, Oklahoma returned a solid quarterback in Watts; a quick, talented, and experienced runner in David Overstreet; a promising young back in Buster Rhymes; and depth at fullback with Weldon Ledbetter and Stanley Wilson. Receivers Bobby Grayson and Steve Rhodes would lead the receiver corps, and Forrest Valora, widely considered the best blocking tight end in America, was back. The offensive line was buttressed by tackles Louis Oubre, Ed Culver, and Lyndle Byford; guards Terry Crouch and Don Key; and center Bill Bechtold. The defensive line was manned by Richard Turner, Johnnie Lewis, Steve Whaley, Scott Dawson, Keith Gary, Orlando Flanagan, and Mike Weddington. Linebackers Mike Coast, Mike Reilly, and Sherdeill Breathett would be supported by defensive backs Darrell Songy, Basil Banks, Byron Paul, Gary Lowell, Steve Haworth, Jay Jimerson, and Ken Sitton.

Fumbles were once more the order of the day as the Sooners trailed the Kentucky Wildcats 7–0 at halftime in the 1980 season opener in Norman. With five minutes gone in the third quarter, Watts left the game with a deep thigh bruise, and Darrell Shepard joined the offense and led it to its first touchdown. After three quarters, the score remained tied at seven when Oklahoma capitalized on a turnover deep in Kentucky territory to score the go-ahead touchdown. The Sooners would need a safety and two more touchdowns to safely distance themselves from their opponents in the 29–7 victory. Although they had managed to salvage a game tarnished by errors against Kentucky, all the king's horses and all the king's men could not put the Sooners back together after losing five of six fumbles on a rain-soaked field against visiting

Stanford the next weekend. The Cardinals, with head coach Paul Wiggin and sophomore quarterback John Albert Elway, Jr., upended Oklahoma 31–14. The Sooners' defensive game plan, in anticipation of Elway's passing, had been to drop eight men back into passing formation, and it had nearly paid off. Merv Johnson comments, "It was John Elway's coming out party, and he had a good game in many ways, but people forget that he put himself in a position to lose. He hit our linebackers and coverage people right in the chest six times, but the balls were all dropped. And then he fumbled a quarterback sneak at the one yard line, but one of their players got it back and they went on to score. It was a game where, although Elway displayed his talents, he could very easily have been the goat."[16]

The Sooners, down 24–0 in the third quarter, marched the length of the field only to fumble the ball through the Stanford end zone for a touchback, a play that became representative of Oklahoma's bad fortune that afternoon. "You knew that John Elway had a special sauce about him," reflects Watts. "We just didn't play well offensively or defensively that day and of course, Elway had something to do with that."[17]

On October 4, Oklahoma traveled to the Rockies to participate in what has become known as the Great Boulder Horse Race. The Sooners vented their frustration over the Stanford fiasco against a woefully lacking Colorado defense by scoring an unheard-of twelve touchdowns, gaining 876 total yards (surpassing the 871-yard NCAA record set by Wyoming in 1949) and rushing for 758 yards (eclipsing the 748-yard NCAA record set by Alabama in 1973) in the 82–42 victory. The eighty-two points set a modern-day Sooner record, and the game as a whole set new NCAA records for most points scored (124) and most touchdowns (18). Adding embarrassment to the Buffaloes' injury, the Sooners rang up 35 first downs and averaged 10.4 yards per play.[18] "I remember Coach Switzer just feeling horrible about the Colorado game that year," remembers Watts. "We were running up and down the field on his former boss and friend, so he told Galen Hall not to run any more option plays and to stay away from the corners—he didn't want it to look like he was running up the score. He was just hurtin' for Fairbanks."[19]

The OU offense, supremely confident after the Colorado game, headed to

Dallas with a tailwind of momentum. But it did not take long for Texas to take the wind out of the Sooner sails as Oklahoma, committing six turnovers in the first half alone, entered the halftime locker room down 10–0; it was the third time in 1980 that OU had been shut out in the first half. Texas would finish the afternoon by extending its winning streak to two straight against Switzer with a 24–13 win. After the loss, the Sooners held a 2–2 record after four games—the worst early season mark posted by any Oklahoma team since pre-Wishbone days. They had plummeted to number seventeen in the AP poll amidst conference partners Iowa State (ranked nineteenth), Missouri (ranked sixteenth), and Nebraska (ranked tenth).

Freshman Buster Rhymes opened the game and the scoring by returning the opening kickoff one hundred yards for a touchdown the following week against Kansas State; his feat surpassed the previous school record of ninety-nine yards set by Jerome Ledbetter against Colorado two weeks earlier. Despite another six fumbles, Oklahoma surged to a 35–21 victory. Iowa State had surprised the conference by starting its season 5–0 in 1980, but it surprised no one when the Wildcats dropped their next game to Kansas and then lost to Oklahoma 42–7 the following weekend.

A rare midseason contest against a nonconference foe was next on the schedule when North Carolina traveled to Norman. Ranked sixth in the nation, the Tar Heels rolled into town on Friday with a 7–0 record and were unceremoniously driven out of town on Saturday in the wake of a 41–7 loss. Super defender Lawrence Taylor, later to gain fame in the National Football League, could do little to stop the Sooners from rolling for 388 rushing yards in the lopsided affair. And then in early November, Oklahoma survived two close calls—in Lawrence against Kansas (21–19) and in Norman against Missouri (17–7)—to set up yet another showdown with Nebraska.

As their team prepared to host Oklahoma, Husker fans' nerves were on edge—and not without good reason. They had witnessed the debacle in 1972 when Dave Robertson and Tinker Owens entered the sanctity of Memorial Stadium in Lincoln and snatched victory from the grasp of defeat in the second half; they had cringed in 1974 as Davis and Washington brought the Sooners back from a 14–7 second-half deficit for a 28–14 victory; they had watched in shocked disbelief as Blevins, Rhodes, and Peacock dashed their dreams in the last minutes in 1976; and though they emerged victorious in 1978, they had been forced to watch helplessly seven weeks later as Oklahoma usurped their enjoyment over that victory by beating them in the Orange Bowl. Tom Osborne—who had ascended to the throne in Lincoln in 1973, the same year Switzer took over in Norman—had only won a single game in the series. On November 22, 1980, the Sooners, a team twice beaten and clutching on to the ninth position in the AP poll, were preparing to square off against the fourth-ranked Huskers, a team that had only lost to Florida State in early October and was in the midst of a tight four-team race for the national title. Since that loss to the Seminoles, Nebraska had steamrolled its way through the Big Eight Conference, laying waste to Iowa State, Kansas State, Missouri, Colorado, Oklahoma State, and Kansas by a total score of 275–38. Oklahoma, installed as a twelve-point underdog, was given little serious hope of winning in Lincoln.

By the end of the first quarter, it appeared that the oddsmakers had been too conservative as Nebraska held onto a 10–0 lead. Late in the second quarter, Watts and Chet Winters each scored a touchdown, sending Oklahoma into the locker room with a 14–10 lead. Although the Huskers did not score, the third quarter belonged to their defense as Oklahoma failed to register a single first down. Midway through the final stanza, Nebraska, capitalizing on a short Sooner punt, crossed the OU goal line to take a 17–14 lead. Then lady luck—historically very fond of Oklahoma in Lincoln—decided to smile on the Sooners. With just over two minutes remaining in the game, Buster Rhymes broke free from his own forty-three-yard line and delivered the ball to the Nebraska fourteen before being tackled. "I just kept telling myself, 'No fumble! No fumble! No fumble!'" said Rhymes.[20] His mantra had worked—he did not fumble—and three plays later, Watts hit Bobby Grayson inches away from the Husker goal line. With fifty-six seconds left on the game clock, Rhymes leapt into the end zone for six points. The Sooner defense helped Nebraska drain the clock, and Oklahoma left town with another victory steeped in Sooner Magic.

The following weekend, Buster Rhymes set a new freshman season rushing record with 659 yards in the 63–14 win over Oklahoma State. The victory had also earned another conference crown for the Sooners and, with it, an invitation to the Orange Bowl for a rematch with second-ranked Florida State. The 10–1–0 Seminoles and the Sooners measured up well offensively—FSU had put 352 points on the board in 1980 compared to OU's 397—but the Seminoles had a clear edge on defense, having held all opponents to a mere 85 points while the Sooners had allowed 199. Florida State enjoyed another intangible advantage: revenge. In his fifth season at the helm in Tallahassee, Bobby Bowden had taken a team that had won only four games since 1972 to a leading role on the eastern gridiron; in 1979 and 1980—his Orange Bowl years—his record on the eve of the forty-seventh Miami classic stood at a resounding 21–2–0, exactly the same as Pittsburgh's and better than Penn State's 17–6–0 over the same time period. Among his losses at Florida State were two to the Sooners. The first, in 1976, had understandably come in Bowden's first season, but the second loss in the 1980 Orange Bowl, had been difficult; it had spoiled FSU's perfect season, a feat that, had it been accomplished, would have been the first in school history.

Two missed field goals resulted in a scoreless first quarter, but with forty-nine seconds remaining in the half Seminole running back Ricky Williams found a seam and lanced the Sooner defense for ten yards and a 7–0 lead. But as the clock ticked its last seconds away in the half, OU's Mike Keeling belted a fifty-three-yard field goal through the uprights, bringing Oklahoma to within four points at the break; the kick set a new Orange Bowl record, beating the previous mark of forty-four yards set by Penn State's Chris Bahr in 1974.

Watts led the Sooners on a seventy-eight-yard touchdown drive to open the third period, giving Oklahoma its first lead of the evening; but the advantage was short-lived as OU gave the ball back to Florida State minutes later deep in Sooner territory. The gift resulted in a Seminole field goal and a 10–10 tie. With neither team able to consistently move the ball, the rest of the third quarter remained scoreless. While attempting a punt early in the fourth period, Keeling mishandled the center snap, allowing the ball to shoot behind him and into the end zone, where Florida State recovered for the go-ahead touchdown. Trailing 17–10 and with a faltering, inconsistent offense, the situation appeared bleak for Oklahoma while across the field the FSU sideline erupted in celebration.

They had stifled the Sooner offense for most of the game and, knowing that they had not allowed a single fourth-quarter point in 1980, the Seminoles were confident that the game was all but over. Florida State continued to shackle Oklahoma's offense until the Sooners took possession of the ball on their own twenty-two-yard line. With 3:19 remaining, Watts entered the huddle. "I remember it as though it was yesterday," he recounts. "I don't think there was anybody in the huddle who didn't expect to win that game." Defying odds, Watts broke the 'Bone and embarked upon a tactic that no one suspected the Sooners could use successfully and consistently: the forward pass. Overcoming three third-and-long situations while deftly utilizing a mixture of scrambling and passing to Rhodes, Winters, and Rockford, "Caesar" led his legions to the Florida State twenty-one-yard line. "In that last drive I almost threw a couple of interceptions," says Watts. On a fullback screen pass, he had rolled out to his right, had looked back to his left, and suddenly had seen a defensive lineman bearing down on him. "And then I saw Weldon (Ledbetter) open and tried to get it to him, but I threw it to a noseguard instead. Thankfully, he didn't catch it—that's why those guys play defense and not wide receiver," remarks J. C.[21] The FSU player who dropped the interception was Garry Futch. "Always," said Futch, "That play will *always* be in my dreams."[22] After Futch's drop, Watts scrambled to the Florida State ten-yard line with less than a minute-and-a-half to play. Two plays later, he hit a diving Steve Rhodes in the end zone for the touchdown. With 1:25 left in the game, Oklahoma trailed Florida State 17–16. Watts describes what happened next: "After we scored there was no question that we would go for two; our field goal kicker wasn't even warming up. I remember Coach Switzer signaled us from the sidelines, just waving us back onto the field, saying, 'Hey, go for it!' We ran what we called the '741,' which was just a reverse-fake-option; the tight end blocks down like it's a run, and releases; and then there was old Forrest, just wide open in the end zone."[23]

Valora, who had been used primarily as a blocking back in the Wishbone, had been the perfect outlet for Watt's touch-pass. Watts had completed five of six passes on the final drive, giving the Sooners an 18–17 lead and, with it, the victory. It was the second time in the last three games that Oklahoma had been forced to come from behind late in the game against a top-five team with a stifling defense in a hostile environment. "I thought we had the game won," said Bowden. "It was ridiculous for a Wishbone team to throw the ball against us the way they did. They played an excellent game."[24]

J. C. Watts was named the Orange Bowl Most Valuable Player for the second consecutive year, an unprecedented achievement that has never been duplicated. In his two seasons as starting quarterback, Watts's Sooners compiled a 21–3–0 record and finished third in the nation each year. He had taken the baton from the class of Lott, Roberts, and King, preserved its integrity, and passed it on. And there were further honors for Switzer. For the job he had done by taking a team that had started the year with only three returning defensive starters and lost two of its first four games before turning it around and winning both the Big Eight Conference and the Orange Bowl, he was given the Football News Coach of the Year Award. But for the next three seasons, greater challenges would be in store for him.

18 New Decade, New Formation

JANUARY 1981–JANUARY 1984

"While there were Selmons playing at Oklahoma, I went 54–3–1," smiles Switzer.[1] But he had not done badly without Lucious, Lee Roy, and Dewey, either. After eight years on the job—five of those years without the benefit of a Selmon on campus—Barry Switzer's record stood at 83–9–2, an astounding 88 percent winning record. By comparison, Bud Wilkinson had posted a 73–8–3 record over his first eight seasons, an 87 percent winning record. And while Wilkinson had won one national title during those eight years, Switzer had garnered two, and both coaches had come within a hairbreadth of winning two more apiece—Wilkinson in 1949 and 1954, and Switzer in 1977 and 1978.

Early in the year, Switzer squelched rumors that he might be going to the Houston Oilers to replace fired Bum Phillips. "They fired Bum because he ran the ball too much," he said. "If I had Earl Campbell, I'd give it to him *every* play."[2]

After a brief courtship with John Robinson and USC in early 1981, coveted assistant coach Gary Gibbs decided to remain in Norman and accept a promotion to defensive coordinator, a post recently opened by Rex Norris's departure (Norris would return to the team as defensive line and assistant head coach before the 1981 season began). Gibbs's first defense would be very young but very talented. In the opening game against visiting Wyoming on September 12, 1981, five of eleven defenders would be sophomores. Of Ricky Bryan, Thomas Benson, Dwight Drane, Jackie Shipp, Barrion Walker, and Bob Slater, only Slater was a third-year sophomore—the rest were true second-year players. Johnnie Lewis and Mike Reilly, both seniors, were back; Darrell Songy and John Blake, juniors, played major roles; and sophomore John Truitt and promising freshmen Keith Stanberry, Kevin Murphy, Lawrence Hardin, Elbert Watts, and Tony Casillas would also figure prominently into Gibbs's plans.

On offense, fourth-year junior Kelly Phelps had won the starting quarterback job with Darrell Shepard in close support. Stanley Wilson returned at fullback; Buster Rhymes was at running back; Chet Winters and Weldon and Jerome Ledbetter were on hand; and freshmen Steve Sewell and Alvin Ross would also play supporting roles. The offensive strike team operated behind a senior-dominated offensive line consisting of guards Terry Crouch, Bill Bechtold, and Don Key (a junior), and tackles Lyndle Byford and Ed Culver.

It was mighty Wishbone versus tiny Wishbone on September 12 when Wyoming came to Norman. Cowboy head coach Al Kincaid had visited Norman two years earlier while an assistant at East Carolina to study the Sooners' Wishbone, but the knowledge he had gained could not avert a 37–20 loss to Oklahoma.[3] While Switzer appeared relatively pleased with the 37 offensive points and 515 yards produced by his offense, defensive secondary coach Bobby Proctor had a different slant on his team's performance. "The thing that really disappoints me," said Proctor, "is that our guys didn't bust their tails. We just seemed to be hanging in there and hoping we wouldn't get further behind. It's a shame that we don't have a fine secondary to complement our offense; everybody will be throwing the ball on us (this year)." The closer-than-anticipated victory had dropped the second-ranked Sooners to third in the wire service polls, a situation that seemed to bother the acerbic Proctor less than others. "Polls are for losers," he commented, "just like statistics."[4]

The Sooners had a two-week break before their next game, a bare-knuckles donnybrook with Southern California in the Coliseum. The Trojans, benefitting from tune-up victories over Tennessee (43–7) and Indiana (21–0), were ranked first in the nation while the Sooners had climbed back to second place during their off week. True freshman Keith Stanberry describes the feelings he experienced playing in the Coliseum for the first time: "Walking down the pitch-dark tunnel in the Coliseum, all we could hear was the 'click-click-clicking' of our cleats on the concrete. And then all of a sudden, we walked out of the tunnel and looked up and saw ninety thousand people in the stands—my hometown only had a population of about ten thousand—and the band is blaring that USC fight song; it was awe-inspiring. We were in a sea of cardinal red and gold, and we felt like we were walking on air."[5]

The game, with Keith Jackson and Frank Broyles announcing, complemented by ex-Sooner Steve Davis's sideline commentary, was broadcast by ABC to 90 percent of its affiliates. Switzer's 84–9–2 record made him the nation's winningest active coach by percentage (.895), and Robinson's 52–8–2 made him second (.855).[6]

Oklahoma led throughout the first half, holding on to a 17–14 lead at intermission. And with 13:08 remaining in the game, Darrell Shepard—who had replaced Phelps under center—scrambled across the Trojan goal line to give his team a 24–14 lead. But Southern California, outplayed and outscored the first three quarters, was not to be denied. On their next possession, the Trojans mounted a seventy-four-yard drive ending with a Marcus Allen touchdown, reducing OU's lead to three points. On their next—and final—possession, the Sooners, finding themselves in a fourth-and-one situation near midfield, decided to punt with four-and-a-half minutes remaining. "We had about a foot to go near midfield and we punted," recalls Merv Johnson. "They got the ball, took it seventy-eight yards, and scored. In hindsight, you have to wonder what might have happened if we'd gone for that first down."[7] The Trojans scored the final touchdown with two seconds remaining to win 28–21. Statistically, the game had been reasonably close, but while Oklahoma had notched 444 total yards to USC's 395, there had been a category in which OU had faltered: fumbles. The Sooners had dropped the ball ten times, losing five.

The 1981 Sooners would follow the USC loss with a disheartening 7–7 tie with Iowa State and a 34–14 punch in the jaw from Texas before winning their next four games against Kansas (45–17), Oregon State (42–3), Colorado (49–0), and Kansas State (28–21). Then, standing at the season's crossroads with a 5–2–1 record, seventeenth-ranked Oklahoma traveled to Columbia to play unranked Missouri. The Sooners had won or shared a remarkable nine consecutive conference crowns, and in order to remain in contention for their tenth, they would have to leave Columbia with a victory.

But it was not to be. The game was a microcosm of the year; despite rolling up 398 yards of offense on a touted Missouri defense, Oklahoma laid the ball on the turf nine times, losing six while tossing two interceptions in the 19–14 setback. It was the first time in his career that Switzer had lost more than two games in a season, and the first time in his tenure as head coach that he would lead the team into a game against Nebraska without an opportunity to win the conference title. Nebraska, by virtue of its victory over Iowa State the same afternoon, had already taken the crown.

But the Huskers had not looked like conference champions in early September. After getting off to a 1–2 start, including losses to Iowa in Ames (10–7) and Penn State in Lincoln (30–24), they found themselves on the wrong side of a 3–0 score at halftime against Auburn. Turner Gill, a hotly recruited sophomore quarterback from Fort Worth, was listed third on the Husker depth chart as he stood on the sideline, watching in frustration as his team floundered. The frustrated Osborne, at his wit's end, sent Gill in to begin the second half and watched in wonder as the young quarterback led Nebraska to a 17–3 comeback win. As a result of that victory, Gill was awarded the starting job in Lincoln for the next two years. Gill and backfield mates Irving Fryar and Mike Rozier—the three known as the famed "Triplets"—would lead the Huskers back to dominance. But if things had ended the way Barry Switzer had planned in February 1980, Turner Gill would have made Norman, not Lincoln, his home. Switzer explains:

> I thought we had Turner Gill all along because he committed to me very early on. I've always said that losing him was the biggest mistake of my career, taking him for granted. I went to sign a linebacker on signing day because Gill told me, "Coach, don't worry about me, I'm coming. Go get some other players." I believed him, took him at his word, and went to sign Jeff Leiding, a linebacker from Oklahoma who ended up going to Texas. But I should have been in Ft. Worth with Turner Gill on signing day; I don't give a damn whether he said he was coming or not. I learned a painful lesson that day.[8]

The lesson became more painful for Switzer as the Sooners lost to the Huskers in Norman, 37–14. Emotions on the team ran high after the loss. Stanley Wilson, who had just become the first back to gain 1,000 yards in a season since Billy Sims, commented from frustration, "This is the worst team I've ever played on."[9] In the Sooner locker room after the game, Switzer asked his team whether they wanted to accept an invitation to the Sun Bowl. "We're so banged up I don't know if we can even put a defensive team on the field next week [against OSU] and come back and get ready to play another good team," said Switzer. "But we put it to the team and it was pretty much 100% to go."[10] Oklahoma would recover a significant amount of their self-confidence and pride the following week as they dispatched Oklahoma State 27–3 before preparing for their Christmas trip to El Paso to meet the University of Houston in the Sun Bowl.

The first half ended with Sooner fans' worst fears appearing to be realized as Bill Yeoman's stubborn team left the field with the game tied 7–7. But Oklahoma's young players stepped to the fore in the second half; midway through the third quarter, with the game still knotted at seven, Keith Stanberry stopped a promising Houston drive by batting down a pitchout and recovering it himself. The turnover led to an OU field goal, and the Sooners took control of the game thereafter. Freshman halfback Fred Sims unleashed a torrential downpour of yards on Houston—he would gain 181 in the second half alone—as the Sooners buried the Cougars 40–14. Stanberry describes the events leading up to the Sun Bowl, his first start at Oklahoma:

I had been one of the top three defensive backs in the nation who went to OU in 1981—Elbert Watts from California, Lawrence Hardin from Texas, and me—and of the three, I was third. I worked my tail off and played some my freshman year, but I didn't start; I had to watch the guy in front of me who was struggling, and I got frustrated. So after the Oklahoma State game, I left school and went home to Mount Pleasant. I had talked with SMU and I was planning to transfer, but Coach Gibbs and Coach Selmon had somehow gotten wind of what I planned to do, and both called and talked with my mom. As soon as I got home, she put my bags right back in her car and drove me back to Norman. She told me I wasn't going to quit. And the next week I started in the Sun Bowl against Houston and had a great game.[11]

1981 was the worst season the Sooners had seen since 1966. The offense simply made too many mistakes and, unlike Oklahoma teams in the late seventies, did not have the experience to overcome errors made against quality opponents. "It just never quite all came together that year," reflects Merv Johnson.

"It wasn't the type of year OU fans and coaches wanted to have. We were only average on offense, and one of the reasons was that we never quite determined who 'the man' was at quarterback. We kept alternating between Phelps and Shepard and never gained any true consistency."[12]

Yet the Sooners had come together in the Sun Bowl. Their young team had gained experience and had regained a measure of the confidence that had been lost on the field against Missouri and Nebraska. And 1982 would usher in a shift away from the Wishbone brought about by the arrival of an exciting new player.

⁝

In late 1981, events were beginning to reach a climax that would forever change the way college football would be handled by universities and the way it would be viewed by fans. The ripple that had been sent through the NCAA's pond by the creation of the College Football Association in 1977 was threatening to become a tsunami. Although one of the CFA's major, long-lasting effects would be to end the NCAA's control of television rights, at the time of its inception the organization sought to address other issues that it considered of greater importance. Chuck Neinas explains:

> Initially, we did not organize with television rights in mind; that was not on our early agenda. The first bit of legislation the CFA imposed eventually became Proposition 48, which established scholastic requirements for athletes. The second thing we did was to put a mechanism in place to ensure that athletes *maintained* their eligibility scholastically; we achieved this by implementing a testing procedure to verify that a 4.0 student was truly a 4.0 student. We also proposed legislation which removed the alums and the boosters from the recruiting process, and we established a recruiting calendar reducing the number of recruiting days from two hundred per year down to seven or eight weeks. And although it had not been a top priority, there were indeed problems with the way the NCAA controlled television rights. While trying to be all things to all people, the NCAA was attempting to afford less prestigious schools an opportunity to televise their games, and, consequently, the percentages for television broadcasts involving the marquee schools were, in fact, declining. As the NCAA was

negotiating this contract, Jim Spence of ABC told NCAA executive director Walter Byers, "The only thing you're doing, Walter, is watering down the scotch."[13]

Byers had also argued that increasing the number of televised games would diminish stadium attendance, thereby harming the universities; he had exercised control over these regulations with a large voting body, the member majority of which had not been major college football powers. "Walter Byers comprised his voting committee of presidents from smaller schools who had strong basketball programs and Division II football programs or no football programs at all," comments Switzer. "He didn't include representatives from the Michigans, Oklahomas, or Texas-level programs. And these smaller schools were sharing the revenue produced by the power schools and voting for rule changes that were seldom in the best interests of the bigger institutions."[14]

With knowledge that the television contract between ABC and the NCAA was up for renewal at the end of the 1982 season, the CFA negotiated its own contract with NBC with the goal of breaking free from the broadcasting confines of the NCAA while still maintaining active membership within the organization. Neinas continues:

> To this day, that television contract remains the best ever negotiated; in today's dollars, it would have been worth 450 million. But the NCAA objected vociferously, prompting the president of the University of Texas, Peter Flawn, to become the first to fire a shot across their bow by telling them, "You don't have our TV rights—the TV rights to Texas football belongs to the University of Texas." The NCAA responded by stating that by history and tradition, institutions surrender those rights as an obligation of membership. In an attempt to quell the rebellion, the NCAA threatened all CFA member institutions with probation and ineligibility in postseason play in all sports.[15]

Although the CFA had originally been created with the intent of working within the confines of the NCAA, the issue of television/property rights had finally forced the association to act outside of it. In the summer of 1982, the CFA Governing Committee convened with University of Georgia president Fred Davison serving as president and University of Oklahoma Faculty Athletics Representative Dan Gibbens acting as chairman of the television subcommittee. It was decided that the Oklahoma City law firm of Crowe & Dunlevy would file a lawsuit for the University of Oklahoma and University of Georgia on behalf of the CFA. These two universities became the lone plaintiffs in the action because the majority of CFA member institutions suspected and feared that involvement in the lawsuit might invite punitive action from the NCAA. But as it evolved, the two-school arrangement provided more efficient management of the endeavor. The lawsuit, officially filed in the federal district court in Oklahoma City, asserted that the control exercised by the National Collegiate Athletic Association over their participating members was in violation of the Sherman Anti-Trust Act of 1890. New Mexico federal district judge Juan Burciaga was assigned to the case to avoid any appearance of bias.[16]

Judge Burciaga eventually ruled that the NCAA was indeed in clear violation of the Sherman Act and that their controls offered "unreasonable, naked restraints on competition." The court declared that the NCAA had been acting as a "naked cartel" limiting production and fixing prices and denounced their "rank greed" and "lust for power." However, a stay was granted the NCAA shortly afterwards allowing them to proceed with the first year of their new contract with ABC.[17]

Andrew Coats—who would subsequently become dean of the OU Law School—offered the final oral argument on behalf of the University of Oklahoma and the University of Georgia before the United States Supreme Court; on June 27, 1984, the Court, by a 7–2 vote, ruled in favor of the original district court's decision favoring the CFA, a decision that permanently broke the NCAA's asphyxiating grip on broadcasting rights.[18] "People should be grateful to the University of Oklahoma," remarks Switzer. "Our successful legal action was responsible for the proliferation of televised football games today. And it only happened because we had the courage to challenge the NCAA, an organization that has always had a bur in their saddle for Oklahoma. We've always been a black sheep in their eyes, but in this case we were right, we stood up against them, and we won."[19]

Salient among the problems facing the Sooners as the 1982 season approached was depth on the offensive line. Only Steve Williams, Elbert Graham, and Paul Parker returned from the previous year. Don Key's career had been cut short by major surgery, and graduation had claimed the balance of the offensive clearing crew. In their absence, a number of talented but largely inexperienced underclassmen would be forced into action. Sophomores Scott Leggett, Tim Randolph, Paul Smith, Greg Sims, Troy Fields, Sidney Dodd, Brent Burks, Chuck Thomas, David Dillingham, and Paul Ferrer along with freshmen Eric Pope, Richard Reed, and Travis Simpson would need a crash course in technique before the opening game. With some inexperience on the offensive line, the Sooners would find it increasingly difficult to break their speedy halfbacks into the open field running from the Wishbone, so the I-formation was adopted to showcase their featured backs.

The talented defense with its strong nucleus of underclassmen from 1981 would be called upon to mature quickly in 1982. Rick Bryan, Bob Slater, Kevin Murphy, and John Truitt, led by the only senior, John Blake, would provide muscle and experience up front; Shipp and Benson would back them up; and the secondary, comprised of Keith Stanberry, Darrell Songy, Daryl Goodlow, Scott Case, Dwight Drane, and Steve Haworth, already intimidating in 1981, was expected to improve. Mike Keeling would return to toe the ball.

Kelly Phelps was firmly entrenched at quarterback with Rod Pegues and Danny Bradley watching from the sidelines. Paul Clewis and David Carter would field Phelps's aerials while Johnny Fontenette and Darin Berryhill blocked on the ends. Stanley Wilson would continue at fullback with Jerome Ledbetter spotting him, and, although Alvin Ross had transferred to Illinois, the running back stable was full with Chet Winters, Weldon Ledbetter, Steve Sewell, and Fred Sims. And there was Marcus Dupree.

The Sooners had been one of an incredible two hundred teams vying for Dupree's services in the winter of 1982. The Philadelphia, Mississippi, high schooler had caught the attention and the imagination of college football coaches and fans across the country with his unique physical gifts and spectacular career; the six-foot-three, 220-pound Dupree—a 4.3 sprinter—had rushed for 83 touchdowns and 5,300 yards, averaging over 13 yards per touch while only playing running back his sophomore, junior, and senior seasons (he had played wide receiver as a freshman).[20] As Dupree entered his senior year in the summer of 1981, he was considered the best high school football player to ever play in the deep south and was often compared to Herschel Walker, a high school back who had scored eighty-five touchdowns before his eighteenth birthday.[21]

By early January, the Sooners were given no better than a one-in-six shot at bringing Dupree to Norman as he had narrowed his list of preferred schools to Texas, UCLA, USC, Southern Mississippi, Nebraska, and Oklahoma.[22] The roller coaster ride continued when, on February 2, Dupree publicly announced that he was going to Texas, only to be vetoed by his mother, Cella Connors.[23] Meanwhile, on February 9 highly regarded All-American running back Spencer Tillman from Tulsa's Edison High School, undeterred by the prospect of competing for a job with Dupree, cast his lot with the Sooners.[24] But the game of "musical colleges" came to an abrupt halt when Barry Switzer and Billy Sims arrived in Mississippi in early February to finally persuade Dupree to sign with Oklahoma.[25] "Being a freshman, coming to a big-time university like Oklahoma, and not knowing what to expect was quite an experience," reflects Dupree. "Your eyes are big as you take in all these new experiences."[26]

The Sooners' first opponent would be the West Virginia Mountaineers, led by head coach Don Nehlen. The Mountaineers had closed out 1981 with an impressive 26–6 scalding of Florida State in the Peach Bowl, a victory that had propelled them from the ranks of the unrated to number seventeen in the final AP poll. Friday, before the two teams squared off on Owen Field, Nehlen said of the Sooners, "They are dynamite; we have no way of stopping their offense."[27] And he was right; his defense could not prevent Oklahoma from scoring twenty-seven points. However, the problem was that Oklahoma could not stop West Virginia either as free-slinging quarterback Jeff Hostetler had his way with the Sooner secondary, passing for 321 yards en route to a 41–27 upset.

It had been a difficult loss for Switzer; the travails of 1981 appeared to have followed him into yet another season. After losing to the Mountaineers—the first opening-day loss of his career—he had dropped five of his last thirteen games, and for the first time since becoming head coach at the University of Oklahoma his future appeared tentative. In the locker room after the West Virginia game, he commented, "Everybody's gonna be down for a day or two, but I think they're going to get it back together and realize that while we may be Oklahoma, no one really gives a damn [who we are] unless we *kick* 'em."[28]

The Sooners had little difficulty "kicking" Kentucky 28–9 on September 18, but the following weekend, Southern California would hand the Sooners their first shutout since their 38–0 loss to Notre Dame in 1966. Oklahoma's fledgling I-formation combined with fumbles, interceptions, and drive-killing penalties, had produced only 211 yards against the Trojan defense in the 12–0 fiasco. The next weekend, the Sooners increased the percentage of plays they ran from the I-formation, and it paid off; Wilson, who had only garnered twenty-one yards against USC, gathered in ninety-seven in the 13–3 victory over the Iowa State Cyclones. Additionally, Dupree, who had realized only twenty yards on twelve carries through the first three games, plowed for sixty-two yards.[29]

Then came Texas. The undefeated Longhorns had blasted their first three opponents by a total of 76–19 and were ranked thirteenth nationally; the Sooners, ranked ninth in the preseason, had fallen from the wire service polls after the West Virginia loss and had yet to be invited back. Stanley Wilson, the workhorse in Oklahoma's I-formation, had dislocated a shoulder in Ames and was questionable for the Texas game, so Switzer and Galen Hall had to make a decision on whether to give the nod to Fred Sims, try to start Wilson, or go with Dupree.

Dupree received the nod, and the game was on. When asked before the kickoff about his role in the offense, he remarked, "The offensive line is real young, but all they need to do is hold their blocks and the backs will do the rest."[30] On his first carry in the first quarter, he showed them what he meant as he took the ball and broke through the Texas line for a sixty-three-yard touchdown. "We knew Dupree was something special, but we felt that teams could take him out of the play from the Wishbone," explains Merv Johnson. "That's why we incorporated more I-formation. And from the Texas game on, let me tell you, it was exciting. He had at least one long run for a touchdown and a ton of yards in every game we played."[31] The Sooners continued to lead throughout the game, and the Longhorns continued to keep it close until the clock expired with

Oklahoma on top of a thrilling 28–22 score. Despite Dupree's heroics, the game had been a true team effort; his cross-country jaunt was complemented by runs of fifty-nine and fifty-one yards by Weldon Ledbetter and Freddie Sims. The young offensive line had controlled the more experienced Texas defensive front, the young Sooner defense had not broken, and Kelly Phelps had gone the distance. Referring to the Sooners, Texas coach Fred Akers commented after the game, "That was no 2–2 team out there today."[32] The victory broke a three-game losing streak to Texas and removed some of the weight from Switzer's shoulders. "I've probably had better football teams," he remarked breathlessly in the postgame locker room, "but I want to tell you I have never had a team play as hard and give more effort against a tougher or better opponent than in this game today. This group of players never won a big ball game . . . but they won the big game today. You have to accomplish that to become a good football team."[33]

But the pollsters still were not convinced as OU remained unranked. Yet after the resurgence against Texas, the Sooners proved that they were a good team as they began their march through the conference. Kansas fell behind the Sooners 24–0 at halftime before succumbing 38–14. OU's defense starred in the 27–9 victory over Oklahoma State as it held Ernest Anderson—a back who was averaging over 200 yards per game and who had just become the fourth player in college football history to surpass the 1,000 yard mark after the first five games—to 59 yards. Boulder's thin air had not slowed Dupree down during his seventy-seven-yard punt return, and it had not stopped Ricky Bryan, Dwight Drane, and Keith Stanberry from feasting on Buffalo quarterback Randy Essington's passes in a 45–10 Sooner romp. Kansas State, trailing Oklahoma 14–10 with six minutes left in the game, had its last march toward Oklahoma's end zone foiled by a game-saving interception and touchdown return by Keith Stanberry as the Sooners took the day 24–10. Missouri was repaid for the pride, sweat, and joy that they had usurped from OU in 1981 with a 41–14 slice of Sooner retribution.

Suddenly, Oklahoma was hot. As the Sooners prepared to face their biggest obstacle of the season—a trip to Lincoln to face the third-ranked Huskers—they were on a seven-game winning streak, undefeated in conference play, and ranked eleventh in the nation. Nebraska had climbed to second nationally before losing to Penn State in late September, but by the time the Sooners had deplaned at Lincoln Airport on Thanksgiving Day, NU had moved to third. Switzer referred to the 1981 installment of the Cornhuskers as "the best team we've played since I've been at the University of Oklahoma,"[34] a statement that appeared to be steeped in hyperbole. But upon closer examination, Osborne's Huskers were just that good; they were leading the nation in total offense and scoring offense with six first-team conference players backing their play, and they led the conference in scoring defense and total defense. And against the rush, the Cornhuskers would be pitting their strength against that of the Sooners; they had not allowed an opposing rusher to gain one hundred yards since Stanley Wilson had done it in 1981.

Nebraska appeared to be as good as advertised as they posted three first-half touchdowns to take a 21–7 lead at intermission. But on OU's third play in the second half, Dupree bowled the Husker Blackshirts over on an eighty-six-yard touchdown run. Oklahoma and Nebraska posted one more six-pointer each, and the third period ended with Nebraska clutching on to a four-point lead. The fourth quarter would see the Sooners threaten but falter, and the game would end with Nebraska on top 28–24. Unlike the error-laden early season losses to West Virginia and USC, the Sooners had played well against an excellent opponent. Dupree, who had been listed as "probable" for the game because of an upper respiratory infection, had been the leading rusher in the game with 149 yards. "I had pneumonia before we played Nebraska," recalls Dupree. "I came out of the hospital the week of the game."[35] The phenomenal freshman had finished the regular season as the team's leading rusher, setting a new University of Oklahoma freshman rushing record with 905 yards.

With its loss to the Huskers, Oklahoma was headed for the Fiesta Bowl to play Arizona State. Switzer had anticipated that his team would experience some slight conditioning problems after the three-week layoff, but he had not expected his star running back to check in weighing 240 pounds. "Once everyone was in Tempe, we conducted a series of sprints, and Marcus couldn't finish them," recounts Switzer. "Scott Hill, the coach who was conducting those sprints, was beside himself he was so pissed off because Marcus, the fastest guy on our team, came in last in every damned sprint. He was in horrible condition."[36]

Yet Oklahoma proceeded to dismantle Arizona State's top-rated rushing defense. The Sooners surprised the Sun Devils by mixing their offensive sets, running more often from the Wishbone than from the I-formation, and—late in the first stanza—Oklahoma found itself on the Sun Devil five-yard line after Dupree's fifty-six yard run. Two plays later, Wilson stuffed it into the end zone. In the second quarter, Arizona State tallied two field goals and a safety to take the lead 8–7. Wilson scored OU's second touchdown to give the Sooners a 13–11 halftime lead. Dupree says about his first-half performance, "The Arizona State players were shocked at the way I was running through them. I encountered a few of their players later on—Ron Brown played with the Rams—and he said, 'Man, we couldn't understand how you could do that to us. Our coach set us up ten yards deeper than we usually played to stop your breakaways, or in case you did break out, we would stand a better chance of bringing you down.' And I said, 'I kept wondering why I had such a hard time getting past you guys.' But they had had ten yards on me . . . that was why."[37]

However, promising drives combined with Sooner fumbles killed momentum in the third quarter, and the game finally ended with ASU on top, 32–21. Oklahoma's stable of running backs had embarrassed the Sun Devil stopping unit for a stunning 417 yards; Wilson and Sims busted through and around the A-State defense for 125 combined yards; and Dupree, despite seeing only limited action—he played sparingly in the first quarter and sat out most of the fourth—established a Fiesta Bowl rushing record of 239 yards. After the game, Switzer, frustrated with Dupree's inability to play for four quarters, had vented to the media. He explains the reason for his frustration:

We had the ball sixty-five snaps in the damned ball game and Marcus only played thirty-four of them; he missed thirty-one, and don't you think I don't know these stats by heart?!? Without Marcus in the lineup, we averaged 3.3 yards a carry; with him in the game we averaged 9.2 yards per carry. And in those 34 plays when he's in the game, he carried the ball 17 times—only 17 times!—for 249 yards. That's damned near fifteen yards per carry. But every time he'd make a long run, he'd limp off the field and sit over on the bench holding his leg, taking five minutes to recuperate. If he'd been in condition and had played the other thirty-one snaps, we would've won that game. Arizona State was leading the nation in defense against the rush, and Dupree shredded them. If he'd been in condition and had played the other half of that game, we'd have kicked their asses; hell, he might have rushed for 400 yards. I was pissed off about it then, and I'm still pissed about it today! So I might have come across pretty hard after the game because I was mad; we'd lost the damned game because he'd had four limp-offs.[38]

In Dupree's defense, he stated that he had not fully recuperated from his upper respiratory infection and played the Fiesta Bowl with ailing lungs, bruised ribs, and pulled a hamstring. "I depended on Dupree just like I depended on Joe Washington and Greg Pruitt and Billy Sims," continues Switzer. "You give the ball to your best player, so you bet your ass I depended on him—that's why I recruited him. Marcus Dupree was the most physically gifted back to ever set foot on the field at the University of Oklahoma—more physically mature, bigger, stronger, and faster—but he was out of shape and he never realized his potential."[39]

The Sooners finished 1982 with a respectable 8–4 record and ranked sixteenth in the nation. Their only All-American was Ricky Bryan from Coweta, Oklahoma, but players earning All-Conference honors were Bryan, Paul Parker, Steve Williams, Kevin Murphy, Jackie Shipp, and Marcus Dupree. "In 1982, we should have recognized Dupree's talent before we did," reflects Merv Johnson. "His breakout game was against Texas, the fifth game of the year, and we hadn't involved him much before that. We lost to Southern Cal 12–0 in the third game, and you've got to figure that if we had let him carry the ball twenty-five times it might have been a different story."[40] But Dupree, for all his failings, had been magnificent and was selected the Football News Freshman Player of the Year; it would be the phenomenal wunderkind's final accolade.

∵

A familiar cast of characters—Nebraska, Oklahoma, and Texas—occupied the top three slots in the 1983 preseason polls. The Sooners' lofty ranking was based primarily on the anticipated strength of their defense, a unit which returned everyone but John Blake and Steve Haworth. Switzer expounded on his returning defensive team:

The strength of our team must be our defense. At tackle we've got Rick Bryan, an All-American, and another player nobody talks about—Bob Slater. I think those two tackles are as good as anyone in the Big Eight. We've got three-year starters at linebacker, too; Jackie Shipp has performed consistently well throughout his career and we're expecting Thomas Benson to have a big year. At defensive end we have three players who've played well for us: John Truitt, Daryl Goodlow, and Kevin Murphy. In the secondary, I think Scott Case is one of the best defensive backs in the league. He has the ability to make the big play and so do Dwight Drane and Keith Stanberry. And replacing John Blake at noseguard we have Tony Casillas; he's young but he could be a real good player because of his size and strength.[41]

The offensive line was rock-solid, anchored by Chuck Thomas and Paul Parker; receivers Buster Rhymes and Paul Clewis were back complemented by freshman Derrick Shepard; Johnny Fontenette returned at tight end; Darren Atyia would do the punting; and freshman Tim Lashar would win the placekicking job by late September. The offensive backfield was led by junior Danny Bradley, who had stepped into the quarterback spot; redshirt freshman Spencer Tillman started at fullback; and Marcus Dupree was expected to continue his record-breaking assault on the national record books from the I-back position. But all was not well with Dupree. The coaches were displeased when he returned to campus in August out of condition. "He came back his sophomore year seriously out of shape," describes Keith Stanberry. "We ran quarter miles and he just couldn't do it. He couldn't even finish a sprint; they had to hose him down to cool him off."[42] Yet Dupree, although not able to score on a cross-country run without being caught from behind, was still a scintillating runner and a threat to chew up chunks of yardage against most defenses. "I was surprised at the role reversal; they expected me, playing fullback at 197 pounds, to get down in a four-point stance and block for Dupree, who weighed about 240," recalls Tillman.[43]

Over the past seven years, opening games had been rough going for the Sooners. In 1976 and 1977, they needed strong fourth-quarter performances to subdue subpar Vanderbilt teams; in 1978, they had to hold on to win a six-point decision over what would prove to be a mediocre Stanford team in Palo Alto; in 1979, they struggled to beat an eventual 5–6–0 Iowa team in Norman; in 1980 and 1981, they would need big second halves to control Kentucky and Wyoming; and in 1982, they lost to West Virginia. Therefore, Oklahoma fans everywhere were experiencing justifiable anxiety when their Sooners traveled west to Palo Alto to exact a measure of revenge for the 1980 loss in Norman. Switzer knew that his team would face a smooth pro-set offense with a sophisticated passing game, so certain personnel shifts needed to be made in a defense that had allowed eleven touchdown passes in five nonconference games in 1982. Jackie Shipp was switched to strongside linebacker, Thomas Benson was switched to the weakside, and Scott Case was moved from corner back to free safety. The changes combined with a strong showing by the Oklahoma defensive line wreaked havoc on the Stanford offense, giving the Sooners a 27–14 opening-day win. The OU offense had blocked well for the backs, enabling Dupree—who was shut down in the first half—to finish the game with 138 yards, Earl Johnson with 96, Spencer Tillman with 95, and Danny Bradley with 65. The Sooner defense applied a tourniquet to the Cardinal running game, allowing the team nothing—minus one yard, actually—on twenty-two attempts. Rick Bryan and Kevin Murphy posted eight tackles apiece as repeated boos emanated from the slide-rule section of Stanford Stadium.

The following week, the situation altered radically for Oklahoma when sixth-ranked Ohio State made its first trip to Norman and left with a 24–14 victory. The vaunted Sooner ground game produced less than two hundred yards, and Dupree, who only played for the first twenty minutes, left the game with a bruised nerve in his leg and only thirty yards under his belt. While ugly to Sooner fans, the 24–14 result had not accurately reflected the lopsided nature of the game. The Buckeyes had earned more first downs than Oklahoma, 24–14; they had controlled the football 60 percent of the time; and they had been successful on ten of seventeen third down conversion attempts while the Sooners only converted three of thirteen opportunities.

The loss to Ohio State was followed by a disappointing performance against the University of Tulsa the following week. Without Dupree, the Sooners played well early in the game, taking a 28–0 lead into halftime; but the second half was the polar opposite. Although Earl Johnson gained 143 yards before exiting the game in the third quarter with an injury, Oklahoma managed only 78 yards rushing, 9 yards passing, and 5 first downs in the second half before eking out a 28–18 victory. "In my 17 years of coaching," declared Switzer after the game, "this second half was the worst 30 minutes of football that has ever been played by a team I have coached. We threw interceptions, we didn't block anybody, we didn't run and we didn't make anything happen."[44] The next opponent, Kansas State, continued to perplex the ninth-ranked Sooners. Entering the game as eleven-point favorites, the Sooners sleepwalked to a 10–0 halftime deficit before bolting back to win 29–10. Dupree played—his knee bolstered by a protective pad—and gained 151 yards and scored three six-pointers, but the highest accolades from Kansas State head coach Jim Dickey went to Tillman, who had sprinted and slashed for 131 yards and a touchdown. "Everyone talks about Dupree but we think Tillman is their best back," he commented.[45]

The Sooners would need a healthy Dupree, a motivated Tillman, and every ounce of talent at their disposal to defeat their next opponent, the second-rated Texas Longhorns. The defense had stepped up over the past few weeks, and before the Texas game Switzer had challenged the offense to join it. But the Texas defensive line had its way with the Oklahoma offense in the 28–16 Longhorn victory. In spite of OU's playing a game against the Horns without losing a fumble for the first time since the Wilkinson era, a relentless Texas

Spencer Tillman, 2010. Courtesy Spencer Tillman.

defense shackled the Sooners all afternoon. Faced with thirteen third down conversion situations on the day, Oklahoma managed only a single first down. Tillman gained only forty yards—his lowest output as a Sooner—and Dupree, who managed to play most of the game, gained but fifty yards and suffered a mild concussion late in the contest. Merv Johnson reflects on the 1983 Red River Rivalry:

> We had a terrible game against Texas that year. We had way too many motion penalties, eight or ten—maybe more, but what happened was the Texas defensive linemen were shouting out numbers during our snap count, which really messed us up. The officials claimed they never heard them doing it, but drive after drive was stopped by those motion penalties. The defensive tackles were in tight with our center, so they would shout "hike!" or whatever, and it threw us off. Our players were about ready to fight each other, me, and everyone else they were so frustrated. It was easily my worst day as a coach.[46]

After Texas, Switzer had traditionally allowed the team to take the following Sunday off before reporting for duty. But Dupree was also absent on the ensuing Monday. By Thursday, Dupree had still not returned to the team and the press took notice. At that time, Switzer announced that Dupree had been suspended for going AWOL. Later that day, Dupree announced from Mississippi that he would not be returning to Oklahoma, claiming that he could not seem to satisfy Barry Switzer, and that he had originally had his priorities mixed up. He had wanted to play on national TV while winning a Heisman and a national championship, he stated, but he had not given any thought to what it might be like to be so far from home. "The only thing I know is that Marcus doesn't want to play football anymore," commented Switzer. "He's tired of it and that's a tragic waste. He has great talent, as we all know, but the young man has some problems."[47] As difficult as it was for Sooner fans to believe, it had happened; Marcus Dupree, one year after capturing everyone's imagination with a blistering sixty-three-yard touchdown gallop on his first carry against Texas, was gone.

The following weekend, Oklahoma traveled to Stillwater to play a resurgent Oklahoma State squad. The previous weekend, the undefeated Cowboys had hosted second-ranked and undefeated Nebraska and had come within a referee's whistle of the upset before finally succumbing 14–10. Oklahoma also came within a poorly communicated onside kickoff of losing to Oklahoma State. With just under fourteen minutes remaining in the game, the shockingly inept Sooners found themselves mired in a 20–3 hole. In order to have any chance to win, they would have to score, and quickly. On the second play of their next possession, that is precisely what they did as Derrick Shepard hauled in a seventy-three-yard touchdown pass—OU's longest aerial of the season—from Danny Bradley, bringing the score 20–10. Oklahoma State punted after three plays, and on OU's next possession Bradley moved the team to the OSU two-yard line before his pass was picked off with 6:22 left. But two minutes later, the Cowboys were forced to punt again, and Oklahoma took possession close to midfield. A combination of Bradley passes and Earl Johnson dashes took the Sooners into the OSU red zone, setting up a five-yard Tillman scoring trot. Eschewing the conversion kick, Switzer ordered a two-point play, and moments later Bradley pegged Earl Johnson in the back of the end zone. Score: Oklahoma 18, OSU 20.

Then Sooner Magic made a sudden reappearance. Oklahoma prepared to kick off with 2:50 remaining on the clock. "We wanted to kick it away and let our defense stop them, which I had no doubt we could," says Switzer.[48] So the Sooners lined up for the kickoff with every man on special teams looking for the deep ball except for one: the kicker, Tim Lashar. "Nobody told me I was supposed to kick it long," said Lashar. "Guys were switching back and forth, running around, and I didn't know what they were doing so I just kicked it onside."[49] The whistle blew, Lashar squibbed the ball onside, and when the dust cleared Scott Case had recovered for the Sooners. Oklahoma moved the ball to the OSU twenty-nine-yard line, where, with seconds remaining, Lashar lashed a perfectly centered field goal through the uprights, and the Sooners prevailed with a very unlikely 21–20 victory.[50] Bob Hersom of the *Daily Oklahoman* wrote, "The Sooners made 23 mistakes in Stillwater that afternoon. Twenty-two consisted of a school record 15 penalties, six lost fumbles, and a pass interception; but the 23rd error helped them win the game."[51]

The confidence gained after the topsy-turvy victory in Stillwater, followed by victories over their next two games against Iowa State (49–11) and Kansas (45–14), was dashed as the Sooners suffered their second shutout in the past eighteen games, losing to Missouri in Columbia, 10–0. Oklahoma was held to minus seven yards rushing in the first half and finished the game with a season-low eighty-four. The loss to Missouri had effectively ended OU's hopes for a conference championship, a trip to the Orange Bowl, or a consolation journey back to Tempe. The following week, the Sooners took their frustrations out in a 41–28 shelling of Colorado. As the Sooners held on to a second-place tie in the conference with Missouri, they realized, with a 7–3 record and a Thanksgiving Week game against Nebraska looming, just how tentative their situation had become.

Nebraska had begun its season with an impressive 44–6 vengeance whipping of Penn State in the Kickoff Classic played in East Rutherford, New Jersey. By the time the Cornhuskers found themselves packing their gear for their trip to Norman, they were sporting an 11–0 record, a number one ranking in the AP poll, and a confidence level not seen on campus since Jerry Tagge and Johnny Rodgers graced the sidelines in 1971. The Huskers, behind Turner Gill, Irving Fryar, and the man who would win the 1983 Heisman Trophy, Mike Rozier, had bested all eleven opponents by a composite score of 516–165, a 54–15 per game average. In addition to their thirty-eight-point defeat of Penn State, they had destroyed Minnesota in Minneapolis 84–13 and Syracuse 63–7; and in the four weeks preceding their game with Oklahoma, they had blistered Colorado 69–19, dismantled Kansas State 51–25, embarrassed Iowa State 72–29, and mangled Kansas 67–13. A victory over Oklahoma would give them three consecutive seasons without a loss in the Big Eight, the longest conference-winning streak of any team since Bud Wilkinson's run from 1947 through 1958.

Nebraska entered the game ranked first in the country, and Oklahoma was unranked—a situation that had never happened before in the history of the rivalry. It was also the first time that Nebraska would visit Norman installed as a two-touchdown favorite. "No one thought we had a chance to win this game except our coaches and players," said Switzer.[52] The Huskers scored halfway through the first quarter to take a 7–0 lead, but, after two Oklahoma field goal attempts misfired in the second quarter, the Sooners finally scored on a thirty-nine-yard Tillman trot to knot the score at seven apiece. On Nebraska's next possession, Thomas Benson picked off a pass, giving the Sooners the ball at their own twenty-seven (after a fifteen-yard unsportsmanlike foul was assessed against OU on the play). On the very next snap, Bradley lofted a beautiful seventy-three-yard spiral to Rhymes, giving Oklahoma a 14–7 lead with just over two minutes remaining in the half. But the Huskers were not done; it took them a scant 1:29 to mount a seventy-three-yard drive of their own to tie the game at halftime 14–14.

Midway through the third quarter, Oklahoma broke the tie when Tillman slashed for an eighteen-yard touchdown; but as they had done earlier, the Huskers struck back with lightning speed less than a minute later and again on their next possession to take a 28–21 lead into the fourth period. With five minutes remaining, the Sooners began a methodical drive that took them to the Nebraska two-yard line before a procedure penalty set them back to the seven. On the next play, Bradley was sacked for a three-yard loss. On third down, Bradley lofted a pass to Derrick Shepard at the NU goal line, but Husker cornerback Neil Harris was there to break it up. On fourth down, with forty-two seconds remaining, a Bradley pass to Rhymes in the back of the end zone was once again deflected by Harris, and Nebraska took possession of the ball and the game. "Oklahoma is a great football team," declared Husker head coach Tom Osborne after the game. "There's no doubt that's the best defense we've seen all season. They also have the most underrated offense."[53]

The bowl prospects for the Sooners came into focus after the Nebraska game, and the outlook was not positive. In the 2009–2010 season, thirty-four bowl games hosted sixty-eight teams—eight more than the copious number invited to the March Madness basketball tourney—but in 1983, only seventeen bowl games existed, making the invitation process a bit more selective. And the Sooners, with their 7–4–0 record in tow, simply did not possess their trademark cachet. Additionally, the Sooners had scheduled a first-ever twelfth game in 1983; they were to travel to Honolulu to play the University of Hawaii on December 3. Switzer had declared the game to be the Sooners' "bowl game," and it became both a road trip and a beach vacation for the Oklahoma fans able to make the journey. But it also gave bowl committees pause; they feared that should Oklahoma be invited to a late-December bowl game, its usual traveling contingent of supporters, spent from their trip to Hawaii, would not accompany the team. So Oklahoma did not lobby for a bowl trip; it would be the first time a bowl-eligible Sooners squad had not gone bowling since 1969.

Oklahoma was installed as a twenty-eight-point favorite against Hawaii, a team that had finished fifth in the Western Athletic Conference. However, once again expectations and reality flip-flopped as Oklahoma found itself in a 10–0 hole at intermission. The Sooners shook off the doldrums for a white-knuckled 21–17 victory. Oklahoma returned to the top twenty for the first time in a month, tied with Baylor at the twentieth position.

Although the Sooners had finished the season by nearly upsetting the number one team in the nation and beating Hawaii, the criticism of Switzer within the state became increasingly vociferous; losing three straight games to Nebraska and four of the last five to Texas had not sat well. Since 1981, Oklahoma had played eleven ranked teams and had lost to all but Iowa State—whom they tied—in 1981 and Texas in 1982. At the conclusion of the 1983 season, Rick Bryan was named the Big Eight Conference Defensive Player of the Year and Spencer Tillman the Top Offensive Newcomer. Dupree had set a new freshman rushing record in 1982 with 905 yards, Earl Johnson had broken it 1983 with 945 yards, and Spencer Tillman had broken Johnson's record the same year with 1,047 yards. And although Switzer had won 67 percent of his games that year, his 8–4–0 Sooners had tied Missouri for second place in the conference and had tied Oklahoma State for second place in their own state; Tulsa had placed first with their 8–3–0 mark. The wolves were clearly at the gate. After the loss to Ohio State, the *Daily Oklahoman*'s Jim Lassiter wrote, "It's been going on too long now just to be a mild recession. Oklahoma football is in a deep depression. Frighteningly, the bottom may have to fall out before the Sooners get off the deck. The Sooners can't win a big football game anymore simply because they have fallen behind the times. College football is in the Space Age and the Sooners are still in the Bronze Age."[54]

But Lassiter's appraisal of the team, like that of the average fan, was long on emotion and short on perspective. From 1973 through 1980, the Sooners had compiled an 83–9–2 record while winning 88 percent of their games, but since the dawn of the new decade, Switzer's Sooners had only managed a 16–9–1 record while winning 62 percent of their contests, far below the level to which Oklahoma supporters had become accustomed.

Switzer was being hoist with his own petard much as Bud Wilkinson had been for the same reason; they had both won at an unsustainable pace, creating unrealistic expectations. As Chuck Fairbanks and Gomer Jones came to realize, broad perspective becomes strained and fans become impatient when their teams begin to lose. And when losing to high-profile opponents consistently, as Switzer had to Texas and Nebraska, coaching careers are often unfairly jeopardized. Despite Lassiter's loosely constructed simile, the Sooners were not a Bronze Age team struggling through a Space Age environment; they were a Space Age team struggling for the right fuel formula.

They were to find it nine months later.

19 Back to the 'Bone and Back to the Top

JANUARY 1984–JANUARY 1986

Despite entering the 1984 season with a number of positives—the Sooners welcomed back nine offensive and four defensive starters—Barry Switzer was a coach under siege. His 106–21–3 record made him the winningest active coach in the nation, but Switzer's 23–12–1 record over the past three years had exposed him to criticism. Critics asserted that he was spending too much time with his outside business interests and not enough developing and maintaining his team. Some also claimed that his involvement with Sun Belt Oil Company and the Penn Square Bank controversy not only distracted him but adversely affected his image. So the university broke tradition by not extending his four-year contract to five years. Switzer responded to his detractors: "There was nothing to that—only to those [who] wanted to make something out of it. When I am a partner and have a vested interest in some company I'm not involved in the day-to-day management of it. Other people who have expertise in running companies are there, but I'm not. During recruiting months I'm gone every day on the road and I don't even think about outside interests. The only business I was ever in was the insurance company and we sold that three years ago and we dissolved Sun Belt two years ago."[1]

Entering the 1984 season, Barry Switzer recommitted himself to football. "It's not that we weren't winning, we just weren't winning enough," he continued. "I think the one thing that disappointed everybody, myself included, is that we didn't look good last year. That bothered me." The Sooners had *not* looked good in 1983. Among other problems, they had set both school and conference records by accruing ninety-five penalties in twelve games. Therefore, Oklahoma initiated a new academic monitoring program, and the Sooners became only the twelfth team in the nation to voluntarily impose drug testing. Bed checks were rigorously reimplemented, and classroom attendance checks were approached with vigor. "We would have done these things whether the regents had extended my contract or not," said Switzer. "I didn't have to have that to motivate me; we just needed to get this done. We had to get better and the only way you can do that is to work, work, work."[2]

That work ethic was temporarily disrupted with the departure of Switzer's longtime offensive coordinator and friend, Galen Hall, who, along with Switzer, was the last holdover from Jim Mackenzie's original 1966 staff. To replace him, Switzer hired thirty-three-year old Mack Brown, who had just finished his first and only year as head coach of the Appalachian State Mountaineers. The Sooners, with their entire backfield returning, planned to revert to the basic Wishbone formation, but with a twist. Switzer describes the difference: "We implemented some flex-wing sets by shifting the flanker out on the wing. But it basically wasn't any different from the Wishbone set. Our new offensive coordinator, Mack Brown, didn't want to run a triple option; he'd never been a part of that scheme and he wasn't comfortable with it. He preferred to run the outside Veer with Danny Bradley, which we did and did effectively. We lined up in the Wishbone, but we weren't a true triple-option football team."[3]

With the offensive plan in place, the Sooners turned to their defense. Rex Norris left Oklahoma to accept the defensive coordinator position under Darryl Rogers at Arizona State. With headliners Ricky Bryan, Scott Case, and Thomas Benson gone to the Atlanta Falcons, Jackie Shipp to the Miami Dolphins, Bob Slater to the Washington Redskins, and both Dwight Drane and Daryl Goodlow to the USFL, Keith Stanberry, Kevin Murphy, Jim Rockford, and Tony Casillas were the only returning starters. Although linebackers Shipp and Benson were gone, Paul Migliazzo and Brian Bosworth would not miss a beat in replacement roles. But with underclassmen filling in critical gaps, the coaching staff found themselves relying on younger, untested players. "Sometimes freshmen and sophomore play better than seniors because of their youthful enthusiasm," said Switzer. "To win, we're going to have to have that because we're inexperienced."[4]

Oklahoma kicked off the 1984 season ranked sixteenth in the AP poll, the first time the team had opened the season out of the top ten since 1973. Their first opponent, Stanford, threw a scare into packed Memorial Stadium as the team drove fifty yards for the opening score. But the worm turned for the Cardinals after their opening drive as the young Sooner defense stopped their passing game and shut down their ground attack, holding their runners to only ninety yards on twenty-eight attempts in the 19–7 victory. Oklahoma's next opponent, Pittsburgh, had opened the season ranked third in the nation before being humbled by Brigham Young. Despite the absence of Tillman, Johnson, Murphy, and Tupper, Oklahoma would take the Panthers to task, drubbing them 42–10. Quarterback Danny Bradley appeared to be coming into his own as he ran for two touchdowns and passed for two more. The victory brought the Sooners to 2–0 and shot them five spaces up the AP ladder to number eleven. The ascent would continue the next two weeks as victories over Baylor (34–15) and Kansas State (24–6) lifted Oklahoma to the third spot in the AP poll and second place in the UPI. The young Sooner defense, counting seven freshmen and nine sophomores among its top twenty-two players, was playing dominating football as Oklahoma faced yet another showdown with number one Texas south of the Red River.

Injuries were a major concern for the Sooners during the two-week layoff leading up to the Texas contest. Sooner trainer Dan Pickett expressed concern over the condition of both Earl Johnson and Spencer Tillman. Johnson, who was still suffering from the cracked kneecap he had sustained in the 1983 Nebraska game, would play against Texas with a protective kneepad, and Tillman, who had been battling a pulled hamstring and had yet to play in 1984, was far from full speed. Adding to Oklahoma's concerns, Pickett declared that All-American defensive end Kevin Murphy would miss the game with a severely bruised foot.[5] The game would also mark the first time in the history of the series that both quarterbacks would enter the fray ranked among the nation's top-ten passers; Longhorn signal caller Todd Dodge was second in passing efficiency while OU's Danny Bradley was eighth.[6]

The game was played under the worst possible conditions, with driving rain making both footing and ballhandling difficult. Texas capitalized on two Sooner miscues, scoring a touchdown after Mike Winchester dropped the ball trying to punt and a field goal resulting from a Tillman fumble. The Longhorns led 10–0 at the half as the rainfall intensified. On the Longhorns' first possession in the third quarter, Texas's Terry Orr had the ball jarred loose by Brian Bosworth, Keith Stanberry recovered, and Steve Sewell scored on the next play.

On the Horns' next possession, their center, Terry Steelhammer, snapped the ball over the head of his punter and through the end zone for a safety, reducing Texas's lead to a single point, 10–9.[7]

And then, late in the third quarter, the Sooner Schooner started to roll. Taking the ball at its own nineteen-yard line, OU marched eighty-one yards in ten plays, capped by Sewell's eleven-yard touchdown run. "The most valuable player on that 1984 team, in my opinion, was Steve Sewell," reflects Tillman.[8] Bradley's two-point conversion pass was knocked down, and Oklahoma led 15–10. The Sooner defense, ranked second in the nation, continued to frustrate the Longhorns until the final six minutes of the game when Texas's Kevin Nelson broke free for a fifty-eight-yard run ending at the Oklahoma two-yard line. After four attempts to crack the OU line produced no points, the Sooners took over on downs with 3:51 remaining, but they were equally unable to move the chains, and Switzer elected to take an intentional safety. "Taking the safety was a sound strategy," declared Danny Bradley. "Our punter hadn't had a great punt all day so we figured we'd give them the safety and punt from the 20 and make them go 70 or 80 yards."[9] After the punt, Oklahoma led 15–12 as the Horns took over at their own forty-four-yard line.

What happened on the following series of plays rivaled the infamous "Jack Sisco Affair" in notoriety.* During the Longhorns' final drive, there were three questionable calls, each going Texas's way. On first down, Todd Dodge threw a pass to tight end Jerome Jones, who caught the ball and was hit by Paul Migliazzo. The ball was dislodged and recovered by Tony Casillas. Although television replays clearly showed that the ball had been fumbled while in play, the officials declared that his knee had been down—hence, there was no fumble. The second questionable call came when Keith Stanberry was called for pass

---

* In 1947, Texas and Oklahoma were tied at seven apiece when, just before halftime with Texas on the Sooner three-yard line, the clock had apparently run out. But referee Jack Sisco intervened, claiming that one second remained on the clock, and gave Texas another opportunity to score. On the play, Texas back Randall Clay took the ball, fumbled, recovered it himself, and was visibly down by contact as his knee touched the turf before he continued into the end zone, giving his side a 14–7 halftime advantage. Sooner fans were enraged, and even the normally reserved Wilkinson charged onto the field, berating Sisco for his questionable call. The animosity generated by the incident caused resentment and anger in both fan bases to the degree that cancellation of the rivalry was considered.

interference on a visibly uncatchable ball, keeping the Longhorns' drive alive. And the third call came with nineteen seconds remaining in the game when, from the Sooner eleven-yard line, Dodge tossed a ball into the right corner of the end zone. Horn receiver Billy Boy Bryant mishandled the ball, which then bounced off the hands of Sooner Andre Johnson before careening into the grasp of strong safety Keith Stanberry. Stanberry grasped the ball to his chest, planted his feet well inside the sideline, and hydroplaned on the wet surface out of bounds. Although the replay plainly indicated an interception, both officials disallowed the catch.[10] Stanberry recalls the episode:

Their first two pass attempts were incomplete, and the third one was the one I intercepted, the controversial one. I picked it off in the end zone and slid out of bounds, and when I got up I *knew* I'd intercepted that ball. But as I was running over to the sidelines thinking we'd won the game, I saw the two refs making their conflicting calls; one of them said I didn't catch it, and the other said I did but that I was out of bounds. The sideline went nuts after that interception was waved off, and Switzer went running after the ref to let him know he'd blown it; he was madder than I'd ever seen him. But we didn't have a chance to argue for long because they were hurrying to line up for their field goal. [Texas made the kick in the final seconds, and the game ended in a 15–15 tie.] When I went into the locker room after the game, Coach Switzer and Coach Gibbs were going ballistic. Everybody felt like we'd been ripped off, which we had.[11]

Later in the locker room, Switzer fumed to reporters, "A Southwest Conference official took the game away from us. He's the ref and he controls the game. If that ain't homing, I don't know what is."[12] Switzer was proven correct the next week when Bruce Finlayson, the supervisor of Big Eight Conference officials, contacted him. "He officially apologized to us for the call having been blown," remembers Stanberry.[13]

Apology notwithstanding, the Sooners still left Dallas with a 15–15 tie. On Sunday they advanced to second place in both the AP and UPI polls while Texas dropped from first to third. The following week in its game against Iowa State,

Oklahoma faced the challenge of defending a pass-happy team showcased by the Alex Espinoza–to–Tracy Henderson tandem. The Sooners also faced two other challenges: overcoming the doldrums caused by their ill-deserved tie against the Longhorns and dealing with the traditional slump that often occurs the week following the big game in Dallas. The twenty-eight-point landslide victory predicted by the pundits never materialized. With three minutes remaining, Oklahoma trailed the Cyclones 10–6 before Tillman scored on a seven-yard pitchout. The Sooners relied upon their top-ranked defense to fight a holding-action retreat from Ames in their 12–10 victory. "We came in flat and just didn't play well," said Bradley after the game.[14]

Tillman burns Iowa State. Courtesy Spencer Tillman.

The following Saturday, the Sooners suffered twin disasters; they lost to Kansas 28–11, and they lost Keith Stanberry and Andre Johnson for the season in a postgame automobile accident. The Sooners were hobbled by injuries to Tony Casillas, Earl Johnson, Patrick Collins, Kevin Murphy, and quarterback Danny Bradley—who sat out the KU game with a severely sprained ankle and torn ligaments in his right index finger. True freshman Troy Aikman started under center, becoming the first true rookie to start at quarterback at Oklahoma since World War II.[15] Despite entering the game with a 2–4 record, including an embarrassing 24–7 loss to modest Kansas State, the Jayhawks took the Sooners to task, winning 28–11. "Troy was just about to turn eighteen when he was thrown into that game," recalls Merv Johnson. "I think Kansas scored three touchdowns on us in the second half without gaining a single first down."[16] The Sooners dropped from second to tenth in the AP poll after the loss—a particularly galling development considering that Oklahoma State had risen to seventh.

With Bradley and a contingent of injured players back in the lineup, Oklahoma cleared the next two conference games with victories over Missouri (49–7) and Colorado (42–17) before once again tossing a monkey wrench into number one–ranked Nebraska's machinery by the score of 17–7. The following weekend witnessed an unprecedented event in the history of Oklahoma football; the Sooners hosted the Cowboys with both ranked among the nation's top five teams—OSU was rated second and OU third. The two teams fought to a 7–7 tie at the half, and the Cowboys stretched their lead to 14–7 in the third quarter before the Sooners notched the final seventeen unanswered points in their 24–14 victory. "I think we're a great football team," roared Switzer. "We've been excellent offensively since the Kansas loss and defensively we've been the best team in the country all year."[17] With the regular season complete, Danny Bradley was named the Big Eight Conference Offensive Player of the Year by the Associated Press, Tony Casillas earned All-American honors, and Bradley, Casillas, Darrell Reed, and Brian Bosworth were All-Conference selections.

Oklahoma had earned its first conference title since 1980 and its accompanying berth in the Orange Bowl, this time to play Don James's Washington Huskies. Heading into bowl season, Oklahoma once again found itself in a position to vie for a sixth national crown. Brigham Young was ranked first, Oklahoma was second, Florida was third (the Gators were on probation and ineligible to go to a bowl), and Washington was fourth.

It did not take long after the game commenced for the Huskies to establish their credibility as they scored two unanswered touchdowns to take a 14–0 lead. Oklahoma came roaring back in the second period to score its first touchdown after Jim Rockford intercepted a tipped pass, and its second—and final—touchdown on the half's last play, a sixty-one-yard Bradley-to-Shepard pass. Neither team drew blood in the third period, but early in the fourth, Lashar hit a twenty-two-yard field goal to break the 14–14 tie. And then the controversy began. When the officials signaled that Lashar's field goal was good, the RUF/NEKS wheeled the Sooner Schooner onto the Orange Bowl field in celebration, only to be flagged for unsportsmanlike conduct (Switzer would later refer to the incident as "unhorsemanlike conduct"). Though Oklahoma had been granted permission to allow the Schooner to roll during the game by Dan McNamera of the Orange Bowl Committee, the officials had not been consulted.[18] The field goal was disallowed, and the ensuing attempt—from fifteen yards further back—failed. Washington would score two second-half touchdowns to take the day 28–17. Brigham Young won the national title, Washington hugged them tightly from second place, and Oklahoma wrapped up the year ranked sixth. "We had a good year in 1984," comments Switzer. "We beat Nebraska and should've beaten Texas."[19] After twelve years at the helm, Switzer's record of 115–23–4 was still tops among the nation's active coaches, and for the first time since the late seventies the Sooners were back on track. Spencer Tillman reflects on the factors contributing to Oklahoma's emergence from the slump of 1981–1983:

I think the biggest differences between the Sooner teams in the early eighties and the 1984–1985 teams were the lack of continuity at quarterback and offensive coordinator. The fact that we were tinkering with the I-formation and going through the transition in offensive coordinators in 1983–1985 played a pivotal role. We had Galen in '83, Mack in '84, and Jim Donnan in '85. And then at quarterback we had Watts, Phelps, Shepard, and Bradley all squeezed into that compressed time frame. The continuity—or lack thereof—of the mission-critical positions of quarterback and offensive coordinator had a lot to do with our lack of success in 1981 through 1983.[20]

The Wishbone, having been relegated to an alternate offense in 1981, 1982, and 1983, and then employed without its true triple-option capabilities in 1984, was about to make a stunning comeback.

∵

In the winter of 1985, offensive coordinator Mack Brown departed to take the reins at Tulane and was replaced by Jim Donnan. "When Jim arrived," explains Switzer, "we went back to the true Wishbone with some variations we'd picked up from Air Force. Once again, we became a true triple-option football team."[21] The Sooners welcomed back fifty-one lettermen including fourteen starters—six on offense and eight on defense—but were questionable at the team's most fundamental position: quarterback. Sophomore Troy Aikman, expected to take over the slot, was handicapped by a negative public perception born from the loss to Kansas in 1984; filling in for the injured Bradley, Aikman had absorbed much of the blame for the loss in Lawrence although he had not been solely responsible for it. The competition for quarterback in the spring of 1985 was between Aikman and Kyle Irvin. Freshmen Eric Mitchel and Jamelle Deveron Holieway—George Cumby's cousin—would add further depth when they arrived in August. Holieway, the Los Angeles Times' 4A Player of the Year and one of the nation's most highly prized quarterback prospects, explains how he came to cast his lot with the Sooners:

> I picked Oklahoma because of their tradition and because of Thomas Lott. He wore a bandana underneath his helmet, and I thought that was great, so I started doing it myself in high school. Coach Switzer had also let Joe Washington wear his silver shoes, and I thought that he had to be a cool coach to allow that sort of thing; he let players be themselves. And then I finally met him. He was scheduled to be the guest speaker at our high school football banquet the next evening, so I was the last stop on his recruiting trip. He walked into my house and said, "Jamelle, I'm tired." I asked him if he'd like to have a seat on the couch or in the chair, but instead he said he'd rather just lie down on the floor, so we got down there together, side-by-side, and just talked. Every other recruiter that had come to the house had sat at the dining room table and talked with

me and my parents, but with Switzer, it was just him and me lying there talking, and we got to know each other really well. He told me about the things he liked about the way I played, and we bonded that day. Before he left I told him, "Coach, if you want me, I'll come to OU." After meeting Barry Switzer, I was convinced that Oklahoma was the place for me.[22]

But when Irwin went down with a cracked fibula in the spring, Aikman became the man, and it did not take him long to impress. Offensive coordinator Jim Donnan recognized Aikman's potential early on. He commented, "Troy Aikman is the best-kept secret in America. When [people] think of an Oklahoma quarterback they think of a Thomas Lott or a J. C. Watts or a Danny Bradley, and Troy isn't along those lines. But he's an outstanding athlete with outstanding leadership qualities. He's got the best arm of any quarterback I've had in 18 years of coaching and I coached Gary Huff at Florida State when he led the nation in passing."[23]

In the final spring showdown, the format was changed from a true Red-White game to a 107-play scrimmage because of the large number of players out with injuries. In the game, Aikman excelled completing 15 of 22 passes for 203 yards and four touchdowns. And suddenly, the fans found themselves ready to forget the Aikman of 1984 and adopt the Aikman of 1985.

Oklahoma had been scheduled to open the season early with a September 14 game against highly regarded SMU, but ABC requested that the game be moved to December 7 to accommodate its broadcasting schedule. So the Sooners' first game would be played against the Minnesota Golden Gophers led by Lou Holtz. The game, played on September 28, was the latest scheduled opening game the Sooners had played since their 1961 September 30 kickoff against Notre Dame. Switzer realized that although the schedule modification would benefit his team by affording it an additional two weeks to prepare, it would also give his opponent the dangerous advantage of having played two games prior to hosting the Sooners.

Number one Oklahoma arrived in Minneapolis a damaged team. In the weeks prior to the game, offensive guards Eric Pope and Jeff Pickett had been hobbled by respective ankle and knee injuries; offensive tackle Greg Johnson suffered from a knee bruise; defensive tackles Jeff Tupper and Steve Bryan were also day-to-day; and halfback Damon Stell was slowed by ankle problems. Meanwhile, by the time its bout with the Sooners rolled around, Minnesota had already vanquished Montana 62–7 and Wichita State 28–14. Once again, shortly after kickoff, the seventeen-and-a-half-point favorite Sooners found themselves in an opening-day dogfight. Late in the game and nursing a dangerous 13–0 lead, the Sooners turned the ball over in their own territory, allowing Gopher quarterback Rickey Fogie to lead his team to a touchdown, tightening the score to 13–7. But the Oklahoma defense, so resilient throughout the game, stopped a last-minute Minnesota drive to preserve the win. The 13–7 margin of victory represented a continuation of slow starts for the Sooners; the last full-fledged blowout inflicted by Oklahoma on an opening-day opponent had been in 1975 in a 62–7 blasting of Oregon. Aikman acknowledged after the game that he had not played particularly well, but what he *had* done was more important—he had not turned the ball over, and he had not lost the game. Compounding the postgame anticlimax, there were more injuries. Tillman, who had impressed in the first quarter by plowing through the Gopher defense for seventy-three yards, left the game early in the second period with a hamstring injury that was expected to sideline him for four to five weeks, and Earl Johnson reinjured his kneecap and was lost for the season.[24]

If Aikman had been tentative in his first game of the season, he took command in his second. Switzer realized that the best way to encourage talent was to allow it full range of expression, so he turned Aikman loose through the air against OU's next opponent, Kansas State. Behind Aikman's arm—he passed for 177 yards—the Sooners ran over the Wildcats in Manhattan 41–6. Oklahoma generated 540 yards of offense and 30 first downs against a defense that had been ranked fourteenth nationally. In addition to Aikman's golden arm, he proved he could run the option by breaking off runs of sixteen, eighteen, and twenty-five yards. "I decided to just go out there and throw the ball," declared Aikman. For the second week in a row, an opponent had only scored once on the staunch Sooner defense.[25]

The Sooners journeyed to Dallas as a team on a mission: to defeat Texas and exact revenge for the injustice suffered the previous year. As both teams stood side by side on the ramp waiting to enter the Cotton Bowl, Earl Johnson described how the Texas and Oklahoma players interacted: "You walk down the [ramp] with your opponents, you look at 'em, and you bark at 'em," said Johnson. "That's what we do while they're moo'in at us." Brian Bosworth also spoke of his feelings on OU-Texas day, explaining, "It's the electricity you feel; the tension. It's the hatred for each school. It's something that for myself personally, when I go down that ramp it's such a gut feeling that my stomach ties up in a knot and I just get all upset. It's a total transformation inside [your] personality when you go down that ramp."[26]

The 1985 Oklahoma-Texas game was a typical trench-war affair. With the game scoreless late in the first period, Texas drew first blood by picking off a midair fumble and returning it seven yards for a 7–0 lead. But it would be Texas's only score of the afternoon. On the Sooners' next drive, they lashed back with a forty-three-yard pass from Aikman to Keith Jackson, followed by eight running plays to tie the game at seven apiece at the half. Oklahoma took the lead—and the game—on a forty-five-yard run by Patrick Collins in the fourth quarter. "It was a triple-option play," said Aikman. "I took it outside and surprisingly enough, [the Texas defense] took me; I don't know why they did, but I got the ball over to Collins and he's got such great speed he just out ran everybody to the end zone."[27] But the true star in the 14–7 triumph had been the young Sooner defense, headed by the Big Eight Defensive Player of the Week, Brian Bosworth. Switzer called his defense's effort "the best by an Oklahoma defense in 20 years."[28] Pat Putnam of *Sports Illustrated* wrote:

> Going into the Texas game, the Sooners were first nationally in total defense (146.5 yards allowed per game), first against the rush (39 yards), third against the pass and second in points surrendered (6.5). On Saturday, Oklahoma held the Longhorns to just 17 yards on the ground and 53 in the air. Texas had a grand total of four first downs, none in the second half. "Those statistics are incredible," said Sooner linebacker Paul Migliazzo. "We knew we could stop them. But accomplish that? No way." Moreover, Oklahoma accomplished that without Tony Casillas, its All-America noseguard. On the game's third play, he went down with

a sprained right knee. The Sooner defense, particularly its irrepressible and brilliant linebacker Brian Bosworth, was in high gear. As a freshman last year, Bosworth had said he hated everything in Texas, including the color burnt orange, which reminded him of vomit. "I'd kill to beat Texas" [he said]; Bosworth finished the game with 14 tackles, 11 of them unassisted, and an interception.[29]

It was Oklahoma's first win over Texas since 1982 and only the second victory over the Longhorns since the Sooners' last national title in 1975. As Putnam had indicated, the Sooner defense was playing lights-out—they had only allowed two scores all year long (the third scored against OU had been by Texas's defense following a turnover). Another factor played an important role in OU's success: Troy Aikman. Aikman's performance in the triple option had steadily improved from Minneapolis to Manhattan to Dallas, providing a comfortable and effective complement to the defense. His proficiency in the passing game promised to treat Oklahoma fans to an aerial show unseen since Bobby Warmack left campus. "Troy could run the Wishbone," recalls Tillman. "He was a little tall, but he could execute that offense."[30]

With a 3–0 start, a third-place ranking in the national wire service polls, a bulletproof defense, and a balanced offense, the Sooners were a confident team. Miami coach Jimmy Johnson—who, while coaching at Oklahoma State, had lost all five head-to-head coaching matchups with Barry Switzer—was in his second season in Coral Gables. His first team had finished 1984 with an 8–5 record, and, although the Hurricanes had begun the new season with high expectations, they had dropped their opening game to Florida, 23–35 and were ranked twenty-second in the nation as they journeyed to Norman.

Oklahoma and Miami found themselves deadlocked at 7–7 after the first quarter. Hurricane quarterback Vinny Testaverde burned the Sooner defense with a fifty-six-yard touchdown pass, and Aikman retaliated with a fifty-yard bomb to Keith Jackson followed by a fourteen-yard scoring strike to Shepard. Then, in the second quarter, disaster struck when Miami defensive end Jerome Brown sacked Aikman, fracturing his fibula. Prior to his injury, Aikman had completed 6 of 7 passes for 131 yards and a touchdown and had broken off a

26-yard run to the Hurricane twenty-one. With Aikman under center, Oklahoma had accounted for 220 yards in the first twenty minutes. With their starting quarterback on the sideline, Switzer and Donnan had a decision to make: whether to toss Eric Mitchel or Jamelle Holieway—both true freshmen—into the meat grinder. Holieway, having already played one series against Kansas State, got the nod.

"Coincidentally, the week before the Miami game was the first time I had ever practiced with the number one offense," recounts Holieway, "and I did pretty well. Then Troy broke his leg against Miami, and I had to take over; Switzer figured that if I could hold my own against our top-rated defense, I should be able to do okay against Miami. When I went in, Eric Pope, a senior, told me to relax and just handle it the way I did in practice."[31] Tillman was in the huddle when Holieway entered the game. "I remember Jamelle running in and saying, 'Let's Roll!'" comments Spencer, "and I looked over at two of our offensive linemen and sort of shook my head and thought to myself, 'Alright; What do we have here?'"[32] What the Sooners had was a young Wishbone operative, confident beyond his years. But the matchup between Miami's quick, strong, defensive linemen and Oklahoma's young inexperienced quarterback spelled defeat for the Sooners that afternoon. "Their linebackers weren't that good—we could run past them all day," said Anthony Stafford. "It was their defensive line that made the difference. They were big, strong, and fast. We'd never seen anything like them before."[33]

Although the tenth-ranked Sooners' hopes for a national title seemed gone, the serendipitously premature promotion of Holieway had set them on a path they could not have anticipated on October 19. "We hadn't had the bell cow quarterback in the early eighties, and that was probably the difference between our teams then and in 1985," reflects Merv Johnson. "I think that when you've got the guy you need at quarterback, you know what to do and what offense to run."[34]

Oklahoma's next game—only its second home game of the season—was with Iowa State. Although the Cyclones tugged a mediocre 3–3 record with them to Oklahoma, their defense was ranked sixth in the nation. Along with Holieway, freshman Leon Perry was slated to start at left half in place of the still-injured Tillman. Shortly after taking the field, the Sooners dashed any doubts their fans might have entertained about Holieway's ability to drive the team. After playing for only thirty-four minutes, Oklahoma—with Jamelle at the controls—led 38–7. The five-foot-nine, 175-pound quarterback carried the ball eleven times for seventy-six yards and a touchdown and tossed a seventy-seven-yard touchdown pass to Derrick Shepard. Eric Mitchel entered the game with 10:05 remaining in the third quarter and finished the Cyclones off, 59–14. The Sooner offense had churned out 643 yards—556 on the ground and 101 through the air. Mitchel accounted for 135 on 15 carries, and Perry ran for 132 on 5 totes. The Sooners had been brilliant, but sadly for Troy Aikman, history had repeated itself. Just as Dean Blevins had lost his starting position to Thomas Lott while sidelined with an injury in 1976, Troy Aikman had lost any hope of reclaiming his starting role due to Holieway's mastery of the triple option.

Over the next four weeks, the Sooner caravan rolled over Kansas (48–6), Missouri (51–6), Colorado (31–0), and Nebraska (27–7) before encountering its first true challenge since the Miami game. With a winter storm brewing, Oklahoma traveled to Stillwater to play the 8–2 Cowboys. Lewis Field, in the minutes between warm-up and kickoff, had undergone an astounding transformation. "When we went out to warm up before the game," recalls Anthony Stafford, "the temperature was in the mid to low thirties. We went back into the locker room, and when we came out to play the game about fifteen minutes later, the field was covered with ice."[35] The game, since labeled the "Ice Bowl," presented conditions no other Sooner team had faced before as the players struggled to negotiate the slippery, frozen tundra. A touchdown by Tillman and two Lashar field goals saved the day for Oklahoma in the 13–0 triumph. "In all the time I've known Coach Switzer," laughs Holieway, "he's only lied to me once; when he recruited me he told me it never snows in Oklahoma. And then in my first year, over Thanksgiving weekend, we played in the Ice Bowl against Oklahoma State in Stillwater."[36]

Two days later, second-ranked Iowa was felled by Ohio State, lifting Oklahoma to second in the UPI poll and third—behind Miami—in the AP poll. The Big Eight Conference champion Sooners had earned a berth in the Orange Bowl against Penn State. A victory over the undefeated Nittany Lions would set the stage for OU's sixth national title, but would not assure it. Should the Hurricanes beat *their* Sugar Bowl opponent, Tennessee, they would be in a position to ascend to number one, especially since they had already defeated

Oklahoma in October. But first, the Sooners would have to get by SMU on Pearl Harbor Day. Having lost four of their ten games, the Mustangs, projected as possible national championship contenders in September, had not lived up to expectations, and they proved to be little more than an Orange Bowl warm-up for the Sooners in the 35–13 season finale.

Although the Nittany Lions traveled to Miami unbeaten and untied, they had been installed as seven-and-a-half-point underdogs. It was virtually unheard of for an undefeated team—especially one with a coach the caliber of Paterno—to be listed as a touchdown underdog in a national title contest. Penn State was led by quarterback John Shaffer, who carried a 54–0 lifetime football record into the Orange Bowl, having never lost a game as a starting quarterback from grammar school through college. Penn State also boasted a defense that allowed only 10.5 points per game. But the Sooner defense had allowed only 8.5 yards per outing and had only given up one rushing touchdown in the past seven games. The Sooners were also first in the nation against the pass and second against both rushing and scoring, earning them the best ranking of any college football team in NCAA history. "We knew Penn State had a great team," comments Switzer. "When you're playing in a championship game, you're playing people who are as good or better than you are."[37]

Penn State's big, speedy defenders managed to close the corners on Oklahoma's option game in the first quarter as the Nittany Lions took a 7–0 lead. The Sooners' first first down did not come until the final seconds of the first quarter on a thirteen-yard pass from Holieway to Keith Jackson, and Oklahoma would complete the drive with a Tim Lashar field goal on the second play of the second quarter. Later in the period, Holieway surprised the crowd and the Nittany Lions with a seventy-one-yard touchdown pass to Keith Jackson, giving Oklahoma a 10–7 lead. On Penn State's next two possessions, Shaffer would be picked off by Sonny Brown and Tony Rayburn, setting up consecutive Sooner field goals and upping OU's lead to 16–7. But in the waning seconds of the half, as Holieway scrambled to run out the clock, he fumbled in Oklahoma territory, and Penn State capitalized with a field goal, decreasing Oklahoma's lead and bringing the halftime score to 16–10.

The Nittany Lions took the second-half kickoff and methodically drove seventy yards before Sonny Brown snagged his second interception of the evening, this time in the shadow of the Sooner goal line. Unable to move from inside their five, the Sooners punted the ball to Penn State, but on his return Michael Timpson was separated from the ball by Sooner Jodie Britt, and it was recovered by Mike Mantle (Mickey's nephew). The Sooners added another field goal, lifting their lead to 19–10. The Oklahoma defense continued to frustrate the PSU running game and its quarterback, who had thrown three backbreaking interceptions during the evening. Paterno reluctantly replaced Shaffer with Matt Knizer in the fourth quarter, to little avail; his offense was rendered inert by the Oklahoma defense for the remainder of the game. Finally, with under two minutes remaining, Sooner fullback Lydell Carr removed any and all doubt about the final result with a sixty-one-yard touchdown run, giving Oklahoma the lead, 25–10, and the game. Earlier in the evening, it had been announced over the Orange Bowl public address system that Jimmy Johnson's Miami Hurricanes had forfeited any potential claim to the national title by losing the Sugar Bowl to Tennessee, 35–7.

With the Orange Bowl victory, Oklahoma had wrapped up its sixth national championship, joining Notre Dame and Alabama as the only teams to have won six titles since the Second World War. At the conclusion of the 1985 season, Brian Bosworth took home the inaugural Dick Butkus Award; Tony Casillas won the Lombardi Award and was named the Big Eight Conference Defensive Player of the Year; Bosworth, Casillas, and Kevin Murphy were named All-Americans; and Bosworth, Casillas, Holieway, Anthony Phillips, Mark Hutson, Keith Jackson, Darrell Reed, and Kevin Murphy were selected All–Big Eight Conference players. Switzer had once again adapted. A pure Wishbone proponent and innovator, he had found himself in a position in 1985 to revert to his signature offense and had the personnel with which to do it, and it had paid enormous dividends. "If Troy hadn't broken his leg," he comments, "we *still* would have won the national championship without a doubt. But Holieway was perfect for the Wishbone. In 1985 we exploded as an offensive football team, led the nation in rushing, and never looked back."[38]

Yet *had* Switzer bothered to look back after the 1986 Orange Bowl, he would have seen 118 major college football teams trailing behind.

Epilogue

A TEMPEST PAST

Hours after the final seconds had ticked off of the Orange Bowl clock on January 1, 1986, the last few stragglers had finally filed out and the stadium fell silent and dark. The Sooner coaches and players would celebrate into the night, but their fans would continue their celebration well into the following year and beyond. Barry Switzer would lead the team for three more seasons, capturing conference titles in 1986 and 1987 along with third-place national finishes both years in both wire service polls. Some had suggested in the early eighties that the Wishbone offense had run its course, that other coaches had learned how to solve its intricacies, but in the three seasons following their 1985 national title, the Sooners had clearly proven them wrong. The 'Bone continued to thrive in Norman, Oklahoma.

However, in 1988, storm clouds began to roil over Owen Field. After sixteen years at the helm, Barry Switzer tendered his resignation on the heels of felonies perpetrated by several of his players. On June 19, 2009—the twentieth anniversary of his resignation—Switzer commented on events that culminated in his leaving the university:

Let's set the record straight; I was never fired and no one ever asked me for my resignation. I resigned completely of my own volition. Of all the negative events that happened on my watch, there were really only four bad apples, four troubled players, that created the controversy. When Charles Thompson appeared on the cover of *Sports Illustrated*[1] in that orange jump suit it occurred to me that the story that *should* have been on that cover was that of Jerry Anderson [Anderson, who played cornerback for Oklahoma in 1975 and 1976, was honored for heroically rescuing several Tulsans trapped in flood in 1984 but drowned five years later while saving two young boys from a rain-swollen river in Murfreesboro, Tennessee].[2] He saved those kids but in the effort, he lost his own life.

Those are the stories that mean something. But the felonies perpetrated by those four individuals overshadowed all the good, positive things that hundreds of other young men from this program had done. I recall having a team meeting and an open discussion with our players after those criminal incidents occurred and I suggested that perhaps I'd made a mistake by giving some of these guys second chances through the years, that maybe I should have been more hard-lined with the team. And one of our kids from the back of the room stood up and said, "No you didn't, coach, you didn't do wrong. Thank goodness you gave second chances; you gave me another chance and I took advantage of it." And essentially what he was saying to me was that you never hear about the successful second chances given to players because those kids take advantage of them, they become good citizens, they become good players, they get their degrees, and they move on to be successful in life . . . and yet they're anonymous. It's the ones who fail to take advantage of those second chances that we hear about, that give the program a black eye. Ninety-nine percent of all the kids we recruited were fine kids. Do I have any regrets? [Switzer pondered his reply for a moment]. Nah, what happened is a part of life. I went on, I've had a great life, and I've accomplished a lot since I left. Donnie Duncan told me that there was a life outside football and he was right.[3]

There was indeed life after college football for Barry Switzer. After sitting on the sidelines for five seasons, he moved on to the National Football League in 1994 to become head coach of the Dallas Cowboys, leading the team to a victory in Super Bowl XXX in his second season. Switzer remains one of only two coaches to have taken a college team to a national championship and a professional team to a Super Bowl title (his friend Jimmy Johnson is the other). Additionally, he was inducted into the College Football Hall of Fame in 2001.

But things were not so bright in Norman after his departure. For the next ten years, the Sooners would wander in the wilderness, floundering under three different head coaches. Assistant coach Gary Gibbs followed Switzer as

Barry Switzer at home, Veterans Day 2010. Author's collection.

head coach at the University of Oklahoma in 1989 and, fighting scholarship limitations resulting from further probations, led the Sooners to a 44–23–2 six-year record before his dismissal following the 1994 season. Howard Schnellenberger succeeded Gibbs for a solitary season before resigning on the heels of a 5–5–1 year, and former Sooner player and assistant John Blake took the reins from 1996 through 1998 and, although managing to recruit a wealth of young talent, posted the worst head coaching record in the history of the program, 12–22–0. And perhaps most importantly, the Wishbone had been discarded. Tossed aside by Gibbs, Schnellenberger, and Blake, the offensive set—so devastating for the better part of two decades—had become little more than a glorious anachronism relegated to a historical footnote.

⁘

Whether run from the Split-t or the Wishbone, the triple-option offense was a driving force in college football—a tempest on the playing field—in the last half of the twentieth century. From 1947 through 1963, Bud Wilkinson set the college football world on its ear with the Split-t, and ten years later Barry Switzer took the Oklahoma Sooners back to the summit using the Wishbone. Both coaches were exceptional recruiters, each able to connect with talented young men in his own way. Both understood the intricacies of the triple-option offense, and together they won more national titles with it—six—than any other major college football team. Bear Bryant won crowns at Alabama in 1973, 1978, and 1979 using the alignment, and Darrell Royal won championships at Texas in 1969 and 1970 using Emory Bellard's new formation. If, as Royal stated, Bellard wrote a "sweet song" with the development of his Wishbone, Oklahoma refined that song and expanded it into a magnificent symphony.

As instrumental as the Wishbone offense was in resurrecting Oklahoma's football program in 1970, without the right man at quarterback—the "bell cow," as Merv Johnson put it—the experiment might have failed and the Sooners may well have continued to flounder. But they did have the right man at precisely the right time in Jack Mildren; the talent, speed, skill, and composure Mildren displayed while executing the fledgling offense earned him the nickname "the Godfather of the Wishbone." After his football career ended, Mildren overcame challenges in many areas to' become vice chairman of the Arvest Bank Group and Oklahoma's twenty-second Lieutenant Governor. But at the age of fifty-eight, Jack lost his final struggle. On May 22, 2008, Larry Jack Mildren succumbed to stomach cancer. Services were held at McFarlin Memorial United Methodist Church in Norman, Oklahoma, beneath a Maxfield Parrish sky. The eulogy was delivered by his former head coach, Chuck Fairbanks. Those gathered to pay their final respects consisted of dignitaries, teammates, family, and friends—those who knew him, admired him, and loved him. Among the many bouquets adorning the church stood one that had been sent by members of the 1971 University of Nebraska Cornhuskers. Although the rivalry the two teams had experienced since 1912 had itself become a casualty, diluted by the scheduling conflicts resulting from the formation of the Big Twelve Conference in 1997 and eliminated altogether by the Huskers' defection to the Big Ten Conference in 2010, those men who had participated in the 1971 "Game of the Century" were determined not to allow its memory or its spirit to pass away. The respect they had brought to the contest nearly four decades earlier had not been left on the playing field after the final whistle; it lived on— lives on—to this day. Like Jack, the former Husker players cared about events and individuals beyond the yard lines of college football. As Antonio said to Sebastian in *The Tempest*,[4] "Whereof, what's past is prologue," what has come before in the sport of college football is and shall continue to be a preamble to its future. Rules may change, formations will come and go, but the spirit and dedication of the men who play it will remain.

Notes

General note: Source material contributing to the creation of this book was derived from existing scholarship combined with extensive interviews conducted by the author over a five-year period. The anecdotal information collected and used by the author from these interviews resides in his personal library.

INTRODUCTION

1. J. Brent Clark, *Sooner Century: 100 Glorious Years of Oklahoma Football: 1895–1985* (Coal Valley, Ill.: Quality Sports, 1995), 48.
2. Ray Dozier, *The Oklahoma Football Encyclopedia* (Champaign, Ill.: Sports Publishing, 2006), 74.
3. George Lynn Cross, *Presidents Can't Punt: The OU Football Tradition* (Norman: University of Oklahoma Press, 1977), 5–6.
4. Ibid., 6.
5. Clark, *Sooner Century,* 97.
6. Jay Wilkinson and Gretchen Hirsch, *Bud Wilkinson: An Intimate Portrait of an American Legend* (Champaign, Ill.: Sagamore, 1994), 12.
7. Ibid., 13–16.
8. Ibid., 17–18.
9. Cross, *Presidents Can't Punt,* 36–49.

CHAPTER ONE

1. Jay O'Neal, interview with author, September 2008.
2. Wilkinson and Hirsch, *Bud Wilkinson,* 78.
3. O'Neal, interview, September 2008.
4. James Quirk, *The Ultimate Guide to College Football: Rankings, Records, and Scores of the Major Teams and Conferences* (Urbana: University of Illinois Press, 2004), 129.
5. Cross, *Presidents Can't Punt,* 323–24.
6. O'Neal, interview, September 2008.
7. Helen Thomas, note to author, March 2009.
8. J. D. Roberts, interview with author, January 2009.
9. Jimmy Harris, interview with author, September 2008.
10. Clendon Thomas, interview with author, January 2009.
11. Harris, interview, September 2008.
12. J. D. Roberts, interview with author, March 2009.
13. Harold Keith, *Forty-Seven Straight: The Wilkinson Era at Oklahoma* (Norman: University of Oklahoma Press, 1984), 294.
14. Roberts, interview, January 2009.
15. Wilkinson and Hirsch, *Bud Wilkinson,* 77–78.
16. Cross, *Presidents Can't Punt,* 253.
17. Ibid., 318–19.
18. Wilkinson and Hirsch, *Bud Wilkinson,* 79.

19. Cross, *Presidents Can't Punt,* 319.

20. Roberts, interview, January 2009.

21. Thomas, interview, January 2009.

22. John Tatum, interview with author, December 2008.

23. Ivan N. Kaye, *Good Clean Violence: A History of College Football* (Philadelphia: J. B. Lippincott, 1973), 235.

24. Red Grange, "The Eleven Best Elevens," *Sports Illustrated,* September 21, 1959.

25. Wilkinson and Hirsch, *Bud Wilkinson,* 75–76.

26. Bob Boyd, interview with author, October 2008.

27. Harris, interview, September 2008.

28. O'Neal, interview, September 2008.

29. Dr. D. G. Willard notes, University of Oklahoma Athletics Communications Department files.

30. Boyd, interview, October 2008.

31. Dr. D. G. Willard notes.

32. Ibid.

33. Cross, *Presidents Can't Punt,* 312.

34. Dr. F. R. Hassler to Dr. D. G. Willard, October 9, 1961, University of Oklahoma Athletics Communications Department files.

35. Jay Wilkinson, interview with author, October 2008.

36. "Kansas Muffs 2-Point Play," *Tulsa World,* October 25, 1959.

37. O'Neal, interview, September 2008.

CHAPTER TWO

1. Keith, *Forty-Seven Straight,* 281–82.

2. "Faces in the Crowd," *Sports Illustrated,* March 14, 1960.

3. Jimmy Carpenter, interview with author, March 2009.

4. Dozier, *Oklahoma Football Encyclopedia,* 147.

5. Cross, *Presidents Can't Punt,* 322.

6. Wayne Mason, "Blocked Punt Sets up Win," *Tulsa World,* October 2, 1960.

7. Dozier, *Oklahoma Football Encyclopedia,* 148.

8. B. A. Bridgewater, "Longhorn Power Snares 24–0 Win, Worst Since 1941," *Tulsa World,* October 9, 1960.

9. Jimmy Jones, "Sooner Gridders Calm After Win," *Tulsa World,* October 23, 1960.

10. Leon Cross, interview with author, March 2009.

11. Carpenter, interview, March 2009.

12. Tatum, interview, December 2008.

13. Cross, interview, March 2009.

14. Mervin Hyman, Arlie W. Schardt, and Morton Sharnik, "The Midwest," *Sports Illustrated,* September 18, 1961.

15. Wann Smith, "Jay Wilkinson: A Retrospective," *Sooners Illustrated,* December 2008.

16. Jay O'Neal, interview with author, March 2009.

17. Ibid.

18. Ibid.

19. Keith, *Forty-Seven Straight,* 300.

20. Ibid.

CHAPTER THREE

1. O'Neal, interview, March 2009.
2. Ibid.
3. Mike McClellan, interview with author, April 2009.
4. O'Neal, interview, March 2009.
5. John Tatum, interview with author, April 2009.
6. Ibid.
7. Jay Wilkinson, interview with author, June 2009.
8. Carpenter, interview, March 2009.
9. Jerry Pettibone, interview with author, December 2008.
10. Carpenter, interview, March 2009.
11. Tatum, interview, April 2009.
12. Ibid.
13. Keith, *Forty-Seven Straight,* 313.
14. Wilkinson and Hirsch, *Bud Wilkinson,* 79.
15. Dozier, *Oklahoma Football Encyclopedia,* 151.
16. Keith, *Forty-Seven Straight,* 317.
17. Jay O'Neal, interview with author, May 2009.
18. Ibid.
19. Ibid.
20. O'Neal, interview, March 2009.
21. Larry Schwartz, "Namath Was Lovable Rogue," espn.go.com/classic/biography/s/namath_joe.html.
22. O'Neal, interview, May 2009.
23. Jay Wilkinson, interview with author, September 2008.

CHAPTER FOUR

1. Cross, *Presidents Can't Punt,* 329–31.
2. Jay Wilkinson, interview with author, July 2009.
3. Bobby Drake Keith, interview with author, May 2009.
4. Mervin Hyman, "Football's Week," *Sports Illustrated,* September 30, 1963.
5. Harold Keith, Sooner Press Conference, University of Oklahoma Athletics Communications Department files, September 23, 1963.
6. Jay O'Neal, interview with author, June 2009.
7. Dan Jenkins, "One Hundred Plays in a Hundred-plus Degrees," *Sports Illustrated,* October 7, 1963.
8. Keith, *Forty-Seven Straight,* 339.
9. O'Neal, interview, May 2009.
10. Tatum, interview, December 2008.
11. O'Neal, interview, May 2009.
12. Jerry Thompson, interview with author, May 2009.
13. Keith, interview, May 2009.
14. Ralph Neely, interview with author, January 2009.
15. Keith, interview, May 2009.

16. George Lynn Cross, *Blacks in White Colleges: Oklahoma's Landmark Cases* (Norman: University of Oklahoma Press, 1975), vii–viii.

17. Wilkinson and Hirsch, *Bud Wilkinson,* 73.

CHAPTER FIVE

1. Bill Thomas, "Wilkinson Sets Off Furor with Regents Over Politics Blast," *Daily Oklahoman,* January 19, 1964.

2. Neely, interview, January 2009.

3. Cross, *Presidents Can't Punt,* 347.

4. Leon Cross, interview with author, July 2009.

5. Jay Simon, "Gomer's Staff to Get Salary Hikes in April," *Daily Oklahoman,* March 17, 1964.

6. "'Gomer to Sue over Stickers," *Daily Oklahoman,* September 17, 1964.

7. Bill Connors, "90-Yard Pass Nets Sooners 13–3 Triumph," *Tulsa World,* September 20, 1964.

8. Allan Cromley, "Somebody Got Us Through, Gomer Gasps," *Daily Oklahoman,* September 20, 1964.

9. Dozier, *Oklahoma Football Encyclopedia,* 159.

10. "Effigy of Jones Found in Tree on Campus," *Daily Oklahoman,* October 21, 1964.

11. Bill Connors, "Sports of the World," *Tulsa World,* September 22, 1965.

12. Jay O'Neal, interview, June 2009.

13. Jay Cronley, interview with author, July 2009.

14. Bill Connors, "Pokes End OU Domination," *Tulsa World,* December 5, 1965.

15. Bobby Warmack, interview with author, July 2009.

16. Jerry Scarbrough, Gomer Favors New Face for Successor," *Daily Oklahoman,* December 7, 1965.

17. Cross, *Presidents Can't Punt,* 363.

18. Warmack, interview, July 2009.

19. Glen Condren, interview with author, July 2009.

20. Jim Riley, interview with author, July 2009.

21. Ron Shotts, interview with author, July 2009.

22. Ibid.

23. O'Neal, interview with author, July 2009.

24. J. D. Roberts, interview with author, July 2009.

25. Condren, interview, July 2009.

26. Ibid.

27. Jack Ging, interview with author, July 2009.

28. Wilkinson, interview, July 2009.

29. John Tatum, interview with author, May 2009.

30. Condren, interview, July 2009.

CHAPTER SIX

1. Merv Johnson, interview with author, August 2009.

2. Barry Switzer, interview with author, August 2009.

3. Johnson, interview, August 2009.

4. Switzer, interview, August 2009.
5. Johnny Majors, interview with author, August 2009.
6. Scarbrough, "Gomer Favors New Face for Successor."
7. Leon Cross, interview with author, August 2009.
8. "'I Just Don't Like to Lose,' comments Mackenzie," *Daily Oklahoman*, January 9, 1966.
9. Patricia Weld, "Family Comes First for Coach's Wife," *Daily Oklahoman*, April 20, 1966.
10. Dr. Homer Rice, interview with author, August 2009.
11. Switzer, interview, August 2009.
12. Warmack, interview, July 2009.
13. Larry Lacewell, interview with author, July 2009.
14. Bobby Warmack, interview with author, August 2009.
15. Switzer, interview, August 2009.
16. "More Passing for OU Seen by Mackenzie," *Daily Oklahoman*, March 11, 1966.
17. Volney Meece, "Youngsters Real Battlers, Mackenzie Says," *Daily Oklahoman*, September 20, 1966.
18. "Mackenzie Drills Sooners on Basics," *Daily Oklahoman*, September 28, 1966.
19. Frank Boggs, "Sooners Get Their Kicks Out of Kickers," *Daily Oklahoman*, October 11, 1966.
20. Ibid.
21. "Sooner Boss Pessimistic," *Daily Oklahoman*, October 14, 1966.
22. Rice, interview, August 2009.
23. Switzer, interview, August 2009.
24. Ibid.
25. Rice, interview, August 2009.
26. "Mackenzie Big 8 Coach of the Year," *Daily Oklahoman*, December 1, 1966.
27. "Sooner Spirits Not Chilled," *Daily Oklahoman*, December 1, 1966.
28. Rice, interview, August 2009.
29. Switzer, interview, August 2009.
30. Leon Cross, interview with author, August 2009.
31. Ray Soldan, "OU Won't Soon Forget Big, Smiling Jim Mackenzie," *Daily Oklahoman*, April 29, 1967.
32. Cross, interview, August 2009.
33. Galen Hall, interview with author, January 2010.
34. Johnson, interview, August 2009.
35. Cross, interview, August 2009.
36. Rice, interview, August 2009.
37. Switzer, interview, August 2009.

CHAPTER SEVEN
1. Volney Meece, "We'll Meet the Challenge, New OU Coach Says," *Daily Oklahoman*, May 3, 1967.
2. Rice, interview, August 2009.
3. Bill Connors, "Warmack's Deft Play Sparks Offensive Show," *Tulsa World*, September 24, 1967.

4. Volney Meece, "Chuck Elated Over First Victory," *Daily Oklahoman*, September 25, 1967.
5. Bill Connors, "Texas Reverses Tide as OU Drives Falter," *Tulsa World*, October 15, 1967.
6. Bill Connors, "Warmack's Last-Minute Pass Earns 14–10 Nod," *Tulsa World*, November 19, 1967.
7. Steve Zabel, interview with author, October 2009.
8. Wann Smith, "Sooner Bowl Heroes," *Sooners Illustrated*, January 2008.
9. "3 Juniors, 4 Sophs Wear Big 8 Crowns," *Daily Oklahoman*, December 7, 1967.
10. Ray Soldan, "Sooners' Warmack Honored," *Daily Oklahoman*, December 3, 1967.
11. Ray Soldan, "Sooners One Up on OJ Simpson," *Daily Oklahoman*, December 31, 1967.
12. "Sooners Get Week Off," *Daily Oklahoman*, December 4, 1967.
13. "Dickey Says Sooners and Vols Very Similar," *Daily Oklahoman*, December 20, 1967.
14. Smith, "Sooner Bowl Heroes."
15. Ibid.
16. Dozier, *Oklahoma Football Encyclopedia*, 171.
17. Ray Soldan, "Sooners' Warmack Honored," *Daily Oklahoman*, December 3, 1967.

CHAPTER EIGHT
1. "Sooners 'No. 1' on 25," *Daily Oklahoman*, July 7, 1968.
2. "Fairbanks Sees Thorny Path for OU," *Daily Oklahoman*, July 28, 1968.
3. Barry Switzer, interview with author, September 2009.
4. Eddie Hinton, interview with author, September 2009.
5. Ibid.
6. Ibid.
7. Ibid.
8. Leon Cross, interview with author, September 2009.
9. Ken Mendenhall, interview with author, September 2009.
10. Steve Zabel, interview with author, September 2009.
11. "Bowl Previews," *Sports Illustrated*, December 23, 1968.
12. Switzer, interview, September 2009.
13. Dozier, *Oklahoma Football Encyclopedia*, 175.
14. Ibid., 174.
15. Switzer, interview, September 2009.
16. Ibid.
17. "Mildren or Ripley? Fairbanks Unsure," *Daily Oklahoman*, April 5, 1968.
18. Switzer, interview, September 2009.
19. Larry Lacewell, interview with author, September 2009.
20. "Owens Close to Record," *Daily Oklahoman*, April 11, 1969.
21. Ray Soldan, "Mildren Dazzles Pitt 37–8," *Daily Oklahoman*, September 28, 1969.
22. Bob Hurt, "Sooners Better Than Last Year, Royal Says," *Daily Oklahoman*, October 7, 1969.
23. Bob Hurt, "Texans All Happy Fellers," *Daily Oklahoman*, October 12, 1969.
24. "Statistics," *Daily Oklahoman*, October 19, 1969.
25. "Sooners Get Extra Work to 'Catch Up,'" *Daily Oklahoman*, October 24, 1969.
26. Bill Connors, "Boom! Kansas State 59, OU 21," *Tulsa World*, October 26, 1969.
27. Katherine Hatch, "After 35 Years, K-State Wallops OU," *Daily Oklahoman*, October 26, 1969.

28. Mendenhall, interview, September 2009.
29. Ibid.
30. Switzer, interview, September 2009.
31. Dozier, *Oklahoma Football Encyclopedia,* 178.
32. William Nack, "A Name on the Wall," *Sports Illustrated,* July 23, 2001.
33. Bob Hurt, "OU LEAVES," *Daily Oklahoman,* October 27, 1970.
34. Dozier, *Oklahoma Football Encyclopedia,* 182.

CHAPTER NINE

1. Jimmy Banks, *The Darrell Royal Story* (Austin, Tex.: Shoal Creek, 1973), 120.
2. Ibid., 123.
3. Emory Bellard, interview with author, April 2009.
4. Switzer, interview, September 2009.
5. Jay O'Neal, interview with author, September 2010.
6. Darrell Royal, interview with author, April 2009.
7. Bellard, interview, April 2009.
8. Royal, interview, April 2009.
9. Michael Rosenberg, *War as They Knew It: Woody Hayes, Bo Schembechler, and American in a Time of Unrest* (New York: Grand Central Publishing, 2008), 77–78.
10. Rex Kern, interview with author, February 2009.
11. Archie Griffin, interview with author, February 2009.
12. Bellard, interview, April 2009.
13. Switzer, interview, September 2009.
14. Ibid.
15. Ibid.
16. Hall, interview, January 2010.
17. Lacewell, interview, September 2009.
18. Greg Pruitt, interview with author, October 2007.

CHAPTER TEN

1. Barry Switzer and Bud Shrake, *Bootlegger's Boy* (New York: William Morrow, 1990), 73.
2. Bob Hurt, "Sooner Grads Haunting Fairbanks," *Daily Oklahoman,* October 12, 1970.
3. Switzer and Shrake, *Bootlegger's Boy,* 73.
4. Bob Hurt, "Ready, Set, Second-Guess!" *Daily Oklahoman,* October 11, 1970.
5. Leon Crosswhite, interview with author, November 2009.
6. Switzer, interview, September 2009.
7. Dozier, *Oklahoma Football Encyclopedia,* 183–84.
8. Lacewell, interview, September 2009.
9. Katherine Hatch, "'Poor Aggies' Chant Started Awfully Early at Norman," *Daily Oklahoman,* November 19, 1970.
10. Wally Wallis, "We Should Have Stayed Home," *Daily Oklahoman,* November 29, 1970.
11. Volney Meece, "Sooners 'Respond Real Well in 76 Degrees,'" *Daily Oklahoman,* December 29, 1970.
12. Bill Connors, "Last Gasp Bama Field Goal Attempt Fails in Bluebonnet," *Tulsa World,* January 1, 1971.

13. "OU Athletic Director Dies on New York Trip," *Daily Oklahoman*, March 22, 1971.

14. Rice, interview, August 2009.

15. "Gomer Jones' Services Set," *Daily Oklahoman*, March 23, 1971.

16. Bob Hurt, "Sports Greats Bid Gomer Farewell," *Daily Oklahoman*, March 25, 1971.

17. Crosswhite, interview, November 2009.

18. Volney Meece, "Sooners Have Some Problems but Backfield Isn't One of Them," *Daily Oklahoman*, August 29, 1971.

19. Bill Connors, "OU Puts '30' on SMU Story," *Tulsa World*, September 19, 1971.

20. Greg Pruitt, interview with author, November 2009.

21. Harold Peterson, "Players of the Week," *Sports Illustrated*, October 11, 1971.

22. Switzer, interview, September 2009.

23. "No Words Can Describe It," *Daily Oklahoman*, October 10, 1971.

24. Greg Pruitt, interview with author, September 2007.

25. Ray Soldan, "Call Sooners Off; I'm Duly Impressed," *Daily Oklahoman*, October 18, 1971.

26. Bob Hurt, "Remember K-State? Sooners Sure Do," *Daily Oklahoman*, October 21, 1971.

27. Dozier, *Oklahoma Football Encyclopedia*, 187–88.

28. Ray Soldan, "Sooners Romp After 31–0 Half," *Daily Oklahoman*, January 2, 1972.

29. Bill Connors, "OU Gives Jack Winning Salute," *Tulsa World*, January 2, 1972.

30. Keith, *Forty-Seven Straight*, 214.

31. Barry Switzer, interview with author, March 2010.

32. Ibid.

CHAPTER ELEVEN

1. Leon Cross, interview with author, December 2009.

2. Dave Robertson, interview with author, December 2009.

3. Switzer and Shrake, *Bootlegger's Boy*, 81–82.

4. Ray Soldan, "Sooners Should Be Ranked Number 1," *Daily Oklahoman*, September 17, 1972.

5. Derland Moore, interview with author, December 2009.

6. Ibid.

7. Bob Hurt, "OU Used Granddads' Defense," *Daily Oklahoman*, October 16, 1972.

8. Crosswhite, interview, November 2009.

9. "Up Colorado, On Bouncing," *Daily Oklahoman*, October 22, 1972.

10. Robert B. Allen and Ray Soldan, "Pruitt's Sore Ankle Puts Lump in OU Fans' Throats," *Daily Oklahoman*, October 23, 1972.

11. Cross, interview, December 2009.

12. Pat Putnam, "Neither Rodgers Nor Pruitt Was Able to Do It," *Sports Illustrated*, December 4, 1972.

13. Bob Hurt, "Good Thing Sooners Tinkered with Ends," *The Daily Oklahoman*, October 24, 1972.

14. Ibid.

15. Ibid.

16. Robertson, interview, December 2009.

17. "Sooners Rally," *Daily Oklahoman*, October 24, 1972.

18. Hurt, "Good Thing Sooners Tinkered."

19. Hall, interview, January 2010.

20. "Chuck Doubts USC Could Sweep the Big 8," *Daily Oklahoman*, December 5, 1972.

21. Volney Meece, "Great . . . Sooners Not Sleepy," *Daily Oklahoman*, December 30, 1972.

CHAPTER TWELVE

1. Dozier, *Oklahoma Football Encyclopedia*, 193–94.

2. Volney Meece, "Players Glad Chuck Gets Big Chance," *Daily Oklahoman*, January 26, 1973.

3. Bob Hurt, "OU Aides, Players, Rally Behind Barry," *Daily Oklahoman*, January 27, 1973.

4. Bob Hurt, "OU Athletic Counsel Recommends Hiring Switzer," *Daily Oklahoman*, January 27, 1973.

5. "It's Official—Switzer Hired," *Daily Oklahoman*, February 9, 1973.

6. "Hogs Broyles High on Barry," *Daily Oklahoman*, January 30, 1973.

7. Bob Hurt, "Owens Recalls Switzer's Strategy," *Daily Oklahoman*, January 30, 1973.

8. Switzer and Shrake, *Bootlegger's Boy*, 93.

9. Frank Boggs, "Switzer Wins Nod from Search Panel as OU Grid Coach," *Daily Oklahoman*, January 30, 1973.

10. Hurt, "OU Aides, Players."

11. Barry Switzer, interview with author, September 2010.

12. "Proctor 'Accepts' OU Job," *Daily Oklahoman*, April 17, 1973.

13. "It's Official."

14. "Film Verifies That Sooner Stars are Missing," *Daily Oklahoman*, April 17, 1973.

15. Jimbo Elrod, interview with author, April 2010.

16. Larry Lacewell, interview with author, March 2008.

17. Rusty Weller, "Rumors, Denials Cloud OU Practice," *Daily Oklahoman*, April 20, 1973.

18. Ibid.

19. Ibid.

20. Wann Smith, "The Beginning of an Era," *Sooners Illustrated*, November 2006.

21. Volney Meece, "Switzer Praises Quarterback Davis," *Daily Oklahoman*, April 22, 1973.

22. Cross, interview, December 2009.

23. Smith, "Sooner Bowl Heroes."

24. "The Sooner Scandal, Blow-by-Blow," *Daily Oklahoman*, April 9, 1973.

25. Bob Hurt, "No Doubt, Probation Does Hurt," *Daily Oklahoman*, August 12, 1973.

26. Frank Boggs, "OU Not Throwing in the Towel," *Daily Oklahoman*, August 9, 1973.

27. Smith, "'The Beginning of an Era."

28. Joe Washington, interview with author, January 2010.

29. Dozier, *Oklahoma Football Encyclopedia*, 194.

30. Bob Hurt, "One of the Best I've Ever Seen," *Daily Oklahoman*, October 1, 1973.

31. "A View from the OU Locker Room," *Daily Oklahoman*, August 25, 1974.

32. Barry Switzer, interview with author, August 2007.

33. Ibid.

34. Hank Inman, "Miami Calmed on Blown FG," *Daily Oklahoman*, October 7, 1973.

35. Tinker Owens, interview with author, September 2007.

36. Frank Boggs, "Sooners Rope Steers," *Daily Oklahoman*, October 14, 1973.

37. Barry Switzer, interview with author, October 2006.

38. "A View from the OU Locker Room."
39. Bob Hurt, "This One's Especially Sweet for Barry," *Daily Oklahoman*, November 25, 1973.
40. Switzer, interview, October 2006.

CHAPTER THIRTEEN

1. Starting in 1973, teams on probation were not eligible for ranking in the UPI Coaches' Poll, and coaches associated with those teams were not eligible for Coach of the Year honors.
2. "Sooners' Switzer Prefers the Players' Poll, Anyhow," *Daily Oklahoman*, January 4, 1974.
3. "Trojans Say Sooners No. 1," *Daily Oklahoman*, January 3, 1974.
4. Charlie Smith, "Big 8 Scribes Display Awe for Sooners," *Daily Oklahoman*, August 29, 1974.
5. Chuck Davis, "Here's a Good Line on OU—The Line," *Daily Oklahoman*, September 6, 1974.
6. Elvis Peacock, interview with author, August 2010.
7. *Baylor Magazine,* September 2004.
8. Tinker Owens, interview with author, February 2010.
9. Mike Inman, "Switzer Worried Over Mistakes, Not Ratings," *Daily Oklahoman*, September 17, 1974.
10. Jimbo Elrod, interview with author, February 2010.
11. "Sooners Save 28–11 Victory in Late Surge," *Daily Oklahoman*, September 25, 1974.
12. Elrod, interview, February 2010.
13. Inman, "Switzer Worried Over Mistakes."
14. Dozier, *Oklahoma Football Encyclopedia,* 197.
15. Pruitt, interview, September 2007.
16. Pat Carter, "Writers' Feelings Mixed on Sooners," *Daily Oklahoman*, October 14, 1974.
17. Tony DiRienzo, interview with author, September 2007.
18. Wann Smith, "Red River Rivalry Heroes," *Sooners Illustrated*, October 2007.
19. DiRienzo, interview, September 2007.
20. Walt Jayroe, "One-Arm Shoate National Honoree," *Daily Oklahoman*, October 16, 1974.
21. Barry Switzer, interview with author, April 2010.
22. Frank Haraway, "Buffs Become Believers," *Daily Oklahoman*, October 20, 1974.
23. Walt Jayroe, "Sooners Didn't Expect Iowa States' Wishbone," *Daily Oklahoman*, November 4, 1974.
24. "Switzer Says Sooners Act Too Loose," *Daily Oklahoman*, November 8, 1974.
25. Walt Jayroe, "All No. 1 OU Teams Feasted on Missouri," *Daily Oklahoman*, November 11, 1974.
26. Dozier, *Oklahoma Football Encyclopedia,* 199.
27. Switzer and Shrake, *Bootlegger's Boy,* 111.
28. Dozier, *Oklahoma Football Encyclopedia,* 200.
29. Owens, interview, February 2010.

CHAPTER FOURTEEN

1. Leon Cross, interview with author, November 2009.
2. Wade Walker, interview with author, December 2008.
3. Barry Switzer, interview with author, February 2010.
4. Robertson Travel Post, Inc. Advertisement, *Daily Oklahoman*, March 9, 1975.
5. "'Every Team Scares Me,' Switzer Says," *Daily Oklahoman*, September 7, 1975.
6. Bob Hurt, "New Recruiting Rules to Widen OU Territory," *Daily Oklahoman*, August 17, 1975.
7. Robert B. Allen, "Hollis Gets Royally Upset with Darrell," *Daily Oklahoman*, August 16, 1975.
8. Victor Hicks, interview with author, December 2010.
9. Hank Inman, "X's, O's Important with Shoate Gone," *Daily Oklahoman*, September 3, 1975.
10. Steve Davis, interview with author, December 2007.
11. Owens, interview, February 2010.
12. Ibid.
13. Scott Hill, interview with author, February 2010.
14. "Elrod Tops on Defense," *Daily Oklahoman*, October 7, 1975.
15. Bob Hurt, "Nervousness Makes Comeback at OU," *Daily Oklahoman*, October 8, 1975.
16. Walt Jayroe, "OU, Texas Naturally High," *Daily Oklahoman*, October 7, 1975.
17. "Joe, Defense Worry Royal," *Daily Oklahoman*, October 7, 1975.
18. "Littrell to Stay Home," *Daily Oklahoman*, October 8, 1975.
19. Hank Inman, "Jayhawks Cause 11 Oklahoma Disasters," *Daily Oklahoman*, November 10, 1975.
20. Hill, interview, February 2010.
21. Owens, interview, February 2010.
22. Ray Soldan, "Sooners Balloon Popped," *Daily Oklahoman*, November 9, 1975.
23. Davis, interview, December 2007.
24. Joe Washington, interview with author, July 2007.
25. Hank Inman, "It Ain't Much Fun to Lose," *Daily Oklahoman*, November 9, 1975.
26. Hank Inman, "Jayhawks Caused 11 Oklahoma Disasters," *Daily Oklahoman*, November 9, 1975.

CHAPTER FIFTEEN

1. Hill, interview, February 2010.
2. Elrod, interview, February 2010.
3. Mike Treps, interview with author, February 2010.
4. Owens, interview, February 2010.
5. Washington, interview, July 2007.
6. "Players Pick Nebraska," *Daily Oklahoman*, November 21, 1975.
7. Jack Fried and Jim Fried, *The Winning Edge: Oklahoma's Sooners—Why They Win* (Oklahoma City: n.p., 1976), 251–52.
8. Ibid., 268–71.

9. Ibid., 274–76.

10. Bob Hurt, "Switzer Has Sharp Words for Sooners," *Daily Oklahoman*, December 27, 1975.

11. Davis, interview, December 2007.

12. Archie Griffin, interview with author, March 2010.

13. Davis, interview, December 2007.

14. Ibid.

15. *Oklahoma Sooners: 1975 National Champions.* DVD. The Computer Group, 2004.

16. Elrod, interview, February 2010.

17. Skip Bayless, "Leach Convinced OU Deserves to Be No. 1," *Daily Oklahoman*, January 2, 1976.

18. Davis, interview, December 2007.

19. Walt Jayroe, "Joe Becomes All-Time Big 8 Rushing Leader," *Daily Oklahoman*, January 3, 1976.

20. Owens, interview, September 2007.

21. Hank Inman, "Sooners Probation Draws to a Close," *Daily Oklahoman*, January 3, 1976.

22. Elrod, interview, February 2010.

CHAPTER SIXTEEN

1. Bob Hurt, "Turnover Adds Some Uncertainty for OU," *Daily Oklahoman*, September 5, 1976.

2. Hill, interview, February 2010.

3. Steve Rhodes, interview with author, March 2010.

4. Kenny King, interview with author, March 2010.

5. Ibid.

6. Larry Lacewell, interview with author, April 2010.

7. Hank Inman, "Dean Seeks Fresh Start," *Daily Oklahoman*, September 16, 1976.

8. "Victory Doesn't Satisfy Sooners, Blevins," *Daily Oklahoman*, September 13, 1976.

9. "Switzer Uncertain About Sooners' Future," *Daily Oklahoman*, September 27, 1976.

10. Ray Soldan, "Sooners, Cowboys Hang On," *Daily Oklahoman*, October 3, 1976.

11. Gene Hochevar, interview with author, March 2010.

12. Dean Blevins, interview with author, March 2010.

13. Thomas Lott, interview with author, March 2010.

14. Dozier, *Oklahoma Football Encyclopedia,* 205.

15. Lott, interview, March 2010.

16. King, interview, March 2010.

17. Bob Hurt, "OU Fills Defensive Holes," *Daily Oklahoman*, October 20, 1976.

18. Hill, interview, February 2010.

19. J. Carl Guymon, "Buff Offense No Surprise, Switzer Says," *Daily Oklahoman*, October 31, 1976.

20. Lott, interview, March 2010.

21. Bob Hurt, "Sooner to be Obstacles in Huskers' Title Drive," *Daily Oklahoman*, August 29, 1976.

22. Switzer and Shrake, *Bootlegger's Boy,* 130–31.

23. Lacewell, interview, April 2010.

24. Rhodes, interview, March 2010.
25. Blevins, interview, March 2010.
26. Bob Hurt, "OU Feasts on Cowboys," *Daily Oklahoman*, December 26, 1976.
27. Elvis Peacock, interview with author, December 2007.
28. Chuck Neinas, interview with author, August 2010.
29. Ibid.
30. Lott, interview, March 2010.
31. Dozier, *Oklahoma Football Encyclopedia*, 208.
32. Hochevar, interview, March 2010.
33. Ibid.
34. King, interview, March 2010.
35. Billy Sims, interview with author, April 2010.
36. Lott, interview, March 2010.
37. Blevins, interview, March 2010.
38. Uwe von Schamann, interview with author, February 2010.
39. Sims, interview, April 2010.
40. Hochevar, interview, March 2010.
41. King, interview, March 2010.
42. Walt Jayroe, "Switzer," *Daily Oklahoman*, September 25, 1976.
43. Billy Sims, interview with author, March 2010.
44. Dan Lauck, *Newsday Long Island*, September 25, 1976.
45. Lacewell, interview, April 2010.
46. King, interview, March 2010.
47. Bob Boyles and Paul Guido, *Fifty Years of College Football: A Modern History of America's Most Colorful Sport* (New York: Skyhorse, 2007), 786.
48. Larry Lacewell, interview with author, March 2010.
49. Hochevar, interview, March 2010.
50. Dozier, *Oklahoma Football Encyclopedia*, 212.
51. J. Carl Guymon, "'If Kinlaw Can Stay Healthy . . .'" *Daily Oklahoman*, September 1, 1978.
52. King, interview, March 2010.
53. Sims, interview, April 2010.
54. Switzer, interview, April 2010.
55. "Sooners Send Texas Reeling," *Daily Oklahoman*, October 8, 1978.
56. Dozier, *Oklahoma Football Encyclopedia*, 213.
57. Sims, interview, April 2010.
58. Lott, interview, March 2010.
59. King, interview, March 2010.
60. Dean Bailey, "Surprise! Oklahoma vs. Nebraska!" *Daily Oklahoman*, November 19, 1978.
61. King, interview, March 2010.
62. Sims, interview, April 2010.
63. King, interview, March 2010.
64. Switzer, interview, April 2010.
65. King, interview, March 2010.
66. Sims, interview, April 2010.

CHAPTER SEVENTEEN

1. Volney Meece, "OU Offense Is Unchanged," *Daily Oklahoman*, August 26, 1979.
2. Barry Switzer, interview with author, May 2010.
3. "New Sooner Must Sit Out Season," *Daily Oklahoman*, August 7, 1979.
4. J. Carl Guymon, "Blake Ends Brief Stint at Fullback," *Daily Oklahoman*, August 16, 1979.
5. "Sooners Begin Practice with Two Surprise Players," *Daily Oklahoman*, August 21, 1979.
6. J. C. Watts, interview with author, April 2010.
7. Rhodes, interview, March 2010.
8. Watts, interview, April 2010.
9. Merv Johnson, interview with author, May 2010.
10. Dozier, *Oklahoma Football Encyclopedia*, 217.
11. Switzer, interview, May 2010.
12. Dozier, *Oklahoma Football Encyclopedia*, 218.
13. Al Carter, "Billy and Barry Differ on Vote," *Daily Oklahoman*, December 4, 1979.
14. Watts, interview, April 2010.
15. Al Carter, "Heberts Heroics Spurs Sooners," *Daily Oklahoman*, January 2, 1980.
16. Johnson, interview, May 2010.
17. Watts, interview, April 2010.
18. Dozier, *Oklahoma Football Encyclopedia*, 221.
19. Watts, interview, April 2010.
20. Dozier, *Oklahoma Football Encyclopedia*, 223.
21. Watts, interview, April 2010.
22. Floyd Stanley, "Seminoles Butler Thought His Team Had the Game Won," *Daily Oklahoman*, January 3, 1981.
23. Watts, interview, April 2010.
24. Al Carter, "Frantic Drive Wins It for OU," *Daily Oklahoman*, January 3, 1981; and Stanley, "Seminoles Butler."

CHAPTER EIGHTEEN

1. Switzer, interview, May 2010.
2. "Switzer Staying Where He's At," *Daily Oklahoman*, January 1981.
3. Al Carter, "Wishbones Will Cross Paths," *Daily Oklahoman*, September 12, 1981.
4. Al Carter, "OU Coaches Have Minds on USC, not Polls," *Daily Oklahoman*, September 14, 1981.
5. Keith Stanberry, interview with author, May 2010.
6. "OU at USC," *Daily Oklahoman*, September 26, 1981.
7. Johnson, interview, May 2010.
8. Switzer, interview, May 2010.
9. Jim Lassiter, "Huskers Wreck Sooners 37–14," *Daily Oklahoman*, November 22, 1981.
10. Al Carter, "OU's Dominance of Series Ended," *Daily Oklahoman*, November 22, 1981.
11. Stanberry, interview, May 2010.
12. Johnson, interview, May 2010.
13. Neinas, interview, August 2010.
14. Barry Switzer, interview with author, June 2010.
15. Neinas, interview, August 2010.

16. Dan Gibbens, interview with author, June 2010.
17. Andrew Zimbalist, *Unpaid Professionals: Commercialism and Conflict in Big-time College Sports* (Princeton, N.J.: Princeton University Press, 1999), 98.
18. Gibbens, interview, June 2010.
19. Switzer, interview, June 2010.
20. "Mom Overturns Dupree's Decision—For Now," *Daily Oklahoman*, February 2, 1982.
21. Smith, "Sooner Bowl Heroes."
22. Al Carter, "Five Games on TV Were More Than Fans Could Handle," *Daily Oklahoman*, January 17, 1982.
23. "Mom Overturns Dupree's Decision."
24. Jim Lassiter, "Tillman Gets OU Off to a Fast Start," *Daily Oklahoman*, February 10, 1982.
25. "Sooners Corral Marcus Dupree," *Daily Oklahoman*, February 13, 1982.
26. Marcus Dupree, interview with author, December 2007.
27. Tim Cowlishaw, "West Virginia's Mountain: Preparing for Oklahoma," *Daily Oklahoman*, September 10, 1982.
28. Volney Meece, "Philosophic Switzer Finds Positive Side to Disaster," *Daily Oklahoman*, February 12, 1982.
29. Tim Cowlishaw, "Sooners Dot the I, 13–3," *Daily Oklahoman*, October 3, 1982.
30. Ibid.
31. Johnson, interview, May 2010.
32. Ray Soldan, "That Was No 2–2 Team, Texas Coach Says of OU," *Daily Oklahoman*, October 10, 1982.
33. Volney Meece, "OU's Effort Best Ever, Barry Says," *Daily Oklahoman*, October 10, 1982.
34. Jim Lassiter, "Switzer Extols NU to Skies, and Maybe a Little Beyond," *Daily Oklahoman*, November 24, 1982.
35. Dupree, interview, December 2007.
36. Switzer, interview, May 2010.
37. Dupree, interview, December 2007.
38. Switzer, interview, May 2010.
39. Ibid.
40. Johnson, interview, May 2010.
41. Bob Hersom, "Switzer Hopes Defense Will Offset Back Woes," *Daily Oklahoman*, September 4, 1983.
42. Stanberry, interview, May 2010.
43. Spencer Tillman, interview with author, June 2010.
44. Bob Hersom, "OU Survives Worst Half to Down TU," *Daily Oklahoman*, September 25, 1983.
45. Bob Hersom, "Sooners Sputter but Drop K-State," *Daily Oklahoman*, October 2, 1983.
46. Johnson, interview, May 2010.
47. Bob Hersom, "Suspended Dupree Still in Seclusion," *Daily Oklahoman*, October 13, 1983.
48. Switzer, interview, May 2010.
49. Bob Hersom, "Onside Kick Just Another Mistake," *Daily Oklahoman*, October 16, 1983.
50. Tom Kensler, "4th Quarter Rally Rescues OU," *Daily Oklahoman*, October 16, 1983.
51. Hersom, "Onside Kick Just Another Mistake."

52. Bob Hersom, "OU's Best Effort Falls Short," *Daily Oklahoman*, November 27, 1983.

53. Ibid.

54. Jim Lassiter, "Jim Lassiter," *Daily Oklahoman*, September 18, 1983.

CHAPTER NINETEEN

1. Bob Hersom, "Football's Fun for Barry Again," *Daily Oklahoman*, May 13, 1984.

2. Ibid.

3. Switzer, interview, June 2010.

4. Bob Hersom, "OU Attack Deemed A-," *Daily Oklahoman*, May 6, 1984.

5. "Brown Brings Fresh Look to OU–Texas Battle Plan," *Daily Oklahoman*, October 9, 1984.

6. Bob Hersom, "We'll Find Out Who's Best," *Daily Oklahoman*, October 13, 1984.

7. Bill Cromartie, *Annual Madness* (Nashville: Rutledge Hill Press, 1982), 453.

8. Tillman, interview, June 2010.

9. Volney Meece, "Sooners Say Refs Helped Texas Tie," *Daily Oklahoman*, October 14, 1984.

10. Cromartie, *Annual Madness*, 455.

11. Keith Stanberry, interview with author, September 2007.

12. Cromartie, *Annual Madness*, 455.

13. Stanberry, interview, September 2007.

14. Volney Meece, "'Great Play' Saved Day for OU," *Daily Oklahoman*, October 21, 1984.

15. Bob Hersom, "OU Bites the Dust in Kansas, 28–11," *Daily Oklahoman*, October 28, 1984.

16. Merv Johnson, interview with author, June 2010.

17. Volney Meece, "Switzer Comes to Praise OU, Not 'Barry' Them," *Daily Oklahoman*, November 25, 1984.

18. "Bowl Officials Cleared Schooner, But Not Refs," *Daily Oklahoman*, January 2, 1985.

19. Switzer, interview, June 2010.

20. Tillman, interview, June 2010.

21. Switzer, interview, June 2010.

22. Jamelle Holieway, interview with author, June 2010.

23. Bob Hersom, "QB Problem?" *Daily Oklahoman*, April 4, 1985.

24. Bob Hersom, "Win Costly: Johnson Done, Tillman Shelved," *Daily Oklahoman*, September 30, 1985.

25. Bob Hersom, "A Passing Fancy: OU 41–6," *Daily Oklahoman*, October 6, 1985.

26. Bob Hersom, "OU–Texas Preview," *Daily Oklahoman*, October 6, 1985.

27. Volney Meece, "Barry Shouts It: 'We're the Best!'" *Daily Oklahoman*, October 13, 1985.

28. "Big 8 Honors Bosworth," *Daily Oklahoman*, October 15, 1985.

29. Pat Putnam, "The Big D Was a Big Deal in Big D," *Sports Illustrated*, October 21, 1985.

30. Tillman, interview, June 2010.

31. Holieway, interview, June 2010.

32. Tillman, interview, June 2010.

33. Anthony Stafford, interview with author, June 2010.

34. Johnson, interview, June 2010.

35. Stafford, interview, June 2010.

36. Holieway, interview, June 2010.

37. Switzer, interview, June 2010.

38. Ibid.

EPILOGUE

1. *Sports Illustrated*, February 27, 1989.
2. "Heroic Death." *Orlando Sentinel*, May 29, 1989. http://articles.orlandosentinel.com/keyword/jerry-anderson
3. *Tulsa World*, September 7, 2010.
4. William Shakespeare, *The Tempest*, ed. Jonathan Bate and Eric Rasmussen (New York: Modern Library, 2008), act 2, scene 1, 36.

Bibliography

Banks, Jimmy. *The Darrell Royal Story.* Austin, Tex.: Shoal Creek, 1973.

Boyles, Bob, and Paul Guido. *Fifty Years of College Football: A Modern History of America's Most Colorful Sport.* New York: Skyhorse, 2007.

Clark, J. Brent. *Sooner Century: 100 Glorious Years of Oklahoma Football: 1895–1985.* Coal Valley, Ill.: Quality Sports, 1995.

Cromartie, Bill. *Annual Madness* Nashville: Rutledge Hill Press, 1982.

Cross, George Lynn. *Blacks in White Colleges: Oklahoma's Landmark Cases.* Norman: University of Oklahoma Press, 1975.

———. *Presidents Can't Punt: The OU Football Tradition.* Norman: University of Oklahoma Press, 1977.

Dozier, Ray. *The Oklahoma Football Encyclopedia.* Champaign, Ill.: Sports Publishing, 2006.

ESPN. *ESPN College Football Encyclopedia.* New York: ESPN Books, 2005.

Fried, Jack, and Jim Fried. *The Winning Edge: Oklahoma's Sooners—Why They Win.* Oklahoma City: n.p., 1976.

Hassler, Dr. F. R., to Dr. D. G. Willard. October 9, 1961. University of Oklahoma Athletics Communications Department files.

Kaye, Ivan N. *Good Clean Violence: A History of College Football.* Philadelphia: J. B. Lippincott, 1973.

Keith, Harold. *Forty-Seven Straight: The Wilkinson Era at Oklahoma.* Norman: University of Oklahoma Press, 1984.

———. Sooner Press Conference, September 23, 1963. University of Oklahoma Athletics Communications Department files.

Lapchick, Richard. *100 Pioneers: African-Americans Who Broke Color Barriers in Sport.* Morgantown, W.V.: Fitness Information Technology, 2008.

McCallum, John, and Charles Pearson. *College Football, U.S.A., 1869–1971.* Greenwich, Conn.: Hall of Fame Publishing, 1971.

Oklahoma Sooners: 1975 National Champions. DVD. The Computer Group, 2004.

Quirk, James. *The Ultimate Guide to College Football: Rankings, Records, and Scores of the Major Teams and Conferences.* Urbana: University of Illinois Press, 2004.

Rosenberg, Michael. *War as They Knew It: Woody Hayes, Bo Schembechler, and American in a Time of Unrest.* New York: Grand Central Publishing, 2008.

Schwartz, Larry. "Namath Was Lovable Rogue." espn.go.com/classic/biography/s/namath_joe.html.

Shakespeare, William. *The Tempest.* Edited by Jonathan Bate and Eric Rasmussen. New York: Modern Library, 2008.

Smith, Wann. "The Beginning of an Era." *Sooners Illustrated*, November 2006.

———. "Sooner Bowl Heroes." *Sooners Illustrated*, January 2008.

Snook, Jeff. *What It Means to Be a Sooner: Barry Switzer, Bob Stoops and Oklahoma's Greatest Players.* Chicago: Triumph Books, 2005.

Switzer, Barry, and Bud Shrake. *Bootlegger's Boy.* New York: William Morrow, 1990.

Watterson, John Sayle. *College Football: History, Spectacle, Controversy.* Baltimore: Johns Hopkins University Press, 2000.

Wilkinson, Jay, and Gretchen Hirsch. *Bud Wilkinson: An Intimate Portrait of an American Legend.* Champaign, Ill.: Sagamore Publishing, 1994.

Willard, Dr. D. G. Notes. University of Oklahoma Athletics Communications Department files.

Zimbalist, Andrew. *Unpaid Professionals: Commercialism and Conflict in Big-time College Sports.* Princeton, N.J.: Princeton University Press, 1999.

Index

Aikman, Troy Kenneth, 283, 285–91, 293

Akers, Fred, 216, 264

Alabama, University of: vs. Oklahoma 1963 Orange Bowl, 49–51; vs. Oklahoma 1970 Astro-Bluebonnet Bowl, 130–31

Allen, Marcus LeMarr, 255

Allison, Carl, 14, 73

Anderson, Ernest, 264

Anderson, Jerry, 199, 202, 206, 210, 213, 295

Andros, Dee (Andrecopolous, Demosthenes), 7, 13, 117

Andros, Plato (Andrecopolous, Plato), 117

Arizona State University: vs. Oklahoma 1983 Fiesta Bowl, 265–67

Arkansas, University of: vs. Oklahoma 1978 Orange Bowl, 226–29

Arnold, Claude, 7, 13, 26

Arnold, Jerry, 172, 182

Auburn University: vs. Oklahoma 1972 Sugar Bowl, 139

Aycock, Steve, 116, 133, 134

Babb, Mike, 183, 206, 213, 223, 230

Baccus, Gary, 133, 142, 145, 153

Baer, Jack, 220

Baldischwiler, Karl, 206, 220

Banks, Basil, 230, 238, 244, 245

Banowsky, William, 239

Barrett, Steve, 86, 234

Bechtold, Bill, 245, 254

Bell, Gordon, 200, 202, 203

Bell, Roy, 111–13, 116, 117, 125, 138, 140

Bellard, Emory Dilworth, 120, 122–24, 298

Benson, Thomas, 253, 261, 268, 269, 273, 278

Bierman, Bernard W. "Bernie," 4, 5, 62

Biletnikoff, Fred, 69

Blaik, Bob, 33

Blaik, Earl Henry "Red," 13, 33, 62

Blake, John, 239, 253, 261, 267, 268, 297

Blevins, Dean, 206–12, 219, 221, 230, 238, 248, 291; on 1976 Nebraska game, 216; on Ohio State game, 222, 223

Boggs, Frank, 168

Bolinger, Bo, 7

Bosworth, Brian Keith, 278, 279, 283, 288, 289, 293

Bowden, Robert Cleckler "Bobby," 209, 244, 249, 251

Boyd, Bob, 21, 22, 25

Boydston, Max, 7, 66, 132, 204

Bradley, Danny, 261, 268, 269, 272, 274, 278–80, 282–86

Brahaney, Tom, 133, 141

Brewer, George, 7, 132

Brooks, Billy, 167, 177, 180, 190, 202, 204, 206

Brown, Hal, 137

Brown, Ron 266

Brown, Sidney, 203, 206, 213

Brown, Sonny, 292, 293

Brown, William Mack "Mack," 278, 284, 285

Broyles, John Franklin "Frank," 79, 80, 83, 84, 94, 101, 119, 155, 157, 254

Bruce, Earle, 179, 237

Bryan, Ricky, 253, 264, 267–69, 275, 278

Bryant, Anthony, 173

Bryant, Paul William "Bear," 14, 49, 50, 51, 54, 73, 80, 81, 85, 94, 130, 134, 197, 298

Burgar, Jim, 86, 88, 110

Burget, Grant, 142, 148, 149, 161, 172

Burris Brothers (Kurt, Lynn, Paul "Buddy," Robert "Bob"), 7

Byers, Walter, 16, 259

Byford, Lyndle, 245, 254

Calame, Gene Dan, 7, 26, 46

Campbell, Earl Christian, 177, 190, 226, 253

Carpenter, Jimmy, 26, 27, 30, 40, 42, 43

Carr, Lydell, 293

Carroll, John, 133, 136, 137, 139, 140, 142, 146, 147, 149, 177

Case, Scott, 261, 268, 269, 272, 278

Casillas, Tony Steven, 253, 268, 278, 280, 282, 283, 288, 289, 293

Catlin, Tom, 7

CFA. *See* College Football Association

Chandler, Albert, 116, 129, 133, 138, 141, 142

Chez Paree Supper Club incident, 20–23

Claiborne, Jerry, 80

Claphan, Sammy Jack, 220, 224, 237

Clark, Waymon, 161, 162, 165, 172

Clewis, Paul, 261, 268

Coats, Andrew, 260

College Football Association (CFA), 217, 218, 258–60

Collins, Patrick, 282, 288

Condren, Glen, 44, 72, 75, 77

Connors, Bill, 71, 98, 139

Cornell, Bob, 14, 24, 54, 73

Cox, Tom, 25, 33

Cromwell, Nolan, 191–93

Cronley, Jay, 70

Cronley, John, 39, 70

Cross, George Lynn, 4–6, 11, 16–18, 44, 51, 53, 71, 72, 79, 97, 101

Cross, Leon, 15, 25, 30, 31, 33, 45, 48, 49, 54, 65, 81, 92–94, 97, 107, 108, 132, 141, 148, 160, 183

Crosswhite, Leon, 116, 117, 127–29, 131, 133, 140–42, 146, 149, 153

Crosswhite, Rodney, 86, 88

Crouch, Terry, 237, 245, 254

Crowder, Eddie, 7, 13, 15, 18, 21, 26, 53, 54, 63, 73, 113, 132, 136, 137, 146, 147, 157, 158

Culbreath, Jim, 190, 203, 206–208

Cumby, George, 183, 184, 206, 230, 236, 237, 244, 285; transferring from OU, 207, 208

Daugherty, Hugh "Duffy," 10, 11, 27, 61, 62, 124

Davis, Kyle, 153, 172, 182

Davis, Steve, 99, 100, 141, 156, 159–62, 164, 165, 167, 168, 172, 175, 177, 180, 181, 187, 190, 192, 193, 196, 199–203, 207, 247, 254

Deer, Monte, 31, 33, 43, 45, 48

Derr, Bruce, 109, 113, 131

Devaney, Robert Simon "Bob," 48, 49, 68, 70, 89, 91, 100, 109, 147, 150, 161, 214

Devine, Daniel John "Dan," 23, 39, 41

Dickey, Don, 25, 27, 32

Dickey, Doug, 79, 101

Dickey, Jim, 270

Dickey, Lynn, 114, 128, 129

Dickson, George, 54, 73

DiRienzo, Tony, 176–78, 180, 190, 191, 206

Ditka, Michael Keller "Mike," 27, 28

Dittman, Barry, 230, 237

Dodd, Bobby, 12, 80, 94

Dodge, Todd, 279, 280, 281

Donnan, Jim, 284–86, 290

Dooley, Vincent Joseph "Vince," 79

Dorsett, Anthony Drew "Tony," 188

Drane, Dwight, 253, 261, 264, 268, 278

Duncan, Donnie, 157, 229, 237, 296

Dupree, Marcus L., 261–71, 275

Elliott, Peter R. "Pete," 13, 14, 132, 165

Elrod, James Whittington "Jimbo," 157, 161, 175, 189, 196, 202, 204, 206

Elway, John Albert, Jr. "John," 246

Eschbach, Al, 58

Evans, Chez, 206

Fairbanks, Charles Leo "Chuck," 38, 62, 73, 92, 94, 98, 101, 103, 105, 107, 108, 110–12, 114, 115, 117, 118, 123, 124, 127, 129–33, 137, 141, 142, 148, 150, 152, 155, 156, 158, 160, 171, 240, 246, 276, 298; promotion to head coach, 97; resignation, 153, 154

Faurot, Donald Burrows "Don," 4, 5, 121

Fehring, William Paul "Dutch," 13

Feldman, Rudy, 34, 53, 54, 73

Ferragamo, Vince Anthony, 198, 199

Finefrock, Paul, 92, 93

Finlayson, Bruce, 281

Fisher, Ada Lois Sipuel, 60

Fletcher, Ron, 44

Florida State University: vs. Oklahoma 1965 Gator Bowl, 68, 69; vs. Oklahoma 1980 Orange Bowl, 243, 244, 248–51

Flowers, Nehemiah, 61, 205

Foster, Eddie, 133, 141, 153

Franklin, Willie, 129, 133

Fry, John Hayden, 61, 109, 134, 239

Fryar, Irving, 256, 273

Fulcher, Rick, 144–46, 149, 153, 165, 167

Futch, Gary, 250

Gass, Floyd, 130, 132

Gautt, Prentice, 7, 25, 60, 61, 205

Gibbens, Dan, 260

Gibbs, Gary, 153, 186, 229, 237, 253, 257, 281, 296, 297

Gibson, Vince, 128, 137

Gill, Turner, 256, 273

Ging, Jackie Lee "Jack," 7, 75

Goodlow, Daryl, 261, 268, 278

Graham, Otto Everett, 63

Grange, Harold Edward "Red," 20, 21

Gray, Billy, 83, 92, 97

Gray, Edmund "Beaky," 7, 9

Gray, Tommy, 7

Grayson, Bobby, 245, 248

Greathouse, Myrle, 7

Greenlee, Wayne, 7

Green Merrill, 7, 63

Griffin, Archie Mason, 123, 201

Grisham, Jim, 44, 54, 64, 67, 69

Hadl, John, 32

Hall, Galen, 73, 83, 93, 97, 125, 148, 150, 157, 159, 201, 228, 237, 246, 263, 278, 284

Hamilton, Raymond "Sugar Bear," 133, 142, 145

Harmon, Mark, 141

Harper, Gary, 86, 90

Harper, Mike, 86

Harper, Warren, 97, 175, 186, 237

Harris, Jimmy, 7, 10, 13, 14, 17, 21, 22, 26, 46, 74, 132

Harris, Sen. Fred Roy, 65

Harrison, Bob L. "Hog," 7

Harrison, Jon, 116, 133, 137, 138, 141

Hart, Ben, 61, 86, 91, 205

Hartline, Ronnie, 25

Haskell, Lawrence E. "Jap," 4

Haworth, Steve, 245, 261, 267

Hayes, Wayne Woodrow "Woody," using the Wishbone, 122, 123; 137, 172, 201, 218–20, 222–25, 237

Hearon, Darlan "Doc," 7

Heath, Leon "Mule Train," 7

Heatly, Dick, 14, 73

Hebert, Bud, 183, 206, 223, 224, 230, 244

Henderson, Zac, 206, 207, 213, 234

Hicks, Victor, 183, 184, 186, 196, 206, 232, 237

Hill, Scott, 155, 156, 192, 196, 198, 206, 207, 213, 214, 237, 265; Tony Dorsett collision, 188

Hinton, Eddie, 86, 89, 102, 105–107, 110, 205

Hobby, Brewster, 14, 21, 25, 73, 132

Hochevar, Gene, 172, 173, 210, 219, 220, 224, 229

Hoffman, Wayne, 172, 182, 185

Holieway, Jamelle, 285, 286, 290–93

Holtz, Louis Leo "Lou," 226, 228, 229, 286

Hornung, Paul, 9

Houston, University of: vs. Oklahoma 1981 Sun Bowl, 257

Hover, Lee, 199, 206, 209

Hughes, Randy, 143, 153, 161, 182

Humm, Dave, 149, 180, 215

Hunt, Daryl, 183, 184, 186, 192, 206, 230, 236, 237

Hutson, Mark, 293

Ice Bowl, Oklahoma vs. Oklahoma State (November 30, 1985), 291

Ivory, Horace, 190, 206, 207, 211, 212, 217

Ivy, Frank "Pop," 13, 14, 63

Jack Sisco Affair, 280n

Jackson, Keith Jerome, 288, 289, 292, 293

Jackson, Kerry, 141, 153, 156, 161, 173, 175; probation, 158, 159

James, Don, 283

James, Pat, 80, 83, 85, 90, 94, 97, 112

Jennings, Bill, 13, 16, 42

Jimerson, Don, 97, 160, 219

Jimerson, Jay, 219, 221, 222, 230, 245

Johnson, Andre, 281, 282

Johnson, Earl, 269, 270, 272, 275, 279, 282, 287, 288

Johnson, Greg, 286, 287

Johnson, James William "Jimmy," 157, 241, 289

Johnson, Pres. Lyndon Baines, 66

Johnson, Merv, 79, 80, 93, 237, 241, 246, 255, 257, 258, 263, 267, 271, 283, 290, 298

Johnson, Wallace "Wally," 61, 205

Jones, Gomer Thomas, 12–14, 17, 40, 43, 54, 58, 60, 63, 64, 67–73, 75, 76, 79, 81, 84, 276; death of, 131, 132; promoted to head coach, 65; resignation, 77

Jones, Mike, 111, 237

Jordan, Lee Roy, 49–51

Kalsu, James Robert "Bob," 86, 91, 100, 116

Keeling, Mike, 238, 243, 244, 249, 261

Keeton, Durwood, 153, 161

Keith, Bobby Drake, 14, 54, 59, 63–65, 73, 132

Kennedy, Pres. John Fitzgerald, 11, 12, 18, 44, 49, 59

Kennedy, Attorney Gen. Robert Fitzgerald, 59

Kern, Dr. Rex William, 122, 123

Kerr, Sen. Robert S., 53

Key, Don, 245, 254, 261

Kiffin, Monte, 16, 228

Kimball, Bobby, 183, 230, 237

King, Glenn, 116, 133, 134

King, Kenny, 183, 184, 206, 212, 215, 217, 220, 221, 223, 225, 230, 231–37, 251; on 1978 Orange bowl, 227, 228; transferring from OU, 207, 208

Kinlaw, Reggie, 183, 184, 206, 213, 222, 230, 236–38

Kinney, Jeff, 138, 139

Krisher, Bill, 7, 9

Lacewell, Larry Wayne, 73, 83–85, 112, 125, 129, 145, 154, 208, 215; on 1978 Orange Bowl, 226–29; recruiting Lucious Selmon, 157, 158; resignation, 230

Lashar, Tim, 268, 272, 284, 291, 292

Lea, Paul, 31, 45, 47

Leach, Rick, 200–203

Leake, John E., Jr. "Buddy," 7, 15, 66

Ledbetter, Jerome, 254, 261

Ledbetter, Weldon, 238, 245, 247, 250, 254, 261, 264

Lee, Swede, 83, 97

Lee, Wayne, 31, 33, 45, 49

Liggins, Granville "Granny," 86, 105, 205

Littrell, Jimmy, 153, 167, 172, 181, 187, 190, 197

Looney, Joe Don, 45–49, 56–58

Lott, Thomas, 183, 206, 211–13, 215, 217, 219–22, 229, 230, 232–37, 239, 251, 285, 286, 291; transferring from OU, 207, 208

Luster, Dewey "Snorter," 4, 30, 62

Lytle, Rob, 202

MacKenzie, James Alexander "Jim," 73, 79, 80–95, 97, 101, 103, 105, 112, 237, 278

MacLeod, John Matthew, 131

Majors, Johnny, 81, 188

Mallory, Bill, 178, 189

Manley, Leon "Willie," 7, 132

Mantle, Mickey, 83, 293

Maris, Roger, 83

Marshall, Everett, 114, 116, 117

Mathis, Reggie, 183, 230, 236, 237

Mayhue, Charley, 15, 44

McClellan, Mike, 25, 38, 39, 41, 42

McClendon, Charles Yeomans "Cholly Mac," 80, 137, 243

McDaniel, Wahoo, 25

McDonald, Tommy, 7, 9, 15, 17, 140

McKay, John Harvey, 54, 55, 79, 153, 162, 164, 172, 218

McPhail, Coleman "Buck," 7, 63

McQuarters, Ed, 44, 61, 205

McReynolds, Joe, 156, 189, 190

Meece, Volney, 39

Melendez, Jaime, 206, 207, 220

Mendenhall, Ken, 86, 108, 110, 114, 115

Michaels, Bill, 159

Michigan, University of: vs. Oklahoma 1976 Orange Bowl, 199–203

Migliazzo, Paul, 278, 280, 288

Mildren, Larry Jack, 110–14, 116, 117, 125, 126, 128, 129, 131–34, 136–41, 160, 298, 299

Miller, Terry, 234

Milstead, Karl, 25, 27, 29

Mitchel, Eric, 285, 290, 291

Mitchell, Jack "General Jack," 7, 13, 23, 26, 28, 29, 48, 58, 64, 73, 98

Moore, Derland, 116, 133, 142, 144, 145

Moore, Robert W. "Bud," 191, 232, 233

Mosley, Wendell, 142, 207, 237

Munn, Clarence Lester "Biggie," 124

Murphy, Kevin, 253, 261, 267–69, 278, 279, 282, 293

Namath, Joseph William "Joe," 49–51

Neely, Ralph Eugene, 15, 44, 59, 64, 69

Neinas, Chuck, 217, 218, 258, 259

Nelson, Roger, 7

Newman, Howard, 37, 89

Neyland, Robert Reese "General Bob," 3

Nixon, Freddie, 206, 230, 232, 237

Noble, Lloyd, 4, 5, 62

Norris, Rex, 229, 237, 253, 278

Nystrom, Buck, 97

Ohio State University: vs. Oklahoma
    (September 24, 1977), 218–25

O'Neal, Benton, 7

O'Neal, Jay, 7, 12–14, 21, 24, 26, 33, 34, 37–39,
    46–51, 53–58, 63, 65, 69, 73, 74, 76, 121

O'Neal, Pat, 7

Onofrio, Albert Joseph "Al," 195

Osborne, Dr. Thomas William "Tom," 90,
    168, 183, 197, 214, 215, 235, 243, 248, 256,
    265, 274

O'Shaughnessy, Steve, 116

Oubre, Louis, 237, 245

Overstreet, David, 230, 234, 238, 245

Owen, Benjamin Gilbert "Bennie," 3, 60, 88, 95

Owens, Charles Wayne "Tinker," 148–51, 165,
    166, 168, 172, 174, 175, 182, 187, 191–93, 196,
    197, 199, 202, 204, 206, 247

Owens, Jim, 7, 63, 73, 81

Owens, Steve Everett, 98–100, 102, 103, 105,
    109–15, 124, 125, 132, 148, 155, 171

Page, Bob, 22, 26, 33, 40, 42, 43, 45

Pannell, Tommy, 46, 47

Parilli, Vito "Babe," 80

Parker, Paul, 261, 267, 268

Parrington, Vernon Louis, 171

Parseghian, Ara Raoul, 20, 107

Paterno, Joseph Vincent "Joe," 151, 292, 293

Payne, Ronny, 25, 27, 33, 42, 43

Peacock, Elvis, 173, 175, 181, 186, 190–92, 199,
    206, 207, 215–17, 221, 227, 248

Pegues, Rod, 239, 261

Pell, Charles Byron "Charley," 243

Penn State University: vs. Oklahoma 1972
    Sugar Bowl, 139; vs. Oklahoma 1986
    Orange Bowl, 291–93

Perry, Leon, 290, 291

Perryman, A. G., 127

Peters, Tony, 161, 162, 213

Pettibone, Jerry, 41, 97, 183, 229

Phelps, Kelly, 239, 253, 255, 258, 261, 264, 284

Phillips, Anthony, 293

Phillips, Mike, 158, 159, 173, 197, 206

Phillips, Oail Andrew "Bum," 253

Pope, Eric, 261, 286, 290

Pope, Kenny, 143, 153

Powers, Clyde, 143, 153, 161, 162, 167

Pricer, Billy C., 7

Proctor, Bobby, 157, 206, 237, 254

Pruitt, Gregory Donald "Greg," 116, 125, 126,
    129–31, 133–37, 139–43, 147, 148, 153, 175,
    176, 267

Qualls, Albert, 116, 133

Quantrill, William Clarke, 89

Rawlinson, Ken, 131, 132

Ray, Darrol, 230, 234, 236, 238\

Rayburn, Tony, 292

Rector, Joe, 14, 73, 132

Reed, Darrell, 283, 293

Reilly, Mike, 245, 253

Rentzel, Thomas Lance, 44, 54, 64, 66, 67, 69

Rhodes, Steve, 206, 207, 215, 216, 223, 230,
    232, 237, 239, 240, 245, 248, 250

Rhymes, Buster, 245, 247, 248, 254, 268, 274

Rice, Dr. Homer, 73, 82, 86, 89, 92, 94, 97, 132

Riley, Jim, 72, 86, 87

Ringer, Mike, 55, 66

Ripley, Mickey, 109, 111

Roberts, Greg, 183, 206, 220, 230, 236, 237, 251

Roberts, John David "J. D.," 7, 12, 14, 15, 17, 18, 73, 74, 132

Robertson, Dave, 141–43, 148, 149, 152, 153, 156, 247

Robertson, Port, 25, 97

Robinson, Brooks, 83

Robinson, John Alexander, 253, 255

Rockford, Jim, 250, 278, 284

Rockne, Knute Kenneth, 62

Rodgers, Franklin C. "Pepper," 98, 99

Rodgers, Johnny Steven, 138, 147, 273

Rogers, Jimmy, 206, 230, 234

Roush, John, 153, 172, 182

Royal, B.R., 185

Royal, Darrell K., 7, 11–13, 26, 28, 44, 56, 64, 67, 73, 79, 81, 83, 87, 108, 113, 119, 120, 122–24, 127–29, 132, 136, 144, 146, 159, 165, 168, 178, 185, 190, 216, 234, 298

Rozier, Michael "Mike," 256, 273

RUF/NEKS, 284

Ruster, Dan, 116, 133, 143

Ruth, George Herman "Babe," 37

Sales, Roland, 227, 228

Sandefer, J. D. III, 7, 54

Saxe, John Godfrey: *The Blind Men and the Elephant*, 19

Sayers, Gale, 58, 67, 138

Schembechler, Glenn Edward "Bo," 202, 203

Schnellenberger, Howard, 243, 297

Schwarzwalder, Ben, 47

Selmon, Dewey, 143, 153, 154, 157, 161, 175, 182, 203, 204, 206, 253

Selmon, Lee Roy, 143, 153, 157, 161, 175, 182, 198, 203, 204, 206, 253

Selmon, Lucious, 133, 142, 149, 153, 157, 158, 161, 229, 237, 253, 257

Sewell, Steve, 254, 261, 279, 280

Shaffer, John, 292, 293

Shakespeare, William: *The Tempest*, 299

Sharp, Dr. Paul, 154

Shepard, Darrell, 239, 245, 253, 255, 258, 284

Shepard, Derrick, 268, 272, 274, 284, 289

Shepard, Woodie, 183, 206, 215–17

Shimek, Bill, 237

Shipp, Jackie, 253, 261, 267–69, 278

Shoate, Rod, 143, 153, 161, 175, 178, 182, 186

Shotts, Ron, 74, 86, 87, 91, 100, 110

Sims, Billy, 183, 184, 199, 204, 206, 221, 224, 225, 230–36, 238, 239, 241–45, 256, 262, 267

Sims, Fred, 257, 261, 263, 264, 266

Sims, Greg, 261

Skidgel, Wes, 69

Slater, Bob, 253, 261, 268, 278

Smith, Charles Aaron "Bubba," 61

Smith, Laverne, 192, 193

Smith, Norman, 44, 64

SMU. *See* Southern Methodist University

Solem, Oscar Martin "Ossie," 5

Songy, Darrell, 245, 253, 261

Southern Methodist University: vs. Oklahoma 1968 Astro-Bluebonnet Bowl, 109, 110

Stafford, Anthony, 290, 291

Stallings, Eugene Clifton Jr. "Gene," 110, 111

Stanberry, Keith, 253, 254, 257, 261, 264, 268, 278–82

Stanley, James L. "Jim," 181, 206

Steinbeck, John: *The Grapes of Wrath*, 62

Stell, Damon, 287

Stephenson, Bobby, 86, 88, 89, 102, 105

Stidham, Thomas E. "Tom," 3, 60

Stoops, Robert Anthony "Bob," 38, 240

Stram, Henry Louis "Hank," 184

Struck, Mike, 153, 157

Sullivan, Patrick Joseph "Pat," 139

Surratt, Charlie, 7

Swann, Lynn, 162

Switzer, Barry, 38, 62, 73, 80, 85, 86, 89, 90, 92, 94, 95, 99, 105–107, 109–11, 115, 120, 122, 127, 128, 132–34, 136, 140, 142, 146, 156–58, 160–65, 168, 169, 171, 172, 174–88, 190, 191, 193, 195–98, 200, 204, 206–10, 213–17, 219, 222, 223, 225, 231, 232, 235–39, 241, 242, 245–48, 250, 251, 253–57, 259, 260, 262–76, 278, 281, 283–93, 296, 299; installing the Wishbone, 123–26; military service, 83–84; Penn Square Bank/Sun Belt, 277; promotion to head coach, 154–55; promotion to offensive coordinator, 97; resignation, 295

Switzer, Don, 83

Tabor, Paul, 183, 184, 206, 220, 232

Tabor, Phil, 183, 184, 206, 230, 236, 237

Tatum, James M. "Jim," 4–7, 15, 60, 62, 71, 95, 121

Tatum, John, 19, 31, 39–42, 44, 45, 47, 54, 56–58, 76

Taylor, Lawrence, 247

Taylor, Sherwood, 206, 230, 238

Teaff, Grant Garland, 161, 174, 231

Tennessee, University of: vs. Oklahoma 1968 Orange Bowl, 101–103

Testaverde, Vincent Frank "Vinny," 289

Thomas, Chuck, 261, 268

Thomas, Clendon, 7, 9, 13, 14, 17, 140

Thomas, Helen, 12

Thompson, Charles, 295

Thompson, Jerry, 14, 25, 49, 54, 59, 73

Tillman, Spencer, 262, 268–70, 272–75, 278, 280, 282, 284, 287, 289–91

Treps, Mike, 162, 196

Truitt, John, 253, 261, 268

Tubbs, Gerald J. "Jerry," 7, 9, 10, 17, 132

Unruh, Dean, 133, 139, 141

Vachon, Mike, 86, 88, 91, 99, 102

Valora, Forrest, 237, 243, 245, 250

Van Burkleo, Bill, 33

Vaughan, Mike, 153, 172, 204, 206

Vermillion, Larry, 49

Vessels, Billy, 7, 34, 109, 132, 200, 201, 204

Von Schamann, Uwe Detlef Walter, 183, 206, 216, 221, 225, 226, 230, 234, 236, 237; "The Kick," 223–224

Walker, Herschel Junior, 262

Walker, Wade, 7, 15, 73, 154, 183

Walsh, William Ernest "Bill," 232

Ward, Dallas "Dal," 29

Warmack, Bob, 71, 72, 84–91, 98–100, 102, 103, 105–107, 109, 110, 216, 289

Washington, Joe Dan, 142, 149, 150, 153, 161, 165, 168, 172, 173, 178, 179, 181, 182, 187–93, 196, 197, 203, 204, 206, 247, 267, 285; 1973 punt return vs. USC, 162, 163

Washington, University of: vs. Oklahoma 1985 Orange Bowl, 283, 284; "unhorsemanlike conduct" penalty, 284

Watts, Julius Caesar "J. C.," 229, 230, 232, 239–41, 243, 245, 246, 248, 251, 284, 286; 1980 Orange Bowl, 244; 1981 Orange Bowl, 249, 250

Weatherall, James "Jim," 7

Webb, Terry, 153, 172, 182, 186, 204

Welch, Tim, 142, 153, 154, 164

White, Billy, 25, 33, 71

White, Charles, 233, 242, 243

White House, The: Sooners' 1964 visit, 66

Wilkinson, Charles Burnham "Bud," 4, 5, 7, 9–15, 17, 19–21, 22–35, 45, 46, 48, 49, 51, 53–56, 60–64, 71–77, 81, 87, 94, 95, 100, 119, 121, 126, 132, 139, 182, 184, 205, 239, 253, 270, 273, 276, 280, 298; Coach of the Year clinics, 10, 11, 18; declares his 1961 squad will win final five games, 37–44; promoted to head coach, 6; resigns as athletic director, 65; resigns as head coach, 59

Wilkinson, Jay, 11, 32, 40, 51, 53

Wilkinson, Pat, 32

Willard, D. G., 22, 23

Williams, Steve, 261, 267

Wilson, Stanley, 237, 241, 244, 245, 253, 256, 261, 263, 265, 266

Winchester, Mike, 279

Winters, Chet, 238, 248, 250, 254, 261

Wood, Arthur L.: 1958 probation, 16, 17

Wylie, Joe, 116, 117, 125, 129–31, 133, 134, 140, 142, 145, 148, 153

Wyoming, University of: vs. Oklahoma 1976 Fiesta Bowl, 216, 217

Yaralian, Zaven, 148, 149

York, Marshall, 27, 92, 93

Zabel, Steve, 99, 100, 105, 107–10